WRITING WITHOUT WORDS

Writing without Words

Alternative Literacies in Mesoamerica and the Andes

Elizabeth Hill Boone and Walter D. Mignolo, Editors

DUKE UNIVERSITY PRESS Durham and London 1994

Second printing, 1996
© 1994 Duke University Press
All rights reserved
Printed in the United States of America on acid-free paper ∞
Typeset in Optima by Tseng Information Systems
Library of Congress Cataloging-in-Publication Data
Writing without words : alternative literacies in Mesoamerica and the Andes /
Elizabeth Hill Boone and Walter D. Mignolo, editors.
Includes bibliographical references and index.
ISBN 0-8223-1377-4 (cl : acid-free paper).—ISBN 0-8223-1388-X (pa :
acid-free paper)
1. Indians—Writing. 2. Indians of Mexico—Writing. 3. Indians—Art.
4. Writing—History. I. Boone, Elizabeth Hill.
II. Mignolo, Walter.
E59.W9W75 1993
497—dc20 93-4531 CIP

Contents

Preface and Acknowledgments

This volume stems from a roundtable held on March 23–24, 1991 at Dumbarton Oaks titled "Art and Writing: Recording Knowledge in Pre-Columbian America." The roundtable brought together a group of twenty-six scholars who had been thinking about and working on graphic systems of recordkeeping in the New World, and it culminated a year's thought and discussion at Dumbarton Oaks about the ways Pre-Columbian societies recorded and preserved information. The meeting was intended not as a formal symposium but as an informal discussion; we wanted simply to spend a few days considering and talking about graphic systems of recordkeeping.

To give structure to the meeting, twelve of the participants agreed to give relatively short presentations that were theoretical in nature and intended to open up areas for general consideration. We fully intended, however, for the meat of the roundtable to be in the discussions that followed each paper. The first day, our attention was devoted to the iconic and pictorial systems of Mesoamerica: Elizabeth Boone, John Pohl, and Peter van der Loo talked about the presentation of time, sequence, and narrative in these systems; Mary Elizabeth Smith, Barbara Mundy, and John Monahan spoke about the graphic presentation of space and territory. Then Tom Cummins opened the question of conventional systems such as the Andean quipu, where meaning is encoded without pictorial images; perhaps because he was alone in speaking about the Andean system or perhaps because we knew less about it, his comments sparked the greatest discussion. In the second day we turned to the hieroglyphic systems and texts of Mesoamerica. George Stuart, David Stuart, and Javier Urcid all explained the early inscriptions from La Mojarra and Monte Albán, after which Stephen Houston looked broadly at the Maya system. Walter Mignolo then carried the conversations into the colonial period and raised the fundamental question of writing and "the book." The participants who fleshed out the discussion were Anthony Aveni, Bruce Byland, Flora Clancy, Susan Evans, Heidi Fogel, Jill Furst, Mark King, Tim Knab, James Langley, Dana Leibsohn, Carlos Rincon, Jeanette Sherbondy, Barbara Tedlock, Dennis Tedlock, Gary Urton, and David Webster. It was an intense two days of thinking and talking about issues none of us had sufficiently considered before. We all came away invigorated and stretched by it.

Although this volume grew from the roundtable, it does not reiterate the presentations given there. Some of the talks addressed a specialized Mesoamerican audience and are being published in other forms elsewhere; some of the speakers and participants were too pressed with other commitments to prepare a contribution. Too, the focus of this volume is less on hieroglyphic systems, such as those of the Maya and the Zapotec, and more on the pictorial and conventional systems that are further from spoken language. We have added articles by Mark King and Dana Leibsohn, discussants at the meeting, as well as a contribution by Joanne Rappaport because they offer important complementary perspectives. Although Rappaport was in Italy during the roundtable, she joined the ongoing discussion of writing in postconquest Latin America upon her return. Dennis Tedlock and Gary Urton commented insightfully on an earlier version of this volume and gave us many valuable suggestions, for which we are grateful. We also thank Tedlock for pushing us to confront the issue of writing head-on and to change the title from "Records without Words" to "Writing without Words."

Elizabeth H. Boone, Dumbarton Oaks
Walter Mignolo, Duke University

WRITING WITHOUT WORDS

Elizabeth Hill Boone

Introduction: Writing and Recording Knowledge

The visual systems of recording and/or communicating information in Pre-Columbian America have always been difficult to categorize. Equally, the topic has been difficult to articulate in a single word or phrase, because the Pre-Columbian situation seems to defy the usual meaning of words such as "art" and "writing." In organizing the roundtable, "Art and Writing: Recording Knowledge in Pre-Columbian America," the first part of the title, "Art and Writing," was constantly a problem. Because there is that tendency to think of writing as visible speech and an evolutionary goal, the word "writing" when it pertains to Pre-Columbian America begs to have quotation marks around it. In indigenous America, visible speech was not often the goal. The word "art," too, carries with it modern Western notions of art as something visual to be appreciated and enjoyed but something separate from communication. Thus, the word combination "Art and Writing" seems to polarize the two and set up an either/or situation, where a visual system is either "art" at one end or it is "writing" at the other. The intention, of course, was the opposite. What I wanted to convey is that art and writing in Pre-Columbian America are largely the same thing. For example, the Nahuatl word *tlacuiloliztli* means both "to write" and "to paint" (Molina 1970: second pagination 120). They compose a graphic system that keeps and conveys knowledge, or, to put it another way, that presents ideas. And it is this view of Amerindian recordkeeping systems that should replace the old, limited notions that have previously been advanced.

In this essay I mean to focus on *systems* of writing—one could say the structure and technology of writing—rather than the *meanings* of writing, social or otherwise. Writing is much discussed these days particularly by semioticians, literary theorists, and anthropologists who are interested in issues of sign and meaning, hermeneutics, "literacy" and orality, and writing and power, to name but a few topics.[1] There are rich paths to be followed here with respect to Pre-Columbian America, but they would take the discussion in other directions and diffuse my purpose, and they are premature in this introduction. Walter Mignolo profitably walks some of these roads in his closing essay. My own purpose here is more fundamental. Most of the scholars who think and write about writing consider writing to be alphabetic writing, normally referring to one of the modern alphabetic scripts; this tends to rest as a basic assumption from which their arguments grow. My intent is to confront this common definition of "writing" and our notions of what constitute writing systems, to explode these assumptions. We have to think more broadly about visual and tactile systems of recording information, to reach a broader definition of writing.

Jacques Derrida in *Of Grammatology* has argued this position on a much wider and more theoretical level. Acknowledging the fundamental ethnocentrism, the logocentrism, that has controlled the concept of writing, he argues for the invalidity of the traditional definition of writing as a utensil to express speech, noting that "writing no longer relates to language as an exterior or frontier." Instead, he explains that "the concept of writing exceeds and comprehends that of language"; it embraces language but goes beyond it (Derrida 1976: 3, 6–9, 30–52). Derrida's philosophical project carries the issue of writing much farther than I can possibly hope to approach in this introduction. Here, my intent is much more straightforwardly practical; it is the reformation of a definition of writing that allows us to consider both verbal and nonverbal systems of graphic communication. Once we have achieved this, we will be in a position to address the extended literary and social questions.

Limited Notions of Writing

We are all aware of the commonly held belief among those scholars and particularly linguists who focus on Europe and Asia that Pre-Columbian cultures did not yet develop "true writing." We have heard terms such as illiterate, nonliterate, and preliterate applied to these peoples. Clearly the term "illiterate," with its meaning of "uneducated," is simply a pejorative misuse of the word. The term "nonliterate" implies that Amerindian cultures lacked something important—that something being writing—and it implies more subtly that this "lack" held them back in some way and caused them to be culturally deficient. The term "preliterate," of course, carries with it evolutionary expectations; it conveys the sense that humankind is characterized by a "will to writing," that writing is a universal cultural goal, and that all cultures are somewhere along the road to writing. The Pre-Columbian peoples simply had not yet arrived there, except that perhaps the Maya were further along.

We see this in most studies of writing—from Isaac Taylor's two-volume history of writing in 1899, to Leonard Bloomfield's classic study *Language* in 1933, throughout Isaac Gelb's authoritative *A Study of Writing: The Foundations of Grammatology* of 1952, in David Diringer's overview *Writing* of 1962, and even in 1989 with John DeFrancis's polemical treatment, *Visible Speech*. These all expound the common view of writing as written language, and they fashion various evolutionary models for the "development" of writing that culminates in alphabetic script.

Just as people and nations fashion their histories to eventuate in themselves,[2] writing specialists have constructed the history of writing to result in modern alphabetic systems. In these histories, indigenous American systems lie either at the beginning of or outside the developmental sequence. It is worth examining these points of view in order, firstly, to point up the unconscious bias toward Western European culture that seems to drive them and, secondly, to put us closer to understanding the relation of American recordkeeping systems to the others.

Almost all the scholars who have looked seriously at writing systems in their general sense have defined writing as spoken language that is recorded or referenced phonetically by visible marks. Since many of these scholars are linguists, it would seem natural for them to tie writing to speech. Bloomfield (1933: 283) used the term "real writing" to specify systems whose characters represent language. Gelb, whose influential study sought to "lay a foundation for a new science of writing," reserved the term "full writing" to designate the "vehicle through which exact forms of speech could be recorded in permanent form" (1963: 12).[3] Archibald Hill, Walter Ong, and anthropologist Jack Goody, too, consider writing as recorded speech, as do historians like Michael Camille and M. T. Clanchy, who have examined the phenomena.[4] The Chinese-language specialist John DeFrancis has perhaps been the most adamant on this point. His "central thesis is that all full systems of communication are based on speech. Further, no full system is possible unless so grounded," and he dismisses all nonspeech writing as "Partial/Limited/Pseudo/Non-Writing" (DeFrancis 1989: 7, 42).

New World specialists have been somewhat divided in their perspectives on writing, depending largely on whether their work analyzes hieroglyphic or pictographic texts. Mayanists, who work with language-based glyphic texts, tend to share the view of writing as recorded language. Linguist Floyd Lounsbury (1989: 203), for example, thinks of writing "in a sense broad enough to encompass the employment of word-signs of nonphonetic derivation (as well as of phonetic), but narrow enough to exclude the employment of such signs, or signs of any variety, when not generally disposed in such a manner as to represent the constituent elements of compound expressions in the user's language." Anthropologist Michael Coe (1992: 13) opens the first chapter of his book *Breaking the Maya Code* with the statement "Writing is speech put into visible form. . . ." Their definitions of writing include the Maya hieroglyphic system but exclude the more pictorial systems of the Aztec and Mixtec.

Aztec and Mixtec specialists, on the other hand, clearly do consider these pictorial systems to be writing, although these scholars (including myself) have tended to shy from giving hard definitions of what is writing. An ambiguity persists because only parts of these largely pictorial systems record language, and one senses an unease with defining writing outside of language. In her classic study of Mixtec place signs and maps, for example, Mary Elizabeth Smith (1973: 7) gets around the ambiguous position of Mixtec "picture writing," by stating that "the manuscripts to be discussed are pictographic expressions of this [Mixtec] language," and then showing how the conventions and structure of Mixtec picture writing convey meaning without necessarily expressing language. Joyce Marcus's recent and important *Mesoamerican Writing Systems* accommodates this ambiguity in a similarly encompassing way. Because she is concerned that writing not be blurred with iconography, she sees writing as having "a *format* and a *correspondence to spoken language,* which allows us to distinguish it from complex iconography," and she thus speaks of Aztec and Mixtec systems in terms of "the text [the language-based labels or captions] and accompanying scenes" (Marcus 1992: 17, 61). The characteristics she itemizes for early Mesoamerican writing systems are based on the glyphic elements, but the scope of the book embraces the entire glyphic and pictorial package (Marcus 1992: 29, 47–67). The problem Smith and Marcus have encountered and maneuvered around is the fundamental difficulty of speaking about writing without tying it to language.

Writing, in most people's minds, is graphically recorded language. The foundation on which this definition rests is the notion, as expressed by DeFrancis (1989: 7, 5), that "speech has evolved as the fullest and most efficient means of conveying thought," for "only full spoken language enables us as human beings to express any and all thought." Since "full writing" records speech, it is, then, the only system "that can be used to convey any and all thought." Thus, in most views, the most advanced writing systems convey speech the most exactly and clearly.

Implicit in this definition of writing is an evolutionary model that shows "more advanced writing systems" (those that record speech most exactly) developing from the more rudimentary ones. Invariably, the pinnacle of development is reached in modern alphabetic systems. It is not incongruous that this basic evolutionary model was solidly born in the scientific positivism of the late nineteenth century, a time when evolutionary models were being pushed throughout the natural and social sciences.[5] In 1899 Isaac Taylor presented a five-stage sequence for the development of writing, which he explained as progressing from pictures to pictorial symbols, verbal signs, syllabic signs, and ultimately alphabetic signs (Taylor 1899, 1: 5–6). Just about all subsequent students of writing have adopted the general directional thrust of Taylor's model, if not its exact stages or linearity, and there have been few to question this. Bloomfield (1933: 283) spoke of the "progress from this use of pictures to the use of real writing." Later, Gelb (1963: 190–192) charted "the direct road toward a fully developed writing" from "No Writing" to "Forerunners of Writing" to "Full Writing" (which is phonetic) in a rigidly linear progression. DeFrancis's developmental tree has more branches, but the writing systems he categorizes still evolve from pictures via rebus symbols and syllabic systems (1989: 58, 268).

If, in these views, the most developed writing systems replicate speech the most efficiently and completely, where, then, do the largely pictorial systems of Pre-Columbian America figure? Gelb (1963: v) located them at the beginnings, placing "the so-called 'Maya and Aztec writing' not under writings proper but under forerunners of writing." DeFrancis (1989: 47, 57) has accepted Maya hieroglyphs as writing under his "morphosyllabic system" category, but he has denied pictorial systems totally as writing, condemning them to the orphaned category of "Nonwriting":

> The forthright answer to how pictographs work as a system is that they don't. Pictographic writing is not a system. It is at best exceedingly limited in what it can express and who is able to understand it. . . . And it should not be called writing without the clearly expressed reservation that it refers to a very restricted type of communication. . . . While it may be legitimate to discuss pictography in a comprehensive study of human communication, to include them in works devoted to writing only obscures the issue unless they are clearly and categorically dismissed as limited, dead-end means of communication.

Other scholars of writing and memory have characterized these systems as limited (e.g., Connerton 1989: 74–75).

It is telling that the denial of pictographic writing systems as "real writing" has generally been accompanied by an insidious pejorative tone, which reveals an inability and unwillingness to understand other systems. In the 1930s, Bloomfield was clearly uncomfortable with pictographic systems, finding them impoverished and difficult, if not outright troublesome, and his approach to them was dismissive (1933: 284–285):

> [In] situations . . . that do not lend themselves to picturing; the picture-user resorts to all sorts of devices that will elicit the proper response. . . . The Ojibwa represented 'ill omen' by an owl, in ac-

Figure 1. Second section of the Dumbarton Oaks Concerto (Concerto in E Flat for chamber orchestra) by Igor Stravinski, 1938. The abstract symbols, their relationships to each other, and their positions relative to the staffs convey messages about both sound and time. Garden Library, Dumbarton Oaks. Photograph courtesy of Dumbarton Oaks.

> cordance, no doubt, with some tribal belief. When the picture-user was confronted by a problem of this kind, we may suppose that he actually spoke to himself, and tried out various wordings of the troublesome message.

Twenty years later Gelb echoed and reinforced this view by tending unconsciously to depreciate those who did not record information phonetically: "There was a time when man did not know how to write. . . . Primitive man is similar in this respect to a child, who no sooner learns to crawl than he begins to scribble on the wallpaper or to draw crude pictures in the sand" (Gelb 1963 [1952]: 24). And he, like Bloomfield, dismissed, without studying them, those recording systems that were not linguistic (Gelb 1963: 24, 4): "All the reports about the alleged use of the *quipu* for the recording of chronicles and historical events are plain fantasy. Neither the Peruvian nor the modern knot writings . . . have any other aim than that of recording the simplest facts of statistical nature."[6] Just as DeFrancis (1989: 45) dismisses pictography as a "limited, dead end means of communication" and places it in his category of "non-writing," he describes the users of pictographic systems as "living in culturally limited societies."

What is most alarming about these statements and views is that they are based on harmfully narrow views of what are *thought* and *knowledge* and what constitutes the expression of these thoughts and this knowledge, and they summarily dismiss the indigenous Western Hemisphere. It is time that we realize that such views are part of a European/Mediterranean bias that has shaped countless conceptions—such as "civilization," "art," and the "city"—that were defined according to Old World standards and therefore excluded the non-Western and non-Asian cultures. An expanded epistemological view would, and should, allow all notational systems to be encompassed. If the indigenous American phenomena are to be considered objectively, a broader view is required.

It is easy to see the fallacy of the assumptions on which most definitions of writing are based.

The notion that spoken language is the only system that allows humans to convey any and all thought fails to consider the full range of human experience. Certainly speech may be the most efficient manner of communicating many things, but it is noticeably deficient in conveying ideas of a musical, mathematical, or visual nature, for example. It is nearly impossible to communicate sound through words; instead, one uses a musical notation that has now become standard in "Western cultures" (Figure 1). Dance, too, cannot adequately be described verbally; instead, the subtle details of choreography can be recorded through one of several dance notations (Owen 1986: esp. fig. 8.15).

The notational systems of mathematics and science were also developed precisely because ordinary language could not "express the full import of scientific relationships," as Stillman Drake has explained.[7] Drake reminds us that although Isaac Newton originally advanced his force law as "The change of motion is proportional to the motive force, and is made in the direction of the straight line in which that force is impressed," we are taught it as "F = kma," an equation that is not only more precise but also more comprehensive (1986: 141). Mathematics and modern physics are now comprehended only through mastery of their own notational languages, which lie outside the normal spoken word (Figure 2).

$$\sigma_X^2 = \frac{1}{n}\left\{\sum_{i=1}^{n} X - n\overline{X}^2\right\}$$

Figure 2. Formula for calculating the variance of a sample. Symbol, size, and relative placement all contribute to the specific meaning.

Such special languages succeed where ordinary languages do not because of the human ability to "grasp certain relationships visually at a glance but not to describe them in words with anything like equal precision" (Drake 1986: 136). And this ability to understand relationships that are graphically presented has led to more pictorial and diagrammatic recording systems, especially in chemistry, which is "dominated by problems of structure and combination" (Drake 1986: 150). Since "structure is generally more effectively depicted than described," complex structural diagrams and even three-dimensional models function instead of words and sentences to convey information. Such diagrams "led to the very complex three-dimensional models required in the solution of the double-helix structure of DNA. . . . The line between notations and models is no longer sharp, nor is the line between theories and models. Thus we see how special notations may become equivalent to theories and serve science in the place of words and sentences" (Drake 1986: 153). As Drake (1986: 147) has summarized: "The pictures we form in science may be ordinary grammatical statements or they may be special notation systems or they may be quite literally pictures drawn to represent structural relations among external objects, actual or hypothetical. Structural relations are frequently perceptible at a glance when they would be very cumbersome to describe in words, and might not be as efficiently conveyed by equational or other mathematical notations. Pictorial notations are often valuable in physics, as for instance in crystallography. They are still more useful in chemistry, which in its beginnings in modern form was faced with problems different in kind from those of early modern physics—problems of structure and combination rather than of motion and force."

Even outside the natural sciences proper, diagramming systems are the choice for "describing, interpreting, and communicating complex phenomena difficult to encompass with verbal or mathematical language" (Wrolstad and Fisher 1986: 131). As Charles Owen (1986: 156) points out, "the diagram is special in its ability to render the invisible visible." It can be efficient and precise, and it can make a powerful statement.

Maps, for example, express spatial relationships especially well. They have no equal in their ability efficiently to describe relative and actual size, form, and placement. I could explain verbally the geographic situation of the cultures whose recordmaking systems we are considering in this volume, but no quantity of words would have the same ease and precision as the map in Figure 3.

Maps and diagrams are part of the way we "envision information," to use Edward Tufte's term. As Tufte (1990: 33) has said, "We envision information in order to reason about, communicate, document, and preserve that knowledge." By envisioning it instead of recording it in alphabetic writing, we clearly recognize that spoken language is not always the best medium for communicating thought.

Figure 3. Map identifying the general location of the major Mesoamerican and Andean writing systems discussed in this volume. Aztec and Mixtec systems are concentrated in Central Mexico, with the Maya extending farther to the south and east into modern Honduras and El Salvador. The *quipu* was used throughout the Inca empire.

As Jacques Derrida has expressed it, "it is a peculiarity of our epoch that, at the moment when the phoneticization of writing . . . begins to lay hold on world culture, science, in its advancements, can no longer be satisfied with it." The writing of theoretical mathematics "has never been absolutely linked with a phonetic production. Within cultures practicing so-called phonetic production, mathematics is not just an enclave. . . .

This enclave is also the place where the practice of scientific language challenges intrinsically and with increasing profundity the ideal of phonetic writing. . . . But beyond theoretical mathematics, the development of the *practical methods* of information retrieval extends the possibilities of the "message" vastly, to the point where it is no longer the "written" translation of a language. . . ."[8]

For those thoughts that *are* best communicated through spoken language, however, we should examine the notion that syllabic and alphabetic writing records this speech. Although this assumption underlies the standard definition of writing as "visible speech," written language is never an exact transcription of spoken language. As Derrida succinctly says, "phonetic writing *does not exist.*"[9]

On one level, writing and speaking are different discourses. With some languages, like Arabic, the written and spoken spheres are distinctly separate (Sampson 1985: 26). Studies of writing and speaking in the United States also show that written prose is almost always different from spoken prose.[10]

On another level, when writing consciously attempts to replicate speech, it can only approximate its goal. Gelb, Hill, Sampson, and other specialists in writing have noted that writing is only a partial system, for it leaves some of the linguistic structure out of the record, failing "to indicate adequately the prosodic features" such as "quality (or length), accent (or stress), tone (or pitch), and pauses," except that "the latter are partially . . . expressed by word division and punctuation marks. . . ."[11] These limitations have been of special concern to playwrights and ethnologists alike.

In advocating the use of a tape recorder to preserve the stories that are recounted to him, Dennis Tedlock (1982: 3) highlights the difference between hearing speech that is being recorded and hearing speech in order to write it down: "The [listening] ear will mostly hear the *music* of the voice, the rises and falls of pitch and amplitude, the tone and timbre, the interaction of the sounds and silences. In short, the mythographer who postpones the use of pencil and notebook [who uses a tape recorder] will hear all the dimensions of the voice that the spelling ear tunes out." Tedlock (1982: 4) notes that the major difference between the original speech and the textual transcription is in the temporal dimension, for the transcription does not record "the internal timing of the performance and the accompanying events . . . in its sequences but also in the proportions of its durations." Thus, his own transcriptional form uses a combination of orthographic devices, spatial markers, capitals, and parenthetical guides to tone in order to preserve as much of the full performance as possible. Even still, the written word fails to convey the fullness of speech.

A final assertion made by historians of writing that should be examined is the evolutionary model. Conventional thought has it that writing developed from pictures to abstract signs to phonetic characters. In the most general sense this may have been the case in the ancient Near East, where Babylonian-Assyrian writing and Egyptian writing began with pictographic systems that then became more abstract and ultimately more phonetic.[12] It would be a mistake, however, to assume that this evolutionary model should hold universally for all systems. Denise Schmandt-Besserat has argued that writing developed in Uruk from the use of abstract clay tokens, in the form of spheres, cones, disks, cylinders, and tetrahedrons; thus, the earliest permanent recordkeeping system developed from the abstract to the pictorial, instead of the other way around.[13] In Mesoamerica, too, there is cause to rethink the evolution from picture to abstract character, for the Aztec and Mixtec writing systems of the fourteenth and fifteenth centuries are almost entirely pictorial, while the earlier Maya hieroglyphic system of the third to the tenth centuries was much more abstract. Thus, as Walter Mignolo (1989: 62) has noted, "the history of writing is not an evolutionary process driving toward the alphabet, but rather a series of coevolutionary processes in which different writing systems followed their own transformations."

An Inclusive Definition of Writing

In relatively recent years the narrow view of writing as visible speech and the correspondingly limited view of literacy as the ability to read and write in alphabetic script have increasingly come under attack. Many Pre-Columbian specialists have long ago disregarded these limited views,[14] but now more and more scholars in other fields are actively calling for a reappraisal of the standard definitions and the ethnocentrism behind them. Merald Wrolstad and Dennis Fisher's edited volume, *Toward a New Understanding of Literacy,* is one attempt to look newly at "how we create and use visible language, and how these connect with the way we think and shape our world." Although they do not redefine literacy, they do suggest that "it is time for a general reassessment," and several of the papers in the volume stress the potential of using the complete "graphic catalogue," not just verbal and mathematical notation.[15] Specialists in ancient languages and modern literacy are now seeing that the old classifications of writing do not fit.[16]

Given the proliferation of visual forms of communication, there is even the suggestion by M. T. Clanchy (1979: 8) that alphabetic script "may be entering its final century." Foreseeing the demise of the book, André Leroi-Gourhan predicts that "reading will still retain its importance for some centuries to come, . . . but writing [understood in the sense of linear inscription] seems likely to disappear rapidly. . . . It is absolutely certain that if scientific reasoning has clearly nothing to lose with the disappearance of writing, philosophy and literature will definitely see their forms evolve."[17]

A broader, more encompassing definition of writing is clearly needed. Looking back at what has already been written about writing, we can find in several studies the raw materials for this definition. Some of the same authors who considered writing narrowly also discussed nonverbal systems. Thinking alphabetically, they just chose the narrower and more evolutionary view. Gelb's history of writing includes a stage that he calls "semasiographic," "in which meanings—not words or sounds—are suggested by signs." Although he goes on to say that "This symbolism is outside of our normal system of writing," he adds that "Equally outside of our normal phonetic system of signs are the conventions employed in mathematics, logic, and some other sciences" (Gelb 1963: 11, 15).

Hill, too, narrowly defines writing as representing language, but his typology of language is broad enough to include "discourse systems" as well as morphemic and phonemic systems. Hill's discourse systems convey meaning directly through pictographs and symbols. Although he considers them "primitive," he justifies their inclusion by saying that they "are basically the same as more advanced types. The purpose of writing can be said to be the unique identification of an utterance. All systems leave some of the linguistic structure out of the record. . . . Since each system is therefore, partial, each system relies on the reader's previous knowledge to supply the necessary background for successful identification" (Hill 1967: 93–94). He goes on to argue that, "In these terms, the mnemonic element in *quipu* or pictorial representations is different only in degree not in kind, from background knowledge demanded of a modern reader. . . . All writing systems seek to perform their central task as efficiently as possible, leaving out all information beyond that necessary to identification. The primitive systems [ie., discourse systems] leave out the most information, it is true, but leaving out information is characteristic of all systems" (Hill 1967: 95).

Geoffrey Sampson's volume, *Writing Systems,* comes closest to giving us a good working definition of writing. He recognizes the problem of viewing "writing as a phenomenon essentially parasitic on spoken language" and tries out several definitions of writing in order to be as inclusive as possible and still distinguish writing from art. His first definition—"to communicate relatively specific ideas by means of permanent, visible marks"—and his second definition—"to communicate ideas in a conventional manner"—both have limitations, which he points up (Sampson 1985: 26–28). By combining them, however, these problems fall away. We then can define writing broadly as *the communication of relatively specific ideas in a conventional manner by means of permanent, visible marks.*

The focus in this definition is on communication, on the structured use of conventions, and on the element of permanency. In this definition, writing is like language in being able to communicate meaning by "*structures* of symbols defined by their interconnections," for, as Sampson (1985: 12) continues, "What gives any particular element of a language its role in the language is not its superficial physical properties but, rather, the relationships it enters into with the other elements of the language." The meaning of the symbols or script can be understood by those who have learned the conventions (or the grammar) for interpreting them. And much of the point of writing is that it is permanent (Sampson 1985: 26, 17). Using this definition, two basic kinds of writing can be distinguished.

One is what Sampson calls glottographic systems, because they represent speech; they compose the traditional definition of writing. Gelb (1963: 11, 191, 250) calls them "phonographic" or "phonetic" and considers them to be "full writing," and DeFrancis (1989: 58) groups them under his equivalent category of "syllabic systems," which he also equates with writing. Hill (1967: 93) divides them into "morphemic" and "phonemic."

The other category, and the one of greatest interest to us here, is what Sampson, like Gelb, calls "semasiographic systems." The term combines the Greek word *semasia* meaning "meaning" with a "graphic" presentational style to indicate those graphic systems of communication where marks communicate meaning directly and within the structure of their own system. Semasiographic systems of communication convey ideas independently from language and on the same logical level as spoken language rather than being parasitic on them as ordinary scripts are. They are supralinguistic because they can function outside of language. Hill labels these systems as "discourse systems," choosing "discourse" over the Greek "semasia" to indicate systems that have their own internal structures and conventions to give meaning. These systems are far from being the dead ends DeFrancis sees. They actually seem to be on an ascendancy these days in an increasingly international and multilingual world. As articulated by Hill (1967: 94) there are two types of semasiographic systems.

One is conventional, where meaning is indicated by the interrelationship of symbols that are arbitrarily codified. Mathematical notation (Figure 2) is one example of such a conventional system, where the numerals, letters, and plethora of specialized signs are conventionally understood as numbers, things, and actions. In these systems, meaning is also conveyed by relative placement, by the spatial relationships of the parts to each other. Scientific notations belong to this category, as do musical and some choreographic notations (Figure 1).

The other type of semasiographic system is iconic. We are seeing more and more of this as our culture becomes increasingly visual. The body of international road signs, signs for travelers in airports, and even cleaning instructions in garments are largely iconic systems that carry meaning without a detour through speech; so, too, is the system of "icons" that signals different functions on my Macintosh computer. In these systems there is generally a natural relationship between the image and its referent, such as a human shown shoveling to signal a construction zone. They have an iconic foundation, but usually they also involve arbitrary conventional elements, so that they tend to blur the distinction between conventional and iconic systems. The system of road signs, for example, combines iconic images with conventional shapes and colors: the red hexagon to mean "stop" or "halt," the yellow triangle to signal caution, the rectangle for messages about speed.

Such semasiographic systems can be understood outside of language once one understands the logical system (a system comparable to a grammar) that drives and orders them. The instruction panel for operating a hand dryer in a university gymnasium (Figure 4), for example, achieves meaning through the interplay of images, abstractions, and sequence, all understood because of the context in which they appear and because the audience has learned how to read such messages. The two images of the hands would probably be recognized by their intended audience in any context, but the button and the three wavy lines (painted red) are abstractions that achieve specific meaning because they are part of this instruction panel on an air dryer. Sequence is established by the side-by-side presentation of the frames, which the audience automatically knows to read left-to-right. Iconic systems such as this have been taking over the domains of public communication because they convey meaning regardless of the language one speaks, and they are quickly understood by those participating in the same general culture.

Michael Coe (1992: 18–19) has recently argued that these semasio-

Figure 4. Instructions for operating a forced-hot-air dryer, of the type found in public wash facilities. The message is conveyed by the sequential presentation of recognizable images and abstractions, understood in the context of the machine. Courtesy of the World Dryer Corporation.

graphic systems are not divorced from language because (a) their meaning still has to be learned through the medium of language, and (b) individuals mentally speak a language when they see such signs. I would argue to the contrary. Certainly a reader can verbally phrase the meaning of a mathematical formula or an informational sign, but another person can offer a different phrase that has the same meaning; more often, individuals simply understand the meaning at a glance. The point is that one does not have to go through spoken language to comprehend the message.

Sampson indicates that it is a matter of choice whether or not to include semasiographs in the definition of writing (1985: 29–30, 32). I feel it essential that we do include them. If we are to consider thought and communication broadly, we must recognize the supralinguistic ways of presenting knowledge. If we are ever to understand the structural principles that govern such systems, we must realize that they operate with their own grammar.

Writing Systems in Pre-Columbian America

Pre-Columbian peoples used both glottographic and semasiographic systems. At different times, several cultures in Mesoamerican and Andean South America wrote with hieroglyphics, pictorial images, and abstract signs, combining elements of all three to different degrees. These indigenous American writing systems have been difficult to place in general histories of writing because they are so varied, and they are poorly understood by most writing specialists.

Maya writing (Figure 5) is by far the best known, especially recently since advances in its decipherment have attracted much scholarly and general attention, and it is the New World system most easily categorized as writing. It is a glottographic system, considered even by traditionalists as close to being "real writing." Hill (1967: 95) and DeFrancis

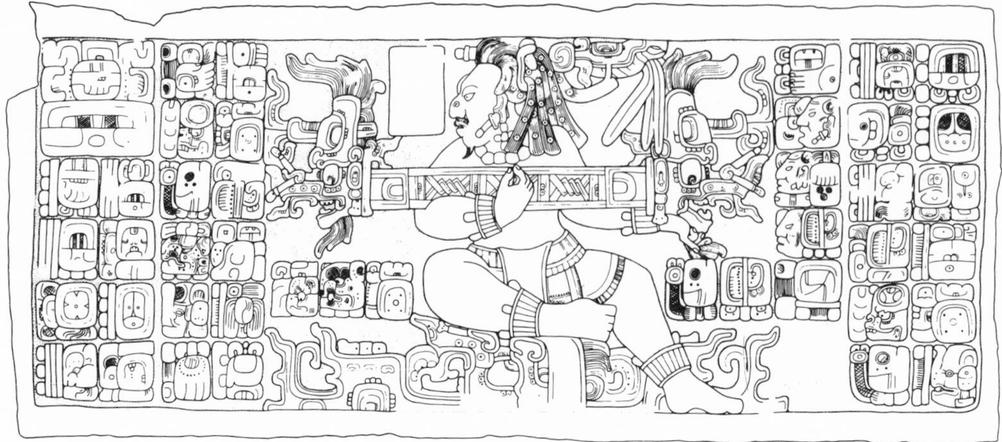

Figure 5. Drawing of a carved wall panel from Lacanha, Mexico. The Maya ruler of Lacanha is pictured seated and holding the ceremonial bar of his office. The surrounding hieroglyphic texts tell of his ancestry, give his titles, and relate (with dates) the important events in his life. Robert Woods Bliss Collection, Dumbarton Oaks, no. B-145. Drawing by David Stuart, courtesy of Dumbarton Oaks.

(1989: 58) classify the Maya script along with Sumerian and Chinese as a morphemic or morphosyllabic system because of its strong phonetic component. As a mixed hieroglyphic system, it employs a combination of logograms representing whole words, phonetic signs, and semantic qualifiers, which together reproduce a verbal text. The individual glyphs feature large central main signs with smaller affixes attached to one or more of the four sides. These affixes function largely as complementary ideograms to the main signs (indicating color, for example), as semantic determinatives, and as carriers of phonetic information to enable the main signs to be correctly interpreted. Organized to be read in a preordained and largely unchanging order, the glyphs are usually found in paired columns, that are read upper left, upper right, lower left, lower right, and so forth down the columns.

Maya writing was well developed by the first century A.D. By this time, several other Mesoamerican cultures, notably in the Gulf Coast and in Oaxaca, had also developed similar hieroglyphic systems. These, too, seem to be language-based, but since much fewer examples of these have survived, they are less well known.

The other Pre-Columbian writing systems are semasiographic. In Mesoamerica, the Mixtec and Aztec recordkeeping systems are highly pictorial (Figure 6). Often called picture writing, they can be classified as iconic systems within the larger semasiographic category. Where Maya hieroglyphs are predominantly phonetic, the Mixtec and Aztec systems are largely ideographic. They are characterized by a high proportion of visual description, but like other iconic systems they also use some arbitrary conventions. Meaning is carried by pictorial and conventionalized

Figure 6. Detail from the Lienzo of Zacatepec (upper left corner). The Mixtec culture hero Lord 4 Wind (seated on the platform on the left) conveys the authority of rule on Lord 11 Jaguar (seated opposite him), in a ceremony attended by various officials (seated and/or simply named to the right); thus begins Lord 11 Jaguar's pilgrimage before he eventually enters the territory of Zacatepec and establishes his rule. The pictorial elements name the participants, specify the events, date and locate them, and give genealogical information for Lord 11 Jaguar. Photograph after Lienzo de Zacatepec 1900: pl. 2.

images, by their relative placement, and by the contexts in which they participate. The precise reading order is not firmly set, so that different readings are possible. Phonetic elements may be present—especially in personal names and place names—but they often operate across language. Aztec (Nahuatl-speaking) scribes from Central Mexico could therefore read the Mixtec histories of southern Oaxaca, giving them voice in their own language. Like other semasiographic systems, the Aztec and Mixtec writing systems are intelligible to those who share a general cultural base even though they might speak different languages.

In Mesoamerica, one feature that distinguishes hieroglyphic systems (such as those developed by the Maya and Zapotec) is that there is a distinction made between images and texts. Although certainly one sees glyphs being introduced onto and within the figures in a pictorial scene—this is apparent in the codices as well as on the relief panels and sculptured monuments—it is clear that parts of the text intrude or enter into what is essentially the space of the images. Generally there are texts on one hand (usually in text blocks, with their own reading order and structure), and there are pictures on the other. They complement each other, they have slightly different meanings, and they are closely tied to each other in providing the full meaning of the sculptural or painted effort, but they are nonetheless two parts acting in harmony. And they tend to occupy separate sections of the surface.

In the semasiographic systems of the Mixtecs and Aztecs, the pictures *are* the texts. There is no distinction between word and image. Individual or composite glyphs are used to indicate personal names and place names, but they are fundamentally a part of the pictorial presentation. And it is the relationship of the disparate pictorial elements that carries the meaning. As Sampson (1985: 12) has said about writing in general, meaning is conveyed by the relationships and the interconnections of the elements.

While Gelb saw semasiographic systems as precursors to glottographic/phonographic systems, in the New World we know this not to have been the case. Hieroglyphic systems that were glottographic developed early in Mesoamerica—perhaps as early as 500 B.C. in Oaxaca and certainly by A.D. 100 in the Gulf Coast and the Maya region—and they were widely known. But the Teotihuacanos, contemporaries with the Maya between *circa* A.D. 200 and 750, never adopted one of these systems and did not develop their own version, just as the Aztecs and Mixtecs five hundred years later eschewed hieroglyphic writing for their own pictorial systems. Clearly, visual systems of permanent communication in the New World functioned differently from those in the Old World; the need to record speech was not universally felt.

This is even more apparent in Andean South America. There the Inca recording system, the *quipu,* is not known to have any phonetic component (Figure 7). Created of cotton and wool cords that were colored, spun, twisted, and knotted in different ways and combinations, Andean *quipus* hold and convey knowledge separate from language. *Quipus* have been almost universally excluded from the larger family of writing systems, even by Mesoamericanists (who see them as codes or counting devices),[18] because they seem to lack linguistic referents of any kind.

Figure 7. Inca *quipu,* one of the more complex examples here spread out radially to reveal better the details of cords and knots. Meaning is carried by knot type and placement, as well as by the color, size, placement, spin, and ply of the cords. Museo Nacional de Antropología y Arqueología, Lima, Peru. Photograph after Ascher and Ascher 1981: 34.

Because none has been deciphered, there is the tendency to see them as indecipherable mnemonic devices. Their physical nature—being fashioned three dimensionally of fabric rather than being two-dimensional marks on a flat surface—also sets them apart and works to deny them the status of writing. Our inability to read them should not, however, make us unable to see them as writing systems. Like Aztec and Mixtec writing, *quipus* function semasiographically. But unlike these Mesoamerican pictorial systems, their elements are conventional rather than iconic. *Quipus* abstract information through color, texture, form and size (of the knots and the cords), and relative placement, but they do not picture things or ideas. In this way, *quipu* writing is like mathematical and scientific notation, and somewhat like musical notation, where arbitrarily codified symbols hold meaning according to their interrelationships. It should therefore be no surprise that *quipus* have been explained largely from a mathematical perspective.[19]

One thing shared by all these indigenous New World systems is that they give accountability. Because they are permanent, or relatively so, they functioned for their societies to *document* and to *establish* ideas. As records, they are memory that can be inspected by others. The hieroglyphic text and the pictorial-iconic presentation could be read or interpreted by many people other than their creator. Andean *quipus* may not have been universally readable, but they certainly could be read by others once the categories of encoded knowledge were conveyed. Most importantly, all were accepted as valid documents.

What interested those of us who gathered over the weekend of the roundtable is: What were these Pre-Columbian writing systems? How did they function generally? What kinds of information did they convey? And how specifically did they convey this information? And finally, what was the audience of these systems, and how were they received? We did not fully answer even one of these questions at the roundtable, but I believe we came closer than any of us anticipated, and, more importantly, we opened a road of inquiry, thought, and dialogue that may enable us and others to answer them.

Notes

1 See, for example, Barthes (1967), Derrida (1976, 1978), Ricoeur (1981). On literacy and orality see in particular Clanchy (1979), Ong (1982), Tannen (1982), Camille (1985), and Goody (1982, 1986), as well as his critic Halverson (1992); on writing and power see Goody (1987), Larsen (1988), Mignolo (1989), Marcus (1992).

2 Handler (1985), Florescano (1993), and Errington (1993) are only some of the scholars who have explained how nations and ethnicities have presented their past to validate the present.

3 Originally published in 1952, the second edition appeared in 1963.

4 Hill 1967: 93; Ong 1982: 84; Goody 1987: 8–12; Camille 1985: 28; Clanchy 1979. Although Derrida has argued for the primacy of writing over speech, he, too, thinks of writing as ultimately tied to speech; see Yates's discussion of this (1990: 211–213, 222).

5 See, for example, Darwin 1859 and Morgan 1877.

6 This latter statement discounts the ethnohistorical records that indicate the Inca used knotted cords also to record histories, other narratives, and songs; Locke (1923: 33–45) reviews these sources.

7 Drake 1986, 131, 135–141; see also Cajori 1974.

8 Derrida 1976: 4, 9–10 (Derrida's italics).

9 Ibid., 39 (Derrida's italics).

10 Scholars like Ong (1967, 1982) and Tannen (1982), among others, have pointed out the different narrative and grammatical structures, and the different vocabularies, of spoken and written communications.

11 Quoted from Gelb 1963: 14. See also Hill 1967: 93; Sampson 1985: 26; and Derrida 1976: 88.

12 See Friederich 1957: 35.

13 Schmandt-Besserat 1978, 1982; see also Larsen (1988), who makes a similar argument.

14 Dibble (1971), Smith (1973), and Berlo (1983, 1989) are a few of the scholars who have approached this issue directly.

15 Wrolstad and Fisher 1986: ix. Especially pertinent are the articles by Owen, Drake, Twyman, and Aveni.

16 E.g., Larsen 1988: 173; Harbsmeier 1988: 273–274.

17 Leroi-Gourhan, *Le geste et la parole* (1965), 2: 261–262, quoted from Derrida 1976: 332–333 n. 86 (Derrida's brackets).

18 See Coe 1992: 19; Marcus 1992: 26–27.

19 See Locke 1923; Ascher and Ascher 1981.

References

Ascher, Marcia, and Robert Ascher. 1981. *Code of the Quipu: A Study of Media, Mathematics, and Culture.* Ann Arbor: University of Michigan Press.

Aveni, Anthony. 1986. Non-Western Notational Frameworks and the Role of Anthropology in Our Understanding of Literacy. In Wrolstad and Fisher 1986, 252–280.

Barthes, Roland. 1967. *Elements of Semiology.* Trans. A. Lavers and C. Smith. London: Jonathan Cape.

Berlo, Janet Catherine, ed. 1983. *Text and Image in Pre-Columbian Art.* BAR International Series 180. Oxford.

———. 1989. Early Writing in Central Mexico: In Tlilli, In Tlapalli before A.D. 1000. In *Mesoamerica after the Decline of Teotihuacan, A.D. 700–900,* ed. Richard A. Diehl and Janet Catherine Berlo, 19–47. Washington: Dumbarton Oaks.

Bloomfield, Leonard. 1933. *Language.* New York: Holt, Rinehart and Winston.

Cajori, Florian. 1974. *History of Mathematical Notations.* La Salle: Open Court.

Camille, Michael. 1985. Seeing and Reading: Some Visual Implications of Medieval Literacy and Illiteracy. *Art History* 8, no. 1: 26–49.

Clanchy, M. T. 1979. *From Memory to Written Record: England, 1066–1307.* Cambridge, Massachusetts: Harvard University Press.

Coe, Michael D. 1992. *Breaking the Maya Code.* New York: Thames and Hudson.

Connerton, Paul. 1989. *How Societies Remember.* Cambridge: Cambridge University Press.

Darwin, Charles. 1859. *On the Origin of Species by Means of Natural Selection, or the Preservation of Favoured Races in the Struggle for Life.* London: Watts.

DeFrancis, John. 1989. *Visible Speech: The Diverse Oneness of Writing Systems.* Honolulu: University of Hawaii Press.

Derrida, Jacques. 1976. *Of Grammatology.* Trans. Gayatri Chakravorty Spivak. Baltimore: The Johns Hopkins University Press.

———. 1978. *Writing and Difference.* Trans. A. Bass. London: Routledge and Kegan Paul.

Dibble, Charles E. 1971. Writing in Central Mexico. In vol. 10 of *Handbook of Middle American Indians,* ed. Robert Wauchope, Gordon Ekholm, and Ignacio Bernal, 322–332. Austin: University of Texas Press.

Diringer, David. 1962. *Writing.* London: Thames and Hudson.

Drake, Stillman. 1986. Literacy and Scientific Notations. In Wrolstad and Fisher 1986, 135–155.

Errington, Shelly. 1993. Progressivist Stories and the Pre-Columbian Past: Notes on Mexico and the United States. In *Collecting the Pre-Columbian Past,* ed. Elizabeth Hill Boone, 209–249. Washington: Dumbarton Oaks.

Florescano, Enrique. 1993. The Creation of the Museo Nacional de Antropología of Mexico and its Scientific, Educational, and Political Purposes. In *Collecting the Pre-Columbian Past,* ed. Elizabeth Hill Boone, 81–103. Washington: Dumbarton Oaks.

Friedrich, Johannes. 1957. *Extinct Languages.* New York: The Philosophical Library.

Gelb, I. J. 1963. *A Study of Writing.* 2d ed. Chicago: University of Chicago Press.

Goody, Jack. 1982. Alternative Paths in Knowledge in Oral and Literate Cultures. In Tannen 1982, 201–215.

———. 1986. *The Logic of Writing and the Organization of Society.* Cambridge, England: Cambridge University Press.

———. 1987. *The Interface between the Written and the Oral.* Cambridge, England: Cambridge University Press.

Halverson, John. 1992. Goody and the Implosion of the Literacy Thesis. *Man,* n.s. 27, no. 2: 301–317.

Handler, Richard. 1985. On Having a Culture: Nationalism and the Preservation of Quebec's *Patrimoine.* In *Objects and Others: Essays on Museums and Material Culture,* ed. George W. Stocking, Jr., 192–217. Madison: University of Wisconsin Press.

Harbsmeier, Michael. 1988. Inventions of Writing. In *State and Society: The Emergence and Development of Social Hierarchy and Political Centralization,* ed. John Gledhill and Barbara Bender, 253–276. London: Unwin Hyman.

Hill, Archibald A. 1967. The Typology of Writing Systems. In *Papers in Linguistics in Honor of Leon Dostert,* ed. William M. Austin, 92–99. The Hague: Mouton.

Larsen, Mogens Trolle. 1988. The Role of Writing and Literacy in the Development of Social and Political Power. In *State and Society: The Emergence and Development of Social Hierarchy and Political Centralization,* ed. John Gledhill and Barbara Bender, 173–191. London: Unwin Hyman.

Locke, L. Leland. 1923. *The Ancient Quipu or Peruvian Knot Record.* New York: American Museum of Natural History.

Lounsbury, Floyd. 1989. The Ancient Writing of Middle America. In *The Origins of Writing,* ed. Wayne M. Senner. Lincoln: University of Nebraska Press.

Marcus, Joyce. 1992. *Mesoamerican Writing Systems: Propaganda, Myth, and History in Four Ancient Civilizations.* Princeton: Princeton University Press.

Mignolo, Walter. 1989. Literacy and Colonization: The New World Experience. In *1492/1992: Re/discovering Colonial Writing,* ed. René Jara and Nicholas Spadaccini, 51–96. Hispanic Issues 4. Minneapolis: Prisma Institute.

Molina, Alonso de. 1970. *Vocabulario en lengua castellana y mexicana y mexicana y castellana.* Ed. Miguel León-Portilla. Mexico: Porrua.

Morgan, Lewis Henry. 1877. *Ancient Society: Or Researches in the Lines of Human Progress from Savagery, through Barbarism to Civlization.* New York: H. Holt.

Ong, Walter J. 1967. *The Presence of the Word.* New Haven: Yale University Press.

———. 1982. *Orality and Literacy: The Technologizing of the Word.* London: Methuen.

Owen, Charles L. 1986. Technology, Literacy, and Graphic Systems. In Wrolstad and Fisher 1986: 156–187.

Ricoeur, Paul. 1981. *Hermeneutics and the Human Sciences.* Ed. and trans. J. Thompson. Cambridge, England: Cambridge University Press.

Sampson, Geoffrey. 1985. *Writing Systems: A Linguistic Introduction.* Stanford: Stanford University Press.

Schmandt-Besserat, Denise. 1978. The Earliest Precursors of Writing. *Scientific American* 238: 50–59.

———. 1982. How Writing Came About. *Zeitschrift für Papyrologie und Epigraphik* 47: 1–5.

Smith, Mary Elizabeth. 1973. *Picture Writing from Ancient Southern Mexico: Mixtec Place Signs and Maps.* Norman: University of Oklahoma Press.

Tannen, Deborah, ed. 1982. *Spoken and Written Language: Exploring Orality and Literacy.* New Jersey: Ablex.

Taylor, Isaac. 1899. *The History of the Alphabet.* 2 vols. New York: Schribner's.

Tedlock, Dennis. 1982. *The Spoken Word and the Work of Interpretation.* Philadelphia: University of Pennsylvania Press.

Tufte, Edward R. 1990. *Envisioning Information.* Cheshire, Connecticut: Graphics Press.

Twyman, Michael. 1986. Articulating Graphic Language: A Historical Perspective. In Wrolstad and Fisher 1986, 188–251.

Wrolstad, Merald E., and Dennis F. Fisher, eds. 1986. *Toward a New Understanding of Literacy.* New York: Praeger.

Yates, Timothy. 1990. Jacques Derrida: "There is nothing outside of the text." In *Reading Material Cultures: Structuralism, Hermeneutics, and Post-Structuralism,* ed. Christopher Tilley, 206–280. Oxford: Basil Blackwell.

Stephen Houston

Literacy among the Pre-Columbian Maya: A Comparative Perspective

Literacy, the ability to link language and script, forms one of the most important topics in twentieth-century linguistics (e.g., Ong 1982). On a practical level literacy relates to matters of pedagogy and societal development (Cipolla 1969; Sanderson 1972; Street 1984), and on a theoretical level to the interaction of spoken and written language and the intensity of cognitive change (Chafe and Tannen 1987; Goody 1987: 263). Still undeveloped, however, is an understanding of literacy in the Pre-Columbian world, particularly among the Maya of Mesoamerica, where scribal arts reached an extraordinary degree of accomplishment and complexity. This essay explores the Maya evidence for literacy against a backdrop of comparative information from other parts of Mesoamerica and the Old World. Its aim: to present a perspective on literacy that goes beyond the particulars of Maya culture, yet enriches the debate on ancient literacy and its consequences with evidence from a region that has been persistently neglected or misunderstood by writers on the subject (e.g., Goody 1987: 22, 23).

Perspectives on Ancient Literacy

The subject of ancient literacy presupposes several questions: Is there a universal definition of literacy, or should literacy be defined in highly variable and culturally determined ways? How does reading depart from writing—that is, to what extent does a text record a complete message, to be studied at leisure in a setting divorced from the oral recitation of that message? By their nature do certain writing systems, particularly those of a logosyllabic kind, inhibit the growth of widespread literacy and reflective mindsets?[1] And how many could read and write in the ancient world?

What makes these questions difficult to answer is the nature of the available evidence. Unlike modern linguists, who have the benefit of living speakers to survey and interview, we cannot study ancient literacy by direct means. In archaeological terms, this stems from the problem of inadequate sampling. Often, the relative lack or abundance of inscriptions reveals little or nothing about literacy, about how many people could write, who could write, and to what degree. Other forms of writing simply failed to survive, so that negative evidence cannot be interpreted as a sign of limited literacy (Harvey 1966: 586, 590; Mann 1985: 206; Johnston 1983: 66). We can escape from this impasse by dealing with the few direct clues that survive and by examining indirect clues—expectations derived from the study of comparable writing systems, from what the ancients themselves said about literacy, and from an understanding of how scripts functioned in society.

Defining Literacy

With such evidence we can address the first question: What are the definitions of literacy? The more abundant data from the Old World reveal an enormous range of meanings (Schofield 1968: 313–314; Thomas 1989: 19–20, 33–34). In the first place, the ability to read was not necessarily the same as the ability to write (Clanchy 1979: 183; Harris 1989: 5), since the latter often involved greater preparation and skill. Ironically, in some societies of Late Antiquity, a person could be regarded as "literate" or even be termed a "scribe," yet show minimal competence; that is, some people could write but not read! The scribes from Fayum, Egypt, barely able to scrawl their names or copy another's script, are notorious in this regard (see also Troll 1990: 113–114); yet witness their anger when characterized as illiterate (Youtie 1971: 248), a situation that compelled the Emperor Justinian to avoid confusion in his notarial system by recognizing various degrees of literacy (Youtie 1971: 254, 261). At the other extreme lies the Chinese conception of "full literacy" (Rawski 1979: 4–5). In imperial China, literacy presupposed a thorough grounding in Confucian learning. Nonetheless, more objective measures of literacy in China signal the widespread ability to use Chinese characters as early as the fifth century A.D., although exegetical skill is likely to have been limited in all periods (Rawski 1979: 5).

The essential point here is that literacy was often defined in cultural terms and in ways that make it difficult to evaluate the meaning of ancient references to the numbers of people who could read or write.[2] For this reason alone, we should adopt a flexible definition of literacy. Attempts to define "full" literacy in rigid terms, such as Eric Havelock's emphasis on a personalized literary tradition recorded in alphabetic script (e.g., Havelock 1982: 6, 27, 57), cast the term in ways that seem tendentious, leading to invidious comparisons with Classical Greece. By liberating the word from Havelock's Classical grip, we can acknowledge not so much different kinds of literacy, as a continuum of scribal practice that ranges along two axes.

The first axis is *production* ("writing"), which extends from the Fayum scribe's crude signature to the calligraphic masterworks of Chinese mandarins. The second axis charts the *response* to an encoded message ("reading"), ranging from the bare perception of meaning or sound to a facility with detailed exegesis. States of literacy may be illustrated graphically by imagining a two-dimensional coordinate system, with production on the x axis and response on the y. If ascending competence is charted from left to right, and from top to bottom, then the lower left and upper right corners represent, respectively, the nadir and pinnacle of scribal accomplishment; the terms of reference are not an absolute standard of literacy, but lie within the tradition itself. A person capable of fluent reading and exegesis, but incapable of effective draughtmanship, would fit into the lower right corner; a craftsman carving a Maya text or a Medieval scribe copying a passage composed by another would fit a slot in the upper left.

There is another point to keep in mind. The biaxial continuum of production and response touches on literacy at both the personal level and within the scribal tradition as a whole. Just as ability shifts within a person's lifetime (not always progressively!), so does the level of scribal expertise change within a single society. In the case of ancient Egypt, such changes occur in response to moments of political and economic transition (Baines 1983: 583). Accordingly, the trajectory of literacy within a single lifetime can be illustrated by a series of positions within the continuum, yielding a distinctive "signature" that might be compared with those of other individuals. On a broader scale, changes within the scribal tradition would also present a distinctive form.[3] By employing the chart for the purposes of qualitative comparison, we have also addressed the question of defining literacy. An acceptable definition is neither binary (literate vs. illiterate) nor inflexible, such as a definition insisting on substantial numbers of people engaged in the habitual reading of literary material (Boring 1979: 1).[4] Rather, literacy varies along the dimensions of reading and writing, and in ways delimited not by universal standards, but by the standards of individual scribal traditions.

Orality and Literacy: The Limits of Writing

Another vital question concerns the relationship between oral performance and writing. In theoretical terms, this question has been with us since Milman Parry first discerned the oral, bardic basis of Homeric poetry (Parry 1971). According to Parry, Homer "improvised," not wrote, the *Iliad* and the *Odyssey* by following strict guidelines of meter and poetic allusion. In other words, although the epics were eventually recorded in alphabetic script, their composition originated in performance; the repetitions, the metrical rigor, assisted the memory of a nonliterate poet composing for an audience in Dark Age Greece.

More recently, Eric Havelock has reemphasized the oratorical nature of early writing (Havelock 1982, 1986), although with a recognition that the Homeric epics represent not pure oral composition, but an attempted reconciliation between spoken poetry and a novel system of writing. To Havelock, literacy was an "act of interpenetration of letters into an oral situation (Havelock 1982: 45).[5] Even early alphabetic script embodied "recitation literacy" (Havelock 1982: 5): reading was not silent, and a tradition of oral discourse, of reciting from memory and of public performance, still represented the principal means of aesthetic and intellectual satisfaction (Balogh 1927; Harvey 1966: 588; Knox 1968: 435; Cartledge 1978: 28; Robb 1978: 32; Stoddart and Whitley 1988: 762–763).[6]

Other evidence suggests the prevalence of recitation literacy in the Classical and pre-Modern world, regardless of the script being used. The earliest Greek writing is likely to have functioned at first as a mnemonic device (Johnston 1983: 67), a means of stabilizing memory. But at the same time feats of memorization continued to be highly prized (Harris 1989: 30–32). In fact, Plato and other authors noted with regret that writing brought "not improved memory but forgetfulness, by providing the literate with an external device to rely on" (Harris 1989: 30; see also Ong 1982: 15; Thomas 1989: 32–33). A similar preference for the spoken word occurs in medieval Europe, where documents were often regarded suspiciously (oral witness being in most cases preferable), and dictation still served as the primary vehicle for literary composition (Clanchy 1979: 211, 219; Doane 1991: xii–xiii). Dictation and vocal reading had the added merit of permitting the nonliterate to participate (Clanchy 1979: 219).

Recitation literacy has other implications as well, the most important being the partial nature of written communication. To many, the chief significance of written texts is that they are compact, canonical, and authoritative (Harris 1989: 39). Direct refutation of their meaning is impossible, for, after "absolutely total and devastating refutation, [a written text] says exactly the same thing as before" (Ong 1982: 79). Yet this understanding places insufficient emphasis on the interplay between writing, reading, and exegesis (as well as being in itself an ill-founded notion, for, as an anonymous reviewer points out, "Texts, all by themselves, don't *say* anything at all"). Often, recorded texts serve as points of departure for performances or further elaborations of their message. They do *not* stand alone, but, rather, must be read by someone with a comprehension of the context and broader meaning, by someone who will take cues from the script. For example, alongside Sumerian cuneiform, there apparently existed a strong oral tradition in which "literate knowledge depended ultimately on oral reformulations of that knowledge (Chafe and Tannen 1987: 397; Heath 1986; Civil 1972). Accordingly, written texts were not so much transliterations of utterances as schematic messages to be fleshed out by recitation and performance (Civil 1972: 21). In practical terms, this meant that, to understand a text fully, the reader of an early Sumerian document had to be familiar with unwritten but tacit information (Civil and Biggs 1966; Larsen 1988: 187). The same holds true for Buddhist scripture, which also depends on oral elaboration. By careful attention to performance and exegesis, the reader gains the full spiritual benefits of the text (Scollon and Scollon 1981: 45).

The conclusion that recitation literacy characterizes much early writing recalls the work of Walter Ong (e.g., 1982), who has proposed the existence of "primary orality" (Ong 1982: 11). This concept pertains to cultures untouched by knowledge of writing or print (McKitterick 1989: 1). Cultures of primary orality transmit messages by bodily behavior and by speech or other sounds (Havelock 1986: 65). By definition, no society with writing can exist within this framework. Yet, to judge from the information assembled above, at least part of the mindset may have continued to operate at different times and varying intensity within much of the Near East and the Classical world (Ong 1982: 11; Thomas 1989: 283–286). The key difference was the presence of writing, which removed by incremental degrees at least some of the pressures to memorize. Eventually, such changes would have resulted in modifications to oral discourse (Havelock 1986: 101), although probably not to the extreme suggested by Ong (1982: 59).

Writing and Technological Determinism

One of the more controversial aspects of Havelock's work (Havelock 1982), as well as that of Goody and Watt (1963; Goody 1977, 1987: 55–56; see also Ong 1982: 78), is their insistence on the revolutionary impact and cognitive consequences of certain scripts. According to Havelock, who, unlike Goody, failed "to modify and qualify as well as expand his earlier views" (Halverson 1992: 301), the alphabet was unique in its sophistication and potential. For the first time it permitted a "wealth of detail," "depth of psychological feeling," personal reflection, and even analytical abstraction (Havelock 1986: 11; Logan 1986: 20–24) that had not been recorded before.[7] The alphabet made this possible through its efficient recording of sounds, its lack of ambiguity, and its ability to relieve the burdens of memorization (Havelock 1982: 61). The result: a form of writing capable of divorcing itself from oral discourse, from public as opposed to internal, private thought—in short, a writing system that created "thinkers" out of "bards" (Havelock 1982: 11). The cognitive impact of the script would be felt gradually, as the link with oral performance became more and more tenuous. In Havelock's opinion, the mere fact that writing was present did not mean the society was "literate"; rather, literacy was a state of mind enabled by a new kind of scribal technology (Havelock 1982: 57; Chafe and Tannen 1987: 392). A second result of the alphabet was that writing became "democratized," since its simplicity permitted ready adoption by an ever-larger circle of people (Havelock 1982: 83; Goody 1987: 55; Cross 1989: 77–78).

Havelock believed the reverse was also true. Other scripts, especially syllabaries, inhibited change, or at least modulated thought in restrictive ways. Their very form, their lack of efficient communication and inferior analysis of sound, made the scripts unwieldy and unlikely to be used by non-elites (Cross 1989: 77). In Chinese, for example, proficiency required a disciplined memorization of complex shapes (Havelock 1982: 52), and the emphasis on calligraphy "narrowed the field of expertise which can recognize and use the script" (Havelock 1982: 53). With syllabic writing it was impossible to escape an attachment to orality; it inevitably paraphrased oral originals, simplified statements or narratives into easily recognizable forms, encouraged an economy of vocabulary, and led to a "cautious restriction of sentiment" (Havelock 1982: 75, 96; 1986: 8–9). This is why translations of syllabic originals into an alphabet are misleading, for they blur and conceal the inherent deficiencies of syllabic script (Havelock 1982: 72).

There is much to criticize here. In the first place, Havelock has clearly been influenced by Ignace Gelb's evolutionary scheme for the development of writing systems (1963). Like Gelb, Havelock views the alphabet as the pinnacle of scribal achievement, a triumph made possible by earlier innovations in the Near East. When he and Gelb discuss other, especially non-Western scripts, they do so with the aim of demonstrating either the derivative nature of these writing systems or their weaknesses relative to Near Eastern and Mediterranean writing (e.g., Gelb 1963: 59).

The result is often misguided and ethnocentric. For example, Havelock takes the position that, for the Japanese, "purely oral habits of thought and experience . . . have survived more tenaciously in . . . Japan" (Havelock 1982: 348) and that "the free production of novel statement in (their) own script will remain difficult" (Havelock 1982: 347). Since Havelock fails to provide any citations to support these remarks, we must assume that he is revealing more about his preconceptions than about his familiarity with the Oriental evidence. In any case, the cultural achievements of Chinese and Japanese civilizations make it difficult to accept the view that Oriental scripts imposed insuperable limitations on analytic thought and philosophical reflection (Gough 1968: 83–84; DeFrancis 1989: 244–47). Remember: it was a logosyllabic script that recorded the Heian *Tale of the Genji,* an account full of exquisite dissections of emotional and aesthetic states (Morris 1964: 183–210).[8]

Other evidence further undermines the hypothesis of technological determinism. Usually it is society, not script, that determines who can read and in what way. In Heian Japan, women used syllabic *kana* because the prestigious Chinese characters were deemed more suitable for "serious" writing (Morris 1964: 212).[9] Despite the inherent difficulties of Chinese script, there is ample evidence that many people were literate (Rawski 1979: 22–23; Sampson 1985: 162), not least because the high prestige of the writing encouraged people to learn it (Keightley 1989: 192).[10] Conversely, the alphabet, which, according to Havelock, democratized literacy, had effects that were neither uniform nor predictable (Stoddart and Whitley 1988: 771). The Spartans used the alphabet, but sparingly, since they did not have the same political uses for writing that the Athenians did (Cartledge 1978: 25; Harvey 1966: 623, 628). In other words, literacy did not come about because a script compelled it, but because auspicious social conditions favored the adoption of reading and writing (Cartledge 1978: 25). Even in areas with the alphabet, the extent of literacy and the rate in which it expanded or declined varied tremendously through time and space (Johnston 1983: 64; Stoddart and Whitley 1988: 771). In all likelihood, these variable patterns were the product of historical and social processes, and not intrinsic to the script itself (Finnegan 1988: 158–159).

There is another problem with Havelock's hypothesis. In characterizing logosyllabic writing as cumbersome and inefficient, Havelock misses the point that writing is only one part of an overall system of communication.[11] If a script is read, its message fleshed out by oral disputation and elaboration, then it can be a more efficient, more complete transmission of that message than if the script were to stand alone in silent ambiguity. Havelock himself mentions the continued importance of oral disputation and recitation literacy in Classical Antiquity, yet describes this not in functional terms, but as a stage of development that preceded full literacy (Havelock 1982: 11).

Perhaps a better way of viewing efficiency is less on an absolute scale, with the alphabet as the final achievement, than according to how writing was used within a particular society (Harris 1989: 324). For example, unlike alphabetic script, which emphasizes differences in language, Chinese writing lends itself to the unification of a linguistically diverse country, the literate portions of which could read the same logograph in different languages (Goody 1987: 282). A similar pattern occurs in Central Mexican writing, which, as an "open" writing system, bridges areas of relative linguistic diversity and cultural homogeneity (Houston 1993b). By alphabetic standards, these scripts are cumbersome—but can it be said that they are inadequate for the purposes defined by their makers? Nor is it clear that nonalphabetic writing, particularly hieroglyphic script, is inherently inefficient in the ways that it conveys meaning. Mayan glyphs contain both phonetic clues and easily recognizable pictorial signs. There is evidence that such signs are difficult to produce, but are they difficult to read? Again, there exists little evidence to indicate otherwise, since a heavily pictorial quality may actually facilitate the direct comprehension of meaning (John Monaghan, personal communication, 1992).

Who Could Read and Write?

A final topic concerns the number of people who could read or write in the Classical and pre-Modern world. For all societies the exact numbers are subject to dispute, yet most authors agree on one point: until relatively recent times, reading and writing accorded with a pattern that Havelock described as "craft literacy" (Havelock 1982: 10, 187–88; Harris 1989: 7–8; see also Parsons 1966: 51). Craft literacy means that reading and writing were the preserve of a relatively small group that excluded most farmers, women, and unskilled laborers; as a skill, it was concentrated in the hands of the elite and of the craftsmen under their control. William Harris would argue that even during the peaks of Classical literacy no more than 10 to 15 percent of the population could read and write (Harris 1989: 328). This situation only changes when strong forces, such as the introduction of the printing press, the reduction of dispersed rural settlement, and the introduction of philanthropic or state support, would begin to encourage literacy, particularly at the level of primary education (Harris 1989: 15).

Nonetheless, the assumptions that underlie such conclusions are in themselves problematic. In this essay we have examined several themes: (1) the wide range of abilities in the production of, and response to, writing; (2) the close interaction between oral and written communication in most pre-Modern societies, regardless of the script involved; and (3) the understanding that most writing systems are less inhibiting and far more flexible and efficient than the partisans of alphabets would recognize.

To put these themes another way, and in answer to the questions posed above, literacy should be defined *within* scribal traditions and in variable ways; writing often fails to convey a complete message, but rather stands in a collaborative relationship with acoustic and bodily messages (see Monaghan, in this volume); and technological determinism is not a useful concept in studies of ancient writing, which must be understood above all in its social dimensions. These observations do not diminish the value of careful work by scholars like Harris, who shows admirable restraint in his quantification of what is essentially qualitative evidence. But they do suggest that the low, if approximate, numbers proposed for the number of literates have several conceptual defects: they blur useful distinctions between reading and writing on the one hand and, on the other, fail to distinguish levels of competence in scribal production and response. The result may be a serious underrepresentation of the extent and impact of literacy.[12]

Maya Literacy

To date, there have been few discussions of Maya literacy. The subject is a difficult one, with even less pertinent information than exists for Old World scripts. Nonetheless, we do have four possible sources of evidence: the comparative information discussed thus far, which gives us a range of possibilities and perspectives; comments by Colonial observers about writing in Mesoamerica and in the Maya region; historical linguistics; and hints from the Pre-Columbian period, particularly the Classic period (ca. A.D. 250 to 900), when, to judge from the number of texts, literacy was at its height.

Colonial Evidence

Among the most trenchant comments are those by Eric Thompson. He saw Maya writing as an *aide memoire* for learned discussions by priests about astronomical matters (Thompson 1971: 19, 20, 27); Maya glyphs were not for the masses, but were rather restricted to members of the nobility (Thompson 1972: 13; Villagutierre Soto-Mayor 1983: 224) and supervised closely by priests at the few centers of learning where books were produced (Tozzer 1941: 27).[13] This remark parallels statements by colonial writers (Tozzer 1941: 28; Thompson 1972: 13), who mention the limited extent of writing, which seldom entered the world of litigation and practical affairs (Tozzer 1941: 231).[14] On the authority of Gaspar Antonio Chi, Diego de Landa, Sánchez de Aguilar, and Bartolomé de Las

Casas, Thompson also notes the close relationship between reading and writing to oral recitation, observing that historical tales and other narratives were often sung or paralleled by oral disquisition—that is, they conformed to a pattern of recitation literacy (e.g., Tozzer 1941: 153).[15] Similar practices existed in Mexico in the years just before the Conquest: "Interpretation of the painted codices depended on intensive memorization by select groups . . . [and] . . . transmission of the extensive bodies of hymns, poems, and chronicles was essentially oral," although the written word represented an especially prestigious channel of information (Kartunnen 1982: 399; see also Sahagún 1950–1982, 3:67; Gillespie 1989: xxvi; Monaghan 1990).

Thompson makes another comment as well: ". . . I feel that [the Colonial writers] refer to a full mastery of the subject . . . but there was surely another group with a limited knowledge of the writing. They might be termed semi-literate" (Thompson 1972: 13). That is, there existed a range of literacy, including some people who, rather like those at Fayum, could barely write and read (Thompson 1971: 27).

Historical Linguistics

Cecil Brown uses historical linguistics to draw his conclusions about hieroglyphic literacy (1991: 495). He suggests that, because the Maya term for "writing" is more broadly diffused than the heterogeneous set of terms for "reading," most people could recognize writing, but could not read. Although ingenious, Brown's evidence does not justify his conclusions about ancient literacy. If people saw writing, and thus devised a term for it, they could also have devised a word for reading, which presumably they also witnessed, at least in the public contexts described by Bishop Diego de Landa (Tozzer 1941: 153). The diversity of terms seems less to represent a condition of rampant Pre-Columbian illiteracy than the extended process of reading in a society with recitation literacy: first, the reader "saw" the paper, then "counted" or construed the signs, and finally "spoke" or "called aloud" from the written page.[16] Thus, Brown's reasoning fails to establish the extent of Pre-Columbian reading and writing, although it does support the presence of recitation literacy among the ancient Maya.

Evidence from the Pre-Columbian Period

Direct evidence from the Pre-Columbian, and especially the Classic period is not only the most speculative but the most relevant, for it refers directly to the question at hand. The evidence has been dealt with in a number of ways. Dorie Reents-Budet, for example, contends that the sculptural presentation of writing may indicate relative degrees of literacy: if the text of a monument faced away from the public, then it signified a small audience for literate communication (Reents-Budet 1989: 196). Her emphasis on the architectural and sculptural placement of writing is a useful one, although it should be stressed that a viewer can easily walk around a monument, and that the positioning of texts has more to do with the order of presentation, ranking, and decorum of images than with literacy (Baines 1983). One stela at the Classic Maya site of Piedras Negras has hieroglyphs on its top, where it is doubtful that anyone could read them (at least not without a ladder!).

Another approach is to examine the characteristics of Maya writing itself. George Kubler believes the pictorial quality of Maya glyphs enhanced their readability, so that even "farmers in the field" could discern, say, the names of rulers (Kubler 1973: 162; Justeson 1986: 453). I have also made this argument about public monuments (Houston 1989: 25), mindful, like Thompson, that there may have been many levels of literacy.[17] My conclusion is precisely the opposite of Havelock's remarks about syllabic script, which Havelock saw as unnecessarily complex and thus inimical to full literacy.[18]

The development of Maya script may also afford some clues about changing degrees of literacy within the trajectory of the scribal tradition. Initially, Maya writing consisted of a linear series of logographs, each occupying a glyph block. Within a few years scribes began to provide phonetic clues, or syllabic reinforcement for the logographs. Through this device, they not only diminished the ambiguity of the logographs by signaling more precisely their reading, but also made an indirect statement about literacy: presumably, a larger circle of readers would require such clues to an extent unnecessary among a smaller group of literates versed in the obscurities of the writing system. Or, to put it another way, the increased use of phonetic clues by the beginning of the Classic period, and, increasingly, purely phonetic spellings reflected not a writing system of heightened inaccessibility, but the existence of a growing number of literates during the course of the Classic period.

Parenthetically, a strong case can be made that the development of Maya script responded less to the unilineal sequences favored by Ignace Gelb than to changing social and cultural conditions. For example, there is no clear evidence of an early stage of pictographic or ideographic writing in Mesoamerica (see Monaghan, in this volume). From all indications, the initial stages were exclusively logographic; virtually all syllabic signs originated in logographs with weak consonants (Justeson 1989: 33). I would even suggest that the whole concept of ideographs needs revision. The few such signs that have been identified in Maya script may be characterized instead as "extended logographs," insofar as they convey words or phrases that are longer than the Consonant-Vowel-Consonant-Vowel-Consonant (CVCVC) form contained in most logographic signs. These signs are both rare and late because of the inherent difficulties in reading them. As for purely ideographic writing, I agree with A. Leroi-Gourhan that "true pictography is recent, mostly dating from after the period of contact with literate societies" (Goody 1987: 301; DeFrancis 1984: 133–148).

There are a few archaeological clues about the extent of Maya reading and writing during the Pre-Columbian period. Perhaps the most direct evidence stems from the number of texts, since presumably a highly literate society would leave more written material than one with little emphasis on writing. Most epigraphers would accept that there survive, as a very rough estimate, between 7,500 and 10,000 hieroglyphic texts, including those on ceramic vessels. Of these, the majority date to the Late Classic period (ca. A.D. 600 to 850), when, at its peak, approximately three million people lived in the southern part of the Yucatan peninsula, where most of the texts occur (Turner 1990: 309). Because of sampling problems and the inherent difficulties of arguing from negative evidence, it is unlikely that the ratio of one text per three hundred people represents a significant figure for understanding Maya literacy (see Boring 1979: 6; Johnston 1983: 66).

John Justeson has discussed a related approach: the use of mortuary offerings, some embellished with hieroglyphs, to "test whether elite persons were systematically more literate than commoners" (Justeson 1978: 320–325). Yet the argument contains a crucial flaw, which Justeson himself recognizes (Justeson 1987: 324, 326). The presence of writing in a grave cannot be regarded as solid evidence for the literacy of the deceased; as a prestige item, examples of script would be logical offerings in such contexts, regardless of the abilities of the person interred in the grave. Nonetheless, the nature of such texts, which have been shown to be dedicatory or proprietary (Houston, Stuart, and Taube 1989), display an intriguing parallel with the earliest alphabetic writing in Greece and the central Mediterranean. In much of the Old World, the use of formulaic expressions may reveal both the cadences of recitation literacy and the limitations of the readers (Robb 1978: 32; Boring 1979: 1; Johnston 1983: 67; Havelock 1986: 85; Wallace 1989: 123–125). To explain: the formulae contain elements that are readily recognizable, although, to be sure, with some virtuosic flourishes; the very existence of the formulae may imply the need to accommodate those with marginal reading comprehension.

But perhaps the best way of evaluating the extent of writing, as opposed to reading, is by examining graffiti. These are marks that result from spontaneous, unforced acts, often done furtively; as such, they not only measure more directly the ability to write but register deviations from canonical spelling (see Wright 1976). In the Classical world, the rich trove of graffiti has been used to examine the extent of writing (Cartledge 1978: 32)—the greater the number of dedicatory and onomastic graffiti, the greater the number of writers (Stoddart and Whitley 1988: 763).

In the Maya area there occur many graffiti, although, regrettably, only a small number have been recorded, and most of these come from the site of Tikal (Graham 1967; Kampen 1978; Trik and Kampen 1983).[19] The numbers are suggestive. At Tikal there appear, as an extremely conservative estimate, some 512 distinct graffiti; 26 of these, or approximately 5 percent, are glyphic, with most displaying an extreme degree of crudity and brevity (Trik and Kampen 1983), and some showing ersatz spellings (Orrego and Larios 1983).[20] At the site of Rio Bec, which lies in an area striking for its paucity of monumental texts, there occur 95 graffiti, of which none are glyphic (Stoll 1979). From this we may deduce regional differences in writing ability that are analogous to the extreme divide between the number of Attic and Cretan graffiti (Stoddart and Whitley 1988: 763). Yet even at Tikal the few graffiti appear to indicate the limited extent of writing among the Classic Maya. The uncertainty that envelops this issue is unlikely to be overcome by the limitations of the evidence: most graffiti at Tikal seem to be quite late—*circa* A.D. 850–900 (Kampen 1978: 169), and thus may not reveal much of value about the extent of writing at the height of the Late Classic period.

Conclusions

This paper has reviewed treatments of literacy in the ancient world and used these studies to understand Pre-Columbian Maya literacy. Its conclusions: that reading and writing should be treated separately, that literacy shifted within a person's lifetime and within the trajectory of a scribal tradition, and that scripts were often ancillary to recitation and performance. Moreover, a focus on the social context of literacy replaces the emphasis that Havelock and others applied to the intrinsic consequences of certain writing systems, although, to be sure, script does record information "far beyond the carrying capacity of human memory, individual or collective" (Halverson 1992: 315) and as such represents a signal advance in human communication.

As for the Maya evidence, all scholars agree that literacy must have been limited at all periods. But disagreement continues about the more subtle questions. I believe Maya writing developed in ways that reflected increased literacy, particularly from the Early Classic on, although from various clues it seems that writing and perhaps reading were still restricted to relatively few people. Writing apparently varied in space, some areas having a vibrant tradition of writing and others, especially small communities but also whole regions, having none. The implications of this are unclear. Perhaps parts of the Maya region did not *need* glyphs to the same extent (see above for discussion about Sparta), a pattern suggesting great regional differences in the social and political contexts of literacy. Another explanation for such variability has less to do with what people needed—with what they did or did not want—than with the fact that others may have made such decisions for them. There exist a few scraps of evidence that monumental writing was under close political control; at the pleasure of the overlord, texts were meted out in small doses to subordinates at subsidiary centers (Houston 1993a). The site of Piedras Negras may even contain direct evidence of the centralized schools that supported this system, which lay embedded within a framework of political control (Satterthwaite 1965). In regard to reading, I agree with Thompson and Kubler that the pictorial features of the writing were maintained—that is, prevented from achieving the abstraction that characterizes Chinese logographs—by the need to preserve superficial reading ability among a larger group of people. However, any reasonable person would acknowledge how tenuous these assumptions are. Further work on graffiti, still much neglected, will provide some hope of elucidating Pre-Columbian literacy, as will a renewed search for the roles of writing in the ancient world.

Notes

In preparing this paper I have benefited from the comments of Michael Coe, Mary Miller, John Monaghan, David Stuart, Norman Yoffee, an anonymous reviewer, and the participants in the Dumbarton Oaks roundtable on writing, organized by Elizabeth Boone in 1991. I thank Elizabeth for asking me to attend and for providing the opportunity to publish my thoughts.

1 Logosyllabic scripts are those that combine "word signs" (often a single morpheme) and "syllabic signs" (often a consonant and a vowel). In Maya script, the syllabic or "phonetic" signs derive from logographs (Houston and Stuart 1992a).

2 An example from Medieval Europe illustrates one such problem of interpretation. According to Franz Bäuml (1980), many people, particularly those of high secular rank, were unlikely to have been literate, despite statements to the contrary. Rather, authors and biographers simply took their cue from Late Antiquity and particularly from the formulaic descriptions presented in the imperial biographies of Suetonius (Bäuml 1980: 240). Such problems aside, Rosamond McKitterick (1989: 272) posits the existence of widespread literacy during the Carolingian period. In her opinion, Christianity established the centrality of the written word by emphasizing the special quality of authoritative texts. Although McKitterick is likely to be correct in her general estimate, Bäuml shows that statements about literacy are not always what they seem.

3 In both cases the signatures are qualitative measures of production and response. Eventually, quantitative values might be assigned to particular coordinate positions on the chart, although there is insufficient space to do so here.

4 In his reflections on Medieval reading and writing, Franz Bäuml defines literacy in terms of social and political advantage (1980: 243). Those with access to the essential knowledge transmitted by writing would gain distinction and prestige; those who did not enjoy such access would suffer disadvantage. The view that writing facilitates political and social hegemony is an old one (Harris 1989: 332). Other scholars would go further and place literacy within a system of control and exploitation, usually exercised by a centralized authority that apportioned the privilege of reading and writing with the aim of monopolizing political discourse (Lévi-Strauss 1955: 342–344; Wheatley 1971: 377; Morison 1972: 2, 14; Clanchy 1979: 263; Larsen 1988): "il faut admettre que la fonction primaire de la communication écrite est de faciliter l'asservissement" (Lévi-Strauss 1955: 344). The use of scripts to facilitate elite control may explain why, as in the Roman empire or in Tokugawa, Japan, the illiteracy of the masses was thought to be a desirable condition, since it "contributed to the stability of the political order" (Dore 1965: 215; Harris 1989: 333).

Nonetheless, an emphasis on the political dimensions of writing can be taken too far. From ancient Egyptian evidence, John Baines deduces a complex, interactive relationship between writing and political control (Baines 1988: 208). With the exception of public monuments, the state could not always supervise the limits or consequences of literacy, which could veer off in ways difficult to contain. In general, the "statist" view of writing—the perspective that script serves solely as a means of political legitimation or control—fails to recognize the multiple functions of writing in both the Old and New Worlds (pace Santley 1989: 96–97).

5 Although Havelock does not mention it, a similar tension between oral composition and written redaction characterizes the epic literature of early Ireland (Jackson 1971: 28).

6 The best-known example of this is Augustine's astonishment in watching Ambrose at his books, reading silently. Yet this illustration of ancient reading

should be taken with a grain of salt: after all, Augustine was a poor African provincial, Ambrose the child of sophisticated and wealthy parents from the center of the empire (Knox 1968: 422). Perhaps silent reading was by then common, as Bernard Knox proposes for Athens during the fifth and fourth centuries B.C. (Knox 1968: 434). For a different view, see Lentz's discussion of silent reading in dramatic contexts (Lentz 1989: 163–164).

7 Brian Stock advances a similar hypothesis in regard to the advent of widespread, alphabetic literacy in northern Europe (Stock 1983: 18, 531). Not since Classical Antiquity had human beings been able to distinguish philosophically between "outer versus inner, independent object as opposed to reflecting subject, or abstract sets of rules in contrast to a coherent texture of facts and meanings" (Stock 1983: 531). The eventual result of these distinctions was the rebirth of hermeneutics in medieval clothing.

8 In discussing three successive works by Jack Goody, John Halverson charts the disintegration of Goody's variant of the "literacy thesis"—the idea that writing instigated a profound cognitive rupture with an oral past (Halverson 1992). Halverson shows that logical syllogisms or abstract thought do not necessarily stem from writing, and that, through time, Goody makes a progressively weaker case for such a connection.

9 "The native syllabary (in Japan) was something called *onnade* or the 'woman's hand' (*otokomojii,* 'men's letters', referring to Chinese characters)" (Morris 1964: 212). The references to female literacy in Heian Japan are noteworthy, for there is a consensus from other parts of the pre-Modern world that relatively few women could read or write (Harvey 1966: 621; Rawski 1979: 22–23; Harris 1989: 329); those that could would have belonged to only "the very best families" (Harris 1989: 280), although direct support for this assumption is elusive. I should mention that one reader of this paper objects to "limited female literacy" as an idea smacking of androcentric bias and weak attention to alternative possibilities. Yet the Maya case is instructive: in Classic art and text women are not once associated with the accoutrements or titles of scribes. We should remember that the issue here is not so much innate ability, as the social conditions that enable literacy.

10 Nonetheless, there are other views about the ease with which people can achieve functional literacy in Chinese script. DeFrancis (1984: 205) strongly questions Rawski's inflation of the numbers of people who could read or write. Rather, like Havelock, he contends that Chinese script is inherently difficult to learn and to retain, making it unsuitable for the needs of modern, literate society (DeFrancis 1984: 220; 1989: 243). Yet we should also remember that DeFrancis spent many years teaching Chinese to American students (DeFrancis 1984). One wonders whether this experience colored his perception of the intrinsic difficulties of Chinese writing.

11 Part of the problem stems from the conception of writing as a technology, as something comparable to the steam engine in its dramatic consequences for society (Havelock 1982: 6; Ong 1982: 81–83). True, writing can be described

as a manual skill with specific objectives—i.e., a technology—but above all it serves as a means of communication that allows production and elicits response. The use of the technological metaphor is regrettable, since it separates script from other kinds of communication.

12 Since our emphasis has been on the cultural and social context of literacy, it might be best to adopt the general sense of "craft literacy" but not the specific label, which remains firmly rooted in the artistic production of Classical Antiquity.

13 Bishop Landa specifically mentions that books were produced under the supervision of the highest-ranking priest and then distributed with minor priests when they traveled to smaller communities to discharge their duties (Tozzer 1941: 28). This suggests, first, that schools were not common and, second, that there were relatively few places where writing was produced.

14 However, this does not seem to have been the case in Post-Classic Central Mexico, where writing had wider uses. According to Fray Bernardino de Sahagún, writing was employed by horticulturists, soothsayers, physicians, and even judges (Sahagún 1950–1982, 8: 55; 10: 29, 31, 42). The contrast with Colonial descriptions of Maya script points to one of two possibilities: that Colonial authors inaccurately emphasized the limited uses of Maya script; or that Colonial writers fairly portrayed the functional differences between Mesoamerican writing systems. Accordingly, the Mexica Aztec—governed by a bureaucratic state—might have had broader uses for writing than did the Post-Classic Maya, who lived within segmentary states of negligible size and bureaucratic development.

15 In precontact Yucatan there existed a close connection between song, dance, and political gatherings. Important officials known as the *Hol Pop* both presided over deliberative bodies (Barrera Vásquez 1980: 228) and supervised dances, singing, and the storage and playing of musical instruments (Tozzer 1941: 93).

16 David Stuart points out that "seeing" may indeed have been the expression for reading during the Classic period, when rulers referred to the act of "seeing" carving stones (personal communication, 1992). Other criticisms of Brown's paper appear in Tedlock (1992), with further comments on Brown and Tedlock by Houston and Stuart (1992b).

17 Cecil Brown construes my remarks to mean that I propose widespread literacy during the Classic period (Brown 1991: 25). My intention was rather to show that the pictorial nature of Maya glyphs had an effect on reading, since it gave to a wider group of people the superficial ability to understand parts of the script. But I also believe that the entire text, and especially its more recondite features, could be produced by only a few people. The crucial distinction, therefore, is between reading and writing. In my opinion, these are categories that must remain separate.

18 Eric Thompson saw a close relationship between the mindset of the ancient Maya and their script. Unlike Havelock, Thompson believed that writing reflected rather than triggered features of thought (Thompson 1971: 15). He did, however,

feel that Maya script was *sui generis,* a unique development that did not compare easily with other writing systems (Thompson 1971: 15). Perhaps this is why Thompson responded so negatively to Yurii Knorosov's studies, which drew upon structural parallels between Maya glyphs and syllabic scripts of the Old World (Knorosov 1958).

19 Karl Taube informs me that graffiti are relatively common in parts of northern Yucatan, although few of these marks have been recorded (personal communication, 1992). There is an urgent need for graffiti to be documented, since many surfaces with Pre-Columbian markings have been heavily damaged by tourists. At Tikal, such wanton destruction mars most of the surviving graffiti. It is also surprising how few accounts there are of graffiti in other parts of Mesoamerica—could it be that people have simply failed to notice them?

20 Another axis of variability is the fact that some buildings have a great deal of graffiti, others little or none. A fuller survey of graffiti in the Maya Lowlands might establish correlations between abundance of graffiti and building type.

References

Baines, John. 1983. Literacy and Ancient Egyptian Society. *Man* 18: 572–599.

———. 1988. Literacy, Social Organization, and the Archaeological Record: The Case for Early Egypt. In *State and Society: The Emergence and Development of Social Hierarchy and Centralization,* ed. John Gledhill, Barbara Bender, and Mogens Trølle Larsen, 192–214. London: Unwin Hyman.

Balogh, E. 1927. Voces paginarum: Beiträge zur Geschichte des lauten Lesens und Schreibens. *Philologus* 82: 84–109, 202–240.

Barrera Vásquez, Alfredo, ed. 1980. *Diccionario Maya Cordemex, Maya-Español, Español-Maya.* Mérida: Ediciones Cordemex.

Bäuml, Franz H. 1980. Varieties and Consequences of Medieval Literacy and Illiteracy. *Speculum* 55: 237–265.

Boring, Terrence A. 1979. *Literacy in Ancient Sparta.* Leiden: E. J. Brill.

Brown, Cecil L. 1991. Hieroglyphic Literacy in Ancient Mayaland: Inferences from Linguistic Data. *Current Anthropology* 32: 489–496.

Cartledge, P. A. 1978. Literacy in the Spartan Oligarchy. *Journal of Hellenic Studies* 98: 25–37.

Chafe, Wallace, and Deborah Tannen. 1987. The Relation between the Written and the Spoken Word. *Annual Review of Anthropology* 16: 383–407.

Cipolla, Carlo M. 1969. *Literacy and Development in the West.* Harmondsworth: Penguin.

Civil, Miguel. 1972. The Sumerian Writing System: Some Problems. *Orientalia* 42: 21–34.

Civil, Miguel, and R. D. Biggs. 1966. Notes sur des textes sumeriens archaïques. *Revue d'Assyriologie* 60: 1–16.

Clanchy, M. T. 1979. *From Memory to Written Record: England 1066–1307.* Cambridge, Massachusetts: Harvard University Press.

Cross, Frank Moore. 1989. The Invention and Development of the Alphabet. In *The Origins of Writing,* ed. Wayne M. Senner, 77–90. Lincoln: University of Nebraska Press.

DeFrancis, John. 1984. *The Chinese Language: Fact and Fantasy.* Honolulu: University of Hawaii Press.

———. 1989. *Visible Speech: The Diverse Oneness of Writing Systems.* Honolulu: University of Hawaii Press.

Doane, A. N. 1991. Introduction. In *Vox intexta: Orality and Textuality in the Middle Ages,* ed. A. N. Doane and Carol Braun Pasternack, xi–xiv. Madison: University of Wisconsin Press.

Dore, Ronald P. 1965. *Education in Tokugawa Japan.* London: Routledge and Kegan Paul.

Finnegan, Ruth. 1988. *Literacy and Orality: Studies in the Technology of Communication.* Oxford: Basil Blackwell.

Gelb, Ignace J. 1963. *A Study of Writing.* 2d ed. Chicago: University of Chicago Press.

Gillespie, Susan D. 1989. *The Aztec Kings: The Construction of Rulership in Mexico City.* Tucson, Arizona: University of Arizona Press.

Goody, Jack. 1977. *The Domestication of the Savage Mind.* Cambridge: Cambridge University Press.

———. 1987. *The Interface Between the Written and the Oral.* Cambridge: Cambridge University Press.

Goody, Jack, and Ian Watt. 1963. The Consequences of Literacy. *Comparative Studies in Society and History* 5 (3): 304–345.

Gough, Kathleen. 1968. Implications of Literacy in Traditional China and India. In *Literacy in Traditional Societies,* ed. Jack Goody, 69–84. Cambridge: Cambridge University Press.

Graham, Ian. 1967. *Archaeological Explorations in El Peten, Guatemala.* Middle American Research Institute, Publication 33. New Orleans: Tulane University.

Halverson, John. 1992. Goody and the Implosion of the Literacy Thesis. *Man* 27: 301–317.

Harris, William V. 1989. *Ancient Literacy.* Cambridge, Massachusetts: Harvard University Press.

Harvey, F. D. 1966. Literacy in the Athenian Democracy. *Revue des Etudes Grecques* 79: 585–635.

Havelock, Eric A. 1982. *The Literate Revolution in Greece and Its Cultural Consequences.* Princeton: Princeton University Press.

———. 1986. *The Muse Learns to Write: Reflections on Orality and Literacy from Antiquity to the Present.* New Haven: Yale University Press.

Heath, S. B. 1986. Literacy and Language Change. *Languages and Linguistics: The Interdependence of Theory, Data, and Application, Georgetown University Round Table on Languages and Linguistics, 1985,* ed. D. Tannen and J. E. Alatis, 282–293. Washington, D.C.: Georgetown University Press.

Houston, Stephen D. 1989. *Reading the Past: Maya Glyphs.* Berkeley: University of California Press.

———. 1993a. *Hieroglyphs and History at Dos Pilas: Dynastic Politics of the Classic Maya.* Austin: University of Texas Press.

———. 1993b. Mesoamerican Writing. In *The Encyclopedia of Language and Linguistics.* Oxford: Pergamon Press, in press.

Houston, Stephen D., and David Stuart. 1992a. Logogramas, fonetismo y la naturaleza de la escritura Maya. *Historia general de Guatemala* Tomo 1. Guatemala: Fundación para la cultura y desarollo, in press.

———. 1992b. On Classic Maya Literacy. *Current Anthropology* 33 (5): 589–593.

Houston, Stephen D., David Stuart, and Karl Taube. 1989. Folk Classification of Classic Maya Pottery. *American Anthropologist* 91: 720–726.

Jackson, Kenneth H. 1971. *A Celtic Miscellany: Translations from Celtic Literatures.* Harmondsworth: Penguin.

Johnston, A. 1983. The Extent and Use of Literacy: The Archaeological Evidence. In *The Greek Renaissance of the Eighth Century BC: Tradition and Innovation,* ed. Robin Hägg, 63–68. Stockholm: Skrifter Utgivna av Svenska Institutet i Athen.

Justeson, J. 1978. Mayan Scribal Practice in the Classic Period: A Test-case of an Explanatory Approach to the Study of Writing Systems. Ph.D. diss., Department of Anthropology, Stanford University. Ann Arbor: University Microfilms.

———. 1986. The Origin of Writing Systems: Preclassic Mesoamerica. *World Archaeology* 17: 437–458.

———. 1989. The Representational Conventions of Mayan Hieroglyphic Writing. In *Word and Image in Maya Culture: Explorations in Language, Writing, and Representation,* ed. William F. Hanks and Don S. Rice, 25–38. Salt Lake City: University of Utah Press.

Kampen, Michael. 1978. The Graffiti of Tikal. *Estudios de Cultura Maya* 5: 155–180.

Kartunnen, Frances. 1982. Nahuatl Literacy. In *The Inca and Aztec States, 1400–1800,* ed. George A. Collier, Renato I. Rosaldo, and J. D. Wirth, 395–417. New York: Academic Press.

Keightley, David N. 1989. The Origins of Writing in China: Scripts and Cultural Contexts. In *The Origins of Writing,* ed. Wayne M. Senner, 171–202. Lincoln: University of Nebraska Press.

Knorosov, Yurii V. 1958. The Problem of the Study of the Maya Hieroglyphic System. *American Antiquity* 23: 284–291.

Knox, Bernard M. W. 1968. Silent Reading in Antiquity. *Greek, Roman, and Byzantine Studies* 9: 421–435.

Kubler, George. 1973. The Clauses of Classic Maya Inscriptions. In *Mesoamerican Writing Systems,* ed. Elizabeth P. Benson, 145–164. Washington, D.C.: Dumbarton Oaks.

Larsen, Mogens Trølle. 1988. Introduction: Literacy and Social Complexity. In *State and Society: The Emergence and Development of Social Hierarchy and Political Centralization,* ed. John Gledhill, Barbara Bender, and Mogens Trølle Larsen, 173–191. London: Unwin Hyman.

Lentz, Tony M. 1989. *Orality and Literacy in Hellenic Greece.* Carbondale: Southern Illinois University Press.

Lévi-Strauss, Claude. 1955. *Tristes Tropiques.* Paris: Librairie Plon.

Logan, Robert K. 1986. *The Alphabet Effect: The Impact of the Phonetic Alphabet on the Development of Western Civilization.* New York: William Morrow.

Mann, J. C. 1985. Epigraphic Consciousness. *Journal of Roman Studies* 75: 204–206.

McKitterick, Rosamond. 1989. *The Carolingians and the Written Word.* Cambridge: Cambridge University Press.

Monaghan, John. 1990. Performance and the Structure of the Mixtec Codices. *Ancient Mesoamerica* 1: 133–140.

Morison, Stanley. 1972. *Politics and Script: Aspects of Authority and Freedom in the Development of Graeco-Latin Script from the Sixth Century B.C. to the Twentieth Century A.D.* Ed. N. Barker. Oxford: Clarendon Press.

Morris, Ivan. 1964. *The World of the Shining Prince: Court Life in Ancient Japan.* Oxford: Oxford University Press.

Ong, Walter J. 1982. *Orality and Literacy: The Technologizing of the Word.* London: Methuen.

Orrego Corzo, Miguel, and Rudy Larios Vallalta. 1983. *Reporte de las investigaciones en el Grupo 5E-11, Tikal, Petén.* Guatemala: Parque Nacional Tikal, Instituto de Antropología e Historia de Guatemala.

Parry, Milman. 1971. *The Making of Homeric Verse: The Collected Papers of Milman Parry.* Ed. Adam Parry. Oxford: Clarendon Press.

Parsons, Talcott. 1966. *Societies: Evolutionary and Comparative Perspectives.* New York: Prentice-Hall.

Rawski, Evelyn Sakakida. 1979. *Education and Popular Literacy in Ch'ing China.* Ann Arbor: University of Michigan Press.

Reents-Budet, Dorie. 1989. Narrative in Classic Maya Art. In *Word and Image in Maya Culture: Explorations in Language, Writing, and Representation,* ed. William F. Hanks and Don S. Rice, 189–197. Salt Lake City: University of Utah Press.

Robb, Kevin. 1986. Poetic Sources of the Greek Alphabet: Rhythm and Abecedarium from Phoenician to Greek. In *Communication Arts in the Ancient World,* ed. Eric A. Havelock and Jackson P. Hershbell, 23–36. New York: Hastings House.

Sahagún, Fray Bernardino de. 1950–1982. *Florentine Codex: General History of the Things of New Spain.* Trans. Arthur J. O. Anderson and Charles E. Dibble. Salt Lake City and Santa Fe: University of Utah Press and School of American Research.

Sampson, Geoffrey. 1985. *Writing Systems: A Linguistic Introduction.* Stanford: Stanford University Press.

Sanderson, Michael. 1972. Literacy and Social Mobility in the Industrial Revolution. *Past and Present* 56: 75–104.

Santley, Robert S. 1989. Writing Systems, Political Power, and the Internal Structure of Early States in Precolumbian Mesoamerica. In *Cultures in Conflict: Current Archaeological Perspectives,* ed. Diana Claire Tkaczuk and Brian C. Vivian. Chacmool, Proceedings of the Twentieth Annual Conferences, 90–99. Calgary: Archaeological Association of the University of Calgary.

Satterthwaite, Linton. 1965. Maya Practice Stone-Carving at Piedras Negras. *Expedition* (Winter): 9–18.

Schofield, R. S. 1968. The Measurement of Literacy in Pre-Industrial England. In *Literacy in Traditional Societies,* ed. Jack Goody, 311–325. Cambridge: Cambridge University Press.

Scollon, R., and S. B. K. Scollon. 1981. *Narrative, Literacy, and Face in Interethnic Communication.* Norwood, New Jersey: Ablex.

Stock, Brian. 1983. *The Implications of Literacy: Written Language and Models of Interpretation in the Eleventh and Twelfth Centuries.* Princeton: Princeton University Press.

Stoddart, Simon, and James Whitley. 1988. The Social Context of Literacy in Archaic Greece and Etruria. *Antiquity* 62: 761–772.

Stoll, Russell F. 1979. Lowland Maya Graffiti: Including a Presentation of the Graffiti at Rio Bec Temple B. Master's Thesis, Division of Graduate Studies, University of the Americas, Cholula, Puebla, Mexico.

Street, Brian V. 1984. *Literacy in Theory and Practice.* Cambridge: Cambridge University Press.

Tedlock, Dennis. 1992. On Hieroglyphic Literacy in Ancient Mayaland: An Alternative Interpretation. *Current Anthropology* 33 (2): 216–218.

Thomas, Rosalind. 1989. *Oral Tradition and Written Record in Classical Athens.* Cambridge: Cambridge Unviersity Press.

Thompson, J. Eric S. 1971. *Maya Hieroglyphic Writing: An Introduction.* 3d ed. Norman: University of Oklahoma Press.

———. 1972. *A Commentary on the Dresden Codex: A Maya Hieroglyphic Book.* Philadelphia: American Philosophical Society.

Tozzer, Alfred Marston, ed. 1941. *Landa's Relacion de las Cosas de Yucatan.* Papers of the Peabody Museum of American Archaeology and Ethnology 18. Cambridge, Massachusetts: Harvard University Press.

Trik, Helen, and Michael E. Kampen. 1983. The Graffiti of Tikal. In *Tikal Report No. 31,* ed. William R. Coe. University Museum Monograph 57. Philadelphia: The University Museum, University of Pennsylvania.

Troll, Denise A. 1990. The Illiterate Mode of Written Communication: The Work of the Medieval Scribe. In *Oral and Written Communication: Historical Approaches,* ed. Richard L. Enos, 96–125. Newbury Park: Sage Publications.

Turner, B. L., II. 1990. Population Reconstruction for the Central Maya Lowlands: 1000 B.C. to A.D. 1500. In *Precolumbian Population History in the Maya Lowlands,* ed. T. Patrick Culbert and Don S. Rice, 301–324. Albuquerque: University of New Mexico Press.

Villagutierre Soto-Mayor, Juan de. 1983. *History of the Conquest of the Province of the Itza.* Culver City: Labyrinthos.

Wallace, Rex. 1989. The Origins and Development of the Latin Alphabet. In *The Origins of Writing,* ed. Wayne M. Senner, 21–35. Lincoln: University of Nebraska Press.

Wheatley, Paul. 1971. *The Pivot of the Four Quarters: A Preliminary Enquiry Into the Origins and Character of the Ancient Chinese City.* Edinburgh: Edinburgh University Press.

Wright, R. 1976. Speaking, Reading and Writing Late Latin and Early Romance. *Neophilologus* 60: 178–189.

Youtie, H. C. 1971. *βραδέως γράφων*: Between Literacy and Illiteracy. *Greek, Roman, and Byzantine Studies* 12: 239–261.

Elizabeth Hill Boone

Aztec Pictorial Histories: Records without Words

In 1541, twenty-two years after the Spanish invasion of Mexico, the Franciscan friar Motolinía made ready to send his recently completed *Historia de los Indios de Nueva España* to his friend and patron Don Antonio Pimentel, Sixth Count of Benavente. Father Motolinía had arrived in Mexico nineteen years earlier with the first wave of Franciscan missionaries, and he had come to know Aztec culture well. In his introductory letter to the count, he credits his sources. In doing so, he characterizes for us the major types of Aztec painted manuscripts.

> I shall treat . . . [of] this land of Anahuac or New Spain . . . according to the ancient books that the natives had of symbols and pictures [*carácteres y figuras*], which is their way of writing, on account of not having letters only symbols. And the memory of man being weak and feeble, the elders in this land disagree in expounding the antiquities and the noteworthy things of this land, although some things pertaining to ancient times and the fixing of the succession of the lords who took possession of and ruled over this great land, have been gathered and explained by their figures. . . .
>
> These natives had five books that, as I said, were written in pictures and symbols. The first [book] speaks of the years and times; the second with the days and with the feasts observed during the year; the third with dreams, illusions, and superstitions, and omens in which the Indians believed. The fourth was the one of baptism and the naming of infants; the fifth, of the rites, ceremonies, and omens related to marriage. Only one of all these books, namely the first, can be trusted because it recounts the truth, although [this truth is] barbarous and not written in letters. . . . Thus they write and picture the achievement of victory and the conduct of wars, the succession of principal lords, bad weather conditions, noteworthy signs in the sky, and pestilences—at what time and under which lord these things occurred. . . . All this the first book relates in symbols and pictures that make the account intelligible. They call this book [*Xiuhtonalamatl*], the Book of the count of the years.[1]

Thus Motolinía describes the continuous year-count annals, the distinctive manuscript form developed by imperial Aztec painters to record and present the Aztec-Mexica story.[2] Although the history is not written in an alphabetic script, Motolinía accepts it as a historical document analogous to the historical documents he knows from the European tradition. Motolinía does not accord the Aztecs writing, but he does accord them recorded histories.[3]

This paper explains the manner in which manuscript painters within and on the edges of the Aztec empire presented history. It first establishes the units of information that are essential to a history and then looks at some of the standard conventions for conveying this information graphically. Standardization and convention allowed most of the pictorial histories to be intelligible across ethnic and linguistic boundaries throughout and beyond the imperium. Then the paper examines how the manuscript painters structured the histories they told. History painters in Late Post-Classic Mexico worked in three different presentational forms. These are the event-oriented history, the cartographic history, and the continuous year-count annals of which Motolinía wrote. Each form conditioned the kind of history that was told.

If one conceptualizes this situation according to a supposed dichotomy between the story (or content) and the discourse (or mode of telling that story), my focus is on the pictorial discourse of Aztec history. This discourse, however, cannot be separated from the story itself. Aztec historical discourse is closely linked to the nature of the history being presented. The kind of story that needed telling in each case seems to have governed the form the discourse took. Equally the discourse itself shaped the history.[4]

The Elements of History

At its simplest, a history is a story about the past. For my purposes here, it does not so much matter whether these stories about the past are mythological or actual, since I am not concerned here with defining and determining truth, or even perceived truth. Instead, I am concerned with identifying the basic informational classes that comprise the stories. To the Aztecs, as to us, histories are created by the combination of four elements: participant, event, location, and time. These are the "who," "what," "where," and "when" familiar to us from journalistic accounts and mystery novels, without the "why" that seems so important to the latter. Histories, in the universal sense, relate events or actions that happen to or affect individuals or groups, somewhere, and at some time. All four elements are required by a story, although one or more of these elements can be assumed or left ambiguous. It is obvious that a history must have protagonists and events, and usually these are specified. Location might seem less important, except that a location is the place where an event occurs; it therefore qualifies both the protagonist and the event, setting it apart from other events. Equally, time is a fundamental dimension because the events in a story cannot all happen at once.

Figure 1. The Aztecs leave their island homeland of Aztlan in the year 1 Flint. Codex Boturini page 1 (after the 1964 edition).

As a minimum, there must be the notion of beforeness and afterness, of sequence; sometimes it is important to convey duration or to indicate a fixed date.

Mesoamerican pictorial histories consist largely of serialized, unmoving images that give a narrative. Invariably the conventional meaning of the images, and their spatial or directional relation to each other, must be known before narrative is understood. There is also the assumption that the interpreter is somewhat familiar with the general story. Page 1 of the Codex Boturini (Figure 1), for example, records and presents the beginning of the Aztec migration from their mythical island homeland of Aztlan, in the year 1 Flint, to the first stop on their migration, Culhuacan, where they erect a temporary reed shelter for their god Huitzilopochtli, who has ordered their migration. The story is pictured with great efficiency on a single page, the images working together to tell who, what, where, and when.

Three participants are pictured. The woman and man seated on the left are presented in the conventional Aztec postures and costumes of their gender; they are quintessential Aztec types, representing the Aztec people living in Aztlan. Yet, she is additionally named; a round shield (*chimalli*) attached by a line to her head identifies her as the priestess Chimalma. Thus, her image conveys the meaning both of an individual and of a group. The next human figure, unnamed and standing in his canoe, functions not as a participant but to convey the action of rowing across the lake. The other protagonist is the Aztec tribal patron Huitzilopochtli, conventionally indicated on the right side by the small human head helmeted with the head of a hummingbird. Our protagonists are, therefore, Chimalma, the Aztecs, and Huitzilopochtli.

The events of the narrative are pictured and implied by the situations of the human figures as much as they are rendered symbolically. On the left, the event is the Aztecs being at rest—or residing—at Aztlan, whence they go by canoe across the lake, after which they travel by foot, footprints showing travel, direction, and sequence. The existence of Huitzilopochtli's shelter implies the activity of constructing it, and the curled speech scrolls rising from his shrine signal his instructions to the Aztec people. Thereafter, footprints carry the Aztecs away from Culhuacan and off the page. Thus, on this relatively uncrowded page, six distinct events or actions together define the principal event which is the migration beginning.

Location is fundamental here; it is the reason for the story in the first place, and it qualifies and justifies the major events of the narrative. Because the city of Aztlan is represented, the singular events of canoeing and travel become the grander event of migrating. This island city, Aztlan, is both described graphically and identified pictographically. Descriptively, it is depicted as a rough circle containing a temple pyramid and conventionalized houses surrounded by a lake; conventionally, it is named by the place sign, composed of the elements reed and water, which are themselves conventionalized signs. Culhuacan, the first stop on the migration, is represented only by its place sign of a curved hill, a phonetic referent to Culhuacan. Distance is unattended because it is not a factor in the story.

Time, however, is a factor. The direction in which the figures face and the action moves, establishes the basic sequence and story line. Since precise time is important to the migration beginning, the year 1 Flint is represented by the single disk and the conventionalized flint knife drawn in the square cartouche. Over and over again in the pictorial histories, 1 Flint is the year the Aztecs initiate great undertakings.[5]

Except for the glyphs composing personal and place names, the graphic components on this page convey meaning without a detour through speech. Functioning outside of spoken language, they help to compose a visual language of graphic convention and spatial relation that is understandable to those familiar with the pictorial conventions.

Structuring History

In setting down stories about the Aztec past, the manuscript painters worked within one of several presentational forms to give structure to their histories. Of the four informational classes that histories relate—participant, event, location, and time—one class generally dominates the history and provides the foundation or structure around which the narrative is presented; the other three classes are then arranged to fit the format provided by the governing class. Each organizational structure requires that sacrifices be made in the other areas.

Most written histories, with which we are familiar, are ordered by events. The intersection of participant and event is the fundamental component of history in Western European thought, and most contemporary histories are organized in this manner. They are structured to present events sequentially, and this in itself helps to establish consequential actions, causes and effects; the participants, the location, and the time are then discussed within the framework of the action and are adjusted to it. A historian of the invasion and conquest of Mexico, therefore, might present the whole of Cortés's stay in Veracruz before relating the confusion his landing caused in the Mexican capital. The historian presents one set of events before changing location and moving back in time to present another.

Other histories are organized more strictly by time. For example, Antonio de Herrera's *Historia general de los hechos de los castellanos,* first published in 1601–1615, is a chronologically ordered history treated too strictly. Herrera divided his history of the Spanish empire in the New World (a history that ran from 1492 to 1554) into eight decades, within which he grouped events that happened in widely scattered locations, abruptly halting a particular narrative at the end of a decade to resume it much later in the next decade. Annals are time-ordered histories.

History painters in Late Post-Classic Mexico used one of three different forms to structure their stories. Those in the Mixteca created event-oriented histories, or what I shall call *res gestae,* literally "deeds done," in which time and place are arranged around the intersection of event and participant. In Central Mexico, the Aztec manuscript painters fashioned either cartographic histories, which are governed by space and geography, or they used the format of continuous year-count annals, in which time provides the armature for the narrative. Occasionally, the Aztec painters also combined the qualities of both annals and *res gestae,* where time is occasionally interrupted to accommodate the narrative requirement of an event.

Res Gestae

The *res gestae* histories are the Mixtec genealogical-historical screenfolds, painted generally on long panels of animal hide to record the dynastic histories of the Mixtec ruling families of southern Mexico.[6] In these, the deeds or events of specific individuals or groups outline the story, and time and place are often given, but they are subsumed. The Codex Selden, a painted screenfold that documents the dynastic history of Jaltepec,[7] reveals the structural principles of the *res gestae* form, how it excels as a representational mode, and what its restrictions might be. Pages 6 through 8 (Figures 2–4) narrate the life of Lady 6 Monkey by presenting in conventionalized form the events in her life that are genealogically and dynastically important. The narrative reads from bottom to top in a boustrophedon fashion.

The first event is her birth (Figure 2, band I, lower right), signaled by her initial appearance, seated and with an umbilical cord attached to her rump, after the conventionalized marriage scene of her parents. She appears ageless, a state she and almost all other Mixtec individuals retain throughout their lives, and she, like them, is easily identifiable by her birth-day name, 6 Monkey, which is pictured attached to the top of her head. Immediately she is counseled by the old wizard 10 Lizard, who warns her of danger, this suggested by the hafted axe painted at the top of his pointed finger. The next event involves her father, 10 Eagle, who successfully defends his city from attack by 3 Lizard (band II). Both are armed with a shield and obsidian-edged club, but 3 Lizard on the left succumbs to the conquest grip of 10 Eagle. The invasion by 3 Lizard is noted by the band of footprints that leads to the place sign behind 10 Eagle; the city, Jaltepec or Place of Sand, is phonetically identified by the glyphic elements of the sign.[8] The date is the day 4 Wind, the year 4 House, the year being marked by the A-O year convention.

The narrative then leaves the victorious father and returns to 6 Monkey. Again the old man 10 Lizard advises of danger or conflict, pictorially amplified now to include a bloody obsidian mirror, an arrow or dart, and down from an eagle, as well as the axe (Figure 2, band III). The supernatu-

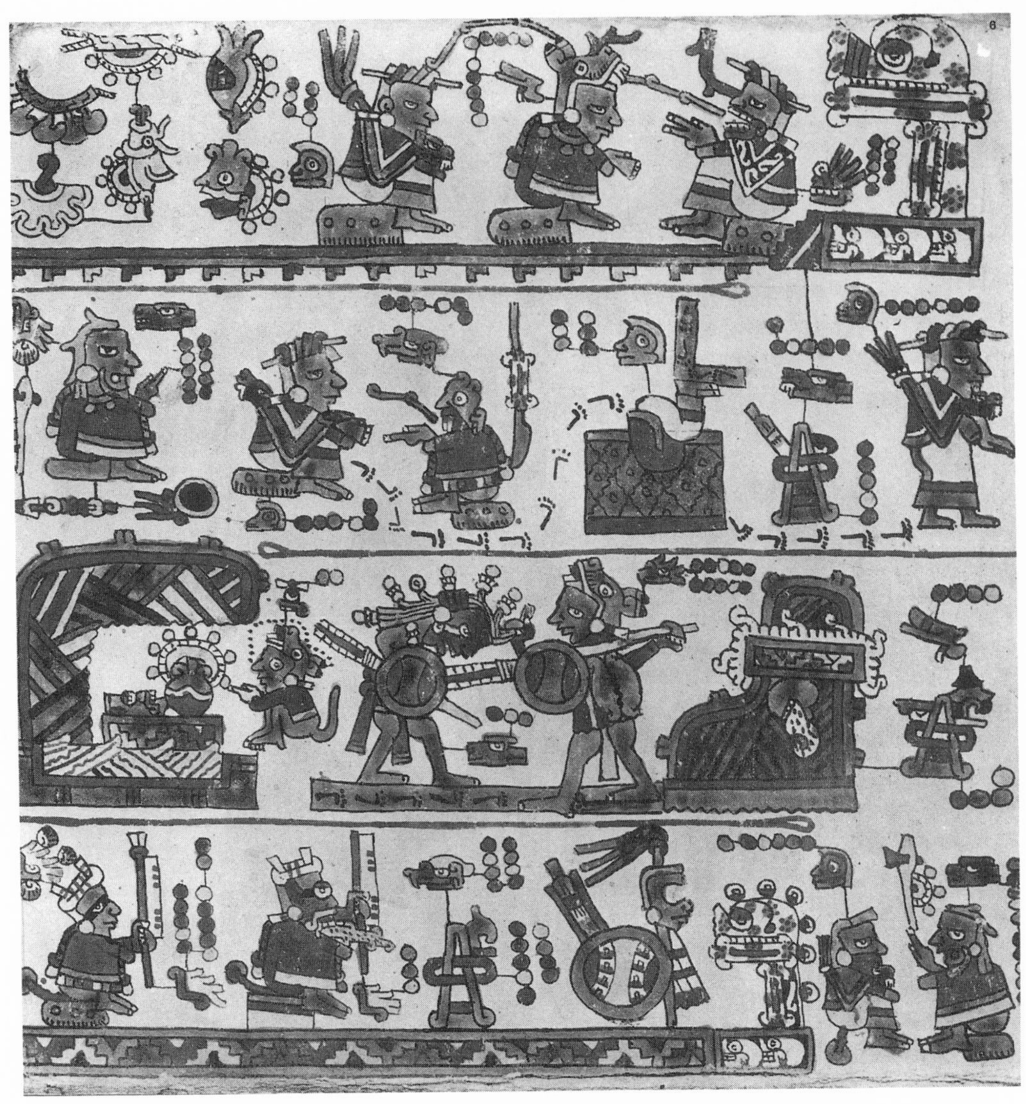

Figure 2. The story of Lady 6 Monkey, Codex Selden page 6 (after the 1964 edition).

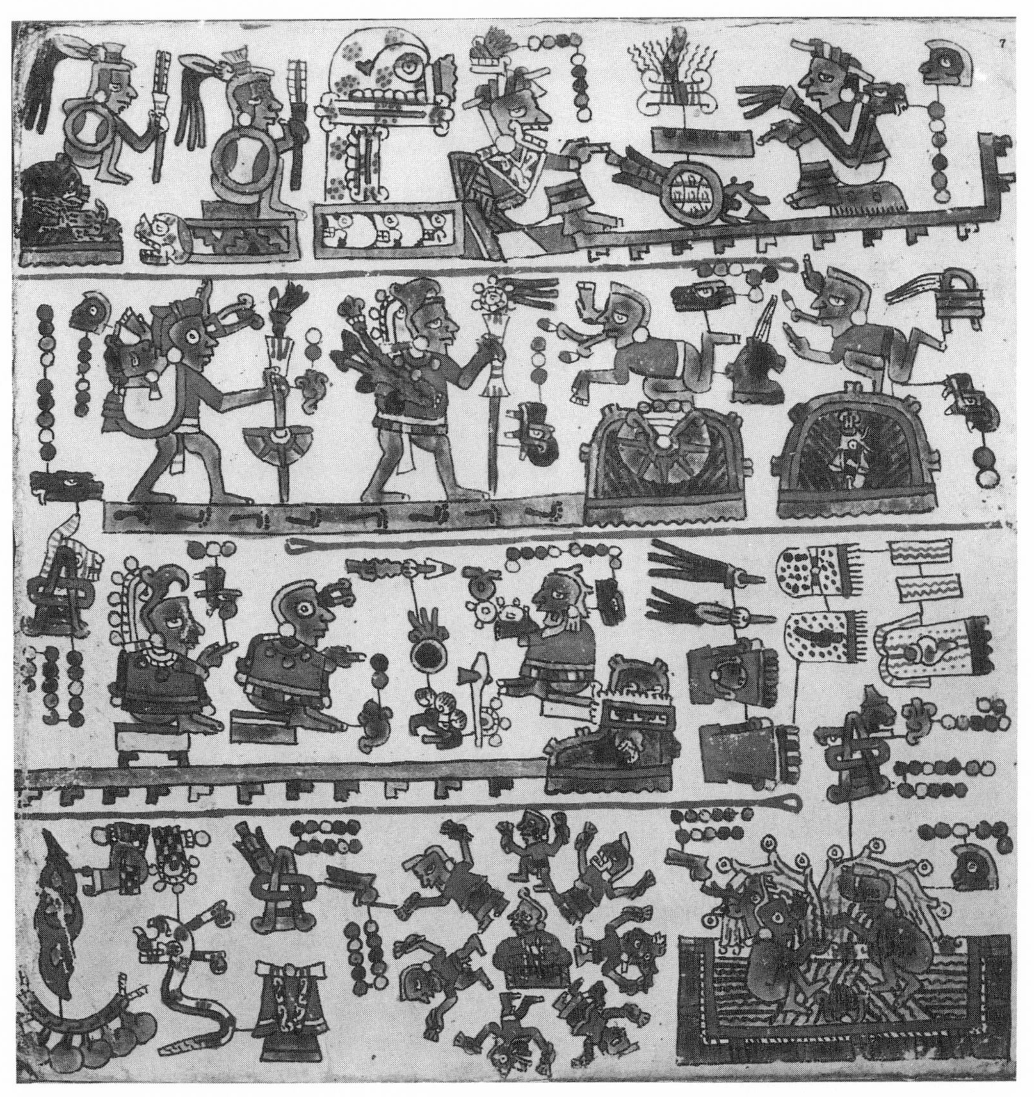

Figure 3. The story of Lady 6 Monkey, Codex Selden page 7.

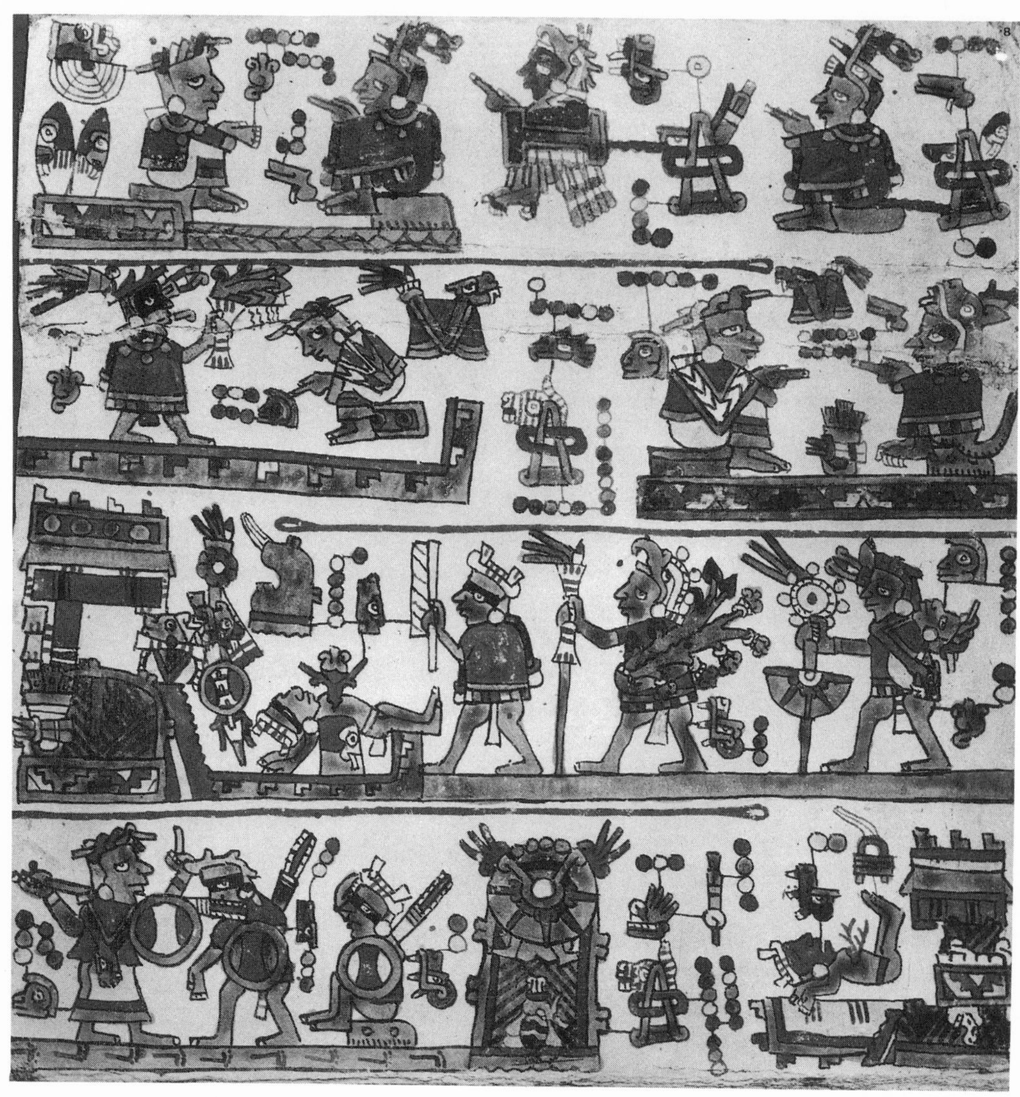

Figure 4. The story of Lady 6 Monkey, Codex Selden page 8.

ral 6 Vulture, whose words roll from his mouth in speech scrolls, tells 6 Monkey to go into hiding, and 6 Monkey promptly does just that, pictorially diving into the earth. After she emerges later, she weds (Figure 2, band IV and Figure 3, band I). Later still, she sends ambassadors to visit two other cities (Figure 3, band III). Pictorially her ambassador 2 Flower carries her name (in the form of her head and her day-name) in a pouch, while the ambassador 3 Crocodile carries her insignia. Their journey, marked by footprints, takes them to two cities identified by their place signs. The rulers of these towns insult 6 Monkey's ambassadors, their sharp speech graphically marked by the small red and white flint knives attached to their speech scrolls. Thus provoked, 6 Monkey prepares for war (Figure 3, band IV), attacks and captures one and then the other at their homes (Figure 4, band I). The event, which lasts 2 days, is significant enough to be dated fully, to the days 3 Grass and 4 Reed, in the year 13 Rabbit. One defeated foe is then taken back to Jaltepec, where he is sacrificed by having his heart cut out (Figure 4, band I), after which the other is carried elsewhere to be sacrificed (Figure 4, band II). Thus victorious, 6 Monkey settles into married life and is pictured wed to her husband (Figure 4, band III), an event that is immediately followed by the birth of her two sons (Figure 4, band IV). After this, 6 Monkey drops totally from the story, which continues with the life of her heirs.

This *res gestae* history is a wonder of pictorial efficiency. All the participants are named pictorially. Events are precisely recorded by well-known conventions and by the poses and gestures of the participants; the action moves quickly from one event to the next. Location is generally stated by the place signs, but it is sometimes described pictorially, too. Time is conveyed by the sequential actions of the story, but individual events are also attached to fixed dates when it is important to do so. The manuscript painters are able to give the particulars of a story in a minimum of space.

The *res gestae* history is a very flexible presentational form. By choosing to structure their narrative around events, the painters are able to move easily from one protagonist to another and from one location to another in order to keep the story flowing. We may have begun our reading with the birth of 6 Monkey, but we quickly switch to her father and then back to her. Just as easily, the story leaves her once she has accomplished everything the dynastic history has required of her—the consolidation of territory, the marriage, and the having of inheriting sons. Just as easily, the narrative moves from one location to another, simply through the convention of the place sign. Time can move forward, but it can also be halted and can move backward to pick up a narrative element that preceded the present events. Thus events are related to each other by cause and effect. This particular pictorial structure comes as close as anything in the Mesoamerican pictorial repertory to indicating consequence. The war carried out by 6 Monkey was the direct result, so we are shown, of her ambassadors being insulted. Thus, this historical form would seem to be the ideal history, and it is what we in the Western world are accustomed to.

Yet it does have limitations. The form conveys no visual sense of the larger whole of the story. Because the presentation is so evenly concentrated throughout, one can become lost in the welter of detail. It is nearly impossible in this form for the painter to develop visually a broader focus or a clearly pictured theme. This form also does not allow the painters to present continuity and duration easily. It provides a sense of much activity, but not development or enduring occupation. And it does not allow the painters easily to show spatial relations.

Cartographic Histories

In contrast to the *res gestae* form, the cartographic history excels both in picturing the whole story as a single statement and in presenting spatial relations. Painted on large panels of hide, bark paper, or cloth, cartographic histories were current throughout Post-Classic Mexico as a viable historical form.[9] In them, geography (or—more accurately—space) provides the organizational structure, with event and time arranged around location. Many of the lienzos and *mapas* fall into this category, as do the Texcocan pictorials Mapa Quinatzin, Mapa Tloltzin, and Codex Xolotl, and the Aztec-Mexica Mapa Sigüenza. Cartographic histories readily present sequential movement and thus provide an ideal format for the recording of migrations, where the narrative is told through a people's wanderings; the Quinatzin, Tloltzin, Xolotl, and Sigüenza manuscripts are all wholly or partially migration histories. Upon an often-stylized geographic panorama, persons and events are depicted, specific locations are identified, and the progression in time is indicated by a directional line or footprints, or it is merely implied by the direction in which the figures face, but actual dates are only occasionally given.

The Codex Xolotl, for example, is an elaborately detailed Texcocan history recording events in the Valley of Mexico beginning with the arrival of the Chichimecs under Xolotl in the year 5 Flint (1224?) through the events leading to the Tepanec war (1427).[10] It is principally a migration history culminating in the pre-imperial period of settlement and expansion. The codex has ten nearly identical maps, each containing

a narrative.[11] The maps were painted to be read as a sequence, so that the passage of time is established both by the movement of the narrative through each map and by the succession of the individual maps.

Figure 5. The coming of the Chichimecs under Xolotl into the valley of Mexico, their exploration and settlement, Codex Xolotl map 1 (after the 1980 edition).

In Map 1 (Figure 5) the geography of the valley of Mexico is established by the lumpy band of conventionalized hills at the top, representing the mountain range on the eastern side of the valley, with the volcano Popocatepetl at the far right (or far southern end). North, then, is on the left side. Nearly paralleling the mountain range toward the bottom of the page is the great system of valley lakes: Xaltocan to the north (left), Texcoco (center), and Chalco and Xochimilco to the south (right). Along this southern edge of the map are already-settled Toltec polities, represented by their place glyphs and their ruling couples, who are likewise named. The Chichimecs enter from the northwest, in the lower left corner, visit Tula and proceed to Xoloque (marked by the head of the animal Xolotl). There the Chichimec leader Xolotl (also named by the animal head) is costumed in the skins and carrying the bow and arrows that are the Chichimec hallmark. He and his son Nopaltzin decide how to reconnoiter the valley, their conversation represented by the conventionalized eyes near their speech scrolls. They travel eastward to investigate five sites marked by place glyphs and confer again about the exploratory expedition. Nopaltzin then leaves Xolotl, meanders southward between the mountains and the lakes until he reaches Texcoco, where he pauses to look over the southern lake; from there he returns directly northward along the lake, passing through Teotihuacan, before he meets Xolotl again at Xoloque. Meanwhile, while Nopaltzin is traveling, Xolotl journeys eastward to inspect a Toltec ruin before he, too, returns to Xoloque. Then they both proceed south to Tenayuca, where Xolotl, surrounded by his vassals, ritually takes possession of the valley. Since the act of taking possession of land involves walking its boundary, footprints take Xolotl around the boundaries of the map (only partially visible where the edges have not been destroyed). Clearly I have omitted much from the story as it is painted, but I think we have enough to consider how this historical form works.

The cartographic history is ideal for migration history, where the fundamental story is the movement of people. The principal narrative is established by locating the protagonists in space and adding directional footprints to provide both the action and the temporal dimension of sequence. If more precise times are required, duration can be indicated by a cluster of blue disks symbolizing the number of years a group has passed in a given place, or the actual year date can be given. At the same time, cartographic histories can readily present simultaneous events. The painter can show Nopaltzin exploring the central valley, while Xolotl visits an old Toltec ruin in the northeast, and still tell us about the Toltec peoples who were then already settled in the southern part of the valley. In fact, time in these cartographic histories is always somewhat ambiguous.[12]

What is not ambiguous is the place any one event or episode has within the larger whole, for the entire story—from entrance to possession—is visible at once on the map. Each part, therefore, is framed spatially by everything else. This unity of expression is particularly noticeable in simpler presentations, such as the Cuauhtinchan maps included in the Historia Tolteca Chichimeca (see p. 171), where the story roughly paral-

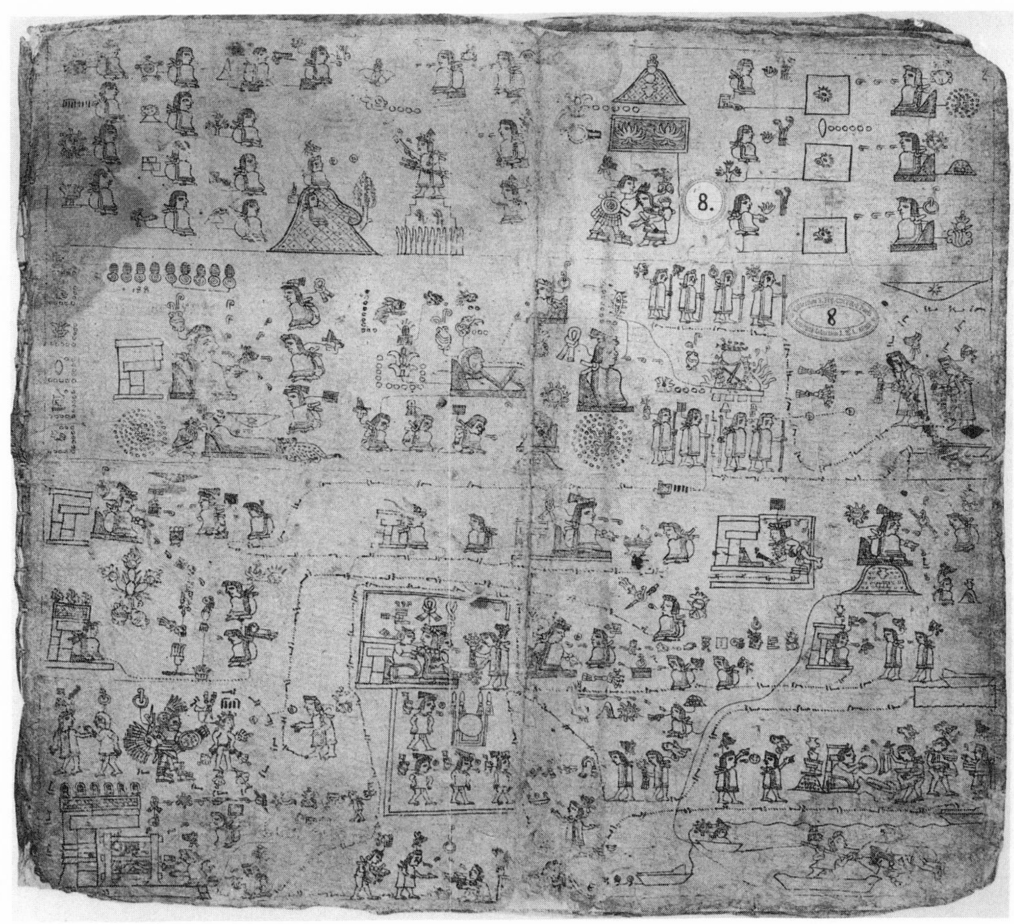

Figure 6. Codex Xolotl, map 8 (after the 1980 edition).

lels Map 1 of the Xolotl in depicting the migration and settling of people into the area. The cartographic form easily accommodates spatial relationships, sequence and simultaneity, duration, and a comprehensive vision. But it is clearly a form with limitations.

The limitations of the cartographic history are obvious in later maps in the Codex Xolotl series (Figure 6). In Map 8 the story has become as complex as that in the Mixtec Codex Selden, and because there is such diversity of event, person, place, and date, the form has difficulty accommodating all that must be included. The larger perspective and the sense of a single comprehensive view dissolves. The field becomes crowded with protagonists intricately connected to a host of locations, action multiplies, and the directional movement becomes confused; any sense of sequence becomes fractured and the narrative impact is lost. Time becomes so ambiguous that it does indeed seem as if everything is happening at once; simultaneity dominates over sequence. The painters of the Codex Xolotl clearly realized this problem, for they adjusted to the liability of the cartographic form by using separate maps to present separate blocks of time. This then freed them to develop contemporaneous episodes and to show their relationships to each other.

By crafting their history in a series of dated maps, the Xolotl manuscript painters recognized the principal benefit of the time-oriented history, which is that it presents the story according to its strict chronology.

Year-count Annals

The time-oriented history is the most prevalent form related specifically to the Aztecs. The Culhua-Mexica or Tenochca Aztecs of Tenochtitlan developed the continuous year-count annals as an efficient and effective way to accommodate and preserve their official and imperial history.[13] It is the historical form, *xiuhtonalamatl,* of which Motolinía wrote.[14] In continuous year-count annals, time is the organizing principle. All the years, whether anything momentous happened during them or not, are painted in a sequence. In the least-acculturated manuscripts—such as the Codex Mexicanus, Codex Moctezuma, and Tira de Tepechpan, the years are generally in a single straight line that reads continuously.[15] In some other relatively unacculturated codices, they are clustered in blocks, probably to save space in representing migrations where there were long periods in which little of importance happened.[16] In some manuscripts exhibiting more European influence, the years are occasionally arranged in short strips to accommodate the European page.[17] Regardless of the arrangement, however, the file of years provides the structure for the history.

Events are painted around the years, often linked to the years by a line or merely painted adjacent to them. Events and actions included in the annals are normally much more varied than in the *res gestae* and cartographic histories. They include natural and climatic phenomena (such as solar eclipses, floods, droughts, and famines), the accession to office and death of rulers, the migration of peoples, the founding of cities, wars and conquests, ritually or mythically important events, and the like. Specific named individuals, with the exception of rulers, are not generally represented, but unnamed humans are often painted in order to represent actions or events. The location of events is assumed—it is assumed to be

Figure 7. Annals for the years 4 Reed to 9 Reed, Codex Mexicanus page 71 (after the 1952 edition).

the place of residence of the people for whom the history is painted—unless an event occurs in another locale, in which case the place sign is given. The locations of conquests or for stops along a migration, for example, are always identified by place signs, for these locations are a fundamental part of the events.

The Codex Mexicanus, although stylistically coarse, is one of the most detailed in its presentation. In Figure 7, the years read from 4 Reed on the left to 9 Reed on the right. On 4 Reed the Aztec ruler Axayacatl has died (his funerary bundle is barely visible), and Tizoc (identified by his name glyph of a striped leg) is enthroned ruler; he begins to renovate the Templo Mayor. In 6 House the Mexica are defeated by the Huexotzinca (an anonymous warrior identified by the place sign for Huexotzinco defeats a presumably Mexica foe). When Tizoc dies in the year 7 Rabbit, Ahuitzotl (identified by the water-beast name sign) is enthroned, and the following year the great temple of Tenochtitlan is dedicated. Moving to the next page (Figure 8), an earthquake (recognized by the conventionalized sign for movement) rocks the land in 10 House, and in 11 Rabbit there is a hail storm so severe that the fish in the lake died. In the next year, 12 Reed, locusts descend to devour the crops, and the year 13 Flint is parched by drought. There follow three uneventful years until another earthquake in 4 Flint (Figure 9). The Aztecs then conquer the people of

Figure 8. Annals for the years 10 House through 2 Rabbit, Codex Mexicanus page 72 (after the 1952 edition).

Xochitlan and Amaxtlan in the next two years, where the conquests are designated by the convention for war (the shield and club) and the place signs of the two polities. A great flood marks the year 7 Reed, and in 8 Flint stone is quarried at Malinalco.

For most of these events, with the exception of Malinalco and the warring cities, the location is not specified. It does not need to be given, because it is understood by the people whose history it is, to be Tenochtitlan. Neither are the protagonists specified. Action and event are indicated by symbols, or they are defined by anonymous actors. Individual accomplishment is rarely a significant element in the Aztec annals, as it is in the Mixtec codices or in the cartographic presentations. The main protagonists of the annals are not the individual rulers but the Aztec-Mexica people; persons are identified only because their activities affect the community's history.[18] In the Codex Mexicanus, the Aztecs and the city of Tenochtitlan are the unmarked categories; they are considered so fundamental and obvious that they need not be named or specifically indicated.

Precise time and the continuity of the years is the central pictorial element. Everything in the annals is structured by the regular and linear march of time, and the very regularity of this time requires that events

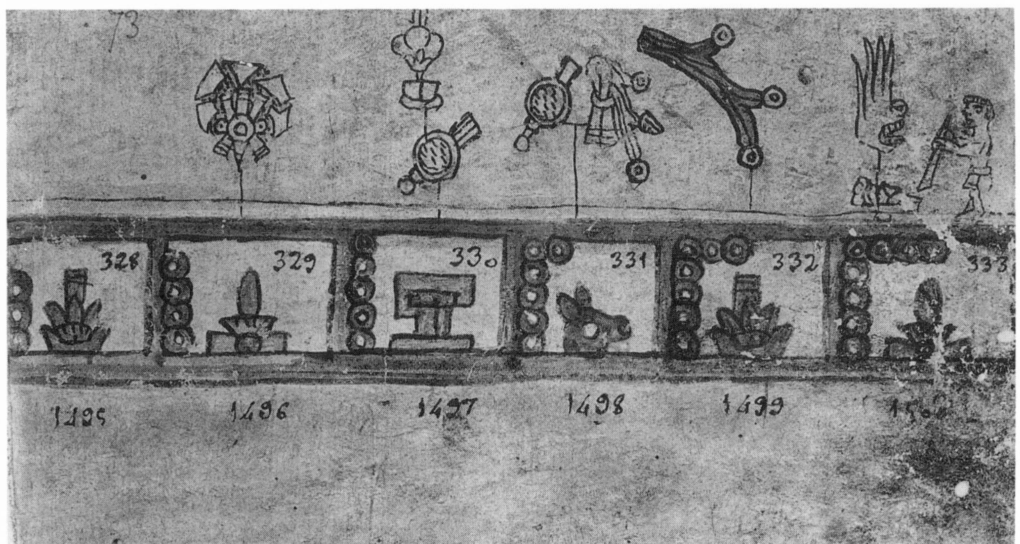

Figure 9. Annals for the years 3 Reed through 8 Reed, Codex Mexicanus page 73 (after the 1952 edition).

be expressed with the utmost efficiency and with the barest of detail—thus location and person fall away.

Why this focus on time? Because time in the Aztec-Mexica pictorial annals is presented as specifically Mexica time, and it symbolizes the empire. At the beginning of the Codex Mexicanus, the Aztecs leave their island homeland of Aztlan to begin their long migration to Tenochtitlan and imperial greatness. History begins at Aztlan, and historical time begins here, too. When the crowd of Aztec men and women leave the marshes of Aztlan, they actually step up onto the band of the year count. The count begins in the portentous year 1 Flint, and it continues uninterrupted through the period of imperial greatness and well past the Spanish invasion and conquest. The Aztecs used the monotonous sequence of the years to present their history and their destiny as an unbroken line. Time was an excellent device to demonstrate the Mexica right to imperial rule and to plant the empire firmly in a deep chronological continuum.

It also carried the implication that the history of the Aztec people would always continue. And the truth of this statement is pictorially reflected in the annals. All the Aztec pictorial annals, except the Codex Mendoza, include the Spanish invasion and conquest of Mexico and then continue with the colonial story. They simply incorporate new rulers and persons of note (such as Cortés and the first bishop Juan de Zumárraga) and new events (such as the great diseases) along with the traditional events.

Tailored Structures

Each of these three historical forms—the *res gestae,* the cartograph, and the annals—has different narrative strengths with concomitant weaknesses. The *res gestae* screenfold presents the personal details of dynastic histories very efficiently as episodes in a series of episodes, but it does this at the expense of spatial relationships, notions of duration and continuity, and of presentational unity. The cartographic history gives simultaneity, spatial movement, and spatial relation at the expense of time. And the annals gives time above all, with its inherent qualities of continuity and duration, but cannot accommodate well the full details of person, place, and event. The painters who worked in these forms were clearly aware of their limitations, and they often blended the different forms to achieve a better presentational balance.

Mixtec painters took the *res gestae* narrative and spread it out over a cartograph, as can be seen in the Lienzo de Zacatepec (Figure 10). Here the foundation is a conventionalized map of the Zacatepec area with an event-oriented history laid over it. The story begins in the upper left, extends to the upper right, and then meanders down the large sheet. Some of the efficiency of the *res gestae* is lost, but the gains are in spatial relationships and the vision of the whole. One sees each episode relationally to those that come before and after, and one can understand the essence of the history at a single glance. It is not incidental that the story being shown is the coming of the people to the area, the founding of Zacatepec, and the establishment of the ruling dynasty, a story virtually parallel to those in the Codex Xolotl and Quauhtinchan Map and requiring a spatial dimension.[19] Migrations are well served by the cartographic form. The manuscript painters in Late Post-Classic Central Mexico clearly recognized this compatibility and took advantage of it by presenting migration stories largely as cartographs.

The limitations of the cartographic history could be overcome by using a series of maps. The ten maps of the Codex Xolotl allowed the painters to concentrate in each map on horizontal and contemporaneous relationships and associations, and to rely on the different maps to provide temporal depth and progression.

In annals, the presentation of time through the continuous progression of the years was its chief liability. There were many years in Aztec history

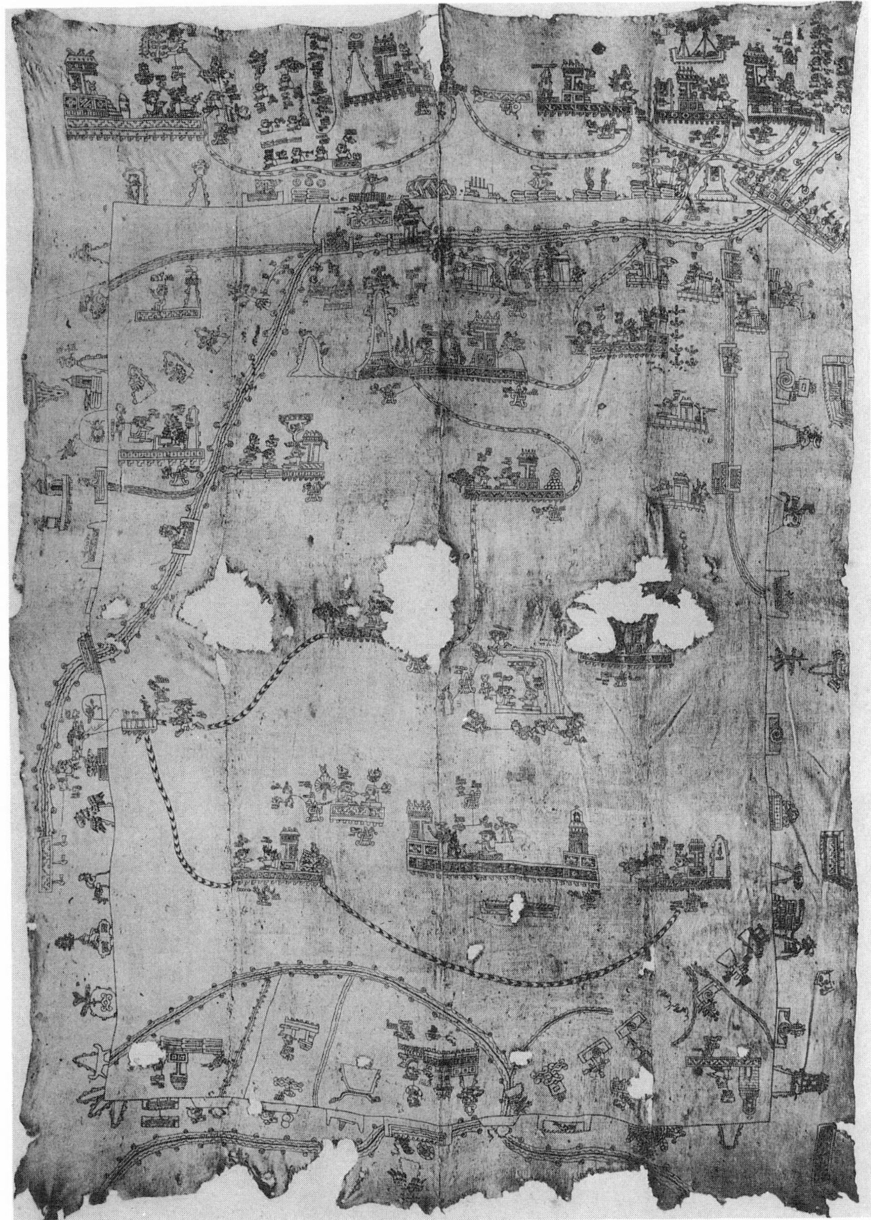

Figure 10. The Lienzo de Zacatepec (after the 1900 edition).

Figure 11. Clustered year counts in the Codex Boturini, page 13 (after the 1964 edition).

when nothing noteworthy happened, yet the annals were still compelled to represent the years, regardless. Sometimes the painters met this problem by clustering the years in blocks (Figure 11). The years still read sequentially, but robbed much less space. This also brought the events closer together and freed more space for the details of the participants and events, so that the modified annals could approximate better the efficiency of the *res gestae*. But the underlying message of continuity and progression that was carried by the annals still remained.

The Aztec continuous year-count annals is a historical form very different from the *res gestae* and cartographic forms. Its subject focus is both broader in some ways and narrower than in the others. It is much less the kind of history with which Western Europeans are familiar, where the story is carried by the intersection of protagonist and event. And there is almost no sense of causality or consequence, which is implied, if not always overt, in the others. The annals form did fit the requirements of the Aztec imperial story, however, just as the *res gestae* history allowed the Mixtec rulers to document their lineage, their alliances, and their territorial claims, and the cartographic form accommodated migrations. The annals, with its temporal spine, excelled as a form to document the continuing story of the corporate body. The focus of the *res gestae* on named individuals and their deeds made that form especially suited to recording dynastic history. And the cartographic history had no equal in its ability to present migratory movements over large geographic spaces. One cannot separate the history being told from the form used to tell it; the story and the discourse relied heavily on each other.

Performing the Histories

I have been speaking about the pictorial histories as if they were isolated from language, as records without words. And I have done this purposefully so that the manuscript forms could be understood as presentational modes in their own terms, as ways of recording stories graphically. Yet these pictorial histories did not remain mute. Aztec historians did not just consult them quietly in libraries or offices, nor did they read the histories to themselves, as we might do with a historical text or reference work. Instead, the pictorial histories are closer to being scripts, and their relation to their readers is closer to being that of a play's script to its actors. The Aztec pictorial histories were read aloud to an audience, they were interpreted, and their images were expanded and embellished in the oration of the full story. The pictorial histories were painted specifically to be the rough text of a performance.

The separate images in Aztec pictorial histories were fashioned as signal references to an oral story. The varied events in the histories are reduced to their epitome, their most essential and distilled visual form.[20] So, too, the participants, the locations, and time are abstracted and conventionalized graphically to the barest essence that still retains identity and meaning. They signal to the reader/interpreter on what events, persons, and places she or he should expound verbally. The Aztec educational process put great emphasis on oral recitation and on memorizing texts and discourses to preserve traditions and knowledge. Those who read the manuscripts had already memorized the histories, the stories, painted therein, and they knew the discourses as familiar roads.

In Nahuatl, according to the Siméon dictionary, *amoxitoa* means "to read a book, to relate, to expound a report," and *amoxpoa* means "to read a book, to relate, to adduce." *Tlatolli* is "speech, discourse, exhortation, history, story."[21] The Colloquies of the Twelve, dating from 1524, describes the *tlamatini,* the learned Aztec priests, as being:

> . . . those who guide us; they govern us, they carry us on their backs, and instruct us how our gods must be worshiped. . . . The experts, the knowers of speeches and orations, it is their obligation. . . . Those who observe [read] the codices, those who recite [tell what they read]. Those who noisily turn the pages of the illustrated manuscripts. Those who have possession of the black and red ink [wisdom] and of that which is pictured; they lead us, they guide us, they tell us the way.[22]

When Aztec scholars "read a book," they did more than receive the messages of the graphic presentational system. The graphic messages triggered in them their understanding or memory of the story, with all its details and with all the verbal requirements and the conventional phrasings of its telling. The images in the manuscript gave meaning, by recording the sense or the gist of the story, and they directed them as readers or interpreters to the elaborate oral exposition of the story they already knew. They told or sung the pictorial histories to an audience. One of the *Cantares Mexicanos* quotes the Nahuatl scholar as saying:

> I sing the pictures of the book
> and see them spread out;
> I am an elegant bird
> for I make the codices speak
> within the house of pictures.[23]

The painted histories kept the migratory, dynastic, and imperial stories sure in their essentials. They refreshed the memory of the elders, and they solved disputes about the past. At the same time they allowed and encouraged embellishment and variation in the telling.

Notes

1 Motolinía 1941: 4–5. The Nahuatl word *xiuhtonalamatl* is given in the fuller *Memoriales* manuscript, which contains a nearly identical passage; see Motolinía 1971: 5. Burrus (1975: 144–145) summarizes the relation of Motolinía's *Historia* and *Memoriales,* both of which are later copies or compilations from lost originals.

2 See Boone n.d. for the argument that the continuous year-count annals was a historical form developed specifically by Aztec painters to relate the official imperial story.

3 This is a paraphrase of the important point Walter Mignolo made in his essay on the book in the Americas.

4 Chatman (1978: 19) synthesizes the structuralist theory of two independent parts to a narrative (story and discourse), seeing them as separate from each other. See B. H. Smith 1981 for a critique of this separation.

5 As one of the dates in the Aztec 52-year cycle, the year 1 Flint recurs every 52 years. On 1 Flint years the first Aztec ruler (Acamapichtli) took office, as did the first imperial ruler (Itzcoatl); see the Codex Mendoza 1979: 2 verso, 5 verso; Boone 1992.

6 These include the Codices Bodley, Colombino-Becker, Selden, Vienna, and Zouche-Nuttall. See Glass 1975b for brief descriptions of these codices, plus their bibliography prior to 1971.

7 Alfonso Caso has written the standard scholarly commentary, "Interpretación del Códice Selden 3135 (A.2)," which accompanies the 1964 facsimile. M. E. Smith (1983) identified the town, formerly called Belching Mountain by scholars, as Magdalena Jaltepec in the Nochixtlán Valley.

8 Jaltepec (literally Sand Hill) is the Nahuatl name for the Mixtec site of Añute (Place of Sand): *"a"* (locative for "place" represented by a mouth) + *"ñute"* ("sand," represented by the scroll of sand coming from the mouth); see M. E. Smith 1983.

9 Although cartographic histories cluster in the states of Puebla, Oaxaca, and Veracruz, extant examples also come from most parts of Central Mexico; see Glass 1975a: 33–36, 39.

10 Charles Dibble has written the standard scholarly commentary, which accompanies the 1980 facsimile.

11 There are additionally two fragments.

12 The sequential placement of simultaneously occurring episodes is left to the reader or interpreter, who chooses which episode to follow first.

13 See Boone (in press) for this argument.

14 Simeon (1981: 770) translates *xiuhtlapoalamatl* as "papeles, libro de la cuenta de los años, historia, cronológia" and *xiuhtlacuilo* as "el que escribe anales, cronista"; Molina (1970: 2nd pagination 160) also gives "cronista" for *xiuhtlacuilo* (literally "year painter"). In addition to Motolinía, Durán (1971: 395–396) describes the content of Aztec annals, and Sahagún (bk. 10, ch. 29, p. 191) mentions them; chapters 9–20 of the *Historia de los Mexicanos por sus pinturas* comprise verbal translations of various annals. Although Aztec annals are conceptually similar to Medieval European annals, they were clearly not European transplants; rather the annals form was already firmly rooted as an Aztec historical genre by the time of the conquest. Lockhart (1992, ch. 8) relates the accretive nature of annals to the general "Nahua tendency to build larger units by the arrangement of discrete parts retaining their distinctness."

15 The unpublished Codex Moctezuma is described by Glass (1975b: 170–171), who also mentions partial publications.

16 For example, the Codex Boturini (or Tira de la perigrinación) and the Codex Azcatitlan. The Codex en Cruz arranges the years in a cross.

17 For example, the Codex Mendoza, Codex Aubin, Aubin-Goupil no. 40, and Aubin-Goupil no. 217; see Lehmann et al. 1981 for the latter three manuscripts.

18 Lockhart (1992, ch. 8) points out that this is the case also with annals written down alphabetically after the conquest, where the *altepetl* or community is the vantage point.

19 See M. E. Smith 1973: 89–121 for the interpretation of the Lienzo de Zacatepec.

20 Brilliant (1984: 52) has explained how the narrative in Etruscan cinerary urns is carried by "the reductive epitome" and "the signal reference."

21 Siméon 1981: *amoxitoa:* "leer un libro, relatar, exponer un proceso"; *amoxpoa:* "leer un libro, hacer relación, aducir" (p. 27); *tlatolli:* "palabra, discurso, exhortación, historia, relato, mensaje" (p. 687).

22 As translated by León-Portilla (1963: 18–19), who also discusses the context and importance of the *Libro de colloquios* (pp. 189–191).

23 As translated by León-Portilla (1969: 11).

References

Boban, Eugène. 1891. *Documents pour servir à l'histoire du Mexique: Catalogue raisonné de la collection de M. E. Eugène Goupil (ancienne collection J. M. A. Aubin).* 2 vols. and atlas. Paris: Ernest Leroux.

Boone, Elizabeth H. 1992. The Aztec Pictorial History of the Codex Mendoza. In *The Codex Mendoza,* by Frances F. Berdan and Patricia Reiff Anawalt, 1: 35–54, 152–153. Berkeley: University of California Press.

———. In press. Manuscript Painting in Service of Imperial Ideology. In *Aztec Imperial Strategies,* by Frances F. Berdan et al. Washington, D.C.: Dumbarton Oaks.

Brilliant, Richard. 1984. *Visual Narratives: Storytelling in Etruscan and Roman Art.* Ithaca: Cornell University Press.

Burrus, Ernest J. 1975. Religious Chroniclers and Historians: A Summary with Annotated Bibliography. In vol. 13 of *Handbook of Middle American Indians,* ed. Howard F. Cline, 138–185. Austin: University of Texas Press.

Chatman, Seymour. 1978. *Story and Discourse: Narrative Structure in Fiction and Film.* Ithaca: Cornell University Press.

Codex Azcatitlan. 1949. Ed. Robert Barlow. *Journal de la Société des Americanistes* (Paris), n.s. 38: commentary on pp. 101–135, with facsimile in a separate album.

Codex Boturini. 1964. Códice Boturini o Tira de la Perigrinación. In *Antigüedades de México basadas en la recopilación de Lord Kingsborough,* ed. José Corona Núñez, vol. 2, pt. 1. Mexico: Secretaría de Hacienda y Crédito Público.

Codex en Cruz. 1981. *Codex en Cruz.* Ed. Charles E. Dibble. 2 vols. Salt Lake City: University of Utah Press.

Codex Mendoza. 1992. *The Codex Mendoza.* Ed. Frances F. Berdan and Patricia Reiff Anawalt. 4 vols. Berkeley: University of California Press.

Codex Mexicanus. 1952. *Codex Mexicanus, Bibliothèque Nationale de Paris nos. 23–24.* Ed. Ernst Mengin. *Journal de la Société des Américanistes* (Paris) 41: commentary on pp. 387–498, with facsimile in a separate album.

Codex Selden. 1964. *Codex Selden 3135 (A.2).* Ed. Alfonso Caso. Mexico: Sociedad Mexicana de Antropología.

Codex Xolotl. 1980. *Códice Xolotl.* Ed. Charles E. Dibble. 2 vols. Mexico: Universidad Nacional Autónoma de Mexico and the University of Utah.

Durán, Diego. 1971. *Book of the Gods and Rites and The Ancient Calendar.* Trans. and ed. Doris Heyden and Fernando Horcasitas. Norman: University of Oklahoma Press.

Glass, John B. 1975a. A Survey of Native Middle American Pictorial Manuscripts. In vol. 14 of *Handbook of Middle American Indians,* ed. Howard Cline, 3–80. Austin: University of Texas Press.

———. 1975b. A Census of Native Middle American Pictorial Manuscripts. In vol. 14 of *Handbook of Middle American Indians,* ed. Howard F. Cline, 81–252. Austin: University of Texas Press.

Herrera y Tordesillas, Antonio de. 1601–1615. *Historia general de los hechos de los Castellanos en las islas i tierra firme del Mar Oceano.* 4 vols. Madrid: Imprenta Real.

Historia de los Mexicanos pur sus pinturas. 1965. *Teogonía e historia de los Mexicanos: Tres opusculos del siglo XVI.* Ed. Angel Ma. Garibay K., 9–14, 23–90. Mexico: Editorial Porrúa.

Historia Tolteca-Chichimeca. 1976. Ed. Paul Kirchhoff, Lina Odena Güemes, and Luís Reyes García. Mexico: Instituto Nacional de Antropología e Historia.

Lehmann, Walter, Gerdt Kutscher, and Günter Vollmer, eds. 1981. *Geschichte der Azteken: Codex Aubin und verwandte Dokumente.* Berlin: Gebr. Mann Verlag.

León-Portilla, Miguel. 1963. *Aztec Thought and Culture.* Norman: University of Oklahoma Press.

———. 1969. *Pre-Columbian Literatures of Mexico.* Norman: University of Oklahoma Press.

Lockhart, James. 1992. *Nahuas after the Conquest.* Stanford: Stanford University Press.

Mapa Quinatzin. 1891. Boban 1891, pp. 219–242, pls. 11–12.

Mapa Sigüenza. 1982. *El territorio mexicano.* Ed. Fernando Zertucher Muñoz and Lenin Molina Tapia, atlas, pl. 3. Mexico: Instituto Mexicano de Seguro Social.

Mapa Tlotzin. 1886. Mapa Tlotzin. Historia de los reyes de los estados soberanos de Acolhuacan. Ed. Joseph Marius Alexis Aubin. *Anales del Museo Nacional de México,* ép. 1, vol. 3: 304–320, folding pl.

Mignolo, Walter. 1987. Signs and their Transmission: The Question of the Book in the New World. Paper presented at the symposium The Book in the Americas. Providence: John Carter Brown Library.

Molina, Alonso de. 1970. *Vocabulario de lengua Castellana y Mexicana y Mexicana y Castellana.* Mexico: Editorial Porrúa.

Motolinía [Toribio de Benavente]. 1941. *Historia de los indios de la Nueva España.* Mexico: Chavez Hayhoe.

———. 1971. *Memoriales o Libro de las cosas de la Nueva España y de los naturales de ella.* Ed. Edmundo O'Gorman. Mexico: Universidad Nacional Autónoma de México.

Sahagún, Bernardino de. 1950–1982. *Florentine Codex: General History of the Things of New Spain.* Trans. and ed. Charles E. Dibble and Arthur J. O. Anderson. 12 bks in 13 vols. Salt Lake City: School of American Research and the University of Utah.

Siméon, Rémi. 1981. *Diccionario de la lengua Nahautl o Mexicana.* Trans. Josefina Oliva de Coll. Mexico: Siglo Veintiuno.

Smith, Barbara Herrnstein. 1981. Narrative Versions, Narrative Theories. In *On Narrative,* ed. W. J. T. Mitchell, 209–232. Chicago: University of Chicago Press.

Smith, Mary Elizabeth. 1973. *Picture Writing from Ancient Southern Mexico: Mixtec Place Signs and Maps.* Norman: University of Oklahoma Press.

———. 1983. Codex Selden: A Manuscript from the Valley of Nochixtlán? In *The Cloud People: Divergent Evolution of the Zapotec and Mixtec Civilizations,* ed. Kent Flannery and Joyce Marcus, 248–255. New York: Academic Press.

Tira de Tepechpan. 1978. *Tira de Tepechpan.* Ed. Xavier Noguez. 2 vols. Mexico: Biblioteca Enciclopédica del Estado de México.

Peter L. van der Loo

Voicing the Painted Image: A Suggestion for Reading the Reverse of the Codex Cospi

Among the few Pre-Columbian pictorial manuscripts from central Mesoamerica which have survived to this day there is a group of five known as the *Borgia Group.* [1] These manuscripts all seem to come from the area that stylistically is usually referred to as the *Mixteca-Puebla* area. Their exact provenance is not known.

This group deals with issues of religion. There are rounds, divisions, and auguries related to the 260-day ritual calendar, which provide a wealth of information concerning the deities related to calendrical events. In addition to the scenes with information on ritual activities and events associated with the calendar, there are also scenes that specifically focus on ritual prescriptions. We will explore a small sample of these scenes, but first we will look at the interpretation and reading of the manuscripts.

Interpreting these manuscripts is a difficult task. The first commentaries, still in use by modern scholarship, were written by the German scholar Eduard Seler (1901, 1904–1909) at the beginning of this century. The next important scholar in the study of the Borgia Group is the Austrian, Karl Anton Nowotny, who published a seminal study of the group in 1961. At present, the publication of new commentaries is being undertaken by Maarten Jansen and Ferdinand Anders. For a further analysis of the history of scholarship on the Central Mexican pictorial manuscripts, I refer to their work (Anders and Jansen 1986). In his important studies of the Mixtec Codex Vindobonensis, Jansen (1982) has shown that these manuscripts can be read as text. Because the message is put down in a pictorial mode, the actual spoken text may differ from reader to reader, but the main content of the message will remain the same to all.[2] Jansen (1982) has also shown that poetic texts and literary figures of speech can be effectively represented in this pictorial system. It may seem that such textual readings are accomplished more easily for the Mixtec codices than for the Borgia group, because the former contain much historic material which lends itself better to conversion to a text, using events, names, and dates to provide a "story line." However, these Mixtec manuscripts provide not only historical facts but also the fundamental religious concepts that explain and justify certain events and the actions of certain persons. This type of historic description is common among many peoples and is usually called *sacred history,* which, in itself, may form part of the sacred stories told and preserved within a religious tradition. The Western reader is probably fairly familiar with this category of sacred history through the description of the history of the Jewish people that is part of the Judeo-Christian holy scripture. Sacred history usually weaves mythic events concerning the beginning of time and the justification of existence seamlessly into historical events that can actually be tracked down through archaeological evidence or other corroborating sources. In the Mixtec codices, for example, myths form the basis for historical claims to prominence of a certain lineage.

In this light, the common designations of the Mixtec manuscripts as "historical" and the Borgia Group as "religious" become less meaningful. So it is with good reason that Jansen (1988: 96) proposes the terms *descriptive* instead of "historical" and *prescriptive* instead of "religious." This brings us to the next question. If the contextual material of descriptive and prescriptive codices is not that far apart, will it then be possible also to find textual readings for the prescriptive manuscripts as was done for the descriptive ones? So far, the interpretation of these manuscripts has usually been limited to a literal description of what is to be seen on a given page. Obviously such a list or tally cannot convey the emotional impact that the opening and reading of these magnificent manuscripts must have had on their original users. If we would want to come to a textual reading, what would be our sources? We would need examples of texts that function in the symbolic field of that same culture. The texts available for such an analysis are sources from the earlier colony and, particularly important for this paper, sources from present-day Mesoamerican rituals.

Looking at the history of Mesoamerica, we can see a continuity in culture that, contrary to popular opinion,[3] reaches across the traumatic experiences of the Spanish invasion. Continuity is the dynamic process that binds a culture throughout its history. In this process a constant incorporation of new elements takes place while at the same time other elements are discarded. A living culture is never static, and cultural continuity never implies an unchanging preservation. After all, a living people are not a museum.

A concept of dynamic continuity that allows for change but recognizes principles that establish the identity of a culture is instrumental in enabling us to understand the pictorial manuscripts.[4] Indeed, closer scrutiny even provides us with an opportunity to construct a text. Hypothetical as that text may be, it is based on the data of the culture that produced the manuscript. For that reason such a text may give us more of a glimpse into the actual meaning and impact of events depicted in a scene than could ever be accomplished by a mere listing of the elements presented in it.

As was mentioned earlier, the manuscripts of the Borgia Group all fall within the general style designated Mixteca-Puebla. Within this overall style, differences between the manuscripts indicate several substyles, but the number of manuscripts is so scant that it does not allow the designation of specific places of origin based on style—as is possible for illuminated European manuscripts, for instance. The Mixteca-Puebla style was widespread in central Mesoamerica during the last autonomous period of indigenous culture. This period is usually termed "Late Post-Classic" and falls roughly between 1150 C.E. and the Spanish invasion. During this time, not only an artistic style but also other cultural features were commonly found in central Mesoamerica. For that reason we see a remarkable similarity in religious beliefs and customs in this region. This does not mean that there were no important regional differences; nevertheless, to this day Mesoamerican religion is characterized by a common and apparently resilient indigenous core.[5] For the Western reader, the situation here is somewhat comparable to the differences between the major Christian denominations, which, in spite of specific divergences all adhere to the same core principles. Note, however, that this comparison is not valid insofar as the different strands of Mesoamerican culture do not condemn each other because of their differences.

The common core of central Mesoamerican religion allows us—following certain precautions[6]—to utilize data from several subareas to attempt an interpretation of the manuscripts of the Borgia group. An example of the successful application of this concept of a common, indigenous core can be shown in the interpretation of the reverse of the Codex Cospi, one of the members of the Borgia Group.

The reverse of the Codex Cospi (pages 21–31) is interesting because it was obviously painted by a different artist from the one who did the front side. As far as artistic skill is concerned, the reverse is clearly inferior in quality. It seems to have been executed by someone who was familiar with the conventions and requirements of the notation system but who was simply not an accomplished draftsman.

The scenes show rituals that are performed for specific deities. In these rituals, bundles of carefully counted sticks or twigs are deposited in patterns. We find this type of ritual not only in the Codex Cospi but also in other members of the Borgia group, namely the Codex Fejérváry-Mayer and the Codex Laud. For some time it has been known that these rituals are related to similar rituals performed today in Mesoamerica, by the Tlapanecs of Guerrero and by the Mixtecs, Mixe, and Chontales of Oaxaca.[7] Of particular importance for the interpretation of the reverse of the Codex Cospi is material that was gathered from the Tlapanecs by the German ethnographer Leonhard Schultze Jena in the 1930s. Based on Schultze Jena's material, Nowotny suggested that we are looking at prescriptions for hunting rituals. This was corroborated by data gathered by the author of this paper in the late seventies and early eighties among the same people. As a result, we can see that the Tlapanec material provides not only a matrix for understanding how these particular pages belong together but also an idea for what a reading of these pages may have sounded like.

The Tlapanec material shows three important elements in the religious complex surrounding hunting. First, we find in the prayers that accompany the rituals a supplication for protection against dangerous animals, specifically animals that bite and sting. Second, in a myth that deals with correct hunting behavior, the dangers of illicit sex for a hunter are explained at length, and it is stipulated that punishments for sexual transgressions will be inflicted through stinging and biting animals.[8] The third important element is the actual supplication for a "kill" by the hunter.

On the reverse of the Codex Cospi, we can see these three elements presented as if in the successive chapters of some exposé.

Pages 21–24. The deities and the bundle patterns are accompanied by stinging and biting animals and plants. Apparently the supplication for protection against those entities is presented here.

Pages 25–26. Both deities involved in the scenes here are goddesses concerned with sexuality and sexual transgressions. It seems likely that these scenes depict the rituals necessary to atone for sexual transgressions or to enable the supplicant to steer clear of any such unacceptable involvement. The latter makes sense because the prevention of this type of transgression is not entirely the responsibility of the hunter alone. The Tlapanecs specify that all sexual transgressions committed by the wife of the hunter, or committed in his house in general, will affect the hunter. So it is useful to seek protection from these occurrences through ritual precautions.

Pages 27–31. Additional signs show the heads of animals with hearts immediately behind them. The heart is an important symbol of life in Mesoamerica. It can be assumed that these particular scenes symbolize the supplication of the hunter to be permitted to kill the animals whose heads are depicted.

We now have an idea of the general pattern followed in the rituals and prayers for hunting, both by the Tlapanecs and by the people who produced the reverse of the Codex Cospi. With these comparisons it is possible to "name" the chapters that have just been described. There are three chapters in which the appropriate deities have been supplicated:

Chapter 1: Protect the hunter from things that bite and sting.

Chapter 2: Forgive illicit sexual acts committed by the hunter or by anyone in his house.

Chapter 3: Permit the hunter to kill an animal, so that he may have sustenance.

Is it possible now to construct a prayer as it may have accompanied one of these pages? This would, of course, be a hypothetical construction, but oral material collected by Schultze Jena provides striking similarities with the visual material presented in the codex. Consequently, this construction is not only justified but also necessary in an attempt to reach a better understanding of the codex.

Schultze Jena (1938) recorded a text, belonging to a ritual with counted bundles, that contains a hunting prayer. The prayer is directed to the type of deity that is usually described as "Lord of the Animals" in the study of religion. The Tlapanecs call their deity "The Old Man of the Mountain." He is the owner of all animals, and he can direct them to the hunter or withhold them, according to the state of purity of the hunter. Other entities addressed are the "Souls without Faith"; these are malevolent beings that must always be placated lest they have a detrimental influence on the hunt or on the conduct of the rituals that are meant to insure a successful hunt. They can also function as the inflictors of punishments for transgressions against the Old Man of the Mountain. To placate these beings, they are always given, as part of the offerings, the bundles that are placed at the corners of the offering table. For the Tlapanecs, these are always the bundles made up of six or nine sticks. In the Codex Cospi we see bundles placed similarly in the corners, but the numbers used are different. The particular Tlapanec prayer fragment quoted here is spoken by the ritual specialist who performs the ritual on behalf of a hunter. In it, retribution is offered for the animals that were killed previously by the hunter, while at the same time a blessing for new endeavors is sought.

I come in the name of the one who has robbed the animals from the Old Man of the Mountain: that is why he brings an expiatory offering, so that nothing may escape him, what he might hear or see, when he prepares himself again, tomorrow to go into the woods.

May he be allowed to see, to hear, to eat; may he not be impeded in hearing, may he not be impeded in seeing.

May the gunpowder not be wet the day he encounters a deer, and may the percussion cap not be wet.

May the bullet from the gun not stray there, where he will look and aim. May (a deer) fall for him again at his hands and feet.

That is why I bring you now an expiatory offering, for that which has before fallen into his hand.

He atones for all of that, for he does not wish that it will be withheld from him, that he will lose, what he wants to see and hear, when he prepares himself in the woods.

May no lightning strike, may no snake lie in ambush, may no (poisonous) caterpillar be sticking to the foliage there, where he prepares himself, where he sets himself up.

May no scorpion be hiding under the tree trunk, at the foot of the tree, where he will set himself up, where he will be on the day that he goes out into the woods.

For these animals are the hands of the evil souls of the dead of the mountain, those whose hands and feet are hot, if the hunter did not bring leaves and flowers, good copal, and warm blood at the feet of the evil souls of the dead. (Schultze Jena 1938: 177)

In several texts gathered by the author, this type of ritual is begun with an invocation of the deity to be addressed, followed by a statement of the ritual specialist in which he explains the meaning of the offering table he has prepared. Also the deity of fire is invoked as the one who will carry the intentions and offerings of the supplicator to the actual deity that is addressed. This makes Codex Cospi page 21 (Figure 1), the first of the scenes in the sequence on the reverse of the Cospi, an interesting object of study. On this page we see the fire god accompanied by counted bundles. As accompanying signs there are the day-name sign 1 Rabbit, a human sacrifice, and five stinging or biting animals (from bottom to top): a jaguar, a snake, a scorpion, a mosquito, and a spider.

If we consider the Tlapanec example, it would make sense to place the fire god on the first page, because he will have to carry the supplications of the ritual to the other deities. With these observations and the text recorded by Schultze Jena in mind, we may come to the following reading for Codex Cospi page 21.

We come before you, 1 Rabbit, Lord of Fire, seated on your throne of fire, with your spear thrower in your hand. We have brought you bundles in the appropriate numbers, so that the hunter will not suffer in the woods. Here is your table of offerings:

Three times nine bundles of eleven each, for you, so you may help us; four times two bundles of twelve, two in each corner, for the malevolent forces, so that they may not interfere.

We also have chosen a man to be sacrificed for you. We offer you the warm blood of his heart.

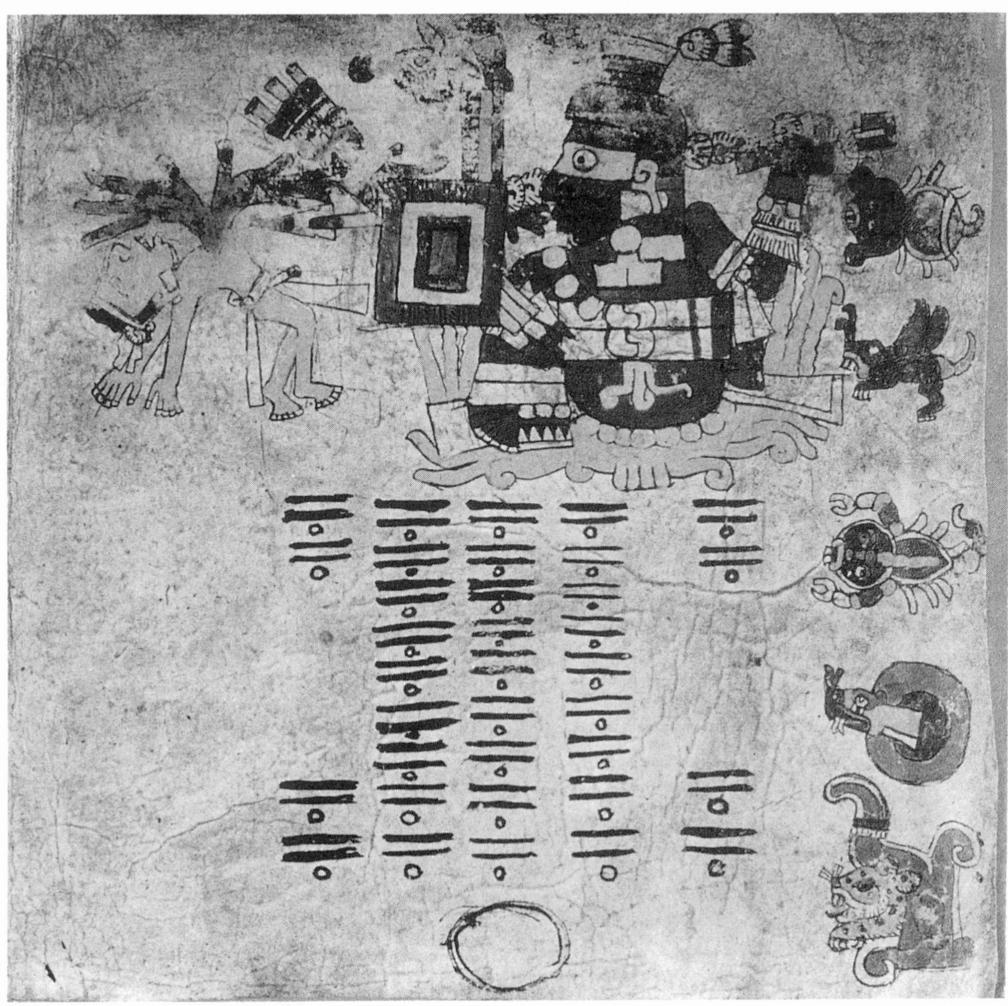

Please help and protect the hunter when he goes out to the woods, when he sets himself up in his place.

May he not be bitten or stung by the animals with big claws and jaws or the animals with venomous teeth or the animals with venomous sting.

May no jaguar suddenly jump out of its hiding to attack the hunter with jaw and claw.

May no snake suddenly strike from its lair to bite the hunter with its venomous teeth.

Figure 1. Codex Cospi page 21. The fire god presides over a hunting ritual with counted bundles. His day name "1 Rabbit" is above his shield. Also shown are a human sacrifice and animals from which protection is sought.

May no scorpion, with its venomous tail, be hiding on the ground at the feet of the hunter when he sets himself up in the woods.

May no mosquito, with its annoying bite, enter the hiding place of the hunter when he prepares himself in the woods.

May no spider, with its poisonous bite, lower itself from the foliage in the place where the hunter sets himself up in the woods.

All these things we beg of you, Lord of Fire, so you may help and protect the hunter. For all these things we have brought you an expiatory offering, an offering also to make recompensation for all the hunter has taken before.

The division into "chapters" and the opening scene featuring the fire god give us some insight into the construction of the scenes on the reverse of the Codex Cospi. The hand that drew the pages, albeit of inferior ability, is that of an individual who knew how correctly to present a coherent group of scenes, arranging them in a deliberate order.

Because we have sources that explain these particular scenes, we can come to a conclusion that the prescriptive or religious codices also contain a text. The core message of that text is unequivocally indicated and is clear to all who are versed in the symbol system used. However, how the text actually sounded depended on both the recitative power and the language of the reader.

This brings us to an important consideration in the interpretation of Mesoamerican writing, and of writing systems in general. It has been shown in this paper how texts from the Tlapanecs fit very well with a particular scene in the Codex Cospi. However, this is not an argument that this codex is Tlapanec. If anything, the more weighty arguments are against such an assumption. Apparently, the Codex Cospi documents rituals that were widely known in central Mesoamerica. By using this pictorial notation system the codex could be read not only by the actual painter but also by many other Mesoamerican peoples who may have spoken very different languages.

In many academic circles writing is still thought of as an evolutionary process that necessarily leads from a lower, pictorial stage through various levels to the highest stage of alphabetical writing. Contrary to this assumption, we must conclude that, in this particular Amerindian writing tradition, a pictorial system is better suited to an environment where a multitude of often unrelated languages is spoken, allowing communication across language boundaries. By nature, alphabetic writing systems lack this flexibility.

Another consideration is that Mesoamerican religions, like most Amerindian religions, do not emphasize dogma. Within the limits of certain basic principles much latitude remains for regional and also personal interpretations of the important elements of the religion. The very fact that the notation system does not fix the text word for word allows the necessary flexibility for regional and personal adaptation.

Finally, the hypothetical text presented here may never win a recitation contest, but it does provide a glimpse into the possible use of the codex. The ability to list the items presented in a scene from a codex is important, but it is only a beginning. If we really want to understand the meaning of the scenes to the people who produced them, then we must try to attain an idea of the emotional impact that the images had. Often it is impossible to reach this goal, usually due to the lack of sources. In the case of the reverse of the Codex Cospi, we have sufficient sources to allow us to attempt a deeper understanding of this manuscript and of the culture from which it came.

Notes

1 The five core members of this group are the codices Borgia, Cospi, Fejérváry-Mayer, Laud, and Vaticanus B (3773).

2 Jansen 1982: 42: *Hay que tener en mente que la pictografía, aunque no* reproduce *las articulaciones del habla, sí* produce *un texto en el momento que un códice es interpretado en voz alta.*

3 For a detailed discussion on the controversy concerning cultural continuity and disjunction in Mesoamerica, see van der Loo 1987: 9–20.

4 For a discussion of and suggestions concerning the methodic requirements of research involving cultural continuity, see van der Loo 1987: 20–26.

5 Since the Spanish invasion, many non-Amerindian elements have been adopted and incorporated into this religion in response to cultural changes. However, the adaptation of the religion to change does not mean that it has ceased to be Mesoamerican in nature.

6 See note 4.

7 For an analysis of the Tlapanec and Mixtec materials gathered by Schultze Jena (1938), see Nowotny 1961: 272–274; 1968: 24–26. For Tlapanec and Mixe materials in the seventies and eighties, see van der Loo 1982; 1987, chs. 13 and 24. For an analysis of the Chontal material gathered by Carrasco (1960), see Nowotny (1968: 24–26). For a further analysis, see the commentary on the Codex Cospi (in press) by Anders, Jansen, and van der Loo.

8 For a full transcription of this myth, see van der Loo 1989.

References

Anders, Ferdinand. 1972. *Codex Vaticanus B (3773).* Graz, Austria: Akademische Druck- und Verlaganstalt.

Anders, Ferdinand, and Maarten Jansen. 1986. *Altmexiko: mexikanische Zauberfiguren; alte Handschriften beginnen zu sprechen.* Graz, Austria: Akademische Druck- und Verlaganstalt.

Anders, Ferdinand, Maarten Jansen, and Peter van der Loo. *Comentario al Códice Cospi.* In print.

Carrasco, Pedro. 1960. Pagan Rituals and Beliefs among the Chontal Indians of Oaxaca Mexico. *Anthropological Records* 20, no. 3. Berkeley.

Codex Borgia. 1976. Facsimile with introduction by Karl Anton Nowotny. Graz, Austria: Akademische Druck- und Verlaganstalt.

Codex Cospi. 1968. Facsimile with introduction by Karl Anton Nowotny. Graz, Austria: Akademische Druck- und Verlaganstalt.

Codex Fejérváry-Mayer. 1971. Facsimile with introduction by Cottie A. Burland. Graz, Austria: Akademische Druck- und Verlaganstalt.

Codex Laud. 1966. Facsimile with introduction by Cottie A. Burland. Graz, Austria: Akademische Druck- und Verlaganstalt.

Codex Vaticanus B (3773). 1972. See: Anders, F. 1972.

Jansen, Maarten E.R.G.N. 1982. *Huisi Tacu; un estudio interpretativo de un libro mixteco antiguo: Codex Vindobonensis Mexicanus I.* Amsterdam: Centro de Estudios y Documentación Latinoamericanos.

———. 1988. The Art of Writing in Ancient Mexico: an Ethno-Iconological Perspective. *Visible Religion: Annual for Religious Iconography* 6: 86–113.

Loo, Peter L. van der. 1982. Rituales con manojos contados en el grupo Borgia y entre los tlapanecos de hoy día. In *Los indígenas de México en la época prehispánica y en la actualidad,* ed. Maarten Jansen and Ted Leyenaar, 232–243. Leiden: Rijksmuseum voor Volkenkunde.

———. 1987. *Códices Costumbres Continuidad, un estudio de la religión mesoamericana.* Leiden: Archeologisch Centrum Rijksuniversiteit Leiden.

———. 1989. Thematical Units in Mesoamerican Religion: Why Deer Hunting and Adultery are a Dangerous Combination. In *The Imagination of Matter, Religion and Ecology in Mesoamerican Traditions,* ed. Davíd Carrasco, 31–51. Oxford: B.A.R. International Series, 515.

Nowotny, Karl Anton. 1961. *Tlacuilolli, die mexikanischen Bilderhandschriften.* Monumenta Americana III. Berlin: Verlag Gebr. Mann.

———. 1968. See Codex Cospi.

Schultze Jena, Leonhard. 1938. *Bei den Azteken, Mixteken und Tlapaneken der Sierra Madre del Sur von Mexiko.* Indiana III. Jena.

Seler, Eduard. 1901. *Codex Fejérváry-Mayer.* Berlin.

———. 1902–1903. *Codex Vaticanus 3773.* Berlin and London.

———. 1904–1909. *Codex Borgia.* 3 vols. Berlin.

John Monaghan

The Text in the Body, the Body in the Text: The Embodied Sign in Mixtec Writing

One of the most important writing traditions to emerge in ancient Mesoamerica was centered in the Mixteca region of southern Mexico, in the present-day states of Oaxaca, Guerrero, and Puebla. The majority of the Pre-Columbian books, or codices, to survive the conquest of the New World are painted in the Mixteca-Puebla style, and native scribes continued to produce documents in this tradition for almost one hundred years after the conquest (see Jansen 1990 for a review of recent research on Mixtec manuscripts).

An example of Mixtec writing can be seen in the place signs on the border of the Lienzo of Ocotepec, a map produced in the late sixteenth century during a land dispute between Ocotepec and some nearby Mixtec cacicazgos. The area in the southern half of the lienzo is today divided between Santa María Yucuhiti and Santiago Nuyoo, former dependencies of Ocotepec, which achieved independence in the Colonial period. Today people in Yucuhiti and Nuyoo can associate place signs on the lienzo with sites in their territory, even though the last scribe died over three hundred years ago. The reason they were able to do this stems from the close relationship between these signs and the Mixtec language. Thus, when people see the sign depicting a grasshopper on top of a hill, they immediately think of a place called *shini tica,* "grasshopper hill" (Figure 1). Likewise, when it is explained to them that the sign next to it is a hill with a depiction of the rain god, they immediately associated it with *yucu savi,* hill of the rain.

Mary Elizabeth Smith has written extensively on Mixtec place signs, and has pointed out that they often function as logographs, that is, they are based on words in the Mixtec language (Smith 1973: 21–22, 172–175). She has also illustrated the different kinds of word signs that are found in Mixtec writing: primary signs, associative signs, signs that utilize the principle of phonetic transfer, signs with phonetic indicators, and motifs found throughout Mesoamerica that function as word signs (Smith 1983: 238–242; King [1990] also makes the argument that syllabic captions can be found in Mixtec writing).

In addition to logographs, Mixtec writing also uses what are often called ideographs and pictographs as a means of conveying information. Unlike Smith's discussion of logographs, work on these signs has been less systematic. This is surprising since logographs in Mixtec writing are largely restricted to a few categories of information, such as personal names and place names. Moreover, these personal and place names usually display a pictographic quality, so that they often can be deciphered without a knowledge of Mixtec (Smith 1973: 173–175). Thus, I can look at a place sign in the Lienzo of Ocotepec, and think to myself "that's a hill with the sign of the rain god on it." I could then ask a Nuyooteco, in Spanish, if there is a place called "cerro de la lluvia," and he or she would then reply, in Mixtec, "Yes, it's called *Yucu Savi.*" The point is, ideographs and pictographs are relatively abundant in Mixtec writing, and may even constitute the majority of signs in the system.[1]

Figure 1. The sign for "Grasshopper Hill" in the Lienzo of Ocotepec (from Smith 1973). Drawing by David Stuart.

But if pictographs and ideographs can be found throughout Mixtec writing, it is also true that the definition of what constitutes a pictograph or ideograph, as others have pointed out, is often vague and contradictory. The reason for this is that what these terms designate is a residual category into which all signs that do not have anything to do with words, or parts of words, or sounds, are placed. It really says nothing about the signs that are in that category themselves, except that they are not based on language.

The question we should ask ourselves then, is what, in the Mixtec case, are they based on? Although current work gives the impression that the answer will involve many different things,[2] an obvious place to start is with nonlinguistic channels of communication. Specifically, Mixtec writing, in addition to having a relationship to the Mixtec language, also has a relationship to the Mixtec body.

The Text in the Body

Recently, there have been several studies, which, building on the observations of earlier scholars, have begun to look at manuscripts like the Mixtec codices not solely as archival documents, which a reader would have silently consulted to discover some item of information, but as scripts to be performed (see Houston, this volume, for a discussion of different kinds of reading). Early Spanish accounts tell us that songs were composed telling of elite genealogies, accounts of battles and feasts, the exploits of nobles, and polity history (Durán 1967: 192, 195; Thompson 1972: 11–12). These are precisely the topics dealt with in the manuscripts, suggesting that they function, in Thompson's words, as "prompt books" for songs and chants (Thompson 1972: 11–12). This perspective has provided some important insights. For example, Mesoamerican texts often seem extremely laconic. The reason for this may have been that they only contain the skeleton of the performance, and the performers were expected to fill in the details themselves (King 1988; Thompson 1972: 11–12). Along these lines, recent research has focused on the poetics of Mesoamerican verbal performance to understand the arrangement of figures in the texts, and as a way of producing more accurate readings of the text (e.g., King 1988; Monaghan 1990). In other words, we are beginning to see performance not just as a framework for understanding how Mesoamerican people used these texts, but as integral to our understanding of the texts themselves: the forms in which they exist, their internal structures, and even the kinds of things they record (see Houston, this volume).

But if we are now coming to the realization that these texts cannot be understood apart from their performance, the focus on song and chant betrays our logocentricity. Were these texts only put into words? Is that the way they were "read?" It is interesting to note that when Durán tells us in his *Historia* about the songs composed by Nahuatl people on their genealogies, history, battles, and feasts, he does so in a chapter entitled "De la relación del dios de los bailes y de las escuelas de danza que había en Mexico en los templos para servicio de los dioses" (it is also in this chapter that he discusses the books of the ancient Mexicans [Durán 1967: 187]). Moreover, in his descriptions of these songs, he does not separate them from dance:

> In their kingdoms songs had been composed describing their feasts, victories, conquests, genealogies, and their extraordinary wealth. I have heard these *cantares* sung many times in public dances, and even though they were in honor of their native lords, I was elevated to hear such high praise and notable feasts.
>
> There were other composers who created chants about the grandeur of and praises to the gods. (Durán 1971: 299)

From this we can see that Durán was unwilling to separate "dance" and "song" in his description of Aztec performance. The translators of the *Historia* attempted to reconcile this apparent contradiction by using the English word "play" for *danza,* perhaps to evoke the idea of the musical, where both dance and song are combined (Durán 1971: 299; see also Bierhorst [1985: 3], who tells us that the Nahuatl name for the genre of "*cantares*" he translates as "ghost songs" is *Netotiliztli,* which, he tells us, is a kind of "dance associated with worldly entertainment"). Although this translation gives us a sense of what these performances were like, Durán is probably not guilty of imprecision.

Dance is, first of all, a Western category. When applied to "human movement systems" in other societies, it can obscure important indigenous categories (Kaeppler 1985: 92–93; Royce 1979: 3–16). For example, in the colonial dictionaries the Spaniards compiled for Yucatec Maya, they translated *ok'ot* as "to dance," and *ok'otba* "to pray." In the same manner *Ah ok'ot* is listed as "dancer," while *Ah ok'otba* is "intercessor, lawyer, mediator," often with the sacred (Barrera Vásquez et al.

1980: 603). Yet we can also read *ok'otba* as the reflexive form of *ok'ot,* so that it translates as "to dance by oneself." On a purely linguistic level, one can see here that a close connection existed for the Yucatec Maya between dance and prayer, and between the dancer and one who mediates with the sacred. The Spanish compilers of the dictionaries, however, appear to have been blind to the connection.[3] One reason is that the Church excluded dance from human interactions with the sacred. Thus in his 1611 dictionary, the lexicographer Cobarruvias, explains the prohibition on dancing in churches by citing the following story:

> . . . In the year 1010, in a village called Colbeche, in the Duchy of Saxony, in the diocese of Magdelburg, while a priest was saying the Christmas Vigil Mass in the Church of Saint Magnus, some eighteen men and fifteen women entered dancing—all aren't in agreement as to the number—and . . . they could not bring themselves to stop, because they had prevented the priest from saying Mass. Our Lord caused them to continue dancing for an entire year, until Heriberto, the Archbishop of Cologne, took them to the church, and praying over them, absolved them, and they were released . . . . (Cobarruvias 1977: 185)

For the sixteenth-century Spanish prelate, dance was a frivolous, even "licentious" activity (Cobarruvias 1977: 185), and God Himself banned it from holy places. One "says" a Mass, and those who "hear" it "chant" responses. The priest does not dance upon the altar, and churches were designed to confine the physical movement of worshipers to standing, sitting, and kneeling.

Another, and perhaps more fundamental, reason the Spaniards resisted the Mesoamerican definition of dance as prayer is that, from the European perspective, the two are physically distinct acts. Prayer after all, involves language, while dance involves the graceful movement of one's entire body, especially one's feet. We can glimpse, however, an alternate vision of the connection between these different activities in the Mixtec verb to dance, *cata tie'e. Cata tie'e* is made up of *tie'e* "foot" and *cata* "to sing" so that *cata tie'e* translates as "to sing with one's feet." What this suggests is that from the Mixtec point of view, "dancing" is a kind of "singing," and, by extension, that linguistic communication should not be treated as a phenomenon that is absolutely distinct from other forms of communication. As Durán's description of Nahua performance also suggests, in Mesoamerica, when one dances, one sings; when one sings, one dances (see also Houston, this volume).

The Mixtec definition of dance as "singing with one's feet" also suggests the possibility that in performance, standardized bodily movements would not only be a crucial component of the performance of a text, but could actually substitute for a verbal reading. The analogy that comes to mind is that of the *mudras* of South Asia, which combine the graceful bodily movements we associate with dancing with a kind of "speech" by the hands. In one genre, Kathakali, there are twenty-four root *mudras,* or hand gestures, which are divided into three possibilities: the same *mudra* in both hands, a *mudra* in one hand only, and different *mudras* in each hand. Using these *mudras* in relationship to the body and facial expression, the Kathakali performer can produce a vocabulary of about nine hundred words (Barba and Savarese 1991: 136).

In Mesoamerica the use of gestures by the elite in communication is well documented (Kurath and Martí 1964: 116–127). In Nancy Troike's study of gestures in the Mixtec codices, she determined that certain ways of pointing one's hands communicate request or assent. She also noted that in the codices, we see at least three different hand gestures, with the two arms in five different positions on both sides of the body (Troike 1982: 184). Although Troike thinks the kinds of things communicated in this way are limited, one could also argue for complex combinations that would have resulted in an expanded gestural vocabulary.

The obvious importance of stereotypical gestures in Mesoamerican interaction highlights the fact that there are many ways that the body can function as a vehicle for communication. My argument here is that if we look at texts (such as the Mixtec codices) as scripts to be performed, then we should not reduce them to verbal presentations in song or chant. Rather, the texts, when performed, were given voice through the entire body: through choreography, through hand gestures, through spacing, and through the clothing worn, as well as through verbal utterances. It may be that in any particular performance one channel of communication may have predominated, or one may have been switched off while the others were on. However, based on the descriptions of early Spanish observers, it appears that all verbal and nonverbal components were important for a proper presentation.

The Body in the Text

If the body plays an important role in the performance or "transmission" of Mesoamerican texts, then it should not perhaps be surprising that the body should also be a basis for the encoding of information in these texts. If one looks at preconquest manuscripts such as the Borgia Group, or at any of the Mixtec codices, literally every page is filled with

Figure 2. Individuals linked by an umbilical cord, Codex Bodley. Drawing by David Stuart.

bodies. There are humans dressed in elaborate costumes making stereotypical gestures. There are anthropomorphized animals and plants, such as birds wearing clothing, snakes with hands, or trees giving birth. Bodily fluids flow freely across entire pages, and body parts appear in unusual contexts. I cannot think of a single scene in any pre-Hispanic Mixtec manuscript where corporeal elements are not the dominant motif. In other words, the vast majority of signs, no matter what else we might call them, are bodies.[4]

The Codex Bodley, a pre-Hispanic manuscript painted on deerskin, illustrates one example. In Figure 2 we see two adults linked by an umbilical cord. How are we to understand this? It is obvious that the Mixtec scribe who produced the manuscript wished to indicate something about the nature of the relationship between these individuals. But the only way we can really comprehend what the scribe wished to communicate about this relationship is if we put it in the context of Mixtec ideas about birth, and the kinds of ties birth establishes between people.

For Mixtecs today a child is first created when the male's semen (*nute kuiji* "white liquid") enters a woman's womb (*soko*).[5] Semen is considered to be blood which flows from all over a man's body when he becomes "hot" during the sexual act. When semen enters a woman in sufficient quantities, it slowly clots (*nakujio ini*) and begins to grow. The sexual act must be repeated up to ten times for a woman to receive enough semen to allow her to become pregnant. As this suggests, the woman is seen as a receptacle in which the fetus grows; she does not contribute in any significant way to the make-up of the child at this stage in its development. It is male blood, in the form of semen, which is crucial. In at least one Mixtec town, people feel that when a child comes out looking very odd, and not at all like its father, it is because the mother had sex with different men while accumulating the necessary mass of semen in her womb, and these varied sources of male blood produced a child equally varied in its characteristics.

Inside the mother's womb, the fetus slowly grows for nine months, where it "swims" in "female liquid" (*nute sɨ'ɨ*) and feeds off its mother's blood. After the child is born (or, as Mixtecs today put it, "when it falls to the ankles of its mother"), the mother is *ki'mu,* "weak, thin, and cold from the loss of blood." Her excessive coldness must be counterbalanced by "hot" things, to move her to the midpoint between hot and cold. For this reason, the midwife gives the mother and her child a sweatbath to heat up her blood (*nasaa nɨñɨ*) and "re-cook" her veins (*nachi'yo tuchi*). This heating of her blood and cooking of her veins is said to have the important effect of converting her blood into a form suitable for the child to feed upon outside her womb, that is, breast milk.

Although males and females contribute substance to their children in different ways—males as they fill a woman's womb with semen, and females as they nurse their child both inside and outside the womb—there is no significant difference in the kinds of things associated with male blood as opposed to female blood. Thus, in Santiago Ixtayutla, a coastal Mixtec community, people do not lexically distinguish between semen and breast milk; they call both "*leche,*" and in Santiago Nuyoo, both mother and father use the phrase "my blood, my milk" (*nu'u nɨñɨ shukuin*) for their offspring, even though only one of them contributes blood in the form of milk to the child. Yet, the idea that males and females contribute blood in different ways does have consequences for

Mixtec ideas about kin relationships. Recall that males transmit blood to their children only at the beginning of the process of reproduction. A woman, on the other hand, transmits blood over a longer period, first as the child matures in her womb and later as it nurses. It sometimes happens that after birth, a child's mother dies, or is unable to produce milk to nurse the infant. To survive, the child must be nursed by another woman. In this case, the child will grow up referring to the woman who nursed it as "mother," in addition to the woman who bore it. The reason the nurse is like the birth mother is because she fed her blood to the child, creating the link of shared substance. This is possible because the process of transmission of fluid to the child occurs both inside and outside the womb, allowing more than one woman to participate. Although it is also true that a child can have more than one father (if a woman has intercourse with more than one male while she accumulates enough semen to become pregnant), this is usually only brought up in the case of an illicit liaison between a woman and a man who is not her husband, and the status of such a man as father is not recognized by the child.

This example is cited here because it highlights an important dimension of Mixtec ideas about kinship: that substance is transmitted through nurturing acts, as well as through sexual intercourse, and that the feeding of one human being by another can create a special bond between them. These acts of nurturance, moreover, define a moral code for transactions among kin.

The word most often used to describe the relationship between parents and children is *nakara.* Mixtec speakers gloss it as "they nurture (me), they maintain (me)," and people consider such acts as feeding (*nsikaji ma,* "he fed him") and clothing (*nsikuniji ma,* "he dressed him") to be specific manifestations of *nakara.* In certain contexts it can be translated as "love," but I think that the phrase "to give the heat of life" best describes its use in most situations, because almost all the things transmitted between persons in relationships informed by *nakara* are spoken of as containing *yɨɨ,* or "heat."

Although parents first "give the heat of life" to their children when they are engendered from their father's blood and when they are fed by their mother's blood, this relationship does not end there, but continues, as parents make every sacrifice to provide a flow of essential resources and vital emotional support to their offspring. When children mature and parents age, roles should reverse, with children becoming "the providers." A crimp in the flow of vital resources and support among kin at any time immediately puts their relationship in question, and implies a growing social distance. Thus, it is usually in terms of a failure to share food or provide clothing that Mixtecs explain the fissioning of households, when one nuclear family leaves to establish a separate domestic unit.

Figure 3. The sign for San Andrés Sachio, Codex of Yanhuitlán (from Smith 1973). Drawing by David Stuart.

Return now to the two adults linked by the umbilical cord. One thing this may represent, of course, is descent, as Arthur Miller suggests for another area in Mesoamerica (Miller 1974). But there is much more to it than this. Recall that the umbilical cord is the organ through which blood is transmitted to children, and that the giving of blood in the womb, where the mother first feeds her child, is the basis of a *nakara* relationship, where parents give their children "the heat of life." In *nakara,* the generation of life, and its sustenance, are inseparably linked, so that parents who have children continue to maintain and nurture them (and vice versa). What this suggests is that when we see individuals connected to one another by an umbilical cord in the codices, the umbilical cord represents an ongoing relationship of *nakara,* as well as a tie of descent. And if the individuals represented in the codices are not just individuals, but also representatives of groups, then what we might see in the umbilical cord is a relationship where one group has separated from another, but the two remain allied, with the "younger" one subordinate and dependent. In this context, it is interesting to note here that in the Kusansum myth recorded by Tozzer in Lancandón country, which plays a key role in Miller's argument, the rulers of the sites of Tulum, Chichén Itzá, Uxmal, and Cobá are said to be linked by an umbilical cord, through which food flows to them. This umbilical cord is in turn linked to the *sakbes,* or "white roads," which connect these sites (Tozzer 1907: 153; Miller 1974: 172). Similarly, Mixtecs today often talk about new colonies being linked to their parents' settlement by umbilical-like tunnels, through which people and supplies pass.[6]

According to such evidence, Mixtecs use corporeal processes, the functions of organs, and bodily products as models for other processes, functions, and products. Thus, when producing a history, or a description of a ritual, or an account of how settlements may be related to one another, the Mixtec scribe was likely to focus on how the event, or practice, or relationship could be expressed in terms of the body.

The Codex of Yanhuitlán contains another example of this corporeal semiotic. Figure 3 is a place sign from the codex which shows a temple platform and a human foot, resting on a hill and frieze. This is the sign for the town of San Andrés Sachio, which translates as "at the base of the temple platform" (Smith 1973: 50).

But why represent Sachio with a foot on top of a temple? Mesoamerican languages commonly mark geographical and physical location, or "locatives," with terms derived from body parts. What the Sachio example illustrates is that Mixtec scribes used the foot as a way of indicating "at the base of" (Smith 1973: 50). In other words, the relationship between head and foot is a model for the relationship of top to bottom. Mixtecs recognize homologies between the body and the world not just for objects related on a vertical plane, but for spatial relationships in general, for the individual's orientation in space,[7] and even for the composition of objects.[8] This is significant in terms of the Mixtec writing system because one of the few domains where the ancient scribes used logographs is in place signs, so that many of the logographs we see in the Mixtec codices—those signs that are explicitly meant to be translated into words—are themselves based on the same set of homologies Mixtecs recognize between the body and the world that we see in the example of the umbilical cord. In such cases, then, the linguistic basis of the sign and the corporeal basis of the sign interpenetrate to such an extent that they cannot be separated from one another.

This discussion of mountains with feet and adults linked by umbilical cords is meant to illustrate the necessity of developing a comprehensive understanding of the Mesoamerican body in order to understand Mesoamerican writing systems. For the Mixtecs, the body is a central metaphor for things ranging from orientation in space to social and political arrangements. The body, however, is a topic that has not attracted much attention from anthropologists and art historians working in Mesoamerica, although the importance of costume and gesture for understanding Pre-Columbian manuscripts has been recognized for some time.[9] Thus, Mary Elizabeth Smith compared the Mixtec codices to a comic strip from the magazine *Punch,* which shows a court jester telling a joke to a king. She points out that we recognize these individuals as king and court jester through their dress. In the same way, the clothing worn by figures in the codices allowed the Mixtec reader to identify who they were and what their functions were. Moreover, just as the story in the comic strip is told through the gestures the characters make, so that when the king places a finger to his cheek, we know that he is thinking, and that the wide eyes of the jester indicate surprise and anxiety, so, too, the figures in the codices are portrayed in stereotypical postures, and are almost always gesticulating in some way (Smith 1973: 20). But to deepen our understanding of what is illustrated in manuscripts such as the Mixtec codices, we need to know much more about Native Mesoamerican ethnophysiology, about how Native Mesoamericans express social, political, and gender relations through the body, about the meaning of gestures, facial expressions, postures, and spacing in Mesoamerica, and we need to put this material in the context of a more general dialogue that views the body as a place upon which conceptual worlds are articulated, communicated, and contested. In other words, we cannot treat Mesoamerican writing, as a form of communication, in the disembodied way that we think of our own writing system.

Notes

A version of this paper was presented at the 1991 Dumbarton Oaks roundtable on writing, organized by Elizabeth Boone. I would like to thank Elizabeth Boone, Mark King, and the other seminar participants for their comments. I am particularly grateful to Steve Houston and Joyce Marcus for their editorial suggestions, and for the conversations we have had on writing and communication.

1 Although scholars who work on Central Mexican and Oaxacan writing systems have long recognized that they contain a strong pictographic or ideographic component, a great deal of emphasis has been placed on finding some phonetic or syllabic element in these scripts. I think one reason for this is that writing systems that are heavily pictographic or ideographic have been spoken of in the way nineteenth-century evolutionists spoke about Australian Aboriginal religion: "primitive" "inefficient," "vague," "incomplete," and even "deficient." The contrast of course, is with phonetic writing, which is seen to lie at the other end of evolutionary development (see Marcus's discussion of Gelb's position on New World writing, in Marcus 1976: 37–38). The great interest in relating Central Mexican and Oaxacan writing systems to language thus may be seen, in part, as an effort to establish the legitimacy of these writing systems.

I think that these feelings of inferiority, however, are misplaced. One can even argue that pictographic systems are, in some respects, more efficient than phonetic writing. For example, a long and cumbersome phonetic text might be needed to reproduce the information contained in a small pictograph. Also, some research has shown that humans learn information more effectively if it is in pictorial form than in writing, and Mesoamerican texts were often used in teaching rituals, myths, history, and genealogy to children (Durán 1967: 191). My point however, is not to engage in name-calling, but to make the observation that the focus on a particular kind of sign relationship, when viewed in an evolutionary framework, gets in the way of our understanding of what a writing system (like that of the Mixtec) is. Instead, these systems must be seen, first of all, in the context of their use. Thus, if writing was used primarily for instruction, then the predominance of pictographs and ideographs makes good sense, in addition to the fact that there was stability and intelligibility over long periods of time.

Along these same lines it is also worth thinking about whether there is something necessary in the transition from pictographic writing to syllabic and phonetic writing systems. It has been argued that humans process pictorial and linguistic information through functionally independent cognitive systems. After all, when comprehending pictorial information we can "think" it without articulating it in language. What this may suggest is that in comparing a system of pictorials to a phonetic writing system we are comparing apples and oranges, and they may not lie on a single evolutionary line, where a pictorial writing system (if such a thing ever existed) must evolve into a phonetic one.

2 Jill Furst has shown us that some signs are based on historical events (Furst 1978). Others are based on hand gestures (Troike 1982). Still others are productive activities, and warfare (e.g., Smith 1983: 243–245). This explains why some of the greatest success stories in decipherment have come through the placing of these signs in the total context of Mixtec culture and experience, often through working with Mixtec populations today (e.g., Pohl and Byland 1990; Jansen 1982; Smith 1973).

3 Moreover, the Spanish compilers of the colonial dictionaries also translated other words as the verb "to dance," such as *tsublal,* which is related to "elegant and fantastic costuming" (Barrera Vásquez et al. 1980: 865). This may suggest that dances were performed for the gods, and that other kinds of dances were not considered by the ancient Maya to be in the same class of acts (Kaeppler 1985: 92).

4 One of the earliest examples of writing in Oaxaca is found on the famous Danzante sculptures of Monte Albán, which probably represent the corpses of captives from conquered towns (Coe 1962: 95; Marcus 1974). This obvious display of power came at a crucial time in Monte Albán's development (Marcus 1983: 90), but what is most interesting is the way these bodies are designed to bear political messages. They are almost all deformed in some way: some have blood scrolls, others have swollen eyes, and still others have been castrated. But in addition to having the power of the Monte Albán polity inscribed upon them through physical torture, these figures also bear inscriptions on their bodies (e.g., Danzante, p. 55; see Marcus 1983: 95). We cannot, unfortunately, fully understand these texts, but it is significant that the body serves as a medium upon which meanings are encoded and transmitted, and with which graphic communication in writing was associated from 600 B.C. onward in Oaxaca.

5 This material is derived primarily from fieldwork in the Mixtec communities of Santiago Nuyoo, Santa María Yucuhiti, and Santiago Ixtayutla.

6 Descent and an ongoing, intimate relationship between people are not the only things communicated by the umbilical cord. The umbilical cord, along with birth, is used by Mixtecs to indicate that a person is anchored to an identity. Thus we see in the codices that people are often attached by an umbilical cord to their names, which are often their supposed birth dates. In Mesoamerican culture, these names are associated with one's destiny, which is acquired by an individual at the moment of birth, and are thought to determine everything from personality to the day of one's death. In a similar way, Mixtecs will bury a girl's umbilical cord under the *comal* in the kitchen, and attach a boy's umbilical cord to a plow—anchoring them, as it were, to their productive roles. In some cases in the

codices, we see individuals linked to place signs by an umbilical cord. Again, this communicates an identity that is tied to "place." At least one old woman in the Mixteca keeps her granddaughter's umbilical cord with her, so that the granddaughter, who is far away, will return "to her proper place."

7 This is most clear in the use of body-part terms as prepositions, where there is an implication of a certain bodily orientation or stance toward the objects designated, or in the activity carried out (Friedrich 1969: 5; Hanks 1990: 14).

8 Thus, when Mixtecs describe a house, the door is its mouth, the sides its ears, and the roof its head.

9 The major exception to this is López Austin (1980). Most ethnographic work on body symbolism has been carried out in the context of medical and ethnomedical research (e.g., Holland 1978; Young 1981). A good review of work on pre-Hispanic clothing is contained in Anawalt (1981).

References

Anawalt, Patricia. 1981. *Indian Clothing Before Cortés: Mesoamerican Costumes from the Codices.* Norman: University of Oklahoma Press.

Barba, Eugenio, and Nicola Saravese. 1991. *A Dictionary of Theatre Anthropology: The Secret Art of the Performer.* New York: Routledge.

Barrera Vásquez, Alfredo, et al., compiladores. 1980. *Diccionario Maya Cordemex.* Mérida, Yucatán, México: Ediciones Cordemex.

Bierhorst, John 1985. *Cantares Mexicanos.* Stanford: Stanford University Press.

Boone, Elizabeth. 1982. *The Art and Iconography of Late Post-Classic Central Mexico.* Washington, D.C.: Dumbarton Oaks.

Cobarruvias, Sebastián de. 1977. *Tesoro de la Lengua Castellana o Española.* Madrid: Ediciones Turner.

Coe, Michael. 1962. *Mexico.* New York: Praeger.

Durán, Diego. 1967. *Historia de las Indias de la Nueva España.* Mexico: Porrúa.

———. 1971. *Book of the Gods and Rites of the Ancient Calendar.* Trans. and ed. Fernando Horcasitas and Doris Heyden. Norman: University of Oklahoma Press.

Featerstone, Mike, et al., eds. 1991. *The Body: Social Processes and Cultural Theory.* London: Sage Publications.

Flannery, Kent, and Joyce Marcus, eds. 1983. *The Cloud People.* New York: Academic Press.

Frank, Arthur. 1991. For a Sociology of the Body: An Analytical Review. In Featherstone et al. 1991: 36–102.

Friedrich, Paul. 1969. *On the Meaning of the Tarascan Suffixes of Space.* Indiana University Publications on Anthropology and Linguistics, Memoir 23. Baltimore: Waverly Press.

Furst, Jill. 1978. *Codex Vindobonensis Mexicanus I: A Commentary.* Albany: Institute for Mesoamerican Studies.

Hammond, Norman, ed., 1974. *Mesoamerican Archaeology.* London: Duckworth.

Hanks, William. 1990. *Referential Practice.* Chicago: University of Chicago Press.

Holland, William. 1978. *Medicina Maya en los Altos de Chiapas.* Mexico: Instituto Nacional Indigenista.

Jansen, Maarten. 1982. *Huisi Tacu.* Amsterdam: Centrum voor Studie en Documentatie van Latijns Amerika.

———. 1990. The Search for History in the Mixtec Codices. *Ancient Mesoamerica* 1: 99–112.

Kaeppler, Adrienne. 1985. Structured Movement Systems in Tonga. In Spencer 1985: 92–118.

Kurath, Gertrude Prokosch and Samuel Martí. 1964. *Dances of Anáhuac: The Choreography and Music of Precortesian Dance.* New York: Wenner-Gren Foundation of Anthropological Research.

King, Mark. 1988. Mixtec Political Ideology: Historical Metaphors and the Poetics of Political Symbolism. Ph.D. diss., Department of Anthropology, University of Michigan.

———. 1990. Poetics and Metaphor in Mixtec Writing. *Ancient Mesoamerica* 1: 141–151.

López Austin, Alfredo. 1980. *Cuerpo humano e ideología: Las concepciones de los antiguos Nahuas.* Universidad Autónoma de México.

Marcus, Joyce. 1974. The Iconography of Power among the Classic Maya. *World Archaeology* 6: 83–94.

———. 1976. The Origins of Mesoamerican Writing. *Annual Review of Anthropology* 5: 35–67.

———. 1983. The First Appearance of Zapotec Writing and Calendrics. In Flannery 1983: 91–96.

Miller, Arthur. 1974. The Iconography of the Painting of the Diving God, Tulum, Quintana Roo: The Twisted Cords.

In Hammond 1974: 167–186.

Monaghan, John. 1990. Verbal Performance and the Mixtec Codices. *Ancient Mesoamerica* 1: 133–140.

———. 1990. Sacrifice, Death, and the Origins of Agriculture in the Codex Vienna. *American Antiquity* 55: 197–199.

Pohl, John. 1984. The Earth Lords: Politics and Symbolism of the Mixtec Codices. Ph.D. diss., Department of Anthropology, University of California at Los Angeles.

Pohl, John, and Bruce Byland. 1990. Mixtec Landscape Perception and Archaeological Settlement Patterns. *Ancient Mesoamerica* 1: 113–131.

Royce, Anya Peterson. 1977. *The Anthropology of Dance.* Bloomington: Indiana University Press.

Smith, Mary Elizabeth. 1973. *Picture Writing from Ancient Southern Mexico.* Norman: University of Oklahoma Press.

———. 1983. The Mixtec Writing System. In Flannery 1983: 238–245.

Spencer, Paul, ed. 1985. *Society and the Dance.* Cambridge: Cambridge University Press.

Thompson, Eric, 1972. *A Commentary on the Dresden Codex: A Maya Hieroglyphic Book.* Philadelphia: American Philosophical Society.

Tozzer, Alfred. 1907. *A Comparative Study of the Mayas and the Lancandones.* New York: The Macmillan Company.

Troike, Nancy. 1982. The Interpretation of Postures and Gestures in the Mixtec Codices. In Boone 1982: 175–206.

Young, James. 1981. *Medical Choice in a Mexican Village.* New Brunswick, New Jersey: Rutgers University Press.

Mark B. King

Hearing the Echoes of Verbal Art in Mixtec Writing

Among the great legacies of Pre-Columbian Mesoamerica are the many writing systems that developed over the course of two thousand years (Marcus 1976). Some of these systems had disappeared or had fallen out of use before Spanish contact, but at least four writing systems were in use when Cortez arrived. From these four systems (Maya, Mixtec, Zapotec, Aztec) only about twenty books remain (Glass 1975: 66–76), a tragic testament to the zealous destruction of native libraries in the sixteenth century.

Nearly half of the surviving Pre-Columbian books were authored by Mixtec writers, residing then in what today is western Oaxaca and southern Puebla, Mexico. Aside from the miraculous fact of the very existence of these books, the Mixtec codices (Figure 1) all represent an extended narrative format having neither the year-by-year characteristics of Aztec chronicles like the Codex Boturini, nor the mantic or almanac qualities of the Borgia Group and Maya codices. Inasmuch as the Maya and Zapotec epigraphic texts are relatively brief by comparison, the Mixtec codices are the only surviving Pre-Columbian texts that represent stories of a more "epic" length, in the sense of the Gilgamesh story, the *Iliad* and *Odyssey,* the Norse sagas, or the *Popol Vuh* of the Quiché Maya. Mixtec codices stand as a unique link to Mesoamerican literary traditions that have, in some cases, been preserved in oral traditions (Gossen 1974; B. Tedlock 1982) or transcribed during the colonial period (D. Tedlock 1985), but have otherwise been lost to us in their original form.

This fact is seldom noticed for the simple reason that we have been unable to decipher much of the content in the Mixtec codices. Although we recognize that the codices contain lengthy histories, most analysts suggest that there are minimal linguistic links between the codices and the histories they represent. Mary Elizabeth Smith compares the writing in Mixtec codices with cartoon-like illustration, but emphasizes that the manuscripts logographically specify proper names, dates, and places (1973a). Indeed, the postcontact, map-like *lienzos* fit this description perfectly, many with little information other than names, dates, and places. But the precontact codices contain much more information, and the articulations with Mixtec linguistic structures are more extensive. While we may never be able to read a Mixtec codex in the same way that we may read Beowulf or the *Popul Vuh,* we will be able to construct a simplified translation, and in some instances a more detailed transcription, preserving aspects of the verbal artistry used in the authoring and recitation of the ancient books.

Treating Mixtec codices as scripts or scores for performance (Monaghan 1990a, 1990b; King 1990) rather than as illuminated historical

Figure 1. The Codex Vindobonensis Mexicanus I, also known as the Codex Vienna. This picture is of the 1974 facsimile, published by Akademische Druck- u. Verlagsanstalt. The book is approximately twenty-two centimeters wide and thirteen meters long, created from strips of deerskin, and is folded into an accordion-like screenfold, with a wooden board attached on both ends. Here, the codex is opened to pages 20 and 19 of the mythological story that covers the entire 52-page obverse.

records forces us to see these books in their cultural and linguistic contexts. They are cultural in the sense that the codices represent an important source of legitimacy for the elite class, helping to support the continuity of social, political, and economic relations within and between elite families, and in the political alliances formed outside the Mixteca—and also in the sense that a performance implies some form of public context, meaning that the symbols and signs filling the pages of the codices do not represent an esoteric ritual and historical knowledge known only to specialists. The signs and symbols on the pages of the codices should be considered political rhetoric, appealing to the values, needs, and concerns of all individuals, couching the political importance of the elite in terms of key religious and social metaphors. Thus, the codices are filled with performance guides that suggest the recitation of community proverbs, agricultural references and allusions, prayer formulae, and direct cues for certain words and syllables.

But if we are to understand the encoding of Mixtec political rhetoric, we must also understand something of the sociopolitical and sociolinguistic contexts that relate to codex production and performance. To these ends, this paper is divided into three parts. First, I will examine the social context by reconstructing aspects of the sixteenth-century Mixtec concepts of "book," "writing," and "performance." In the second part, I consider certain grammatical characteristics of Mixtec writing and how the structuring of the written text relates to its performance. In the concluding section, I present a brief analysis of a scene taken from the Vienna codex, providing a practical illustration of how Mixtec writing combines verbal and visual artistry.

Books, Writing, and Song

While writing is clearly an important part of the support apparatus used by rulers of the Mixtec kingdoms, it represents only one part of a larger system of language-based class support. Ironically, the priests and friars who were so preoccupied with the destruction of Mixtec books were also busy recording the grammar and vocabulary of the language (Alvarado 1964; Reyes 1976), and in the process they left us evidence of linguistic behaviors that have all but vanished in modern Mixtec speech. Most striking is the so-called *iya* vocabulary (Reyes 1976: i–iii, 74–81; Arana 1961; King 1982, 1988; Jansen 1985). The words and expressions comprising this vocabulary represent a conventionalized, but systematic, way of talking about elite-class individuals by non-elites. The elite class was a rigidly endogamous stratum in Mixtec society; this class was so set apart from the non-elite classes that every body part, every action, and every possession was linguistically marked, either by the conventionalized use of a metaphor (e.g., fingernails are "knives") or, at the very least, by the use of a class-distinctive pronoun, *-ya,* which is still productive today as a "deity" pronoun throughout the Mixteca.[1]

Apart from the useful cultural information that these metaphors provide, especially when compared with their non-elite counterparts, the *iya* vocabulary also provides an important link to understanding the categories of speech and communication in Mixtec society at the time of Spanish contact. The elite referential vocabulary was apparently conceived as the language spoken by the very first elites, preserved unchanged since time immemorial (Reyes 1976: i–ii). Rappaport (1979: 202–211) suggests that such language is representative of The Word, lending sanctity, truthfulness, and respect to both the words (and their speakers) and the (often ritual) contexts within which they are used. This agrees with speech categories derived from sixteenth-century vocabulary (King 1982), which can be divided initially into "good words" and "bad words." Good words and appropriate speech form a continuum of subcategories which reflect degrees of meaningfulness and intelligibility. At one end of the continuum are words whose meaning is clear, but insignificant (e.g., gossip and other forms of informal speech); at the other end are words full of meaning yet which are difficult to understand, including prayer, song, and *iya* "speech."[2]

Language data contained in the Alvarado *Vocabulario* (1964) imply that these three varieties of "most proper" speech are but a single category (King 1982). Most important are the data suggesting that the native books are also part of this category. For "to speak with grace, composing from the head," the *Vocabulario* lists "to speak song" or "to speak of family" (*yo-cã'ã-yaa-ndi*), "to speak lineages" (*yo-cã'ã-tũ'ũ-ndi*), and "to speak elite words" (*yo-cã'ã-dzã'ã*).[3] Similarly, the content of the books is described variously as "lineage songs" or "lineage relatives" (*yaa tũ'ũ*), "ancient lineages" (*tũ'ũ yata*), "orderly lineages," and "books of dead rulers." The term for "song" (*yaa*) itself encompasses a number of performance-oriented values, including song, dance, and music (see also Monaghan 1990b), and some entries are especially suggestive. For example, the Mixtec phrase that is given for *bozear ala luna los indios ala luna en su gentilidad* is *yo ca'wi ta-tũ' ũ cani,* "to read long songs of praise."

Hearing the Sacred Music

From the perspectives above, Mixtec books represent sacred texts or scripts for the performance of elite histories, including the ancient, mythic past, especially the genealogy-based stories with which we are most familiar. These scripts are written in what was thought of as an ancient elite-class dialect. But if we are to appreciate the content and composition of the Mixtec books, then we must also examine the meanings of terms associated with the books themselves. The books are most often termed *tacu,* "to paint," "to make designs," and "writing." But a second set of meanings for *tacu* is equally appropriate, including "to hear," or "to listen," implying the oral recitation of books.

Books are also called *tutu* ("page," "design," "to whistle"), a term that is apparently related to the words *toto* ("to sing," "to put in order," "kinship"), *cutu* ("wind instrument," "copal incense"), and *catu* ("whistle," "pipe"), emphasizing the musical or performative aspects of the codices. This musical sense may be related to the syllable *-tu-* in these words. In the broadest sense, *-tu-* and *-tũ-* tend to carry some sense of linearity (King 1988: 147–150), both as the shape (or air pathway) of whistles, flutes, and trumpets and as the conceptual shape of the music itself.

A reasonably explicit example of this metaphoric connection between meaning, sound texture, and symbolism is found on page 48b of the Vienna codex (Figure 2), where we see three of the sixteen "guises" of the culture hero, Lord 9 Wind, who is the source of all social and cultural knowledge. These three individuals might reasonably be called

"singer," "poet," and "painter," representing the three aspects of codex artistry: the ability to compose songs, the ability to perform songs, and the ability to write songs in books. Songs are symbolized by multicolored scrolls, but note in Figure 3 that the smoke issuing from the long-handled incensario held by Lady 4 Dog is symbolized by the exact same scroll form—only the colors are grey and brown instead of blue, green, yellow, and red.

Figure 2. Codex Vienna, p. 48b. Three of the sixteen guises or "roles" of the culture hero, Lord 9 Wind, suggesting skills as singer, poet, and painter/writer. A fourth guise as a "stone man" precedes these in the upper left corner of the figure.

The contextual overlapping of scroll types for the singer in Figure 2, and the incense smoke in Figure 3, can be understood more easily if we look at a second group of terms with linear connotations that relate to this broadened sense of song. We have already noted that the word *cutu* can mean either "wind instrument" or "incense," which is a more logical connection if you consider that *cuu* means "copal (incense) smoke," "incense brazier," and "to ignite copal." Instead of *-tu-*, these terms share the syllable *-cu-*. Perhaps there is some etymological connection to the word *coo,* "serpent" (actual or folk etymology), but here *-cu-* appears to carry more of a sense of "smoke-like scroll patterning" that can be extended to contexts of writing and music-making (playing or singing), as in the verb *coco/saco,* "to write/paint in colors," or *tacu,* "to paint." Inasmuch as scroll symbolism seems to carry a "heated" connotation, I would also suggest that "song" and all song-related activities are spiritually heated in nature. Indeed, in modern day Nuyoo (Monaghan 1987: 487–518), persons who are exceptionally effective and eloquent speakers are said to speak with *yɨɨ* ("masculine heat of vitality").[4]

Consonant with the idea of song as "a spiritually heated offering that rises skyward, the colorful verbal artistry visibly swirling like the sweet smoke of copal" is the association of books with the earth (*ñu'u*). The word for earth, *ñu'u,* has a complex semantic structure, not dissimilar to that for the word *yɨɨ.* If *yɨɨ* represents the heated vitality within individuals, then *ñu'u* can be thought of as the heated spirituality of the earth's body; *ñu'u* can mean "earth" (literally, and in the sense of a specific location), "spirit" (in the sense of the spirit that resides in a given specific location), and "fire" (in the sense of the metaphorical heat associated with these spiritual beings) (Monaghan 1987: 383–459; King 1988: 157–276).[5] The sixteenth-century sources tell us that books are made of "*ñu'u* skin," "*ñu'u* songbooks," and "*ñu'u* tails." Here the connotation is that the books themselves are part of the earth; perhaps this means that the deerskin (or bark-paper) foundation is categorically and conceptually distinct from the writing applied to the surface of the skin. This would make the codices twice-sanctified: once in the sense of the earthly nature of the book itself (and the presumed association of a book

Figure 3. Codex Vienna, p. 18. The ritual greeting for the deity of the East, Lord 7 Flower, who stands at the far right, and who is greeted with offerings of (going left from Lord 7 Flower) a decapitated bird, smoking incense, a burning torch, and conch-trumpet music.

with a specific location), and once in the sense of the "offering" placed on its surface.

To sum up this section on the nature of codices, I turn to a final set of terms relating to codex scribes and the compositions they create. Here again, the similarities in meaning are nearly as striking as the similarities in form: *taa,* "to write"; *tãã,* "to weave or braid"; *yaa,* "(musical) performance"; *ndaa,* "to have a design/writing on something"; and *naa,* "type of drawn figure." Here the resemblance among the terms for "writing or singing something" suggests another variant on the "scrolling" theme, this time as a weaving metaphor. Mixtec writing invariably follows a meandering or boustrophedon pattern that forms one continuous "line," weaving back and forth across the whole surface of a book (Smith 1973a: 217), which is most often made from a long piece of deer hide (as long as fifteen meters) folded, accordion-fashion, into a compact screenfold (see Figure 1). I would suggest that when we look at the range of concepts, words, metaphors, and symbols relating to Mixtec codices, we can begin to appreciate why the Mixtec—and only the Mixtec—wrote texts in a consistent back-and-forth format, creating a visual metaphor for the iconography of song.

The Layers of Meaning in Mixtec Writing

> It was in Santa Cruz, between 1554 and 1558, that members of the Cawek lineage created a new version of the Popul Vuh, writing in the Quiché language but using an alphabetic orthography that had been worked out by the missionary Francisco de la Parra in 1545. If these writers had chosen to transpose the ancient Popul Vuh on a glyph-by-glyph basis, they might have produced a terse, schematic, and highly mathematized text that would have made little sense to anyone but a diviner. What they did instead was to transcribe what the reader of the ancient book would *say* when he transformed the glyphs into what they call his "long performance and account" of "the emergence of all the sky-earth." (D. Tedlock 1985: 71–72)
>
> . . . Marking their act of quotation with such phrases as "This is the account here," they begin before the first dawn, when the world contained only an empty sky and a calm sea. . . . (D. Tedlock 1987: 140–141)

What I want to do here is briefly outline how codices encode certain parameters of performance. I believe the Mixtec codices are precisely what Dennis Tedlock suggests: terse, schematic scripts with ritual and divinatory information interwoven with the facts of the story. In the genealogy-based histories, like the Nuttall, Selden, or Bodley codices, the fusion of historical particulars (names, dates, and places) with mythological and ritual details is so complex as almost to defy analysis. But a contextual analysis of symbolism combined with parallel analyses of linguistic and ethnographic materials goes far in the identification and interpretation of nonhistorical information in Mixtec codices.

Mixtec codices have four basic grammar-like categories of information that can be thought of as layers of meaning. They are grammatical in the sense that these layers encode noun phrases (Smith 1973a; Caso 1977; Jansen 1990; Pohl and Byland 1990), verb phrases, modifiers (King 1988, 1990), and details of discourse structuring (Monaghan 1990b); and layers in the sense that the use of all layers is not obligatory.[6] For example, colonial *mapas* and map-like *lienzos* that use Mixtec writing are dominated by the use of noun phrases and have minimal discursive structuring.[7] While layers are independent in this sense, the combining of the layers in codices gives a distinctly music-like flavor, as if we were looking at a score for four singers. The score would present the independent parts simultaneously, giving a graphic representation of the relative pitch and rhythm of the four for any moment within the piece of music. Although such a score would explicitly state "Quartet for Voices," any individual with the proper musical training could play the score on a piano, make an arrangement for instrumental ensemble, or even "hear" the harmonies by reading the score silently. With this metaphor in mind, I will briefly discuss the layers of information contained in the codices.

Names, Dates, and Places

Nouns and noun phrases are the most obvious, most numerous, and most studied class of glyphs found in the Mixtec codices, and include (1) the names of individuals, both calendrical and personal, (2) date glyphs, and (3) place glyphs (Figure 4). People were named for their birthday in the 260-day ritual calendar (Caso 1977). There is therefore no real difference between these names and date glyphs, except that dates can be year-day combinations or just a day designation (again from the 260-day count). In Figure 4, we see the name of the warrior, 8 Deer, depicted by eight large "dots" connected to the day-sign "Deer" seen as the head of a deer. To the far left of Figure 4 we see a date, Year 4 Reed, Day 10 Vulture. While the "A-O" year symbol with the reed shaft in the center is distinctive, there is nothing to distinguish the day "10 Vulture" from the name "8 Deer" except the proximity of the one to the year sign and

Figure 4. Codex Nuttall, p. 43b–c. Lord 8 Deer "Jaguar Claw," who conquers the location "Eagle Hill" in the Year 7 Reed, on the day 9 Vulture.

the other to the face of the warrior. Furthermore, there is little relationship between this type of temporal information and the Mixtec language; these dates would have been recognized and understood by any scribe in central Mesoamerica, regardless of language (see M. E. Smith 1973a: 22–27). By this I mean that the signs of the Mixtec calendar are virtually identical to Nahuatl calendar signs, even though local divinatory significance of the signs and dates differs.

Personal names (Smith 1973b; Caso 1977; Smith and Parmenter 1991) have a relationship with place glyphs (Smith 1973a: 29–136; Jansen 1982; Pohl and Byland 1990; Smith and Parmenter 1991), and together represent the true class of noun phrases in Mixtec writing.[8] From all published accounts, place glyphs are ad hoc compositions that utilize a core of conventional representations for different types of places, like hills, plains, fields, rivers, and caves. These geographic types are then toponymically qualified with a wide range of glyphs in order to specify which "hill" is being cited. A typical example of a place glyph can be seen in Figure 4 between Lord 8 Deer and the year-day combination to the far left; here, the place is depicted as the "Hill of the Eagle" (an unidentified location). So far, there is little evidence of any "rules" for place-glyph composition, even in the sense that Aztec place glyphs do (Barlow and McAfee 1949). Place glyphs make use of any type of "playful" or poetic device to encode place names, making it impossible to predict (1) how a place name will appear in a codex, or (2) what kinds of linguistic information are being used in any given instance, including pictographic representations, syllables, tone "puns," and other forms of metaphoric association. These facts have made decipherment a painfully slow endeavor. Personal names use a similar range of qualifier glyphs (ballcourts, plants, animals, jewels, spiderwebs, stars, the sun, etc.) to specify a ruler's name, distinguishing them from other elites who share a birthday. In Figure 4 the personal name of Lord 8 Deer is depicted above and behind his head as the claw of a jaguar; thus we might speak of Lord 8 Deer "Jaguar Claw." Together, the warrior, his names, the place glyph, and the date tell of the conquest of "Eagle Hill" by Lord 8 Deer "Jaguar Claw" on the day 10 Vulture in the year 9 Reed. While an arrow in the side of the hill may seem to be an obvious visual device, the phrases for "conquest" in the sixteenth-century Mixtec dictionary actually focus on "putting an arrow in the land" of the conquered people.

Dates, Divination, Captions, and Verbs

Accompanying the "strong lead voice" of noun phrases in the Mixtec codices are divinatory meanings associated with the 260-day ritual calendar. Throughout ancient Mesoamerica, the ritual count functioned as a type of "astrological" tool (hence the birth-date names, for example). Specialists at this form of divination were known as "day keepers" and are known to us from the early ethnohistoric sources, as alluded to by Tedlock, above. Although Mixtec codex scribes were clearly versed in day-keeping practices, we have had little success in the illumination of divinatory information contained in the codices, and aside from the detection of various quasi-mathematical patterns among dates and names, there would seem to be little useful cultural information available to the analyst.[9] While there are almost no modern or ethnohistorical sources pertaining to Mixtec divinatory practice, there is one important resource that reveals a few important properties of ritual day-keeping practices: the vocabulary associated with the calendar.

Unlike the elite "*iya*" vocabulary, discussed earlier, which was preserved by sixteenth-century Dominican lexicographers, the calendar vocabulary is preserved mostly through alphabetically glossed calendar names on *lienzos, mapas,* and codices (Smith 1973: 22–27; Caso 1977, 1: 163–164; Smith and Parmenter 1991). This vocabulary consists of twenty day names and thirteen number terms; the 260-day ritual calendar or cycle represents the repetitive counting through the sequences of numbers and day names, resulting in a set of 260 unique combinations of number and name.[10] What makes the Mixtec calendar terms so important is their strange morphological properties, which have been noticed, but never analyzed:

Day Numbers	*Day Signs*	
1 *ca*	Earth Monster	*quɨwi, quɨ*
2 *cua*	Wind	*chi*
3 *co*	House	*cuayu, cua*
4 *cui*	Lizard	*cuyɨ, cu*
5 *cu*	Serpent	*yoco, yo*
6 *ño*	Death	*maa, ma*
7 *sa*	Deer	*cua'a, cua*
8 *na*	Rabbit	*sayu, sa*
9 *quɨ*	Water	*nduta, ta*
10 *si*	Dog	*waa, wa*
11 *si*	Monkey	*ñuu, ñu*
12 *cua*	Grass	*cuayɨ, yɨ*
13 *si*	Reed	*wiyu, yu*
	Jaguar	*widzu, dzu*
	Eagle	*saya, sa*
	Vulture	*cuii, cui*
	Movement	*quɨ'ɨ, quɨ*
	Knife	*cusi, si*
	Rain	*sawi, wi*
	Flower	*waco, co*

The curiosities here are twofold: (1) few terms bear any resemblance to what are commonly taken to be Mixtec words for either the numbers one through thirteen, or for the day signs ("rain" and "water" excepted), and (2) the number terms are "half-words," by which I mean that Mixtec words are composed of two syllables, and these terms have only one syllable. Likewise each day name is sometimes glossed as a single syllable, in some cases the first syllable, in others the last, but there is *always* the same choice for any single day name.[11]

Special ritual-calendar vocabulary is not an uncommon feature in Mesoamerica and can be found among the Maya (B. Tedlock 1982) and the Zapotec (Marcus 1983; Whitecotton 1990: 146–153); in fact, it may turn out that the Aztecs were more exceptional in their *lack* of special vocabulary for the ritual count of days. Determination of the meanings associated with these special vocabularies is even more challenging, especially in a historical context. Consider the following characteristics of the modern Maya system:

> The [Maya] day names have been "translated" into German, Spanish, and English common nouns by previous researchers, but they cannot be properly glossed except as day names. Even apparently

translatable names such as Batz' ("monkey"), Tz'iquin ("bird"), Ix ("jaguar"), and C'at ("net") are taken by Quiché diviners to be untranslatable proper names within the context of calendrical divination. The day names as understood and used in Quiché communities are not interpreted by linking them to a fixed inventory of static symbols through glosses or etymologies; rather, a given day name is interpreted by means of mnemonic phrases that map the meanings of the days in terms of the social actions that characterize them. These phrases often include the sounds of the day name but not necessarily the name as such. Previous attempts to interpret the 260-day ritual cycle according to the supposed symbolic and metaphoric associations of each day name have treated the names as if they were, in effect, pictographs in a writing system lacking a phonetic dimension. Instead, in actual practice the names are "read" not as words in themselves but as a kind of oral rebus for quite other words; these other words are linked to the day name by means of paronomasia—that is, by means of poetic sound play. (B. Tedlock 1982: 107)

Barbara Tedlock goes on to demonstrate that much of the poetic sound play operates at the level of the syllable, with syllables functioning as the mnemonic connection between the words and phrases related to a day name (1982: 108–126). Considering the strange morphological properties of Mixtec calendar vocabulary, it might be expected that a similar syllabic system of divinatory practice is being reflected since each day name has one emphasized syllable. But the poetics or mnemonics of Maya divination do not extend in the same way to number terms (although the numbers play a crucial role in focusing the appropriate values of day names; see B. Tedlock 1982: 127–131), and there are a number of Mixtec "deity names" written down in Spanish colonial documents that are the product of using the calendar vocabulary as though it functioned as a syllabary.[12] Other evidence also supports the use of the calendar vocabulary as a syllabic system, and the view that the system provides "captions" for the people, places, and activities portrayed in the codices (King 1988, 1990). As we shall see, the words and meanings associated with captions are mostly verbs, a type of linguistic information assumed only to be implied through pictorial conventions (León-Portilla 1992: 318–321), as seen in the "conquest" portrayed in Figure 4.

Both calendar names and date glyphs can function as a caption, but not in the Western sense of a short text. Captions express only a few suggestive words at a time, and from there it is up to the reader to fill in the text with other words and meanings generated through the mnemonics of divination. As with most types of writing, some phonetic details and phonemic contrasts are omitted by the system, just as vowels are omitted from Arabic and Hebrew writing, relying on diacritics to supply vowels when desired; the writing system I am using to write this article fails to note the important phonemic contrasts of stress in English words. Captions do not record tone, word-medial glottals, and vowel nasality, and appear to function as if Mixtec had only three vowels instead of six.[13]

But even within these seemingly generous parameters, only a limited number of Mixtec words can be written using this syllabary. The inventory of syllables is far short of what would be needed to write complete texts. But this is, remember, a divination-based syllabary, and its shortcomings emphasize the fact that ritual-calendar divination was still a vital aspect of day-to-day life when these codices were created. Even if the redundancies in the syllabary are eliminated, there are insufficient "spaces" in the combined thirty-three terms (thirteen number-terms plus twenty day-name syllables) to account for all Mixtec syllables, and the fact that redundancies do exist (see numbers ten, eleven, and thirteen, or day names House and Deer, for example) also speaks for a system that has only been adapted, rather than created, to write verbs; it suggests a system that has more important functions beyond captioning. Thus calendar names and dates tell us (1) denotative information concerning (cyclical, but non-annual) time and, by extension, names of people; (2) divinatory information concerning the character of things, places, and people associated with any given day in the 260-day count (Jansen 1988), with divinatory associations that are likely to be based, in part, on a system of syllable mnemonics; and (3) caption-like information, mostly verbs, that gives a syllabic guide to the oral performance of codices.

In perhaps the most objective sense, the special vocabulary and ritual mnemonics of the 260-day calendar represent the most ancient aspect of writing and the speech genre of song. The first forms of writing to appear in Mesoamerica are calendar names (Marcus 1976), suggesting that the origins of the 260-day count may relate in some way to the origins of sedentary life. The *iya* vocabulary was believed to be the speech of the first rulers, but the vocabulary and mnemonics of the ritual count may actually reflect ancient ritual speech. While this is difficult to substantiate in any detail, the Vienna codex shows that "song" is related to the words a shaman speaks, as in the instance of the culture hero's role as leader of a (psilocybin) mushroom ceremony, seen here in Figure 5 (page 24a), where his speech scroll is identical to that seen in Figure 2, discussed earlier.[14]

To summarize this section, Mixtec writing is composed of complementary layers of meaning (nouns, verbs, and modifiers) structured and arranged in such a way as to illuminate changes in discourse styles. While Mixtec codices clearly represent texts, the writing is more suggestive of a musical score, with a simple, cartoon-like narrative line, visually enhanced by a complex symbolic vocabulary which, in turn, is grounded in the verbal poetics of ritual and divinatory speech. Noun phrases are limited to stylized glyphic representations of proper names and dates; verbs are limited to those that may be composed using the syllables of the ritual calendar vocabulary, excepting visual verbs, such as the "arrow-in-the-hill" = "conquered" verb seen in Figure 4. Modifiers often suggest similarities between nouns and verbs, using a range of poetic devices that tend to relate the visual symbolism of calendar day signs with the mnemonics of the ritual calendar. Earlier in the discussion of writing and song metaphors, I noted that there is a dual patterning of lexical meaning and morphology that is also reflected symbolically; thus, the concept of "music," the syllable "*-cu-*," and "scroll" symbolism are all analogous structures in Mixtec language and writing at the time of the conquest. If we add to this the meaning of contextually associated captions and day-name mnemonics, the nature of these associations becomes more intelligible, and improves our understanding of "song" and codex composition. In the next section, then, I will examine solar associations within the domain of music or song. This includes (1) a consideration of solar "deities" (spiritual personifications), (2) their calendar name captions, (3) the date captions and symbolism used for the first appearance of the sun in the Vienna codex, and (4) a more complete consideration of the symbolic contexts of song scrolls.

The Music of New Life

According to a story from San Miguel el Grande, when the sun first rose, "things happened. A great deal of music was played and the music came along with the sun and it was very hot" (Dyk 1959: 3). Most codex analysts of the past thirty years have taken this information to be an important Pre-Columbian reference and, as we see in Figure 6, the story matches the depiction of the first sunrise as related on page 23b of the Vienna codex. In this scene, the sun rises from the top of a large red-and-white platform; the platform is not smoking, it is "singing" (Jansen 1988) or making music, evidenced by the use of multicolored scrolls, rather than the shades of grey and brown used for smoke. This correlates nicely with the "music is like copal smoke" metaphor, for the modern story relates rising music with rising heat, and visually the scene in the codex relates heat and music through the use of scrolls attached to the platform on either side. The modern story also uses "*tɨwi*" for "play music," meaning "blow on a wind instrument"; note that the scrolls on the platform are like those issuing from the conch-shell trumpet in Figure 3.

But this seems a strange event, so much so that many analysts are prone to call the scrolls "smoke," given the natural qualities of the sun and their effects. And although I have presented several reasons supporting why music and heat are metaphorically related, this does not mean that the sun should necessarily be included within the range of the metaphor. The use of speech or song or musical scrolls in the codices is rare, unlike Aztec manuscripts, which use it like the verb "to speak." Depictions of ordinary communication between individuals almost never use scrolls, and while each "scroll-use event" is important, other events equal or surpass them in historical significance.

The scene in question is from the Vienna codex, the real treasure among the eight surviving Mixtec codices. The Vienna codex is unlike the other seven, and, in fact, unlike any other surviving precontact codex, except for the transliterated version of the Popul Vuh, and similar Maya manuscripts (Roys 1933, 1946). Like the Maya documents, the Vienna codex is an extended origin myth, beginning before the first dawn, in the darkness, when waters covered the surface of the earth, and all the "sky-earth" was chaotic (León-Portilla 1969: 55–57).[15] Like many lengthy origin myths, the content of the Vienna codex reveals hierarchical information concerning the structure and operation of the Mixtec universe.

Origin myths establish categorical distinctions within the universe, organizing cultural existence and providing a logically satisfying hierarchy of things, behaviors, and places (Leach 1962; Burkhart 1989). They are hierarchical in the sense that the "abominations of Leviticus" in the Bible are logically subordinate to fundamental concepts of sanctity taken together with the categorical details of Creation from the opening chapters of Genesis (Douglas 1966: 41–57; see also Rappaport 1979: 97–144). Origin myths often unfold cultural knowledge, defining fundamental categories, their prototype values, and the proper, prescribed ways for elements within the categories to behave, lest social sin be committed, or pollution occur. The Vienna codex unfolds the logical order of the universe, beginning with the timeless, wet, darkness; listed

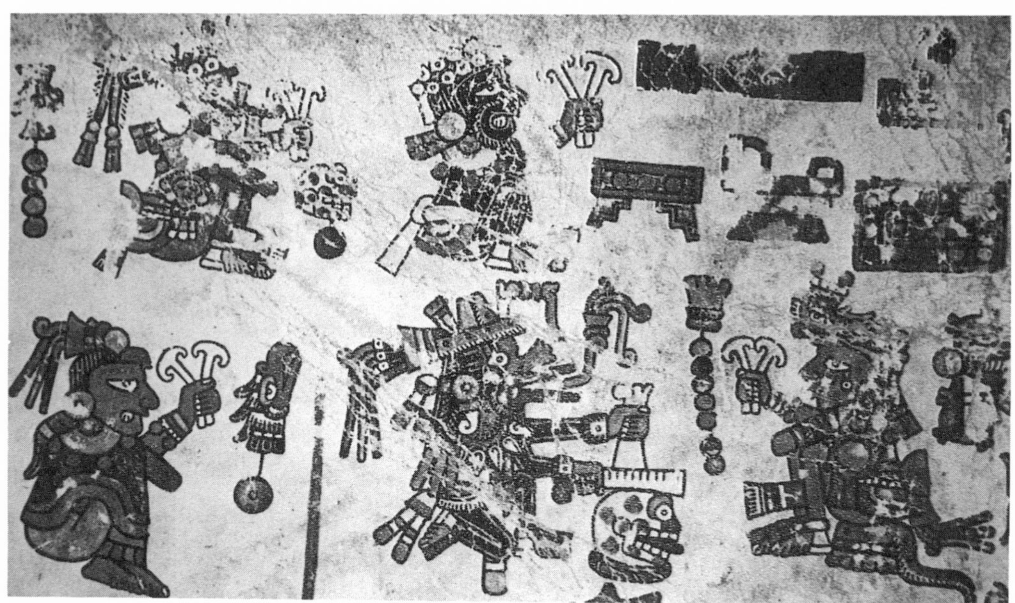

within this darkness are twenty symbols that define the conceptual and categorical boundaries for the entire manuscript. *Everything* that follows this array of symbols is categorically dependent, re-presenting and transforming the fundamental concepts and distinctions in ways that make details of category membership increasingly explicit and coherent. In this way we can use the "progressive," narrative structure of the Vienna codex to help unravel the meanings of symbols, like scrolls.[16]

Figure 5. Codex Vienna, p. 24a–b. Hallucinogenic mushroom ceremony, given in honor of Lord 7 Flower (seated at lower right, facing left). The ritual is led by the culture hero, Lord 9 Wind, who sings and accompanies himself on a skull drum (bottom center). Lords 2 Dog (above 9 Wind), 1 Death (upper left), and Lady 1 Eagle (lower left) are among the other participants. In front of and above Lords 2 Dog and 7 Flower are ritual objects of uncertain meaning.

Singing about Singing

The Vienna codex uses "musical" scrolls in a restricted range of contexts that may be separated into two types of usage: (1) instances where someone is causing music as part of the described actions, and (2) instances where music scrolls are a qualifying or modifying element, as seen in Figure 2, where we are only seeing "roles" or "guises" of the culture hero, not his actual behavior. Instances of the first type of context include (a) part of the ritual preparations for the birth of the first people from the great white tree on page 38c, (b) as part of a community naming ritual following a ritual sweatbath on page 30a, (c) as part of the sacred mushroom ceremony (Figure 5) which immediately precedes the first sunrise, and (d) as "trumpet music" in the ritual greetings for the Eastern and Nadir "deities" on pages 18b (Figure 3) and 20b (Figure 1, right side), respectively.[17]

The common element in these four contexts plus the "musical building" seen in Figure 6 at the first sunrise, is "birth" and the state which immediately precedes a birth ("labor?"), in the sense that three pairs of instances are found in the Vienna codex: (1) two separate instances at the scene of the tree birth (Figure 7), each with the same date caption seen in Figure 6 (Year 13 Rabbit, Day 2 Deer, analyzed below); (2) the first sunrise music, preceded by the mushroom ceremony, which is held in honor of a solar deity named Lord 7 Flower (Figure 5); and (3) the trumpet-music greeting for the solar deity 7 Flower (Figure 3), immediately preceded by a nearly identical set of rituals and trumpet music in the greeting for an individual who may be thought of as a more earthly version of 7 Flower, named Lord 4 Movement, who personifies the "pent-up" heat of masculine vitality.

This leaves only the community naming ritual preceded by ritual sweatbathing (Figure 8). In this context sweatbathing, while not a singing event, may function to increase the type of heat expended during a "birth experience," which we know is true from the modern custom of post-parturition sweatbaths (Ravicz and Romney 1969: 394–395; also illustrated in Nuttall codex, pages 15–16). If this is true, then perhaps the naming ritual emphasizes the beginning of new social identities, taking individuals out of their households and bringing them into their new community contexts and duties. Considering that marriage rituals have no associated music scrolls and that the naming ritual is nearly identical in many respects to the marriage ritual (compare pages 35b and 30a, or 22 and 17b of the Vienna codex), I draw the inference that singing accompanies "births" of a communal nature or of a nature that would affect all households, like the rising of the sun. Even though codices are "elite lineage stories" or "family songs," they relate more than simple genealogies, including the ancient origin-birth stories, which tell how individual kingdoms originated. The codices also tell of the public rituals performed by past rulers on behalf of their subjects to maintain good relations with the forces of nature. In this respect, the codices contain stories of communal interest; the histories of elite dynasties are recorded both as elite genealogy and as the ritual history of communities. The history of rulers becomes the history of communities (King 1988: 334–445).

But most of the contexts for these scrolls are in relation to the sun or things associated with the sun; how might this relate to events like naming rituals? How do we get from the category of sacred speech to the concept of sunrise? A few relationships come to mind: If the speech

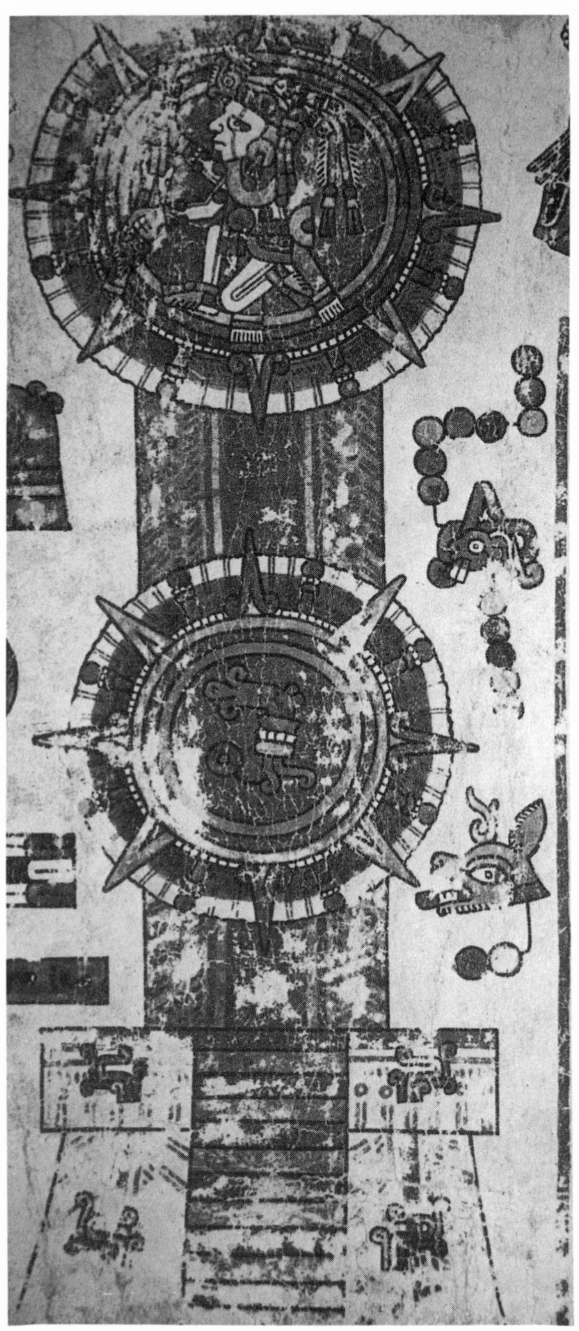

Figure 6. Codex Vienna, p. 23b. The first sunrise, here depicted as two solar disks rising on a red path above a temple adorned with song scrolls. In the lower disk appears the pictorial caption date, 1 Flower; in the upper disk appears a solar deity, with no attached name. To the right side, center, appears a caption date: Year 13 Rabbit, Day 2 Deer.

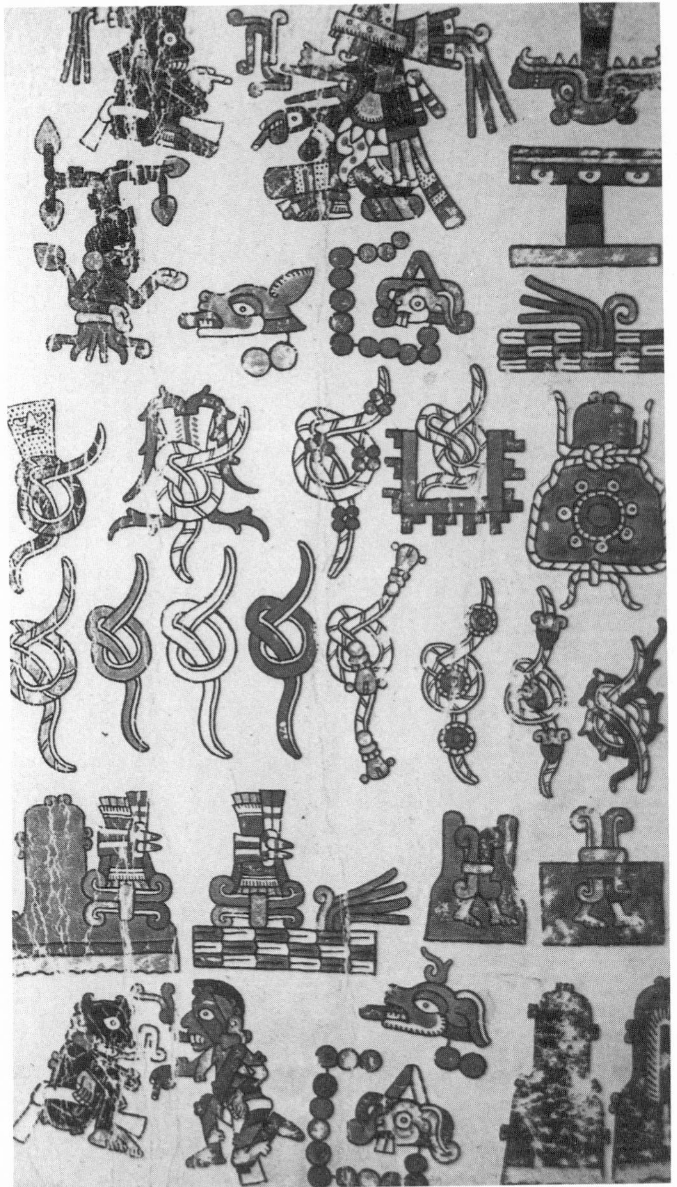

Figure 7. Codex Vienna, p. 38c. Preparations for the birth of the first Mixtec people from a white tree. At the bottom (beginning) of the scene, two stone men sing to one another; at the top (end) of the scene, the culture hero, Lord 9 Wind, sings to a stone man and a tree man. The same date caption appears twice in this scene, once to the right of the stone men at the bottom, and once again below Lord 9 Wind: Year 13 Rabbit, Day 2 Deer. Between these two musical encounters we see twenty symbols of uncertain meaning. Thirteen of the symbols are knotted cords, each with distinguishing characteristics.

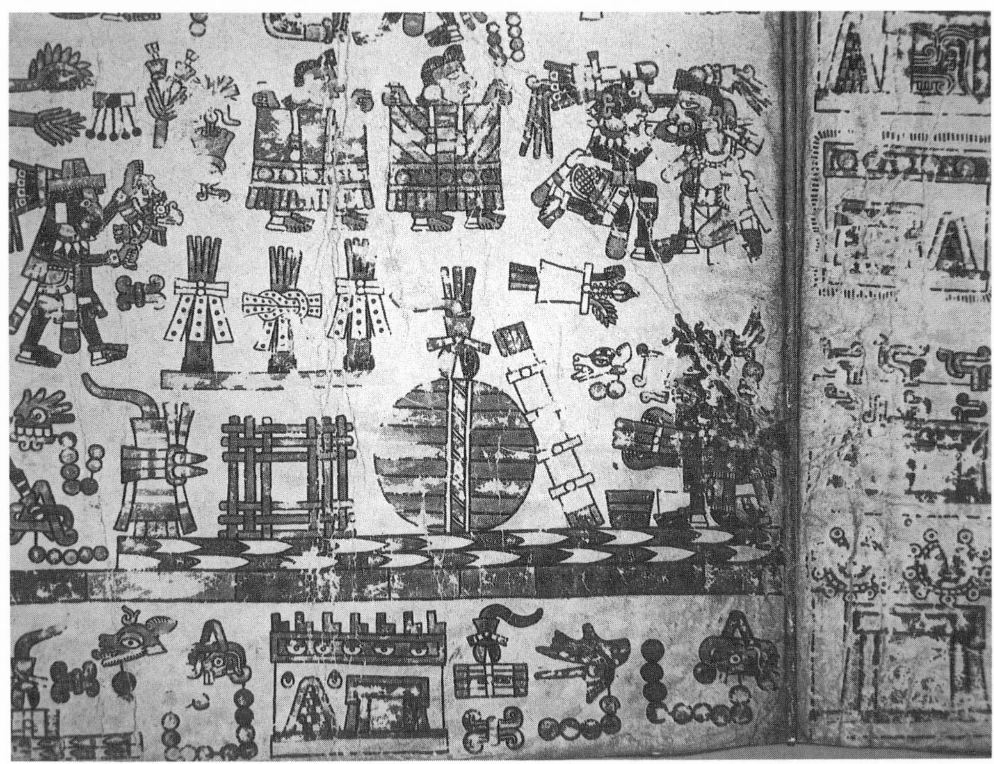

Figure 8. Codex Vienna, p. 31b–30a. The lower two-thirds of the naming ritual; Lord 2 Dog sings in the lower right part of the scene, holding a bundled offering. The caption date, Year 13 Rabbit, Day 2 Deer, appears in the lower left corner, immediately preceding the ritual scene. Along the right side of the figure can be seen a line of sweat-bath structures from the purification scene on the preceding page.

genre of song is related to the divinatory practices of calendar specialists, then a "singing" naming ceremony would necessarily include someone versed in the verbal arts of divination. Since writing seems to have developed out of the same divinatory calendrics, then we also might expect there to be a fundamental connection between "time" and the sun. This can be seen in the year glyph itself, often called an "A-O" year glyph because of the resemblance to an intertwining of the letters A and O (see the center-right side of Figure 6, and in the lower left in Figure 4). This is accepted to represent a "binding of the sun" in the visual sense of a rope tied around a "sun ray" (compare sun rays of the solar disks in Figure 6 with the year glyph to the right).

A somewhat different relationship between sunrise and birth is found in modern and sixteenth-century expressions metaphorically describing birth as "dawning." This elegant metaphor partly hinges on the semantic ranges of the verbs *cana* "to leave the inside," "to bounce back," "to appear," "to scream," "to call out," "to resound," "the song of birds," "speech" (elite *iya* reference), and *nana* "to leave the inside," "to separate," "to sprout," "to produce fruit," "to resound," and "to be born" (elite *iya* reference). The verb *cana* is used in expressions for East, describing the action of the sun's return, but also bears the connotations of birth and loud, clear sounds. Note also that elite-class vocabulary articulates with both of these birth/dawn/music verbs, implying a range of potential elite associations, from solar associations to creative and powerful speech to fertility.[18]

Solar Personifications

In 1959, Alfonso Caso made a stunning breakthrough when he connected the solar pictorial character, Lord 1 Death, with an entry in the Alvarado *Vocabulario* for "(pagan term for) sun": *yya caa ma'a,* suggesting that the special calendar vocabulary was used to speak the names of spirits and, perhaps, ancestors. Since the publication of Caso's article, analysts have been unwilling to stray from the idea that the solar spirit is no more and no less than what we see in depictions of Lord 1 Death. But in fact there is a near twin of Lord 1 Death, found in the Vienna and Nuttall codices, named Lord 7 Flower (seen in Figures 3 and 5), who would appear to be more important, given that 7 Flower appears seven times in the Vienna codex, 1 Death appearing only twice.[19]

Exactly how these two solar characters differ is difficult to determine. Given the near-positive relationship of 7 Flower to the direction "East" in the Vienna codex (Jansen 1982), 1 Death is likely to represent a complementary character. In a ritual scene depicted in the Nuttall codex, 1 Death and 7 Flower are present with three other deities who together represent the four cardinal directions and the center; Lord 1 Death occupies the "West" position, and wears a costume nearly identical to that of 7 Flower (Figure 9).[20] In the Selden codex (page 1), 1 Death plunges downward, also suggesting a "setting" sun complement to 7 Flower's "rising" sun. But these are only guesses; while there is sufficient symbolic data to evaluate the meanings associated with 7 Flower, this is not the case for 1 Death.

One way to examine the differences between the two is by examining their name captions. Lord 7 Flower's name (7 *sa* Flower [*wa*]*co*) gives several appropriate possible translations. First there is *dzacu,* meaning "good," "beautiful," "precious," which describes those things associated with 7 Flower and the East, including birds, gold, jade, chocolate, fine clothing, and the like. The East, the place of song and of the reborn rising sun, relates to a concept of gift giving, or more likely, gift

Figure 9. Codex Nuttall, p. 17b–18a. Lords 7 Flower and 1 Death, as they appear attending a public festival. Note the similarities in costuming.

receiving. Lord 7 Flower represents precious things given to the Mixtec people, including not just material gifts but also things like children, and the abundant fruits of the earth (King 1988).

A second translation of 7 Flower's name caption is the verb *saco/coco,* meaning "to write," "paint in colors," and "compose a song," which relates to the "precious" meanings of *dzacu.* But a second verb is also of interest: *sacu/cuacu,* "to cry" or "sound-out." Here the meanings appear to support the "noisy" first sunrise, but a more explicit connection is found in Figure 5, where 7 Flower sits before the culture hero/shaman/singer, holds two mushrooms, and cries.[21] Note also that 1 Death is one of the eight participants in this ceremony, seen in the upper left of Figure 5.

Lord 1 Death's name caption also presents several potential translations. The Alvarado dictionary gives *yya caa ma'a,* treating both halves as independent words instead of combining number and name syllables into one word. This version reads "Lord who ascends (or escapes or flies up) from the earth's center." If we treat *caa* as one form of the verb *caa/saa,* "to take a sweatbath," then the expression reads "Lord who sweatbathes at the earth's center." The first version suggests a rising sun, the second version a setting sun. Use of the narrowly defined term *ma(')a* suggests associations with openings *into* the earth's interior (King 1988: 176–191); the day sign for "Death" is a skull, which in non-calendrical contexts is the opening through which one passes after death, a metaphor for the mouth of the earth that ultimately consumes us all (Monaghan 1990a). As a syllabic caption, 1 Death translates as the verb *cama/sama,* "to revolve around something," and *ca'ma,* "to resound."

In Figure 6 we see the first sunrise as depicted by two solar disks rising above a singing platform. In the lower disk and to the right are date captions; in the upper disk appears an unnamed male in a warrior-like position. In the Vienna codex, these warrior figures symbolically "start the clocks" (Furst 1978) of both the 260-day count (Vienna codex page 50b-c; King 1990: 146–149), and the 365-day count as seen here in Figure 6.[22] In this instance, the warrior is most likely to be Lord 1 Death, given the diagnostic "fuzzy" tassels behind his headdress (Furst 1978; Jansen 1988). In captions and in symbolism, Lord 1 Death "moves around" while Lord 7 Flower is "attached" to the East. Lord 7 Flower is more closely associated with music and song than is Lord 1 Death, and indeed if it is 1 Death in the upper solar disk, he is physically separated from the music emanating from the platform below him, and the pictorial caption in the lower disk, "1 Flower," states that he has emerged or escaped.

The meaning for the caption "1 *ca* Flower (*wa*)*co*" is quite clear; *cacu* means "to be born" or "safely to escape." If a two-word translation is selected, then the pictorial caption essentially equates with a caption name for Lord 7 Flower: the verb *caa/saa* means "ascends," or "to sob," juxtaposing the syllables for the numbers 1 (*ca*) and 7 (*sa*), with the day-name "Flower," *waco,* "macaw" (a very large, brightly colored, loud, long-tailed type of parrot; see Schoenhals 1988: 420). A different verb, *cã'ã,* "to give voice," gives a similar complement for "macaw." Thus the caption would read: "ascending macaw," "lamenting macaw," or "speaking macaw." Under ordinary circumstances, the specification (and qualities) of a macaw versus some other type of bird would seem unwarranted, but the repeated coincidence of loud sounds, colorfulness, and preciousness suggests otherwise.

The other pictorial caption to the right side of the scene is the date Year 13 Rabbit, Day 2 Deer, a "date" (Furst 1978; King 1988, 1990; Jansen 1988) found in many of the same contexts as song scrolls, including the tree-birth scene (once for each of the two instances of song depicted in this scene on page 38c; see Figure 7), and immediately preceding the beginning of the naming ritual on page 30a (Figure 8). The year "13 *si* Rabbit *sa*(*yu*)" reads *sisa,* "make a sound like that of a roaring fire," or the verb *sisa/cusa* "to become mature," "to be confirmed," "to call invitingly, to invite"; the day "2 *cua* Deer *cua*(*'a*)" reads: *cuaa cuaa,* "remove from the completely matured, ripened field," or "to separate and move about." Both halves of this caption emphasize the sonic and separating aspects of the first sunrise.

A text could be proposed or constructed for this scene (King 1990; Monaghan 1990b) based on the content of the associated captions together with the metaphors and connotations related to music scrolls, the sun, and birth. But the description in the story recorded by Dyk (1959: 3) saying that there was "great heat and much music" is an excellent text (if more terse) by itself for this scene. However, I would like to draw the reader's attention to one more line of evidence concerning the association of sunrise with song, this time taken from meanings and words related to modern marriage negotiation.

> . . . the boy's wedding party sets out early in the morning so as to arrive at the girl's *ve'i* [house] just after first light. The timing is important, and is referred to during the marriage negotiations, when the ambassador, or a member of the boy's family may say:
>
> The dawning word,
> The time of first light
> We come.
> This is not a dark word;
> Rather it is a clear word.
>
> Light and its source, the sun, are associated with truthfulness, integrity, honor, and good faith. Thus, when the speaker asserts that the boy's party is speaking "the dawning words," he is saying that they have come in all sincerity for the girl, and are making the request in the manner established by tradition. (Monaghan 1987: 201)

Modern Mixtecs use the same types of conceptual metaphors (Lakoff and Johnson 1980) that their ancestors did five hundred years ago, and the thematic metaphors of speech are reflected in the symbolism of the codices. The "Life is Heat" cultural metaphor intersects with a variety of other cultural schema, like eating and cooking, birth and death, good and evil, justice and injustice, illness and health, community exchange, sacrifice, and the culture hero 9 Wind (now Jesus) (Monaghan 1987; King 1988). In the sense of "colored scrolls" in the codices, heat is compared to song in the context of precious "new" life. The Vienna codex provides us with the prototype contexts for the occasion of song, and in the process tells us why the book itself relates to song. As the Nuyootecos might say, these books contain "dawning words," and carry the same sincerity, reliability, and honor as such words carry in Nuyoo today. The back-and-forth textual structure and the screenfold compression of the books strongly alludes to the depiction of song with scroll symbolism. The books also contain divinatory words (an illustrated context for colored scrolls), and they are filled with information of communal interest, suggesting that song and ritual speech spiritually support community welfare in much the same way that public symbols support communal identity. The mythic meanings (Friedrich 1986: 16–53) embedded in the actions, words, and symbols of modern Mixtec festivals embody the ideals and moral ethics of community existence (Monaghan 1987: 519–664). But more than that, festivals channel spiritual heat from the natural world into the community, metaphorically transforming the many interdependent households within a community into one large, harmonious household, for spiritual heat is not only transferred in sacrifice and community exchange, it is also produced, yielding a net increase in the amount of heat in the course of a transaction (Monaghan 1990a, 1990c).

Appreciating the nature of the Mixtec "heat" metaphor also helps unravel the symbolic structure of the codices. I have emphasized how smoke and music scrolls (*yaa*) share a common symbolic form, distinguished only by color and from where the scrolls issue. There is also an analogous relationship between feather symbols and fire symbols, as can be seen in Figure 3, where the flames (*yaa*) on the torch held by the dog-faced attendant are nearly identical in form to the feathers that adorn the back of his headdress. Again, the flames are naturally colored red and yellow, whereas these characteristic bundles of four feathers (one short scrolled feather and three long feathers) found on the headdresses of many individuals are multicolored (see Figures 2, 3, and 5), analogous to how colored music scrolls compare to grey-brown smoke scrolls. Given the broad range of contexts discussed earlier that relate birds with precious things and the sun, it is also possible to understand why feathers and fire have a similar scroll-like symbolic relationship. Nuyootecos believe birds are "the purest and most beautiful of animals" (Monaghan 1987: 449); this beauty and purity is metonymically related to bird feathers, which are thought to be an index of male sexuality and virility (i.e. the heat of *yɨɨ*).[23] Again, to extend the Nuyooteco metaphor, feathers symbolically represent birds as "dawning creatures." In similar ways, virtually every kind of scroll symbolism relates to the fundamental Mixtec metaphor, "Life is Heat" (King 1988: 191–276).

Summary

Beginning with the semantics for "book," "writing," and "song," I have attempted to unravel a few aspects of Mixtec writing and its pre-Hispanic cultural significance. By examining the grammatical and compositional qualities of Mixtec writing, I have attempted to illustrate how the codices give performance guides, directing the singer in ways suggestive of musical notation. Nouns and verbs are systematically woven onto the surface of the deerhide books, and the symbolic modifiers provide linguistic harmonies in both conceptual and phonological senses; this is to say that a symbolic modifier like a scroll carries visual and semantic associations connecting the domains of color, birds, song, heat, music, the sun, birth, and precious things, while at the same time emphasizing and highlighting the syllables "*-cu-*" and "*-tu-*." Ultimately reflecting on the polysemous nature of Mixtec lexical structure, we can see that the meanings associated with the word *tacu* ("book," "to write," "to hear," "to know," "to be alive," "to begin life") are all different aspects of the idea of "song." Far from being the esoteric archives of the priesthood, a manuscript like the Vienna codex represents a song-story that strengthened community identity and helped maintain "moral warmth" in the exchange relations between the ruler's household and the other households in the community who helped provide spiritual and material support for the ruler.

But while the stories are public, the skills of the singer and writer are not, and represent a divinatory tradition that most likely extends back to the dawn of Mixtec cultural identity in the words and prayers of the shaman. Modern Western attempts to read these texts, then, must be made accordingly, seeking the cultural metaphors mutually reflected in the symbolic vocabulary, in the Mixtec lexicon, and in the logic of modern sociocultural behavior. If we limit our inquiries to simple historical accounts, we miss the opportunity to see and hear the details of pre-Hispanic words and thoughts that have remained mute for five hundred years. Although colonial resources pertaining to Mixtec society and culture are meager when compared with the copious resources available for the Valley of Mexico or for the Maya region, the extant number of pre-Hispanic Mixtec books is without rival. With the special contextual structuring presented in the Vienna codex origin story, it is possible to analyze aspects of Mixtec society and religion with near-ethnographic detail, providing a framework for cultural logic that illuminates and complements the ambiguities and gaps found in the archaeological and ethnohistorical records.

Notes

Support for this research was provided through a fellowship from the American Council of Learned Societies, made possible, in part, by a grant from the National Endowment for the Humanities. I would like to thank Elizabeth Boone for her invitation to the "Records Without Words" roundtable at Dumbarton Oaks, and for helping me to appreciate the importance of some of the more obvious structures of Mixtec codices. Thanks also to the many participants who provided the weekend at Dumbarton Oaks with exceptionally stimulating discussion.

1 The *iya* vocabulary has apparently all but vanished in modern Mixtec speech, except for the pronoun now used for spiritual entities. The only exception I have encountered is a pair of expressions for "to be born" still used in Xayacatlán, Puebla (near Acatlán). Here, both the old *"iya"* and the non-elite verbs for birth are still used except that their referents have changed. The old elite term is now the common verb for human birth, while the old non-elite term is now exclusively used for non-human (animal) birth (K. Wistrand 1984, personal communication).

2 Support for this reconstructed continuum of meaningfulness versus intelligibility was recently found by John Monaghan (see Monaghan 1990b). After recording a "prayer to copal (incense)" as recited by a shaman from Santiago Ixtayutla, he asked a number of individuals from the town for a translation of some of the more difficult passages. The response many people gave, upon hearing the recording of the prayer, was that they recognized all the words, but that they did not quite understand their meaning.

3 Regarding the phonological transcription used in this paper: vowels with a tilde are nasal; in the sixteenth-century sources, this is denoted with a raised "n" in word-final position. These sources also appear to make a distinction between "t" and "tn" (and perpetuated by Arana and Swadesh 1965), when this is actually only "t" when paired with an oral versus nasal vowel. While nasal vowels are distinct phonemes, there is little support for this distinction being utilized by the Mixtec scribes. Indeed they make extensive metaphoric use of words that vary only in (1) vowel nasality, (2) tone contour, and (3) word-medial glottal stops (e.g. *ñuu* vs. *ñu'u, ini* vs. *i'ni*). The vowel "ɨ" represents a high, middle, unrounded value; a majority of the instances in the sixteenth-century sources indicate this vowel with the letter "e."

4 The spiritual heat of *yɨɨ* "is a property of the individual organism, as evinced in its vigor, heat, blood and *anima. Yɨɨ* is also a property of groups, as groups exchange and pool *yɨɨ* in *saa sa'a* [inter-household reciprocity], in marriage, in *tequio* [communal labor], and in *tinu* [*cargo* hierarchy of offices]. Finally, *yɨɨ* is what circulates between men and the gods, in the form of rain and crop fertility on the one hand, and sacrifice on the other" (Monaghan 1987: 519–520).

5 It is interesting to note that the meanings of "earth" and "fire" for *ñu'u* are two aspects of the same lexical form; the words do not differ by tone. The ideas of earth-spirituality and fire appear to have been conceptually linked for, perhaps,

twenty centuries or more, given the fact that fire and earth are variant meanings for a single form in the Cuicatec language, too. Cuicatec is most closely related to Mixtec of all the languages in the Otomanguean family.

6 Modern Arabic and Hebrew writing reflect an ancient regional tendency to ignore vowels, whether the system is syllabic or phonetic. In both modern cases a second layer of information has been developed in the form of diacritics used to annotate vowels over the standard script. Newspapers commonly do not use the diacritic markings.

7 By this I mean that maps don't tell stories very well. This is *not* to say that *lienzos* and other map-like documents can't tell a story (e.g., see Caso 1949, 1958; Burland 1955), but rather that these documents are limited by their contextual nature as bits of "land-history" composed for presentation in Spanish courts in land dispute cases. Vocabulary for these documents makes the distinction quite clear; if codices are strips of the earth's skin, *lienzos* are merely "cloths." There was no need to make extensive use of verbal artistry in these compositions.

8 I remind the reader here that "noun phrase," in a structural-linguistic sense, includes not only nouns but also whatever other words or dependent clauses are used to modify the meaning of the noun.

9 Certainly there is a long analytical tradition for focusing on the divinatory system's meanings, stretching from the great Eduard Seler (Nicholson 1972) at the turn of the century, to the present-day work of Jansen (1988). But unlike the Aztec case, where we have abundant ethnohistorical data regarding divination, or the Maya, for which there is a rich surviving tradition of divination (B. Tedlock 1982), there is, at present, virtually no Mixtec data on divinatory practice. This forces a reliance on models synthesized from other Mesoamerican sources. While this affords a better appreciation of how the codices reflect different types of meaning, it brings us no closer to understanding Mixtec divinatory meaning or practice.

10 The idea here is to begin with "1" + "day name 1," continuing through "13" + "day name 13," the next day being "1" + "day name 14," and so forth until a completed set of permutations is accomplished and the cycle begins again. This 260-day count operates simultaneously with a 365-day conventional calendar; every 52 years, the two calendars coincide, an event widely celebrated in Mesoamerica by a "new-fire ceremony" that functions ritually to reorder and maintain the universe.

11 The range of Mixtec lexical forms can be characterized as two syllables, each with an obligatory vowel and optional preceding consonant, that may or may not be separated by a glottal stop: (C)V(')(C)V. The values for the numbers and day names given here represent a comparative reconstruction in some cases. For example, we have both "*ca*" and "*co*" as glosses for "one"; similarly some of the day names or their short forms just happen to have been glossed less often, overall, than in other cases. The number variation may represent some aspect of divinatory and/or regional practice, but in all cases I have endeavored to

give what appear to be "standard" forms. For more detailed information, please consult King (1990, 1988: 124–417).

12 Jansen (1982) notes that the *Relación de Tilantongo* cites that the deities for the place are *"sayo"* and *"cuiyo,"* which reflects the syllabic values of their calendar names in the Vienna and Nuttall codices: 7 Serpent and 4 Serpent.

13 Again, I should hasten to point out that the writing system I use here has only five vowel signs to express more than three times that many vowel phonemes found in English. Mixtec vowels, in the poetic sound play of the codices, tend to blur the distinction between "u" and "o," "i" and "ɨ," and "a" and "e." These three pairs of vowels represent what Josserand calls "strong/weak pairs" (1983: 269–270), and reflect how vowels tend to shift dialectologically. Since there probably have always been a few coexisting dialectal variants of the Mixtec language, this feature of the writing system would have enhanced the regional intelligibility of books.

14 Ethnographically, mushroom ceremonies are still an important aspect of ritual life in many areas of Mexico and Guatemala (Wasson 1980; Munn 1972). The words spoken at a Mazatec mushroom ceremony are not the words of the healer, but the words of the spirit within the mushroom; to act as a medium for this spirit, the healer must be physically and spiritually "clean," a fact that has tended to inhibit individuals from touching or reading aloud from the Bible, the text of which is categorized analogously with mushrooms, i.e., as a source of sacred speech (Pike and Cowen 1959). The shamanistic context of mushrooms with "song scrolls" in the Vienna suggests a similar Mixtec perspective on the "speech of mushrooms." Note that the culture hero in this scene is accompanying himself on a skull "drum," played with a bone rasp.

15 There are, to date, a few brief Mixtec creation stories that appear to preserve preconquest details. The origin myth recorded by the vicar of Cuilapan in the seventeenth century is one of the very best prose sources we have for the Mixtec culture, but the text is written in Spanish. Ironically, a Mixtec prose text relating stories from the Bible also survives in the local archives of Tilantongo, authored by the Dominican friar Benito Hernandez (who was also a codex burner of legendary stature) in 1568.

16 This is a contextual approach to interpretation, used with excellent results by Furst (1978) in her commentary on the Vienna codex. The use of the technique here adds ethnographic and linguistic information to the symbolic analysis, more like that of Flannery and Marcus (1976) or Marcus and Flannery (1978).

17 These two trumpet-music instances are part of a sequence of seven analogously structured ritual scenes. Nadir and East are the second and third scenes in this sequence. The significance here is that music is offered *only* in these two greetings and nowhere else in this sequence, with one type of exception. Each of these scenes ends with an inventory of place glyphs; in a number of these ritual scenes music scrolls are attached to buildings or structures. In most instances these "singing" buildings are juxtaposed with a similar structure with the "fuzzy"

qualifier found on the headdress of the figure in the upper sun disk in Figure 6 (see also note 20).

18 I stress "potential" elite associations inasmuch as there has been no adequate test of any of these associations, save, perhaps, the connection between elite "speech," birth, and loud noises, which has been examined here in terms of different aspects of "song." Certainly the culture hero, Lord 9 Wind, has a number of obvious solar associations within his inventories of sixteen guises and sixteen costume symbols, and in the contextual analysis of music scrolls, 9 Wind figures prominently. Given that ancestral rulers sometimes reenact deeds of the culture hero, and play the roles of the culture hero (e.g., as singers, poets, and writers, to name only one type of role), then it might be safely assumed that elites are in *some* ways associated with solar concepts. But solar-elite metaphors do not appear to be political "root metaphors" (Turner 1974; Ohnuki-Tierney 1990; Fernandez 1991) as is often the case with chiefly and traditional state societies.

19 Lord 1 Death appears twice: once each in pulque and mushroom rituals; both rituals also are attended by 7 Flower, with the mushroom ceremony being offered in honor of 7 Flower.

20 The one diagnostic difference between the two are the "fuzzy" tassels attached to the back of 1 Death's headdress, seen in Figure 6 inside the upper solar disk. The diagnostic relationship is sufficiently strong that both Furst (1978) and Jansen (1988) believe the unnamed figure in the disk is actually 1 Death (note the near-identical headdress worn by 7 Flower in Figure 5 and by the person in the upper sun disk in Figure 6). Unfortunately we do not know what the "fuzzy" symbolism is supposed to represent (furriness? brilliance? heat? glowing?), but it also appears in regular association with "singing sweatbaths" and other types of structure in the Vienna codex (e.g., pages 31b, 15a; see extreme right side of Figure 8, which shows one pair of "glowing-and-singing" sweatbaths, immediately preceding the naming ritual; see also lower right side of left-hand page in Figure 1 for an analogous pair of ballcourts), so perhaps the relation should read: 1 Death : fuzzy :: 7 Flower : music scrolls (see note 17). Regarding the scene in the Nuttall codex, the other "direction representatives" include: Lord 2 Dog (North), Lady 9 Grass (South), and Lord 9 Wind (Center). Of the five, only Lord 1 Death lacks a direct corroborating directional association in the Vienna codex.

21 The poetic or mnemonic properties of captions is summarized elsewhere (King 1990), but an important feature is the play with stem-changing verbs, seen here in these examples. Often, verbs with two forms (potentiative and completive aspects) "play off" other verbs that also share either of the two stem forms. For example, the verb *saco/coco*, "to paint in colors/write," shares one stem with the verb *cōcō/sīsī*, "to catch fire," an appropriate meaning for a solar spirit, as well as for the "song is like copal smoke" metaphor.

22 This type of stylized warrior pose is found two other times in the Vienna codex: as a guise of the culture hero, and preceding the spiritual insemination of the white tree that later gives birth (page 50c–49a). In this latter instance, the

"throwing weapons" pose of the warriors is metaphorically connected to both the use of a digging stick used to poke holes in the ground to plant seeds and to the use of male genitalia in sexual union; in this tree context, the warriors are explicitly associated with a planting/throwing caption (King 1990). Here, in the scene of the first sunrise (Figure 6), the warrior is associated with an equally explicit "separation" caption. The first scene marks the literal conception of social (household) existence, while this scene marks the inception of interhousehold social interactions.

23 This is arguably why Lord 7 Flower (associated with birds) and Lord 4 Motion (an intensely masculine character associated with intoxicants, warfare, gambling, and playing on the ballcourt) are the only two spirits who are greeted with music in the second part of the Vienna codex story (Lord 4 Motion's ritual scene is seen in Figure 1). Note also that Wasson (1980: 32) records that in the modern town of Juxtlahuaca, sacred mushrooms used to be gathered only before sunrise ("dawning plants"), and this is exactly where the mushroom ceremony is placed in the Vienna codex story: immediately prior to the first sunrise and given in honor of Lord 7 Flower. Lords 1 Death and 4 Motion also attend this ceremony; Lord 1 Death is seen in the upper left of Figure 5, with 4 Motion seated behind him (not visible in Figure 5).

References

Alvarado, Fray Francisco de. 1964 [1593]. *Vocabulario en Lengua Mixteca.* Ed. Wigberto Jiménez Moreno. México: Instituto Nacional Indigenista and Instituto Nacional de Antropología e Historia.

Arana, Evangelina. 1961. El idioma de los señores de Teposcolula. *Anales del Instituto Nacional de Antropología e Historia* 13: 217–230.

Arana, Evangelina, and Mauricio Swadesh. 1965. *Los Elementos del Mixteco Antiguo.* México: Instituto Nacional de Antropología e Historia.

Barlow, Robert H. and Byron McAfee. 1949. *Diccionario de elementos fonéticos en escritura jeroglífica.* Instituto de Historia, Primera Serie, no. 9. México: Universidad Nacional Autónoma de Mexico.

Benson, Elizabeth P., ed. 1973. *Mesoamerican Writing Systems: A Conference at Dumbarton Oaks, October 30th and 31st, 1971.* Washington, D.C.: Dumbarton Oaks.

Burkhart, Louise M. 1989. *The Slippery Earth: Nahua-Christian Moral Dialogue in Sixteenth-Century Mexico.* Tucson: University of Arizona Press.

Burland, Cottie A. 1955. *The Selden Roll.* Monumenta Americana, vol. 2. Berlin: Verlag Gebr. Mann.

Caso, Alfonso. 1949. El mapa de Teozacoalco. *Cuadernos Americanos* 47: 145–181.

———. 1958. Lienzo de Yolotepec. *Memoria de al Colegio Nacional* 3, no. 4: 41–55.

———. 1959. El dios 1 Muerte. *Mitteilungen aus dem Museum für Volkerkunde in Hamburg* 25: 40–43.

———. 1977. *Reyes y Reinos de la Mixteca.* 2 vols. México: Fondo de Cultura Económica.

Cline, Howard F., ed. 1972–1975. *Guide to Ethnohistorical Sources.* Vols. 12–15 of *Handbook of Middle American Indians,* gen. ed. Robert Wauchope. Austin: University of Texas Press.

Codex Nuttall. 1975. *The Codex Nuttall: A Picture Manuscript from Ancient Mexico.* Ed. Zelia Nuttall, with new introductory text by Arthur G. Miller. New York: Dover Publications, Inc.

Codex Vienna. 1974. *Codex Vindobonensis Mexicanus I.* Graz: Akademische Druck- u. Verlagsanstalt.

Douglas, Mary. 1966. *Purity and Danger: An Analysis of the Concepts of Pollution and Taboo.* London: Ark Paperbacks.

Dyk, Anne. 1959. *Mixteco Texts.* Summer Institute of Linguistics Publications in Linguistics and Related Fields, No. 3. Norman, Oklahoma: Summer Institute of Linguistics Press.

Fernandez, James W., ed. 1991. *Beyond Metaphor: The Theory of Tropes in Anthropology.* Stanford, California: Stanford University Press.

Flannery, Kent V., and Joyce Marcus. 1976. Formative Oaxaca and the Zapotec Cosmos. *American Scientist* 64: 374–383.

Flannery, Kent V., and Joyce Marcus, eds. 1983. *The Cloud People: Divergent Evolution of the Zapotec and Mixtec Civilizations.* New York: Academic Press.

Ford, Richard I., ed. 1978. *The Nature and Status of Ethnobotany.* Anthropological Papers of the University of Michigan Museum of Anthropology, No. 67.

Friedrich, Paul. 1986. *The Language Parallax: Linguistic Relativism and Poetic Indeterminacy.* Austin: University of Texas Press.

Furst, Jill. 1978. *Codex Vindobonensis Mexicanus I: A Commentary.* Institute for Mesoamerican Studies, State University of New York, Publication No. 4. Albany, New York.

Glass, John B. 1975. A Survey of Native Middle American Pictorial Manuscripts. In Cline 1972–1975: 14, 3–80.

Gossen, Gary H. 1974. *Chamulas in the World of the Sun: Time and Space in a Maya Oral Tradition.* Cambridge, Massachusetts: Harvard University Press.

Harner, Michael J., ed. 1972. *Hallucinogens and Shamanism.* New York: Oxford University Press.

Jansen, Maarten. 1982. *Huisi Tacu.* Amsterdam: Centrum voor Studie en Documentatie vav Latijns Amerika.

———. 1985. Las lenguas divinas del México precolonial. *Boletín de Estudios Latinamericanos y del Caribe* 36: 69–81.

———. 1988. Dates, Deities and Dynasties: Non-durational Time in Mixtec Historiography. In Jansen, van der Loo, and Manning 1988: 156–192.

———. 1990. The Search for History in Mixtec Codices. *Ancient Mesoamerica* 1: 99–112.

Jansen, Maarten, Peter van der Loo, and Roswitha Manning, eds. 1988. *Continuity and Identity in Native America: Essays in Honor of Benedikt Hartmann.* Leiden: E. J. Brill.

Josserand, J. Kathryn. 1983. Mixtec Dialect History. Unpublished doctoral diss., Department of Anthropology, Tulane University.

King, Mark. 1982. Historical Metaphor and the Communication of Legitimacy in the Mixteca 500 B.C. - A.D. 1500. Unpublished Master's Thesis, Department of Anthropology, Vanderbilt University.

———. 1988. Mixtec Political Ideology: Historical Metaphors and the Poetics of Political Symbolism. Unpublished doctoral diss., Department of Anthropology, University of Michigan.

———. 1990. Poetics and Metaphor in Mixtec Writing. *Ancient Mesoamerica* 1: 141–151.

Lakoff, George, and Mark Johnson. 1980. *Metaphors We Live By.* Chicago: University of Chicago Press.

Leach, Edmund R. 1962. Genesis as Myth. *Discovery,* May 1962.

León-Portilla, Miguel. 1969. *Pre-Columbian Literatures of Mexico.* Norman: University of Oklahoma Press.

———. 1992. Have we really translated the Mesoamerican "Ancient Word"? In Swann 1992: 313–338.

Marcus, Joyce. 1976. The Origins of Mesoamerican Writing. *Annual Review of Anthropology* 5: 35–67.

———. 1983. The first appearance of Zapotec Writing and Calendrics. In Flannery and Marcus 1983: 91–96.

Marcus, Joyce, and Kent V. Flannery. 1978. Ethnoscience of the Sixteenth-century Valley Zapotec. In Ford 1978: 51–79.

Monaghan, John. 1987. "We are People who eat Tortillas:" Household and Community in the Mixteca. Unpublished doctoral diss., Department of Anthropology, University of Pennsylvania, Philadelphia.

———. 1990a. Sacrifice, Death, and the Origins of Agriculture in the Codex Vienna. *American Antiquity* 55: 559–569.

———. 1990b. Performance and the Structure of the Mixtec Codices. *Ancient Mesoamerica* 1: 133–140.

———. 1990c. Reciprocity, Redistribution, and the Transaction of Value in the Mesoamerican Fiesta. *American Ethnologist* 17: 758–774.

Munn, Henry. 1972. The Mushrooms of Language. In Harner 1972: 86–122.

Nicholson, Henry B., 1972. Eduard Georg Seler, 1849–1922. In Cline 1972, 13: 348–369.

Ohnuki-Tierney, Emiko, ed. 1990. *Culture Through Time: Anthropological Approaches.* Stanford: Stanford University Press.

Pike, Eunice V., and Florence Cowen. 1959. Mushroom Ritual versus Christianity. *Practical Anthropology* 6: 145–150.

Pohl, John M. D., and Bruce E. Byland. 1990. Mixtec Landscape Perception and Archaeological Settlement Patterns. *Ancient Mesoamerica* 1: 113–132.

Rappaport, Roy. 1979. *Ecology, Meaning, and Ritual.* Richmond, California: North Atlantic Books.

Ravicz, Robert and A. Kimball Romney. 1969. The Mixtec. In Vogt 1969: 367–399.

Reyes, Fray Antonio de los. 1976 [1593]. *Arte en Lengua Mixteca.* Vanderbilt University Publications in Anthropology No. 14. Nashville: Vanderbilt University Press.

Roys, Ralph L. 1933. *The Book of Chilam Balam of Chumayel.* Washington, D.C.: Carnegie Institution of Washington.

———. 1946. The Book of Chilam Balam of Ixil. *Notes on Middle American Archaeology and Ethnology* 3: 90–103.

Schoenhals, Louise C. 1988. *A Spanish-English Glossary of Mexican Flora and Fauna.* México, D.F.: Summer Institute of Linguistics.

Sherzer, Joel, and Anthony C. Woodbury, eds. 1987. *Native American Discourse: Poetics and Rhetoric.* Cambridge: Cambridge University Press.

Smith, Mary Elizabeth. 1973a. *Picture Writing from Ancient Southern Mexico.* Norman: University of Oklahoma Press.

———. 1973b. The Relationship between Mixtec Manuscript Painting and the Mixtec Language: A Study of Some Personal Names in the Codices Muro and Sanchéz Solís. In Benson 1973: 47–98.

Smith, Mary Elizabeth, and Ross Parmenter. 1991. *The Codex Tulane.* Middle American Research Institute Publication #61. New Orleans: Tulane University.

Swann, Brian, ed. 1992. *On the Translation of Native American Texts.* Washington, D.C.: Smithsonian Institution Press.

Tedlock, Barbara. 1982. *Time and the Highland Maya.* Albuquerque: University of New Mexico Press.

Tedlock, Dennis, trans. 1985. *Popol Vuh: The Mayan Book of the Dawn of Life.* New York: Simon and Schuster, Inc.

———. 1987. Hearing a voice in an ancient text: Quiché Maya poetics in performance. In Sherzer and Woodbury 1987: 140–175.

Turner, Victor. 1974. *Dramas, Fields, and Metaphors.* Ithaca, New York: Cornell University Press.

Vogt, Evon Z., ed. 1969. *Ethnology.* Vols. 7–8 of *Handbook of Middle American Indians,* gen. ed. Robert Wauchope. Austin: University of Texas Press.

Wasson, R. Gordon. 1980. *The Wondrous Mushroom: Mycolatry in Mesoamerica.* New York: McGraw-Hill Book Company.

Whitecotton, Joseph W. 1990. *Zapotec Elite Ethnohistory: Pictorial Genealogies from Eastern Oaxaca.* Vanderbilt University Publications in Anthropology No. 39. Nashville: Vanderbilt University Press.

John M. D. Pohl

Mexican Codices, Maps, and Lienzos as Social Contracts

Introduction

The Mixtec codices are Pre-Columbian-style folded books constructed from strips of animal hide and painted in a dazzling array of color with caricatures of people, places, and things. We know from colonial references that these remarkable art works contained historical and genealogical documentation that was of critical importance to political decision making by the Mixtec and Zapotec kings who ruled Oaxaca between A.D. 1000 and 1521 (Burgoa 1934a: 210; 1934b, 1: 319, 352). The paintings thereby represent the longest continuous dynastic records known for ancient Mesoamerica and as such enable us to scrutinize, in unparalleled detail, a truly indigenous form of Indian history.

The art style in which the codices are painted has been called "Mixteca-Puebla." The term refers to two adjacent culture areas of central and southern Mexico in which the genre is thought to have reached its most intensive manifestation, probably sometime after A.D. 1200 (Nicholson 1960; Nicholson and Quinones Keber in press; Pohl and Byland in press). Some scholars prefer the term "International Style" because of its employment by at least fifteen different cultures from the Maya of highland Guatemala and Yucatan to the Nahuatl- and Otomi-speaking civilizations of the Valley of Mexico (Robertson 1970). Nevertheless, there are very specific language-based applications, particularly with regard to the use of pictographic place signs (Smith 1973). More important to this discussion however are variant usages that reflect differing forms of social organization.

A comparison of the place signs in the Aztec Codex Mendoza with the Mixtec Codex Zouche-Nuttall, for example, reveals very different perceptions of geographical space (Pohl and Byland 1990). Pages 19 through 21 of Codex Zouche-Nuttall portray historical actions that occur at several different place signs. These include references to Hill of Flints, Hill of the Wasp, and Hill of the Sun, to name a few. All of these place signs appear with symbols representing habitations such as palaces or temples. Comparable depictions of some of these same signs appear in Codex Mendoza, a tribute record that lists the names of communities conquered by the Aztec Empire.

Archaeological reconnaissance in the Mixteca now allows us to identify the place signs in Codex Zouche-Nuttall as individual elite citadels or great houses in which a single royal family resided. They lie no farther apart than a few kilometers (Pohl and Byland 1990; Byland and Pohl in press). In contrast, the place signs in the Codex Mendoza represent entire city states and urban centers, some inhabited by many thousands of people (Barlow 1949). While both codices use virtually the same symbol system, the different treatment of space and settlement size is a direct measure of the concerns of the societies employing the pictographic system. Clearly the Mixtec need to document the history of alliances and wars among a localized, segmentary elite differed enormously from the Aztec need to document the collection of tribute from entire populations of conquered people.

The point that I will emphasize in this article is that we should look not simply to iconography or style in our attempts to assign cultural affiliation to codices, but also to variant usages of information that might reflect different social programs as well. I will argue that the political agendas of the different confederations of Post-Classic kingdoms that rose to dominate Oaxaca, Tlaxcala, and Puebla called for different documentary strategies to record territory and history. These strategies are evident in their codices, maps, and lienzos.

The Mixtec Codices

A number of colonial accounts refer to the Aztec use of "pinturas"—either codices or lienzos. The statements of Friar Toribio Motolonía (1903, 1950), who traveled extensively throughout Tlaxcala and Puebla, are most often cited. He describes five types of books. The first concerned the account of the years and seasons, the second prescribed the feasts, the third was for interpreting omens and dreams, the fourth concerned baptism, and the fifth dealt with the ceremonies and omens for marriage.

To Motolonía only the first type of book told the "truth" because it provided a chronological ordering of past events that resembled a Western-style history. These focused on the stories of wars and conquests, the succession of great lords, and significant weather or astronomical events and plagues. Francisco de Burgoa discusses the use of painted books by Oaxacan peoples. In virtually all cases these are references to the historical paintings that we know as the Mixtec codices:

> They had many books made from paper or fabric from the special bark of trees that are found in the hotlands. They tanned and prepared them like bundled parchment, all about the same width. Others were cut and glued together in one piece as long as was needed. . . . The historians inscribed them with characters so abbreviated that a single page expressed the place, the site, province, year, month, and day with all the names of the gods, ceremonies,

> and sacrifices or victories that they celebrated. . . . They were kept by the sons of the lords having been instructed by the priests since infancy on how to form the characters and memorize the histories. (Burgoa 1934a: 210)

A subtle difference in historical format may be detected both through empirical observation and by comparing Motolonía's and Burgoa's comments. Motolonía speaks of the histories as being primarily a year count. His description matches the *xiuhtlacuilolli* or "year paintings" that appear in Codices Telleriano-Remensis, Rios, and Mendoza, in which the year is often portrayed within a turquoise-blue cartouche with the event being pictured below (Nicholson 1971). The term *xiuh* is in fact a contraction of the Nahuatl word *xihuitl,* meaning both year and turquoise (Molina 1977: 159b).

Burgoa, on the other hand, speaks of histories of *"linajes"* or royal genealogies. As the Mixtec codices these histories are somewhat different in format. The year count is secondary to the listing of marriage couples, and for the most part they lack any overt references to diseases or significant astronomical events in favor of focusing on royal lines of descent, some extending over more than twenty generations.

Codices, lienzos, and maps surviving from the colonial period express differences in social application as well. Although some Mixtec cacicazgos produced maps that in many ways represent European-style conventions, they still preserve an indigenous view of landscape perception (Smith 1973: 162–171; Pohl and Byland 1990). Most of these maps are abstractions with the landscape features presented as codex-style place signs arranged around either a circle or a rectangle.

The Mapa de Teozacoalco is a remarkable example (Figure 1). It was prepared by the town of Teozacoalco for submission with its Relación Geográfica, the answers to a questionnaire issued by Phillip II in 1577 (Caso 1949). The cartographic portion of the painting is composed of a radial map surrounded by forty-four outlying communities. The interior of the circle is crisscrossed with roads and rivers that lead to the community borders. Adjacent to the church near the center of this composition is a royal genealogy stemming from a fourteenth-century lord named 2 Dog "Flint Band."

The Teozacoalco genealogy is then followed back in time to two ancestral lines portrayed at the side of the map. The genealogy on the left represents over twenty generations of the royal house of Tilantongo from roughly A.D. 1050 through 1521. The genealogy on the right represents eight generations of the royal house of Teozacoalco before the usurpa-

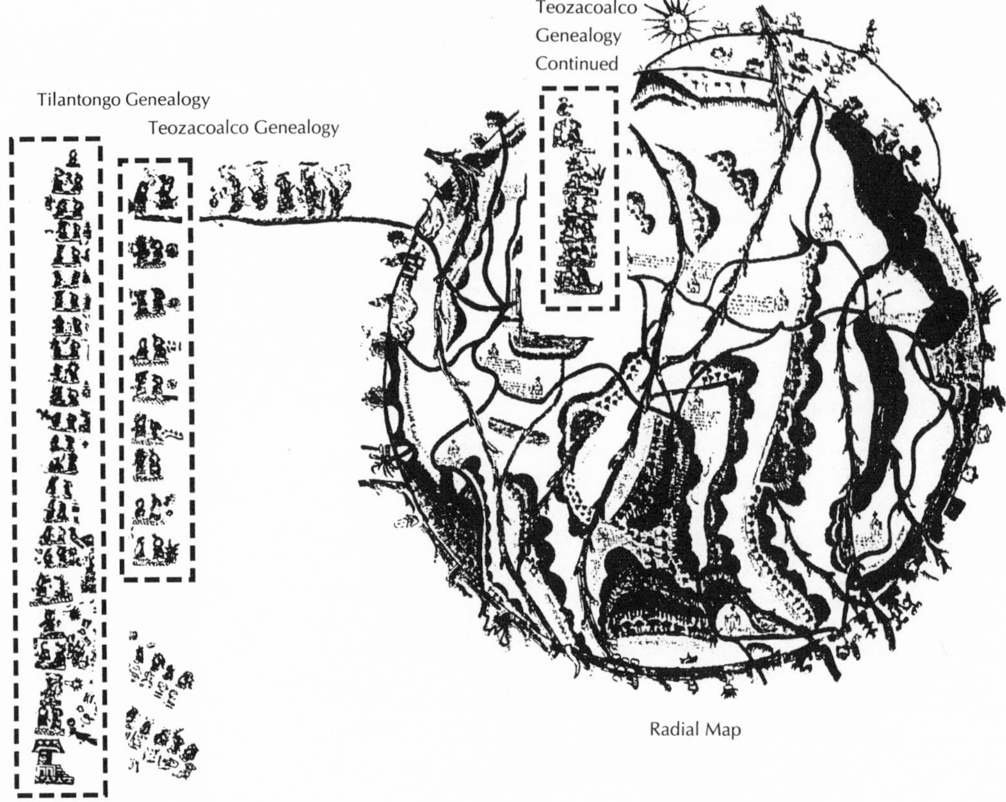

Figure 1. The Mapa de Teozacoalco

tion of Lord 2 Dog, who established the new dynasty portrayed at the center of the map.

The inclusion of the Tilantongo dynasty is meant to enhance Teozacoalco's display of prestige. According to Burgoa (1934b, 1: 276, 369–370), Tilantongo was the residence of the highest ranked royal family in the Mixteca. It was through marriage to this royal house that other kingdoms then evaluated their own positions of seniority among each other. According to the genealogy, Teozacoalco could boast a royal ancestry back to the great Lord 8 Deer himself.

The portrayal of a higher-born family to validate the rank of lesser kingdoms is also found in the Zapotec Lienzo de Guevea (Seler 1960; Jansen 1982a; Paddock 1983; Marcus 1983) (Figure 2). At the top of the lienzo appears a rectangular map of the boundaries of the town of Santiago Guevea located near Tehuantepec. Below the map are two dynasties. The one on the left is that of Guevea, while the one on the right is the royal line of Zaachila, the highest-ranked kingdom of the Zapotecs of the Valley of Oaxaca.

The Mapa de Teozacoalco and the Lienzo de Guevea are documents from the postconquest period, but the Pre-Columbian codices shared this same concern for interweaving a local dynasty's history with the highest royal house. Although Zouche-Nuttall includes not only the principle lines of descent from Tilantongo to Zaachila, an unidentified kingdom called Hill of the Tail/Hill of the Face appears at critical junctures in the epic narrative as if the composers of the manuscript were saying ". . . and we were there."[1] The royal lines of both Tilantongo and Zaachila were in fact the major focus of religious veneration for Mixtec and Zapotec confederations (Burgoa 1934b, 1: 338, 372).

Burgoa reports how the codices were displayed:

> I have heard some elders explain that they fastened these books of cosmography along the length of the rooms of the lords for their own aggrandizement, valuing them and referring to them in their assemblies, in the same way that many Catholics have done with the lives of the saints, adorning their walls with lienzos and figures though more out of interest in the painting than out of their religious devotion. (Burgoa 1934a: 210)

This statement on the presentation of the codices is significant with regard to the Mixtec term for a singer, *tutuyondaayaa,* as "he who holds the song-book" (King 1982). The codex hung upon a wall from which a court poet recited an epic legend can be compared to a storyboard presentation used in film animation or advertising in which artists, actors, and musicians act out a story before hundreds of sequential drawings as a means of evaluating narrative strengths and weaknesses in planning a production. In similar fashion, Burgoa (1934b, 1: 396) speaks of the histories as being dramatized on the days of the major religious festivals. Ten of these were celebrated annually in Tilantongo (Acuña 1984, 2: 232) and we know that such celebrations were usually dedicated to the pantheon of deities and royal ancestors that appear in the Mixtec codices (Jansen 1982b: 283–285).

The genealogical accounts on maps and lienzos appear to be a part of the validation of ownership of the kingdom. They are the pictorial manifestation of a statement found in many Relaciones Geográficas in which a cacique administers the land by "linea recta" or direct line (Acuña 1984, 2: 238, 244; Smith and Parmenter 1991: 20). Direct lines for the royal houses of Jaltepec and Tilantongo appear on Codex Selden and on

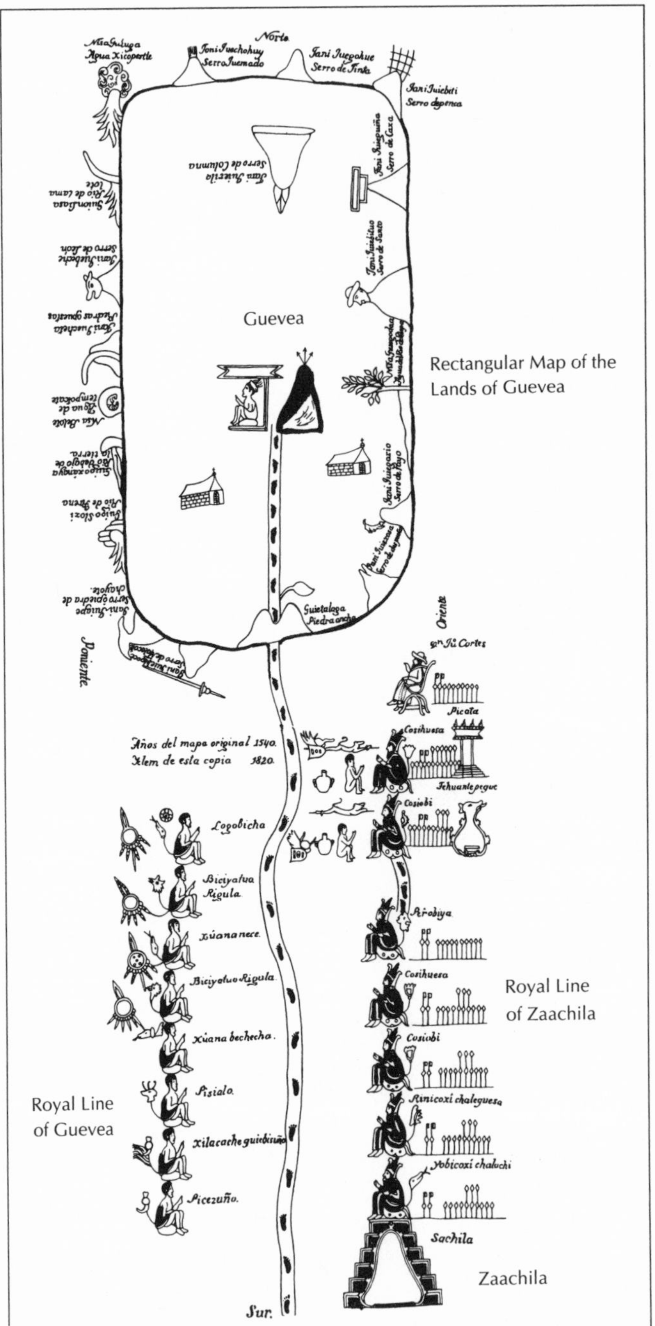

Figure 2. The Lienzo de Guevea

Codex Bodley 1–19, while other narratives may shift geographical location after a prominent marriage with a new royal house. Codex Bodley 40–21 follows a sequence of marriage couples that begins with the emergence of the first ancestors from the rivers at Apoala. The genealogy then moves through different locations that include Red and White Bundle, Jaltepec, Place of Flints, Achiutla, Tlaxiaco, and Cuilapan.

Codex Zouche-Nuttall 22–33 illustrates a line of descent from the royal house of Tilantongo through 8 Deer's son at Teozacoalco and culminates with a marriage between the Teozacoalco princess, Lady 4 Rabbit, and the lord of Zaachila, 5 Flower. The movement through geographical space indicates that the codex could not have validated any single lord's claim to a kingdom, but rather outlines the historical sequence of alliance building that eventually unified the two most powerful Mixtec and Zapotec royal houses in Oaxaca (Figure 3). Elsewhere I have called these social structures "alliance corridors" (Pohl in press; Byland and Pohl in press). They represent a fundamental perception of nationhood beyond the city-state or "great house" level of elite organization.

In summary, although there is considerable variation in the portrayal of landscape and dynasty in the corpus of Oaxacan lienzos, maps, and codices, these documents reflect principles of social organization that were uniquely Mixtec: rule by a plurality of kings who used primogeniture, ancestor worship, and descent reckoning, not only to vindicate rulership but also to determine social rank and alliance organization. The painted books therefore represented the essential records to support this system.

Maps of the Tolteca-Chichimeca

Before the rise of the Aztec empire, Central Mexico, Tlaxcala, and Puebla were dominated by networks of factionalized city-states and kingdoms. These nations had formulated multiple alliance corridors in ways comparable to the Mixtec and Zapotec. The Tlaxcalan chronicler, Muñoz Camargo (1892) stated that before the rise of the Empire of the Triple Alliance, Tlaxcala had been confederated with Huexotzinco, Cholula, Cuauhtinchan, Tepeyacac, Tecamachalco, Tehuacan, Coxcatlan, Teotitlan del Camino, and the Chochos, whose capital was Coixtlahuaca. The communities claimed a common heritage through an origin myth in which the first Chichimeca tribal bands emerged from the seven caves of Chicomoztoc.

According to the Anales de Cuauhtitlan (Velazquez 1945: 3), the Chichimeca were led by four hundred Mimixcoa, warriors originally created

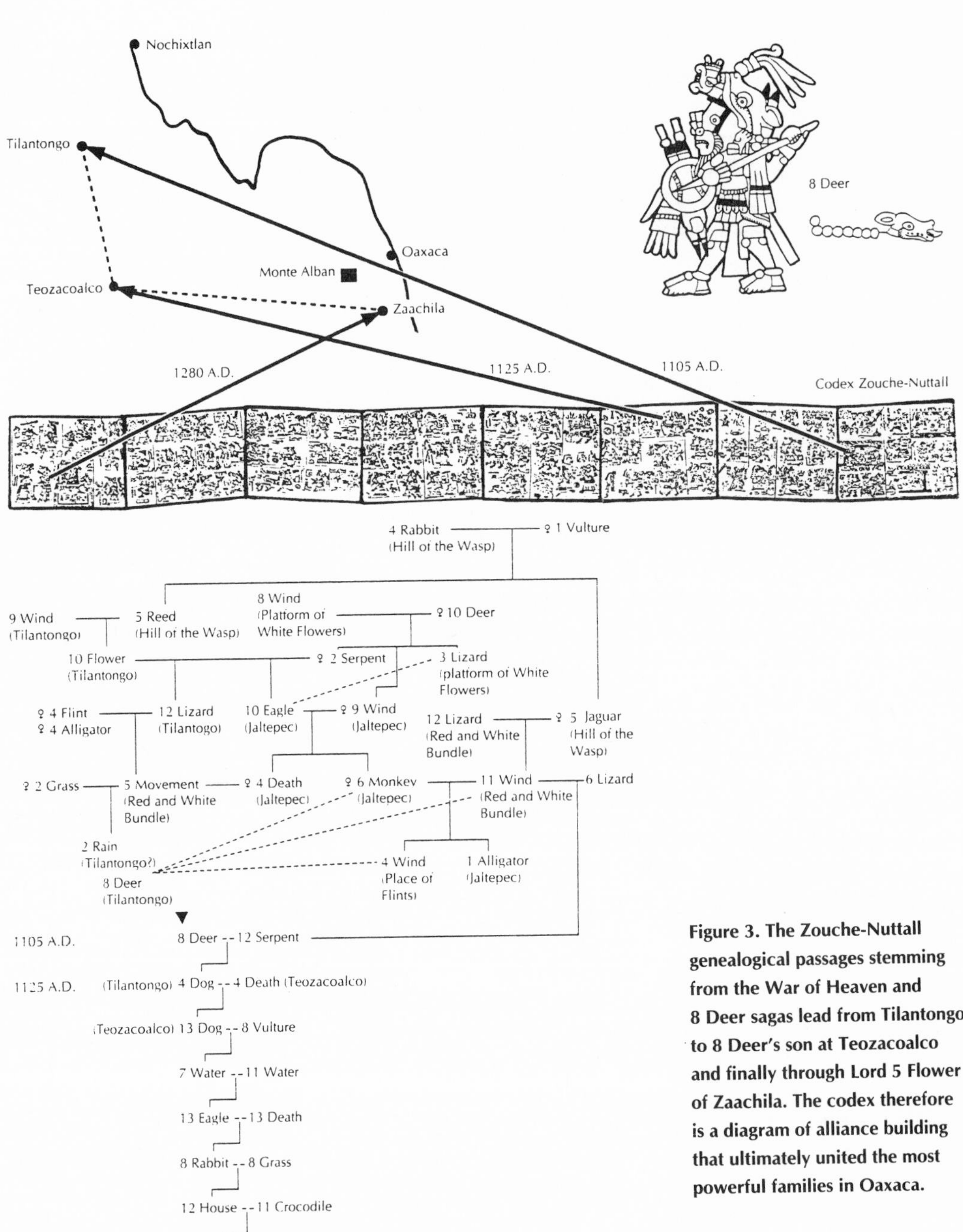

Figure 3. The Zouche-Nuttall genealogical passages stemming from the War of Heaven and 8 Deer sagas lead from Tilantongo to 8 Deer's son at Teozacoalco and finally through Lord 5 Flower of Zaachila. The codex therefore is a diagram of alliance building that ultimately united the most powerful families in Oaxaca.

to provide sustenance for the sun. In the course of their odyssey, they were set upon by a demon called Itzpapalotl, the Obsidian Butterfly, who devoured them. One Chichimec leader named Mixcoatl (also called Camaxtli) escaped and later shot her with arrows. He then freed his brothers and together they killed Itzpapalotl and burned her body. They rubbed the ashes around their eyes as a tribute to their conquest. The Mixtec consequently called them the *Sami Nuu* or "men with burnt faces" (see Smith 1973: 209 on translation).

After a number of harrowing adventures, the Chichimecs entered the Valley of Mexico and became embroiled in local disputes between Toltec city-states. Subsequently Camaxtli-Mixcoatl established a Tolteca-Chichimeca capital at Culhuacan, and later his son, Quetzalcoatl, founded the great ceremonial center of Tula, Hidalgo (Jiménez Moreno 1954–1955). Tula subsequently fell victim to internal strife and was abandoned (Kirchhoff 1955; Davies 1977). The Tolteca-Chichimeca then left Tula to found kingdoms of their own. One group was led by a "son" of Camaxtli-Mixcoatl named Mixtecatl. Mixtecatl's followers eventually settled in Acatlan in the Mixteca Baja (Torquemada 1986, 1: 32; Acuña 1985, vol. 2; Smith and Parmenter 1991). The Nahuatl eponym "Mixtecs" is derived from his name. Another dissident faction, called the Nonoalca, were led south through Cholula, and then on to the Tehuacan Valley by their leader Xelhua (Acuña 1985, vol. 2).

At Cholula, the Tolteca-Chichmeca lords instituted the ceremony by which they and their descendants would be transformed into *tetecuhtin* or "lineage heads," the title that conferred upon them the right to rule their respective kingdoms. A candidate for the title applied through mediation between his parents and two powerful Cholula priests, called the Aquiach or sky lord and the Tlachiach or earth lord. According to Motolonía (1903: 286–292), an eligible prince accompanied by his parents, allies, and other *tetecuhtin* met with the high priests in the temple of Camaxtli-Mixcoatl. Following several days of prayer and penitence, the ears, nose, or lips of the initiate were pierced and an ornament was inserted according to the custom of the kingdom from which the petitioner came. Upon being declared a *tecuhtli,* the prince returned home escorted by agents of the Cholula priests to confirm his right to rule a *teccalli,* or noble estate, as the chief representative of his lineage.

The odyssey of Camaxtli-Mixcoatl's sons and followers in their efforts to establish their royal houses are detailed in the Historia Tolteca-Chichimeca (Kirchhoff et al. 1976). This exceptional work is a *xiuhtlacuilolli* or year count that includes paintings of key events as well as an extensive Nahuatl text. Many of the dated events represent the conquests of towns that the Tolteca-Chichimeca then reestablished under their own authority. Together with four maps called the Mapas de Cuauhtinchan, the Historia Tolteca-Chichimeca remains the definitive source on the origins of the Early Post-Classic Tolteca-Chichimeca confederations.

The Mapas de Cuauhtinchan, however, were composed in order to place the foundation of the kingdom of Cuauhtinchan into the broader context of the great Chichimec migration saga. They structurally resemble the Oaxacan lienzos in that they were painted upon broad sheets of indigenous paper (Bittmann Simons 1968; Reyes 1988). Consequently, the emphasis in the maps is not upon genealogy or even year counts but rather upon the routes that the various Tolteca-Chichimeca factions followed after the breakup of Tula from Tlaxcala to the Tehuacan Valley.

Map No. 1 portrays an assembly of over thirty-five lords at Cuauhtinchan. Four priestly officials appear, wearing not only the deerskin cloaks of the Chichimec but also the distinctive ashen-black face paint of Camaxtli-Mixcoatl. From Cuauhtinchan, footprints indicate the routes taken to communities in the Tehuacan Valley such as Coxcatlan (symbolized by a hill qualified by a shell jewelry collar).

Map No. 2 follows the Historia Tolteca-Chichimeca most closely, including the placement of dates along the migration routes. Not only are portions of southern Puebla included, but the kingdom of Coixtlahuaca in the Mixteca Alta is as well. Map No. 3 portrays a simpler version of the migration story. However, it places more emphasis on the foundation of Tepeticpac, Tlaxcala, by three lords, the first of whom is named Mazatl. This same lord also appears at the founding of his royal house on the Lienzo de Tepeticpac as well (Aguilera 1986). This Tlaxcalan lienzo and others like it (Nicholson 1971a: 51–52) provide us with yet an additional level of information on the status differences between the highest-ranking Tlaxcalan *tecuhtli* or *tlatoani* and the lesser-ranking *tetecuhtin.* Some of these relationships appear to be lineal while others are of an undetermined nature (Figure 4).

The Historia Tolteca-Chichimeca and the Mapas de Cuauhtinchan are also highly unusual portrayals of people, places, and things with regard to what we know of the reality of Early Post-Classic Mesoamerica. For example, the Historia Tolteca-Chichimeca depicts men dressed in deerskin cloaks with bows and arrows walking through the Valley of Mexico as though on a seasonal hunting trip in the desert, hardly an historical reality given the fact that the landscape over which they traveled was settled by thousands of people living in cities, surrounded by hundreds of square miles of cultivated land. The Mapas de Cuauhtinchan extend the metaphor by intermingling scenes of deer hunting with the conquest and defeat of the rulers of Central Mexican and Pueblan city-states. A Nahuatl-language term for a deer trap or snare was even related as the "road to Tollan" (Ruiz de Alarcón 1984: 3).

Consequently, there is a theatrical quality about the portrayal of the epic, as though the story, as painted in both the Historia Tolteca-Chichimeca and the Cuauhtinchan maps, is a charter for a historical reenactment as a hunting adventure. Michel Graulich (1974) has noted that the Camaxtli-Mixcoatl saga was reenacted during one of the eighteen monthly Aztec feasts called Quecholli. The performances not only included ritual deer hunts but also gladiatorial combats and human sacrifices in which the victim was dedicated to Camaxtli-Mixcoatl and carried to the altar for execution in the fashion of a deer (Durán 1971: 140–153; Sahagún 1951, bk. 2: 25–26). Elizabeth Boone (1991) has written on Chichimec migration sagas as ritual performance, demonstrating that there are qualities in the historical narratives that lend an air of carefully planned literary structure. Codex Rios states that the story of the fall of Tula and the construction of the great pyramid at Cholula by Xelhua were sung and performed during a festival called Tulanianhululaez.

The migration stories of the Tolteca-Chichimeca consequently reflect a more traditional system of cognitive mapping in which legends associated with particular geographical features were recounted by tribal chiefs in the course of seasonal hunting migrations. In the interest of emphasizing an "outsider's" divine right to rule, the Chichimec legends thereby became the legitimate means of conceptualizing a political landscape, even though the reality of the people employing the stories had little to do with the hunting strategies to which they were originally adapted. They were, however, ideally suited for lords who needed to emphasize both a common "barbarian" or Chichimec origin to confederations of factionalized city-states as well as the divine rights granted to their *teccalli* as Toltecs. As with the Mixtec genealogical-historical codices, these painted migration stories were the records that supported the political structure.

The Lienzos of the Coixtlahuaca Group

Coixtlahuaca was the capital of a confederation of powerful city-states that dominated the northern Mixteca Alta from the Tamazulapa Valley to the Tehucan Valley in Puebla. The region is known for its tremendous linguistic diversity, with populations speaking Mazatec, Cuicatec, Mixtec, Chocho, Popolocan, and Nahuatl. Although virtually unknown

Figure 4. Mapa de Cuauhtinchan No. 3 portrays the odyssey of the Tolteca-Chichimeca through Cholula to Huexotzinco, Tlaxcala, and other communities in Puebla. The maps therefore illustrate alliance corridors formed between Tolteca-Chichimeca city-states by invoking the foundation of each principal *teccalli* by a son or follower of the culture hero and patron deity, Camaxtli-Mixcoatl. The Lienzo de Tepeticpac provides a more detailed portrayal of the relationship between the highest-ranked *teccalli* of Tepeticpac founded by Mazatl and the lesser-ranking houses of vassal nobility.

Camaxtli-Mixcoatl

Lienzo de Tepeticpac

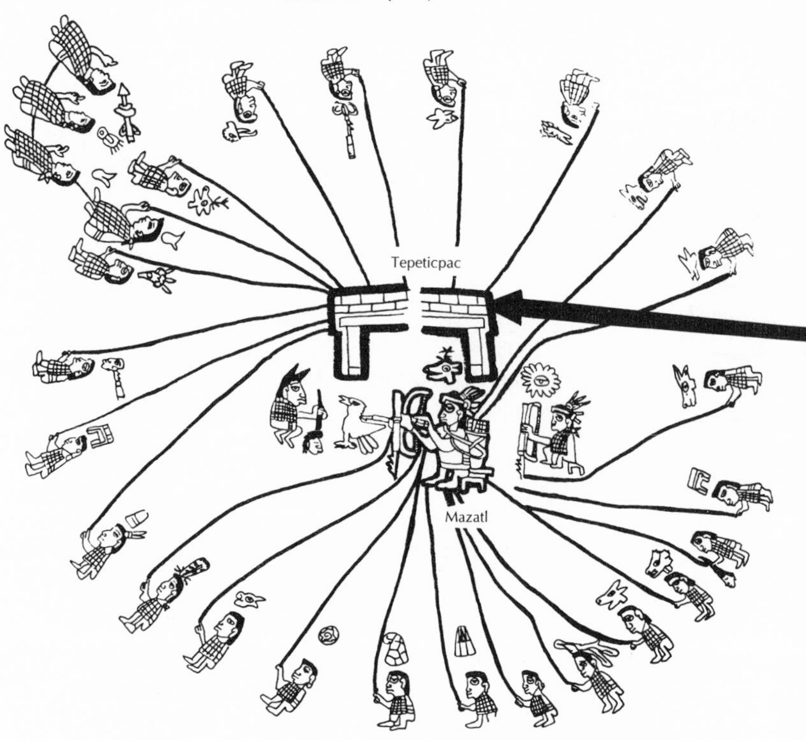

Mapa de Cuauhtinchan #3

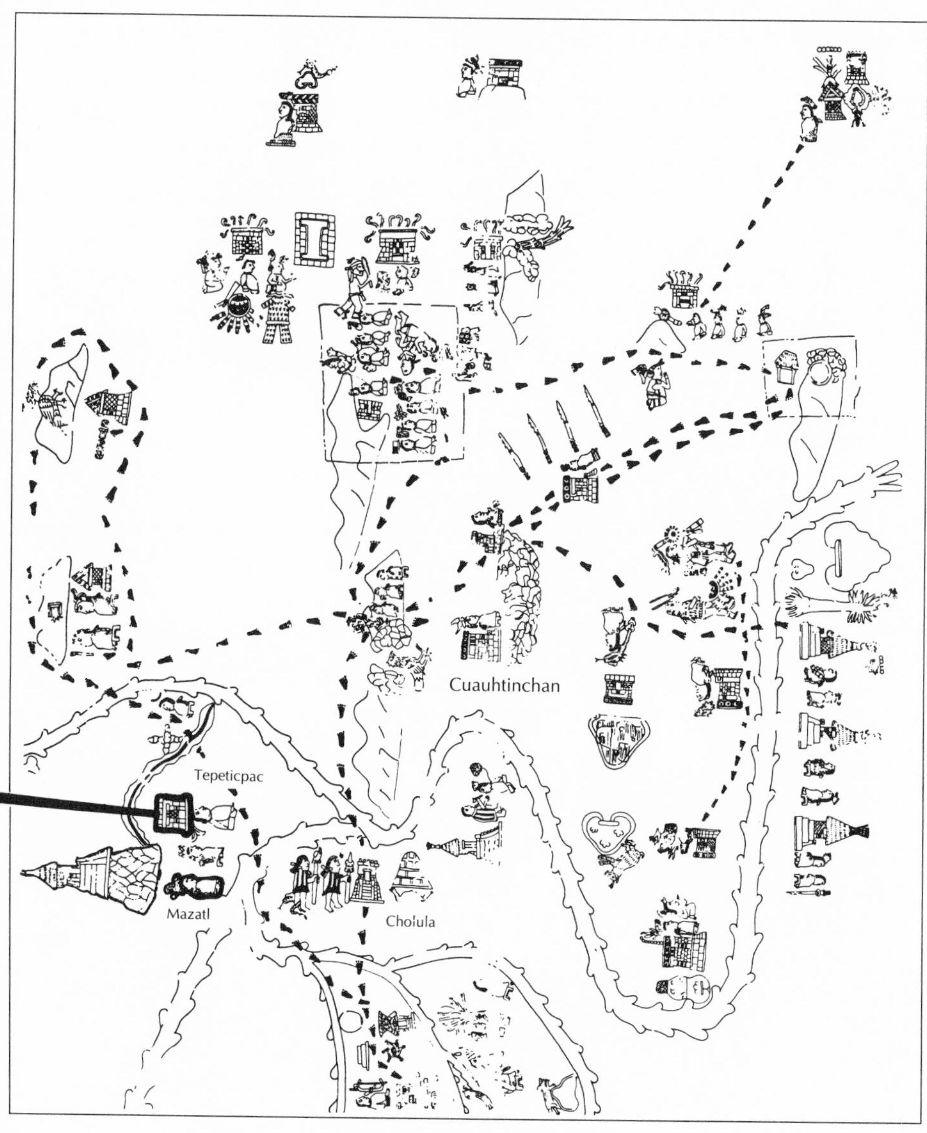

Figure 5. The place sign of Coixtlahuaca on Cuauhtinchan Map No. 2.

archaeologically (see Bernal 1948), an important corpus of over twelve colonial lienzos, maps, and "codices" has been attributed to the area (Caso 1961; Parmenter 1982; Smith 1973: 65–66, 182–184). These have much in common not only with the Cuauhtinchan maps but with the Mixtec and Zapotec manuscripts and maps as well.

Cuauhtinchan Map No. 2 depicts Coixtlahuaca as "Plain/Place of the Serpent" (Reyes 1977: 60) (Figure 5). The place sign is portrayed as a carpet of serpents upon which are seated two couples. One lord is named Atonal, the Tolteca-Chichimeca progenitor of the Coixtlahuaca royal line, according to the Anales de Cuauhtitlan (Velázquez 1945: 15). The couples also represent the founders of a dual system of rulership that is portrayed on several of the Coixtlahuaca lienzos.

Coixtlahuaca and a neighboring kingdom called Tulancingo also appear in the Mixtec codices. It is here that the Mixtec lord 8 Deer sought to elevate his status as usurper to the throne of Tilantongo by having himself transformed into a Tolteca-Chichimeca *tecuhtli* or lord, with the nose ornament ceremony administered by the priest 4 Jaguar, a deity impersonator of Camaxtli-Mixcoatl (Pohl in press; Smith 1973: 70–74) (Figure 6).

The Lienzo de Tlapiltepec (Figure 7) portrays the royal families that ruled Coixtlahuaca from the eleventh century through the time of the conquest (Caso 1961; Parmenter 1982), as well as a Cuauhtinchan map-like journey from Coixtlhauaca through Puebla. Beginning in the lower left-hand corner we see lines running out from the seven caves of Chicomoztoc, past two rivers, to a hill qualified by a net snare or *matlatl* (Caso 1961: A1–A6). The same place sign appears on Cuauhtinchan Map No. 2 near a Place of the Heron or Aztatlan. The lines consequently represent the emergence of the first ancestors from Chicomoztoc and their subsequent migration into an area lying adjacent to the Coixtlahuaca Valley. This much-abbreviated version of the Tolteca-Chichimeca migration story substantiates a passage in the Anales de Cuauhtinchan (Velázquez 1945: 52) in which the fifteenth-century Mixtec lord Atonal claimed Toltec heritage.

The next scene (Caso 1961: A9–A13) portrays the drilling of the first fire to institute the establishment of Tolteca-Chichimeca rule. This was done at a hill with two intertwined serpents. At the center of the hill is a disk inside of which sits a bird. The same scene appears in both Lienzo Seler II and the Selden Roll. In the Selden Roll the object with the bird is held by a woman who forms part of the place sign, possibly a representation of Itzpapalotl herself. Karl Taube (1983) proposes that the disk is a mirror, an object that continues to symbolize community authority in some Mixtec communities today.

Above this scene of the foundation of the realm we see a compound place sign. The first component represents Yucu Cuy or Cerro Verde, a prominent hill above Coixtlahuaca. The second represents Cuauhtinchan. The two place signs together indicate that the royal family of Coixtlahuaca, beginning with Atonal I, was formulated through an alliance between the antecedent to the Place of the Serpent as Coixtlahuaca, and the royal house of Cuauhtinchan. On the Lienzo de Tlapiltepec, the royal line extends through nineteen generations to Atonal II, who was conquered and executed in 1458 by the Aztec Empire. The place sign for the second ruling family at Coixtlahuaca has been destroyed. It runs parallel to that of Atonal I, perhaps even supplanting it after the 1458 Aztec conquest (Carlos Rincon, personal communication) (Figure 7).

The Lienzo de Tlapiltepec narrative then shifts to the right, where a new format is presented; it reverses direction and leads back to the bottom of the lienzo (Caso 1961: C-F, 20–37). At the top right-hand side, we see several place signs loosely arranged as a radial map. The communities include Suchixtlan as Platform of Flowers (Smith 1973: 79), Coixtlahuaca as two intertwined serpents over a rock, Tulancingo as a platform and temple qualified by tule plants, Tamazulapa as a pool of water surrounding a frog, Tejupan as Hill of the Jewel, and finally Yucu Cuy or Cerro Verde as a hill surmounted by lush, leafy plants once again.

From this radial composition representing the Mixteca Alta communities, lines extend to other place signs that are arranged more linearly

Figure 6. Lord 8 Deer petitioned the deity impersonator of Camaxtli-Mixcoatl, 4 Jaguar, for the nose ornament transforming him into a *tecuhtli* or lineage head in the Tolteca-Chichimeca status system (Bodley 9 II). This act expediated his usurpation of Tilantongo. The alliance-making event is later reciprocated by 8 Deer in a traditional Mixtec fashion. Two of his children are dispatched for marriage into the royal line of Tulancingo, a kingdom subject to Coixtlahuaca (see Smith 1973: 73).

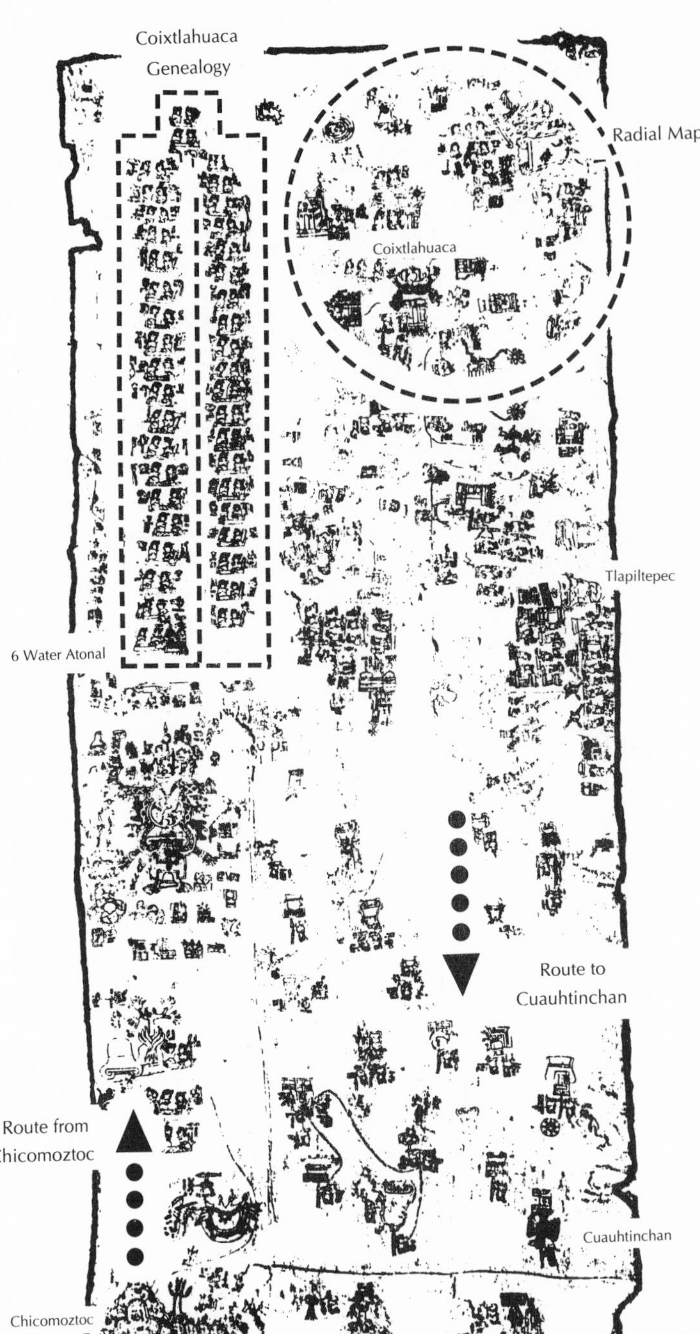

Figure 7. The Lienzo de Tlapiltepec fuses the peregrination layout of the Tolteca-Chichimeca Mapas de Cuauhtinchan with the portrayal of more than twenty generations of Mixtec/Zapotec-style genealogical descent through the royal houses of Coixtlahuaca.

across the cloth like those in the Mapas de Cuauhtinchan. These include Tlapiltepec, Tequixtepec, Tehuacan, Tecamachalco, Tepeyacac, and Cuauhtinchan, to name a few (Jansen and Gaxiola 1978: 14–15). The fact that the lines connect place signs representing towns near Coixtlahuaca with communities in Puebla may refer to an event described in both the Historia Tolteca-Chichimeca and Cuauhtinchan Map No. 2, in which lords from Coixtlahuaca married into the royal house of Cuauhtinchan (Reyes 1988: 56–61; Kirchhoff et al. 1976: 205).

The Lienzo de Tlapiltepec therefore represents a fusion between the format of the migration sagas of a Cuauhtinchan map tradition and the radial map and genealogy of the Mixtec Mapa de Teozacoalco and the Zapotec Lienzo de Guevea tradition. What is significant is the manner in which the two traditions have been joined. The migration saga from Chicomoztoc follows lines drawn to indicate the paths taken into the Coixtlahuaca region. From there the Tlapiltepec narrative shifts to a recounting of the highest-ranked royal line, that of Coixtlahuaca itself. A radial-style layout of Coixtlahuaca and Tlapiltepec is included together with neighboring Mixteca Alta communities, and finally we return to the migration saga format to discuss connections between Coixtlahuaca and Cuauhtinchan.[2]

Discussion

The Mixtec codices and maps, the Historia Tolteca-Chichimeca, the Mapas de Cuauhtinchan, and the Coixtlahuaca lienzos all document a number of factional alliance corridors that once united Tlaxcala, Puebla, and Oaxaca during the Early Post-Classic (Figure 8). These political structures were formed through elite intermarriage, with membership often determined through claims of descent from deified ancestors or reckoned through one of several heroic cosmogonies such as the migrations of the Tolteca-Chichimeca after the fall of Tula. Factions thereby even defined new forms of elite ethnicity that superseded cultural distinctions otherwise maintained by Nahuatl, Popolocan, Chocho, Mazatec, Cuicatec, Mixtec, and Zapotec-speaking peoples. Usage of the Mixteca-Puebla style and iconographic similarities between the Mixtec and Borgia Group codices point to a pronounced mutual influence in religious conceptions as well.

Nevertheless, important differences in the treatment and form of the information conveyed in these art works are found to be the result of differing sociopolitical strategies and belief systems. Central Mexican, Tlaxcalan, and Pueblan city-states and kingdoms, for example, were

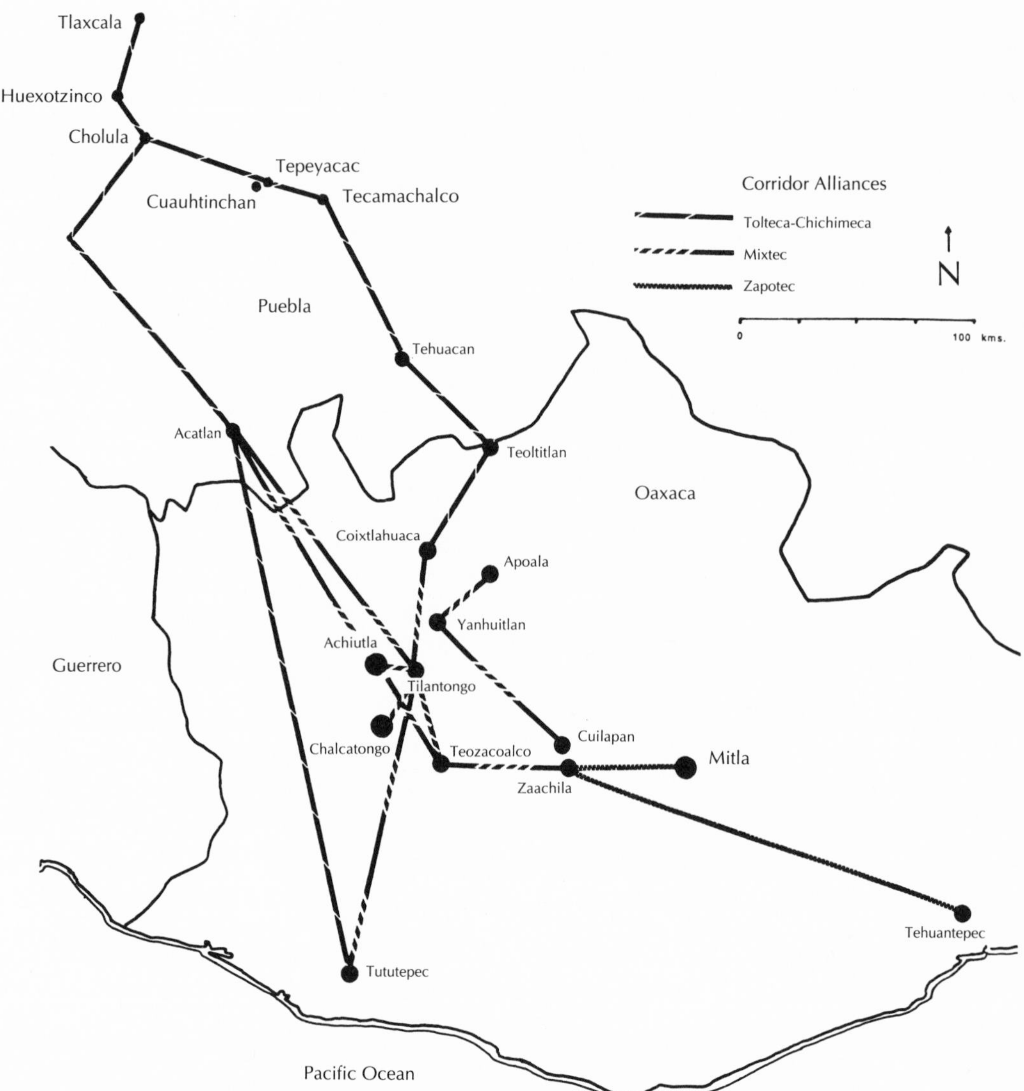

Figure 8. Post-Classic alliance corridors as reconstructed from various Pueblan and Oaxacan maps, lienzos, and codices.

governed by *tetecuhtin* or "lineage heads." According to Pedro Carrasco (1971: 352–354; Carrasco and Broda 1976; Rounds 1977), the title of *tecuhtli* transformed a prince into the head of an Aztec *teccalli* or noble house, a patrimonial landed estate worked by commoners who paid tribute. The title was held for life, with a successor often, although not necessarily, being elected from among the *tecuhtli*'s sons by consent of the highest ranking members of the royal house.

In many respects the role of the *tecuhtli* resembled that of the Mixtec *yya* or the Zapotec *coqui* (Pohl in press). The *yya, coqui,* and *tecuhtli* could claim the paramount position by virtue of descent. Descent reckoning also led to the creation of family hierarchies. Nevertheless, among the Mixtec and Zapotec, primogeniture was the preferred system for passing the paramount position from one generation to the next. The Mixtec Codices indicate that Oaxacan kings gained titles by reckoning direct descent from various divine ancestors born from trees, caves, rivers, heavens, and so forth.

The Tolteca-Chichimeca on the other hand appear to have "elected" the *tecuhtli* with only special consideration being given to a favored son. The royal descent group in general claimed its position through some explicit though not necessarily genealogical connection to either a "son" or follower of the culture hero Camaxtli-Mixcoatl, who emerged from the seven caves of Chicomoztoc (see Motolonía 1903: 9). This implies that the title of *tecuhtli* could represent a fictive kinship term, explaining the absence of genealogical descent lists typical of the Mixtec Codices in the *xiuhtlaquilolli* Historia Tolteca-Chichimeca, for example. Emphasis in this document and the companion Cuauhtinchan maps is on a legendary migration saga that led to the establishment of the principal *teccalli* as political units and not on the patrilineal descent reckoning of individual kings.

Conclusions

By the Early Post-Classic, the great urban centers such as Teotihuacan and Monte Alban had been abandoned. In their wake emerged smaller, factionalized kingdoms and city-states that no longer identified their conceptions of nationhood through allegiance to enormous ceremonial centers but rather through more flexible systems of alliance arranged along primary corridors of cultural and commercial exchange. Far from representing a collapse of civilization, the confederations provided their partners with an unprecedented access to more goods from more distant resources than ever before (Harbottle and Weigand 1992).

Coinciding with these cultural developments was the invention of a new communication system called the Mixteca-Puebla style that superseded regional language-based pictographic or hieroglyphic systems employed by such Classic states as the Zapotec and Maya. The style was widely used by a number of Mexican cultural co-traditions not only in the production of codices but also in wall painting, stone carving, jewelry making, fabric weaving, exquisite ceramic vessels, and other elite craft goods.

This style of pictorial communication was meant to bridge ethnic differences, not magnify them. Thus, the Mixtec codices cannot be attributed to any one kingdom, and several even relate the dynasties of two or three prominent alliance members. We assign them loosely to the Oaxacan confederations on the basis of their being a geographically specific history.

Nevertheless, I have ascertained characteristics that differentiated the usage of information in the production of codices, lienzos, and maps between the Tolteca-Chichimeca and the Mixtec/Zapotec alliances both in Pre-Columbian and colonial times. Divergence in terms of pictorializing the politics of landscape are here discussed as being dependent upon a differential distribution of information between the sacred and the profane. In the Mixtec and Zapotec examples, the recitation of royal descent lines was the highest form of holy liturgy, and the information was communicated through a sacred format as the Mixtec codices. We have no knowledge of any comparable, religiously venerated sources for the Tolteca-Chichimeca confederations, just as we have no records for any equally extensive lines of divine royal descent, invoked to verify the paramount position of authority. Likewise, we have no invocation of great Tolteca-Chichimeca migrations in the Mixtec codices. Rather, Mixtec kings and queens are portrayed being supernaturally born from trees, rivers, rocks, and even the ruins of the Classic period citadels themselves (Pohl and Byland 1990; Pohl in press).

Finally, iconographic hybrids were created by kingdoms that operated regularly in both spheres. These have been identified as members of the Coixtlahuaca lienzos such as the Lienzo de Tlapiltepec, the Lienzo Seler II, and the Selden Roll, and in the Codex Tulane from Acatlan (Smith and Parmenter 1991). Here the royal houses reckoned their status with respect to both systems, invoking equally the migrations of the "sons" of Camaxtli-Mixcoatl and the five hundred-year-old genealogies of the highest-ranked royal houses.

Notes

1 Although many scholars have noted these families and place signs, no one has made any special study of their presence or absence. In Codex Zouche-Nuttall, members of the Hill of the Tail/Hill of the Face dynasty appear on pages 24, 40–41, and 60. Scholars of western European literature have long noted biases in the telling of the Beowulf saga, the Iliad, and the Odyssey, to name a few, that appear to promote the status of certain lesser kingdoms who claimed to have participated in the epic events.

2 M. E. Smith (Smith and Parmenter 1991) notes an unusual fusion of characteristics in the iconography and style in Codex Tulane. While the Relacion de Acatlan says that the kingdom claimed to have been established by the Tolteca-Chichimeca Mixtecatl, the codex portrays the foundation of the kingdom by two Mixtec gods named 9 Movement and 7 Deer, who appear in Codex Vindobonenesis 4 and 26. While the pictorial narrative emphasizes the genealogical lines of descent between the royal house of Teozacoalco and Acatlan, the figures themselves are not painted as Mixtec lords but rather as Aztec-style *tetecuhtin*.

References

Acuña, René, ed. 1984. *Relaciones Geográficas del Siglo XVI: Antequera.* Mexico: Universidad Nacional Autonoma de Mexico.

———. 1985. *Relaciones Geográficas del Siglo XVI: Tlaxcala.* Mexico: Universidad Nacional Autonoma de Mexico.

Aguilera, Carmen. 1986. *Lienzos y Codice de Tepeticpac.* Mexico: Instituto Tlaxcalteca de la Cultura.

Barlow, Robert. 1949. *The Extent of the Empire of the Culhua Mexica.* Ibero-Americana No. 28. Berkeley: University of California Press.

Bernal, Ignacio. 1948. Exploraciones en Coixtlahuaca, Oaxaca. *Revista Mexicana de Estudios Antropologicos* 10: 5–76.

Bittman Simons, Bente. 1968. Los Mapas de Cuauhtinchan y la Historia Tolteca Chichimeca. Mexico: Instituto Nacional de Antropología e Historia.

Boone, Elizabeth Hill. 1991. Migration Histories as Ritual Performance. In Carrasco 1991: 121–151.

Burgoa, Francisco de. 1934a. *Palestra Historial.* Vol. 24. Mexico: Publicaciones del Archivo General de la Nacion.

———. 1934b. *Geográfica Descripción.* Vols. 25–26. Mexico: Publicaciones del Archivo Genral de la Nación.

Byland, Bruce E., and John M. D. Pohl. In press. *In the Realm of 8 Deer: The Archaeology of the Mixtec Codices.* Norman: University of Oklahoma Press.

Carrasco, David, ed. 1991. *To Change Place: Aztec Ceremonial Landscapes.* Boulder: University Press of Colorado.

Carrasco, Pedro. 1971. Social Organization of Ancient Mexico. In Ekholm 1971, 10: 349–375.

Carrasco, Pedro, and Johanna Broda. 1976. *Estratificación Social en la Mesoamerica Prehispánica.* Mexico: Instituto Nacional de Antropología e Historia.

Caso, Alfonso. 1949. El Mapa de Teozacoalco. *Cuadernos Americanos* 8, no. 5: 145–181. Mexico.

———. 1961. Los Lienzos Mixtecos de Ihuitlán y Antonio de Leon. In *Homenaje a Pablo Martinez del Rio en el vigesimoquinto aniversario de la primera edicion de los Origenes Americanos,* 237–274. Mexico: Instituto Nacional de Antropología e Historia.

Davies, Nigel. 1977. *The Toltecs: Until the Fall of Tula.* Norman: University of Oklahoma Press.

Durán, Diego. 1971. *Book of the Gods and Rites and the Ancient Calendar.* Trans. and ed. Fernando Horcasitas and Doris Heyden. Norman: University of Oklahoma Press.

Ekholm, Gordon F., and Ignacio Bernal. 1971. *Archaeology of Northern Mesoamerica.* Vol. 10, pt. 1 of *Handbook of Middle American Indians,* gen. ed. Robert Wauchope. Austin: University of Texas Press.

Flannery, Kent V., and Joyce Marcus, eds. 1983. *The Cloud People: Divergent Evolution of the Zapotec and Mixtec Civilizations.* New York: Academic Press.

Graulich, Michel. 1974. Las Peregrinaciones Aztecas y El Ciclo de Mixcoatl. *Estudios de Cultura Nahuatl* 11: 311–354.

Harbottle, Garman, and Phil C. Weigand. 1992. Turquoise in Pre-Columbian America. *Scientific American* 266, no. 2: 78–85.

Jansen, Maarten E.R.G.N. 1982a. Viaje al Otro Mundo: La Tumba 1 de Zaachila. In Jansen 1982: 87–119.

———. 1982b. *Huisi Tacu: Estudio Interpretivo de un Libro Mixteco Antiguo: Codex Vindobonensis Mexicanus I.* Vols. 1 and 2. Incidentale Publicaties 24. Amsterdam: CEDLA.

Jansen, Maarten E.R.G.N., and Margarita Gaxiola. 1978. *Primera Mesa Redonda de Estudios Mixtecos Sintesis de las Ponencias.* Estudios de Antropología e Historia No. 15. Oaxaca: Centro Regional de Oaxaca, INAH.

Jansen, Maarten E.R.G.N. and Th.J.J. Leyenaar, eds. 1982. *Los Indigenas de Mexico en la Epoca Prehispanica y en Actualidad.* Leiden: Rutgers B.V.

Jiménez Moreno, Wigberto. 1954–1955. Sintesis de la Historia Precolonial del Valle de Mexico. *Revista Mexicana de Estudios Antropologicos* 54, no. 1: 219–236.

King, Mark. 1982. Historical Metaphor and the Communication of Legitimacy in the Mixteca 500 B.C.–A.D. 1500. Unpublished Master's Thesis, Vanderbilt University.

Kirchhoff, Paul. 1955. Quetzalcoatl, Huemac y el fin de Tula. *Cuadernos Americanos* 14: 169–196.

Kirchhoff, Paul, Lina Odena Güemes, and Luis Reyes García. 1976. *Historia Tolteca-Chichimeca.* Mexico: Instituto Nacional de Antropologia e Historia.

Marcus, Joyce. 1983a. The Reconstructed Chronology of the Later Zapotec Rulers. In Flannery 1983: 301–308.

Molina, Alfonso de. 1977. *Vocabulario en Lengua Castellana y Mexicana y Mexicana y Castellana.* Estudio Preliminar de Miguel Leon-Portilla. Mexico: Editorial Porrua.

Motolonía, Toribio de. 1903. *Memoriales.* Luis Garcia Pimentel from a manuscript by Joaquin Garcia Icazbalceta. Mexico.

———. 1950. *History of the Indians of New Spain.* Trans. and ed. Elizabeth Andros Foster. Berkeley: Bancroft Library.

Muñoz-Camargo, Diego. 1986. *Historia de Tlaxcala.* Madrid: Hermanos Garcia Noblejas.

Nicholson, H. B. 1960. The Mixteca-Puebla Concept in Mesoamerican Archaeology: A Re-Examination. In Wallace 1960: 612–617.

———. 1971. *Pre-Hispanic Central Mexican Historiography.* Investigaciones Contemporaneas sobre Historia de Mexico. Memorias de la Tercera Reunion de Historiadores Mexicanos, Oaxtepec, Morelos. 4–7 Noviembre, 1969. (Universidad Nacional Autonoma de Mexico, El Colegio de Mexico, University of Texas at Austin). Mexico.

Nicholson, H. B. and Eloise Quinones Keber. In press. *The Mixteca-Puebla Concept in Mesoamerican Archaeology: Recent Research and Discoveries.* Culver City, California: Labyrinthos.

Paddock, John. 1983. *Lord 5 Flower's Family: Rulers of Zaachila and Cuilapan.* Vanderbilt University Publications in Anthropology No. 29. Nashville: Vanderbilt University.

Parmenter, Ross. 1982. *Four Lienzos of the Coixtlahuaca Valley.* Dumbarton Oaks Studies in Pre-Columbian Art and Archaeology No. 26. Washington, D.C.: Dumbarton Oaks.

Pohl, John M. D. In press. *The Politics of Symbolism in the Mixtec Codices.* Nashville: Vanderbilt University Press.

Pohl, John M. D., and Bruce E. Byland. 1990. Mixtec Landscape Perception and Archaeological Settlement Patterns. *Ancient Mesoamerica* 1, no. 1: 113–131.

Pohl, John M. D. and Bruce Byland. In press. *The Mixteca-Puebla Style and Early Postclassic Socio-Political Interaction.* Nicholson and Quinones Keber.

Reyes, Luis García. 1977. *Cuauhtinchan del Siglo XII al XVI: Formacion y Dessarrollo Historico de un Senorio Prehispanico.* Weisbaden: Franz Steiner.

Robertson, Donald. 1970. The Tulum Murals: The International Style of the Late Postclassic. In *Verhandlungen des XXXVIII Internatonalen Amerikanisten Kongresses,* vol. 2: 77–88. Stuttgart-Munich.

Rounds, J. 1977. The Role of the Tecuhtli in Ancient Aztec Society. *Ethnohistory* 24, no. 4: 343–361.

Ruiz de Alarcón, Hernando. 1984. Treatise on the Heathen Superstitions that Today Live among the Indians Native to this New Spain, 1629, by Hernando Ruiz de Alarcon. Trans. and ed. J. Richard Andrews and Ross Hassig. Norman: University of Oklahoma Press.

Sahagún, Bernardino de. 1981. *Florentine Codex: General History of the Things of New Spain.* Bk. 2, *The Ceremonies.* Trans. and ed. Arthur J. and Charles E. Dibble. Monographs of the School of American Research. Santa Fe.

Seler, Eduard. 1960. *Das Dorfbuch von Santiago Guevea.* Gesammelte Abhandlungen zur Amerikanischen Sprach-und Altertumskunde, vol. 3: 157–193. Graz.

Smith, M. E. 1973. *Picture Writing From Ancient Southern Mexico: Mixtec Place Signs and Maps.* Norman: University of Oklahoma Press.

Smith, M. E., and Ross Parmenter. 1991. *The Codex Tulane.* Middle American Research Institute Publication 61. New Orleans: Tulane University.

Taube, Karl. 1983. The Teotihuacan Spider Woman. *Journal of Latin American Lore* 9, no. 2: 107–189.

Torquemada, Juan de. 1986. *Monarquia Indiana.* Introduccion por Miguel Leon Portilla. Vols. 41–43. Mexico: Editorial Porrua.

Velázquez, Primo Feliciano. 1945. *Codice Chimalpopoca: Anales de Cuauhtitlan y Leyenda de los Soles.* Mexico: Imprenta Universitaria.

Wallace, Anthony F. C., ed. 1960. *Men in Cultures: Selected Papers from the Fifth International Congress of Anthropological and Ethnological Sciences.* Philadelphia: University of Pennsylvania.

Dana Leibsohn

Primers for Memory: Cartographic Histories and Nahua Identity

In the town of Cuauhtinchan, Puebla, three photocopies are taped to the wall behind the mayor's desk in the municipal building. Each of these papers shows a cartographic history painted in that town in the mid- to late-sixteenth century following the Spanish conquest of Mexico (Figures 1, 2, 3). Across from these images, records dating from the sixteenth century to the present have been stacked on shelves reaching to the ceiling. This is the community's archive. Physically, the cartographic histories stand in opposition to the town's written records. At the same time, the images and texts resonate with one another, bracketing the room with signs of Cuauhtinchan's past. In 1991 the people of Cuauhtinchan with whom I spoke could decipher only a few of the place and name glyphs on the photocopies. Yet they were sure that these images represented the town's history. They explained to me that these pictures were about Cuauhtinchan and the things their ancestors did there. The original paintings had been taken from Cuauhtinchan nearly one hundred years ago.[1] Hence, for local inhabitants, it is the photocopies that presently operate as symbols of community pride.

This paper argues that in the sixteenth century, as today, cartographic histories rendered visible a series of ideological propositions. Although they record important events and places from times gone by, cartographic histories do not describe the past in any simple way. Rather these painted images privilege certain memories, setting out a visual framework for indigenous constructions of identity. By focusing on six cartographic histories from the town of Cuauhtinchan as a case study, I will examine how painted imagery structured historical memory and geography in a Nahua community.[2] My argument is that cartographic histories configured identities that were at once corporate in focus and factional in perspective. Moreover, Nahuas did not use this imagery to define themselves in opposition to the Europeans who had begun to inhabit New Spain by the time the paintings were created. Indigenous people living nearby—people with similar histories and claims to territory—were the significant "Other" in these painted histories.

Identity and Altepetl

Individuals forge many kinds of identity over the course of their lives. They draw upon symbols and act out rituals; in so doing, they fashion a series of conflicting and overlapping identities. To speak of "identity" is to evoke a constantly shifting set of positions, a series of interlinked negotiations between self and world. Although no rules exist for establishing identity, certain elements are fundamental. Two of these are self-recognition and memory. A person (or community, or nation) must be able to recognize and name itself to exist as an independent and autonomous entity. And memory makes this self-recognition possible over time.[3] Of course, identity was construed in myriad ways in indigenous communities. In this essay I will trace the relationship among three conceptual categories: the *altepetl,* geography, and history. Not chosen lightly, these categories (*mutatis mutandis*) have figured prominently in Central Mexican constructions of identity over the last five hundred years.

The basic unit of self-definition and affiliation in postconquest Central Mexico was the *altepetl.*[4] A Nahuatl word, *altepetl* combines terms for water (*atl*) and mountain (*tepetl*). In some ways similar to our notion of community, the *altepetl* was a corporate group that possessed and managed specific territory. Each had its own leader: before the conquest and a few years thereafter, rulership was dynastic, while over time *cabildos* with *gobernadors, regidores,* and *alcaldes* became more common. Beyond this, a tradition of ethnic distinctness was put in place (Lockhart 1991: 9). The *altepetl* was understood as a single entity that stood apart from all other similar units; each had its own historical narratives and its own symbols of identity. At the same time, this level of social organization and group affiliation coexisted with other mechanisms for structuring one's place in the world.

James Lockhart has described the *altepetl* as a confederation of constituent parts and argued for a principle of modular organization among Nahuas (1991: 23; 1992: 15–28). If the *altepetl* was an integrated unit bound to certain lands and allied to a single leader, it also incorporated smaller groups, among them were *calpolli* or *tlaxilacalli.* Each *calpolli* was separate, equal (at least in theory), and self-contained, with its own name, territory, ethnic identity, and rulership (Lockhart 1991: 10). Under certain circumstances, *calpolli* might be subsumed under the name of the whole, but they did not forfeit their sense of autonomy. Thus *altepetl* identity was constructed from various ethnic and lineage commitments as well as ties to a larger entity.

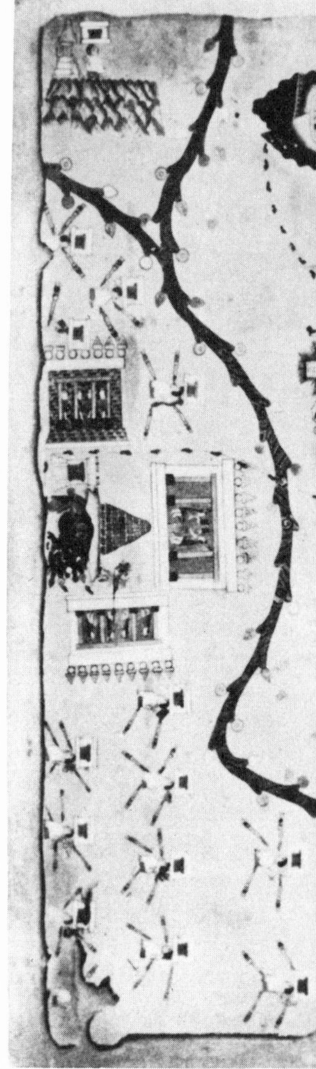

Figure 1. Mapa de Cuauhtinchan No. 1, mid- to late-sixteenth century. At the left, the site of Cholula appears as three buildings flanking a pyramid. The toponym for Cuauhtinchan is nestled among hills toward the center of the painting (Glass 1964).

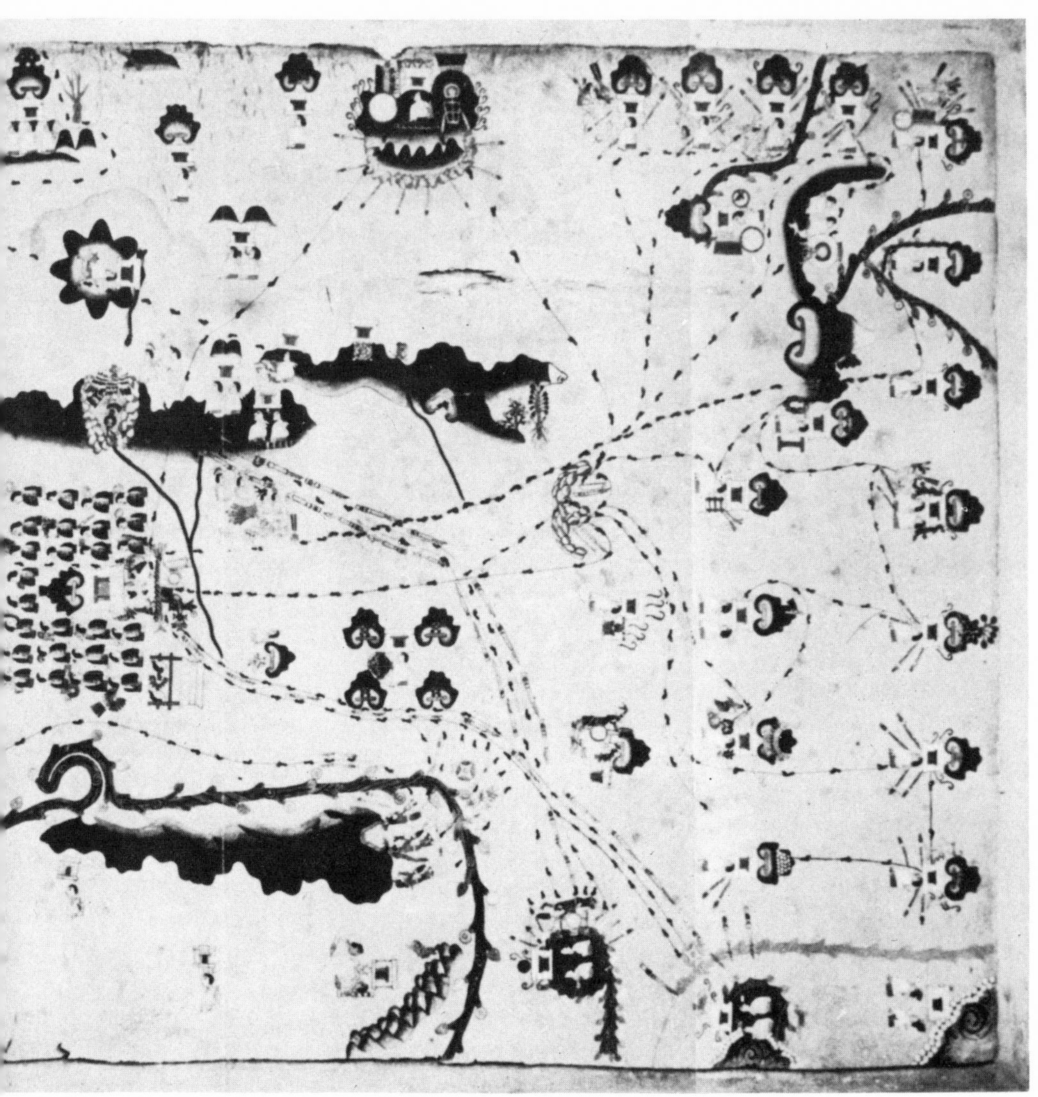

Cuauhtinchan's Cartographic Histories

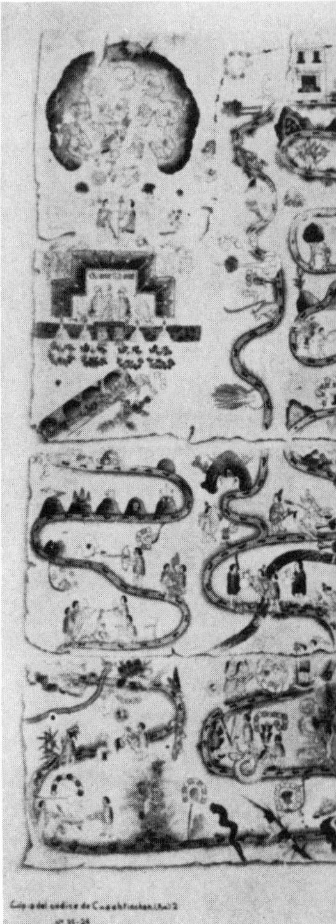

Cuauhtinchan lies just outside the Valley of Mexico, a few miles south of the city of Puebla. Although the *altepetl* of Cuauhtinchan was ethnically diverse, most people living there in the sixteenth century spoke Nahuatl.[5] Soon after the Spanish conquered the area in 1520, the inhabitants of Cuauhtinchan were Christianized and divided between two *encomenderos.* By mid-century a *cabildo* had been established and coinage was used to pay tribute (Gerhard 1972; Kirchhoff, Odena, and Reyes 1976). As was the case throughout much of New Spain, neither total subjection to Spanish ways of life nor explicit resistance to European authority characterized daily life in sixteenth-century Cuauhtinchan.

From this period six Nahua cartographic histories have been preserved.[6] Three of them were painted on indigenous paper and are today called the "Mapas de Cuauhtinchan." These images are rectangular in shape and range in size from .92 × 1.12 meters to 1.09 × 2.04 meters. The Mapa de Cuauhtinchan No. 1 (Mapa 1), No. 2 (Mapa 2), and No. 3 (Mapa 3) all depict a relatively large area surrounding Cuauhtinchan as well as migration routes, conquests, and the founding of several *altepetl* (Figures 1, 2, 3).[7] Around the middle of the sixteenth century, three smaller images were also set down, but these were executed on European paper (Figures 4, 5, 6). One of these is now called the "Mapa Pintado en Papel Europeo y Aforrado en el Indiano" (Mapa Pintado); the other two are part of the historical annals known today as the Historia Tolteca-Chichimeca (Historia). These smaller paintings focus on boundaries, although they also deal with conquests and Cuauhtinchan's founding.

The events represented on all six cartographic histories took place in a time well before the Spanish conquest. Stylistically, as well, the cartographic histories have more in common with pre-Hispanic paintings than contemporaneous European images or maps. Several different "hands" can be identified, but all work with preconquest conventions. The glyphs for personal names, places, and dates, the unmodulated frame lines, the "Aztec" body proportions, and the absence of ground lines suggest that the cartographic histories are redactions or copies of older (perhaps pre-Hispanic) paintings.[8]

Since no sixteenth- or seventeenth-century written documents refer explicitly to the Cuauhtinchan cartographic histories, it is difficult to demonstrate precisely how these images were used before the eighteenth century. Yet we know that these paintings comprised a visual discourse on history and geography. They made it possible for people to recognize

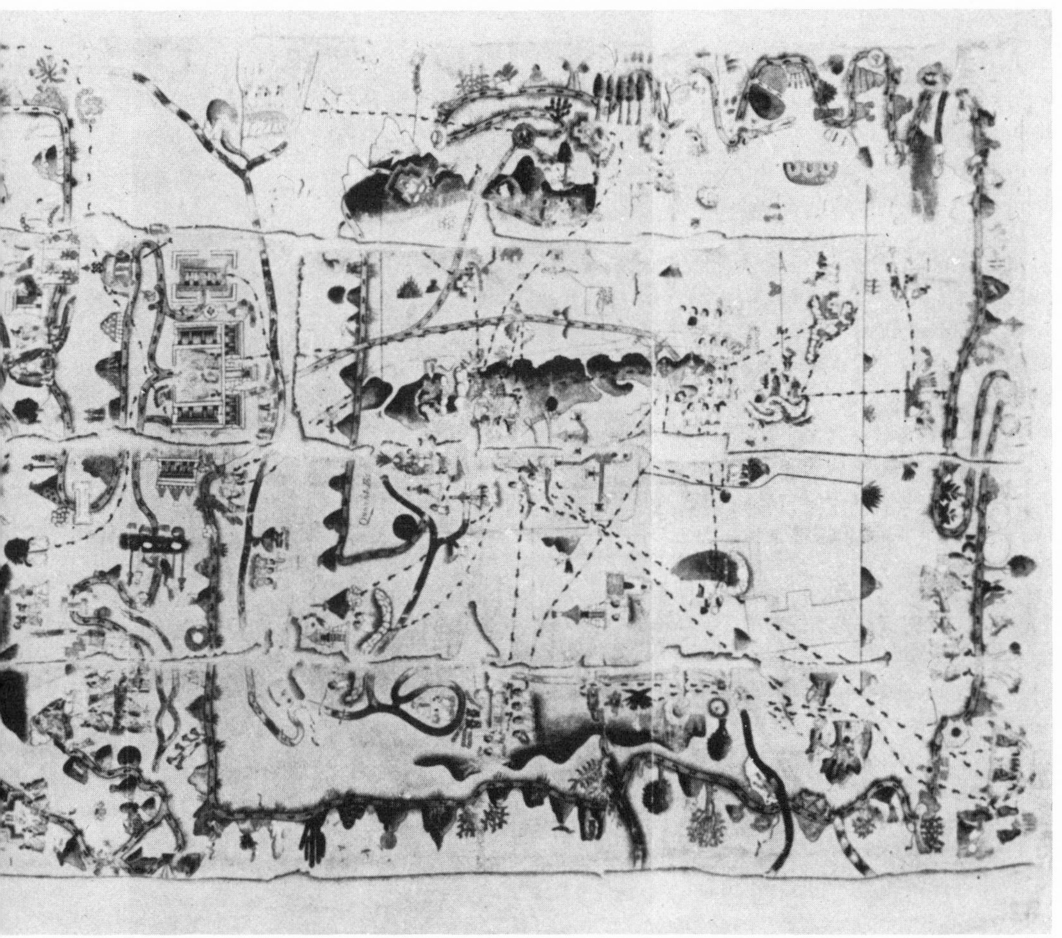

Figure 2. Mapa de Cuauhtinchan No. 2, mid- to late-sixteenth century. Chicomoztoc (Place of Seven Caves), the original home of the Cuauhtinchan people, occupies the upper left-hand corner of this painting. At the center stands Cholula, represented by a complex of buildings. Cuauhtinchan appears within a bank of hills, to the right of Cholula (Glass 1964).

their *altepetl* in visual terms, and to structure particular memories about the past. Toward this end the Cuauhtinchan images use sign conventions common to all cartographic histories. Before turning to the specific identities organized by the Cuauhtinchan paintings, these conventions of sign-use warrant a review.

On Cartographic Histories

In New Spain, indigenous people painted hundreds of maps between 1570 and 1630. By far, the greatest number were legally binding images of territory made for land grants, *visitas,* boundary disputes, and royal questionnaires.[9] Nearly all of these images describe the lands and communities of sixteenth-century New Spain. They were accompanied by written documents and submitted to authorities. In contrast, the remainder—the cartographic histories—record events and places from the distant past. These paintings are distinctive because of their express interest in history and the links they retain with pre-Hispanic visual records. These features, in particular, set them apart from the textual and official channels that governed the conventions of maps created as legal instruments. While cartographic histories were sometimes brought into legal settings to defend claims to territory, their imagery was directed primarily toward indigenous memories rather than colonial officials.

Many groups of people across New Spain produced cartographic histories in the sixteenth century, though most of the eighty-seven known today originated in the regions of Oaxaca, Puebla, and Veracruz (Glass 1975: 39). The themes treated in these painted images are similar, but not identical; some give more attention to genealogy, while others stress migration routes, conquests, and/or boundaries. Minor differences notwithstanding, cartographic histories organize geography and history along four semiotic axes: (1) these images merge two distinct spatial projections; (2) they adumbrate mnemonic cues for historical narratives; (3) they use toponyms to sign place; and (4) they exploit ambiguous blank spaces.

In "Spatial Stories," Michel de Certeau has identified two primary spatial projections: the tour and the tableau (1984: 115–130). The tour is a passage through space that traces an itinerary from one point to the next. Territory is presented as an unfolding narrative of movement. The tableau, on the other hand, depends upon fixed vision. Its spaces are preordered, so territory exists in a stable arrangement regardless of one's travel through it. De Certeau maintains that these spatial projections represent opposites, and visual images grant priority to one system or the other. Cartographic histories, however, simultaneously deploy itinerary

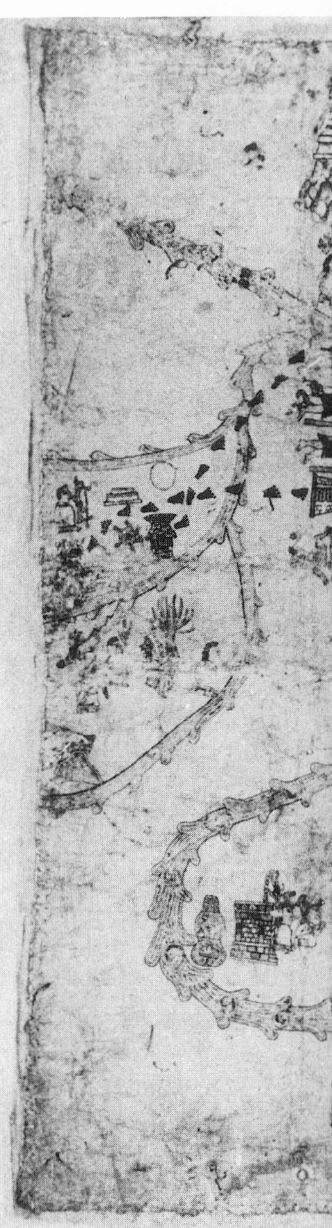

Figure 3. Mapa de Cuauhtinchan No. 3, mid- to late-sixteenth century. At the center of the painting lies a string of hills, split in half. Inside the opening, an eagle has been placed; this is Cuauhtinchan. Across the river to the left, signs for Cholula—a temple and a pyramid—are aligned on axis with those of Cuauhtinchan (Glass 1964).

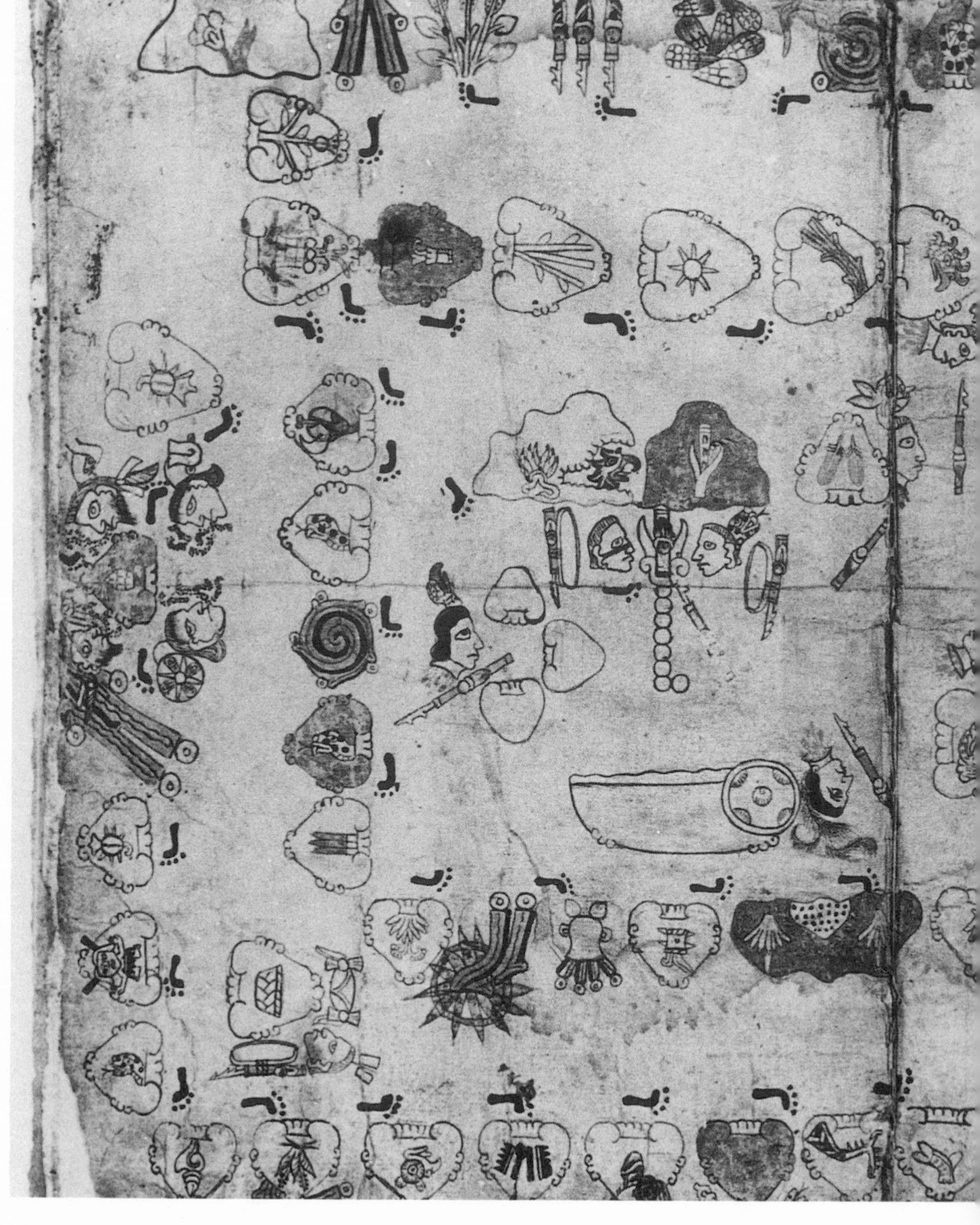

Figure 4. Mapa Pintado en Papel Europeo e Aforrado en el Indiano, circa 1530–1540. Cuauhtinchan is represented by two hill-forms just to the left of the painting's center. At the left and right of the cartographic history, four culture heroes meet to discuss the boundaries of the *altepetl* (Kirchhoff et al. 1976).

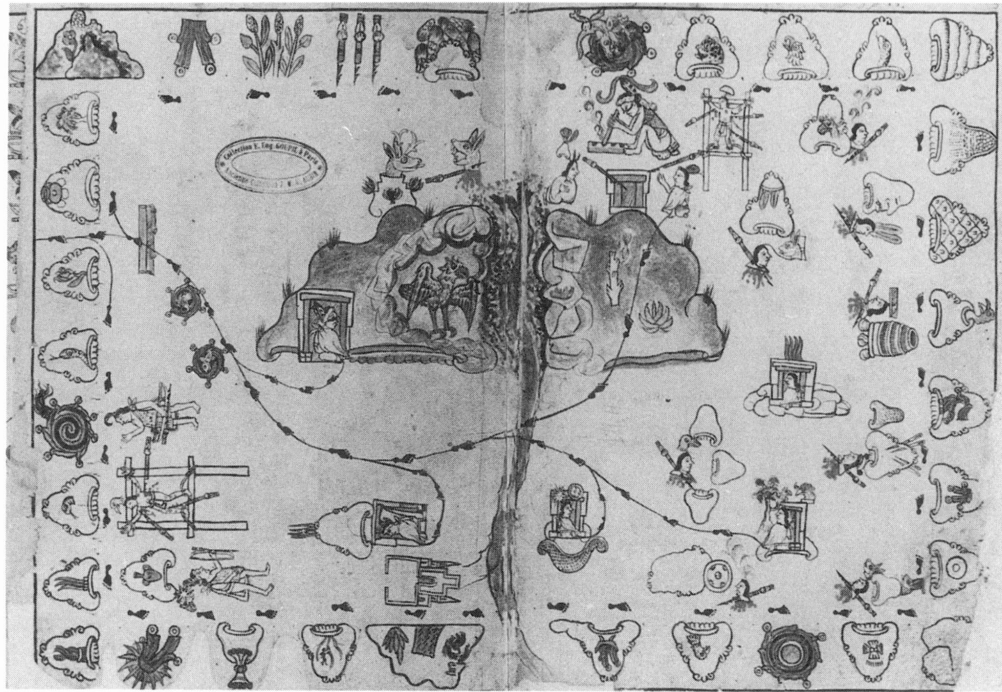

and tableau. These paintings hold the two systems in tension, making no attempt to reconcile the incongruities. Together, the two spatial projections stabilize *altepetl* in place and in time. As tableaux, cartographic histories position *altepetl* within a web of landmarks, situating them amidst preexisting geographical features. The itinerary projection establishes a narrative thread that strings together important places in history. Thus, *altepetl* also take form through a sequence of events that prefaces, and then continues beyond, their founding.

As historical paintings, cartographic histories point the way to sites in memory rather than to particular locations in the landscape. The paintings display signs of a past, although in and of themselves they are not sufficient to summon "history." Narratives are required to make this transformation. In effect, cartographic histories are physical armatures that enable historical reconstructions. The paintings make present to memory that which has begun to fade. Prior to the Spanish conquest, when narratives were strictly oral, paintings functioned as guarantees. Images on paper or cloth ensured that certain events and people would not be forgotten. Cartographic histories painted in the sixteenth century

Figure 5. Cartographic history from the Historia Tolteca-Chichimeca (Mss. 46–50, folio 32v–33r), circa 1545–1563. Cuauhtinchan stands at the center of the painting, surrounded by toponyms that represent boundaries. Footprints joined by solid lines refer to migrations into the region from Cholula. The scenes of conquest refer to battles in which the people of Cuauhtinchan established their right to claim this territory as their own (Kirchhoff et al. 1976).

seem to have played a similar role. They conserved "authentic" memories—keeping the names of people, the dates of their deeds, and the traces of their experiences in permanent form.

Yet no cartographic history records every event in a historical narrative; each is selective, offering visual cues for the knowledgeable reader to expand upon. In this sense, there is a great openness to these paintings. Because they do not discipline their images into a strict narrative line, and because they render only a selection of key events from the past, cartographic histories leave much open to interpretive elaboration. If one set of images could prompt a variety of stories, then historical memory was permitted (if not encouraged) to course with a certain amount of fluidity. As long as narrators used the cues available, the painting served its purpose as guarantor of authenticity.[10] It is immaterial that the painting could not ensure that the telling would be identical each time. Cartographic histories present a secure framework for history, yet the images they employ also support multiple, and perhaps conflictual, recitations. Hence these paintings were symbolic arenas, in which many identities and historical memories were negotiated over time.

Figure 6. Cartographic history from the Historia Tolteca-Chichimeca (Mss. 46–50, folio 35v–36r), circa 1545–1563. Cuauhtinchan appears in the middle of this painting. The date of the *altepetl*'s founding (Year 8 Reed) and two of its founders are shown just below the toponyms. The footprints circling the perimeter of the painting refer to the marking out of boundaries that occurred when the *altepetl* was founded. At the far left and right, two pairs of culture heroes meet to discuss Cuauhtinchan's boundaries (Kirchhoff et al. 1976).

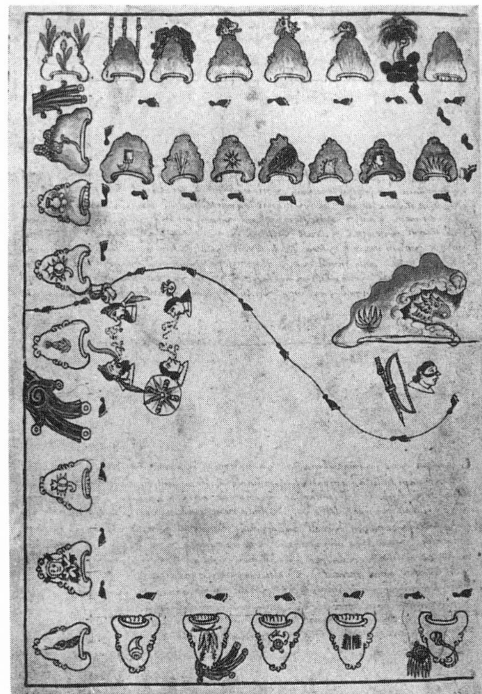

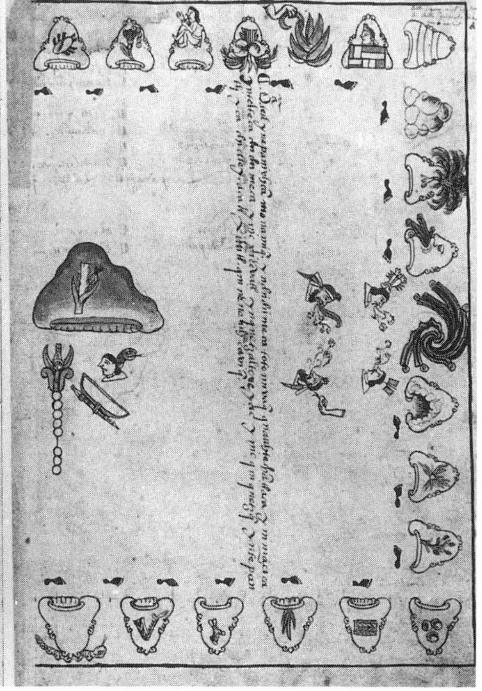

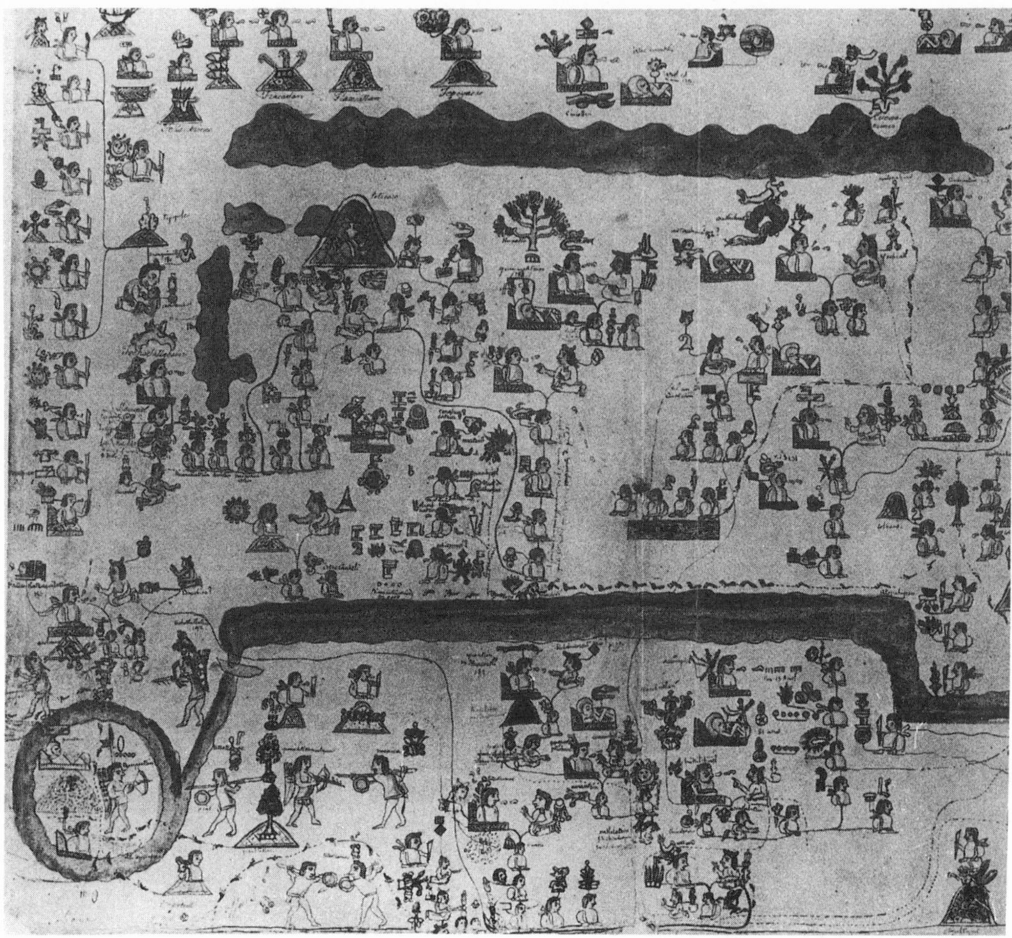

Figure 7. Sheet 5 of the Codex Xolotl, sixteenth century (Dibble 1951).

Cartographic histories give geography form through toponyms. In treating territory as a series of named places, however, the paintings keep description to a minimum. Neither the Lienzo de Zacatepec (see p. 69) nor the Codex Xolotl (Figure 7) reveals much about topography. The stylized rivers that run along the edges of the Zacatepec painting imply landscape, as do the lakes that stretch across the center of page five of the Codex Xolotl. But in both cases the primary signs for place are toponymic. Across Mesoamerica, indigenous toponyms use recognizable pictorial images to cue the names of places. In this way Tenochtitlan—"Place of the Nopal Cactus"—is evoked by a cactus growing out of a stylized stone; likewise a hill-form and grasshopper identify

Chapultepec (Place of Grasshopper Hill) (Figures 8a and 8b). This system allowed a wide variety of locations to be mapped. However, toponyms cannot be taken at face value. Stylized hill-forms appear in nearly every place glyph on the Mapa Pintado (Figure 4). But we know that not all of these sites are hills in the landscape—some are communities and others are natural features. Moreover, the painted sequences of glyphs may mirror the location of places in the physical world, just as they might parallel circuitous migrations that wander in space but appear as straight lines on the map. But this is not always the case. Taken alone, the painted signs describe very little about the "look" of a landscape. Instead, they reveal how territory is named.

Cartographic histories exploit the ambiguity of blank space in complex ways. In the Lienzo de Zacatepec and the Codex Xolotl, the actors, places, and events float against an undifferentiated ground. An absence of signs provides the only structure—emptiness is understood as background separating one place from another. Blank spaces effectively dismiss the topography and relative distance between sites. This occurs in the sequence of place glyphs at the perimeter of the Lienzo de Zacatepec, and again in the center of the painting, where footprints and warpaths (marked by chevrons) traverse an undifferentiated expanse of cloth. These blank spaces refer to interstitial territory. To traverse them is to move across the landscape. Yet the emptiness conforms to no consistent scale—the void signs no distance.

This is also true along the temporal axis. Sometimes dates appear on cartographic histories, providing events with specific temporal markers. More often blank spaces indicate the passage of time. Toward the center of page five of the Codex Xolotl, for instance, there is a conventionalized depiction of a genealogy. A man and a woman sit opposite each other, joined by thin lines to five figures below them (Figure 8c). Descendants of Quiahutzin and Xilocihuatl, the five men appear in a column according to the order of their birth (Dibble 1951). Here the blank spaces between figures mark the passage of time—each man was born *after* the one above him. Near the place glyph for Tenochtitlan there is another example of this. The Tenochca ruler Acamapichtli sits upon a straw mat; just below this scene, the same man appears deceased (Figure 8d). The small blank space separating these scenes does not refer to a change in location—it marks a shift in time. Traveling vertically down the page, one journeys through fifty-one years.[11]

These empty spaces between people function like the years that are set down in annals even when nothing important happened (White 1981). The blankness of the page stands for all the quiet moments in the historical record. They are the periods for forgetting rather than remembering. Yet the size of these spaces is uninformative. In annals, each gap in the record is one year long, but here one cannot tell the quantity of time that has elapsed between events—at least not by sight alone. As with geography, the negative space remains undisciplined by any consistent scale.

The cartographic histories offer few explicit cues for differentiating empty "times" from empty "spaces."[12] This underscores the fact that time and space are inextricably linked. To speak of distance is to evoke implicitly the temporal, and vice versa. Foremost, then, is not the relation of time and space per se, but how the two take form in pictorial terms. In the empty regions of the cartographic histories, relationships between time and space are manifold. By exploiting the ambiguity of

Figure 8. Details from sheet 5 of the Codex Xolotl, sixteenth century (Dibble 1951): (a) Toponym for Tenochtitlan, (b) Toponym for Chapultepec, (c) Descendants of Quiahutzin and Xilocihuatl, (d) Scene of Acamapichtli's Reign.

a

b

c

d

blank space, painters alternatively repress temporal and spatial features. Like the Unconscious, where diverse memories are held in abeyance, the voids of cartographic histories serve as repositories for historical and topographical traces. Blank regions allow other signs to overflow and expand outward—the emptiness collects all that must be forgotten.

This forgetting is pivotal to the ideology of cartographic histories. If the blank support of these paintings stores traces of both place and event, then territory never achieves an originary status. Geography does not lie waiting to be blanketed with human activities, and history is not laid across the landscape. Rather the two are woven together: one comes into being only with the other. This is not to say that indigenous people failed to perceive territory and history as distinct entities. In some circumstances they did and in others they did not, as is the case in most societies. The point here is that in representing geography and history as codependent, these images set out the parameters of an ideological position. In this context, land took on meaning only when engendered with historical event. Cartographic histories made manifest a slippery hermeneusis: places were significant in memory because they were the sites of ancestral deeds, and ancestral deeds were worthy of remembrance because they occurred at significant places.

Toponyms and Identity: Situating Cuauhtinchan

All six Cuauhtinchan cartographic histories are concerned with boundaries. Each frames the *altepetl* with other places, ensuring that it never becomes an extremity or limit. Moreover, the toponym for Cuauhtinchan occupies roughly the same place on each painting: it stands at the center or just above and a bit to the side of the midpoint. Although it is possible to recognize the *altepetl* because its toponym occupies this consistent place, the behavior of Cuauhtinchan's place glyph is not uncomplicated.

In cartographic histories, toponyms are a primary device for configuring identity. Place glyphs perform two functions: first, they situate communities and landmarks in space, and second, they name these sites. In Figure 4, the toponym for Cuauhtinchan occupies a position near the center of the page. In Nahuatl, Cuauhtinchan means "Home of the Eagle," and a bird and cutaway hill glyph have been used to sign this. By cuing its name, the glyph anchors Cuauhtinchan in space, in memory, and in relation to other locations on the painting. The toponym ensures that Cuauhtinchan will not slide into the adjacent *altepetl* of Tepeaca; nor will it slip into a void in memory, for that matter. Through their use of onomastic signs, cartographic histories differentiate each site from its neighbors. Yet they simultaneously imply that all the places on the page are qualitatively similar. Some glyphs stand for towns and others for natural features, but in marking them with one toponymic system these paintings implicitly equalize the sites.

This system of signing place also represses internal difference. Like all naming systems, toponyms single out one feature or name and use it to stand for the whole. In this way the glyphs mask internal variations and assert that each place is a homogeneous entity. Differences within *altepetl*—be they visual, political, or social—are not granted recognition. This raises questions about the ideology inherent in the selection of "conventional" toponyms. We understand something of Cuauhtinchan's ethnic diversity. And we know that identity was organized at the level of the *altepetl* as well as the *teccalli* and the *calpolli.*[13] The issue at hand, then, is: does the use of toponyms eclipse these alternative identities, or can they be acknowledged?

The signifying practice of naming is intimately tied to identity. Names have a deictic function. Yet they also enable memories that, in turn, allow recognition to take place over time. Consequently, naming is akin to recognition, but the two are not identical. Furthermore, different appellations elicit distinct images through connotative association. To call an *altepetl* "Home of the Eagle" is to identify a different place than to call the same *altepetl* "Home of the Eagle and Jaguar." While the two names may have a common object, only the latter is chained to a rich series of Mesoamerican metaphorical associations linking eagles with jaguars. Thus onomastic references to an *altepetl* are neither ideologically neutral nor interchangeable.

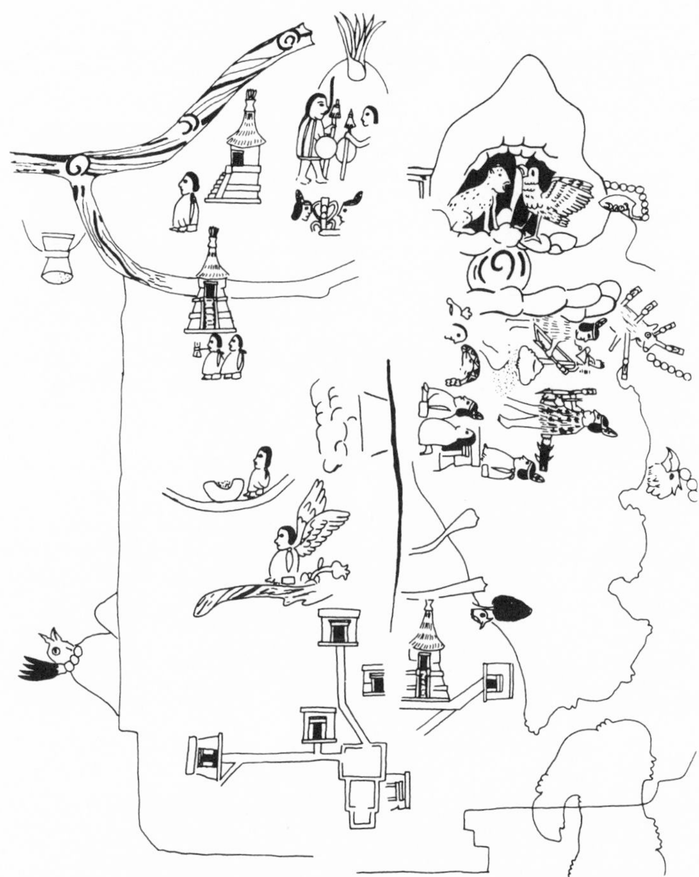

Figure 9a. Toponyms for Cuauhtinchan and Foundation Scene from the Mapa de Cuauhtinchan No. 2, mid- to late-sixteenth century (Reyes García, 1977).

Sixteenth-century Nahuatl documents indicate that "Home of the Eagle" is but one name for the *altepetl* of Cuauhtinchan. Other appellations include Tepetl cotoncan (Place Where the Hill is Broken), Petlazolmetepec (Place of Worn-Out Maguey Mat Hill),[14] Tzouac Xilotepec (Place of the Cactus/Place of Unripened Corn Hill),[15] and Ocelotl ychan (Home of the Jaguar). The cartographic histories refer to these names—but not all in the same way. For example, Mapa 2 shows a rocky cliff with an eagle and a jaguar inside a mountain cave nearby. These images evoke the names Tepetl cotoncan, Cuauhtinchan, and Ocelotl ychan (Figure 9a). In contrast, one of the paintings from the Historia shows two hills separated by a small space: one with an eagle and the other with a small maguey plant, a woody stalk, and an ear of corn. This combination summons the terms Cuauhtinchan, Tepetl cotoncan, Petlazolmetepec, and Tzouac Xilotepec (Figure 9b).

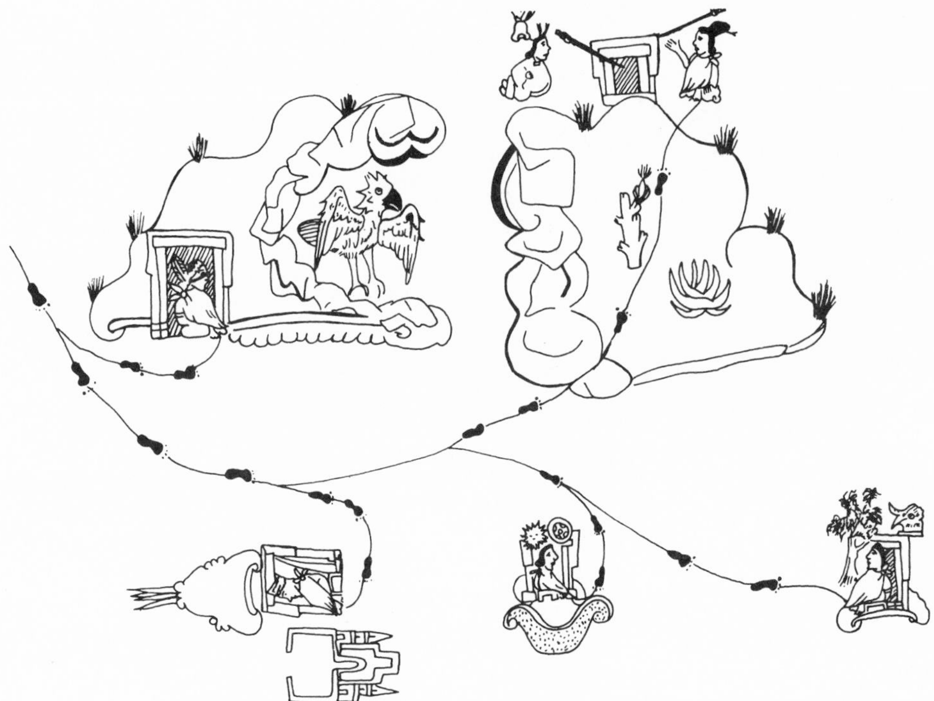

Figure 9b. Toponyms for Cuauhtinchan and Foundation Scene from one of the cartographic histories in the Historia Tolteca-Chichimeca (Mss. 46–50, folio 32v–33r), circa 1545–1563 (Reyes García, 1977).

Comparison of the toponyms for Cuauhtinchan reveals a certain consistency. An eagle and broken rock formation appear in every toponym. The painter may render only the animal's head or set the bird of prey in a cave instead of a rocky cliff, but toponyms for "Home of the Eagle" and "Place Where the Hill is Broken" are always there. Reiteration of these signs lends the appellations Cuauhtinchan and Tepetl cotoncan an importance not awarded to the others. Even though there are several names for the *altepetl,* these clearly take priority. In effect, the repetitious use of toponyms privileges these two names and situates the *altepetl* of Cuauhtinchan within a stable set of identity parameters.

Yet the distribution of toponyms implies that the *altepetl* was not understood as a homogeneous entity. Rather identity—as expressed through names—was negotiable. While all the cartographic histories refer to the town as "Home of the Eagle" and "Place Where the Hill is Broken," only Mapa 1, the Mapa Pintado, and the paintings from the Historia evoke the name Petlazolmetepec. The other cartographic histories refuse this title. Elizabeth Brumfiel has recently argued that opposing factions often use the same symbolic language, competing through the manipulation of a single set of symbols (1989). Such an insight is relevant here. The stability in sign-use on the Cuauhtinchan paintings points to modes of consensual agreement on *altepetl* identity. The variation in toponyms, however, suggests how the cartographic histories negotiated claims through the acceptance or rejection of particular symbols. That differences of opinion existed should not surprise us, for conflicts and subversions always skew constructions of identity.[16]

Territory and Narrative: History as Visual Ideology

While the toponym for Cuauhtinchan occupies a similar place on every cartographic history, none of the paintings depicts an identical array of surrounding sites. Mapa 2 covers the broadest expanse with glyphs for Tenochtitlan, Tlaxcala, Cholula, and Pico de Orizaba. In contrast, the Mapa Pintado and Historia paintings sign none of these places: they emphasize locations nearer to Cuauhtinchan. The differences among the cartographic histories, however, are not strictly those of scale. Each painting combines sites that are close to Cuauhtinchan with those that are some distance away. Moreover, when we examine the immediate environment around the toponym for Cuauhtinchan, we find that each of the paintings frames the *altepetl* with different places.

Some of the variations result from choices in naming. More fundamental, however, is the relationship between territory and narrative. The places represented on each Cuauhtinchan cartographic history vary according to the plot and episodes of the history recorded. This is part of the hermeneusis of place and event that organizes all cartographic histories. Yet the relationship between site and deed is not completely reciprocal. The territory mapped out on the Cuauhtinchan paintings frames important events from the past. But these events do not simply feed significance back into the geography. They determine the very name and breadth of the historical landscape. Visually, identity takes form in a geographic setting molded by the demands of historical event and memory. It is not necessarily constituted around a stable tableau of sites. Nor does it depend solely upon one set of boundaries or landmarks.

If history is integral to the process of self-definition, then it becomes essential to query what kinds of historical narratives the cartographic histories record. Each of the Cuauhtinchan paintings bears the traces of several stories. Clues to these narratives include images of footprints, battles, councils, sacrifices, and *altepetl* foundations. While named individuals appear on all the cartographic histories, there are no explicit references to genealogy. It is events leading to the foundation of Cuauhtinchan and nearby *altepetl,* rather than ancestral connections, that assume priority. Taken together the six paintings present a constellation of sites and deeds.[17] Although there is a fair amount of overlap, no cartographic history replicates any of the others in its entirety. And even when paintings copy each other (as the Historia paintings do the Mapa Pintado), additions and omissions occur. Thus, only in the most general sense, do the cartographic histories reiterate the same tale. These disparities make it clear that people living in Cuauhtinchan preserved not one, but multiple histories. This may seem self-evident: people never have just one story to tell about themselves. But the fact that the cartographic histories supported a multiplicity of narrative strategies is significant.

There can be little doubt that the narratives of the Cuauhtinchan paintings concerned legitimation. Like most historical narration, Nahua histories are partisan and moralizing in nature.[18] In teaching people how things once were, histories also structure what can occur. In this way they mandate a present as well as a future; they take on a prescriptive force. Consequently, historical narration is about more than memory and self-recognition. Who you were in the past plays a determinant role in acquiring power in the present (Rappaport 1991). In sixteenth-century New Spain this was given even more force, as indigenous people justified claims to territory (and hence political and economic integrity) through their histories in legal contexts.[19]

A pivotal scenario in Cuauhtinchan's past that appears in both image and text focuses on Cholula.[20] According to the Historia, it was there that the ancestral leaders of Cuauhtinchan first earned the right (power) to found an *altepetl.* In return for military assistance, the Cholulans granted these leaders lands and women. In this way, the founders of Cuauhtinchan bound themselves to the more sophisticated and prestigious neighbors through marriage and acts of homage. The ideology of Cholulan origins was not unique to Cuauhtinchan; moreover, not every group in Cuauhtinchan claimed direct descent from the renowned place (Kirchhoff, Odena, and Reyes 1976; Reyes García 1977). Nonetheless, all the cartographic histories make the point that Cuauhtinchan originally gained its legitimacy from relations of exchange with Cholula.

The "Cholula connection" is one of the few things referenced on all six paintings from Cuauhtinchan. The Mapa Pintado represents two culture heroes who ruled at Cholula marking out the boundaries of Cuauhtinchan (Figure 4). Mapa 1, Mapa 2, and Mapa 3 associate Cholula with Cuauhtinchan via footprints tracing migrations from one site to the other (Figures 1, 2, and 3). These cartographic histories underscore the ties between the two *altepetl* by placing the two sites on the same horizontal axis. Although the migration route from Cholula to Cuauhtinchan is not always direct, the paintings stress the narrative connections through this axial arrangement of toponyms. As the alignment of Cholula and Cuauhtinchan does not directly parallel the relation of the two sites in the physical world, ideology takes precedence over the accidents of geography.

The treatment of this connection on the cartographic histories reveals that the memory of preconquest events was still essential for sixteenth-century Nahuas. Written documents confirm this. The Historia and the Manuscript of 1553 invoke links with Cholula to justify claims to rights and territory (Kirchhoff, Odena, and Reyes 1976; Reyes García 1988). But Cuauhtinchan does not appear as a unified entity in either text: inter-*altepetl* differences are consistently recorded.

Similarly, the cartographic histories from Cuauhtinchan resonate with both *altepetl*-level interests and more particular investments in the past. Because all of the paintings attend to the "Cholula connection," it is clear that the tie was an integral part of Cuauhtinchan's history. Yet, in visual terms, the link to Cholula took several forms. On Mapa 1, for example, footsteps join Cholula with a part of Cuauhtinchan called Tollan Calmecauacan. In contrast, Mapa 3 depicts similar footprints passing from Cholula to the toponymic sign for Tzouac Xilotepec. These variations reinforce the fact that associations with the celebrated site did not play an identical role for everyone living in Cuauhtinchan. The six cartographic histories affirm through their own visual discourse that legitimating memories remained heterogeneous in the sixteenth century.

Signing the Past: A Semiosis of Nahua Identity

The cartographic histories painted in Cuauhtinchan offer a fundamental lesson in Nahua constructions of identity. This identity—as far as we can read it—held *altepetl* concerns in tension with those of smaller groups. According to the Cuauhtinchan images, this play between *altepetl* unity and factional difference has a long history. All the paintings identify several individuals who were instrumental in the foundation of Cuauhtinchan. They also concur that one of the leaders present was Teuhctlecozauhqui.[21] Beyond this, the consensus begins to break down. Luis Reyes García has convincingly argued that seven groups comprised Cuauhtinchan at the time of its founding (1977), but visually, only Mapa 2 makes this explicit. In this cartographic history, near the toponym for Cuauhtinchan there are seven buildings grouped around a plaza and several distinct clusters of individuals (Figure 9a).[22] All of the other paintings record different renditions of Cuauhtinchan's social structure at the time of foundation: one of the cartographic histories from the Historia shows five men settling *altepetl* (Figure 9b); the others depict two or three people.

Among the paintings, there is visual agreement that Cuauhtinchan was founded by more than one person, and that Teuhctlecozauhqui participated in this event. This concordance points to historical knowledge shared throughout the *altepetl.* Yet the cartographic histories are equally clear that, from its inception, Cuauhtinchan was comprised of multiple subunits—each with its own leader. It is telling that these paintings record the origins of the *altepetl* as a heterogeneous entity. For they reassure us that Nahua identity at the *altepetl* level did not take precedence over other kinds of affiliation at the time of Cuauhtinchan's foundation. When the cartographic histories were painted in the sixteenth century, these differences were (re)recorded, implying that memories of the *altepetl*—as a corporate group of distinct parts—continued to have importance. Thus the cartographic histories preserve and reiterate the tensions between *altepetl* and *teccalli* affiliations.

Two generations after the Spanish conquest, people in Cuauhtinchan were still recording a plethora of historical memories. The events they chose to remember and the ways they pictured them played an integral role in indigenous configurations of identity. The cartographic histories set out the terms necessary to recognize Cuauhtinchan as a stable, but variegated entity. According to these paintings, the very substance of Cuauhtinchan was comprised of narratives about the *altepetl* and its factions, stories about the founding of Cuauhtinchan and legitimating ties to Cholula, and boundaries formed by other, similar *altepetl.*

If the meanings elicited by these cartographic histories have proved to be fragile and fleeting, the images themselves have not. Once stored in the municipal archives, the paintings from Cuauhtinchan are now preserved in the vaults of banks and museums. In the town itself, photocopies have replaced them. People in Cuauhtinchan no longer speak Nahuatl. And although some trace the ancestry of the pueblo to an Indian origin, they do not claim to descend directly from Nahuas. The ties that bind memory, history, and geography are now woven from other fabric.

Today, the photocopied cartographic histories are valued less for the sites and events they represent than as testimony to ancestral knowledge and recordkeeping. Although they are kept with other records attesting to the community's history, the photocopies have a status not granted to written texts. Someone has put them on display, rather than storing them in bundles along with the other documents of the municipal archive. Whether these reproductions will remain on the wall and whether they will retain their distinguished status is, of course, an open question. Regardless of the answer, these images evoke powerful memories that sometimes incorporate and sometimes transcend the changes in politics and ethnicity that have shaped Cuauhtinchan. In the late twentieth century, then, it is still appropriate to ask what kinds of identity are configured through these painted signs of Cuauhtinchan's past.

Notes

For insight and intellectual counsel I thank Daniel Bridgman, as well as Elizabeth Boone, Cecelia Klein, and Joanne Rappaport. I am also grateful to Rachel Hoffman and Daniel Weiss, who read earlier drafts of this paper.

1 Although it is not certain when the original paintings first left Cuauhtinchan, evidence suggests that they remained in the community at least until the late nineteenth century (Yoneda 1981: 21–22). Today, the Mapa de Cuauhtinchan No. 2 is held privately in Mexico City, Mapa de Cuauhtinchan No. 1 is housed in the Bibliothèque Nationale in Paris, and Mapa de Cuauhtinchan No. 3 resides in the Museum of the Instituto Nacional de Antropología e Historia in Mexico City.

2 Nahuas were the largest group of indigenous people living in Central Mexico at the time of the Spanish conquest. Nahuatl, the native language of Nahuas, is still spoken today in some communities. As for the cartographic histories from Cuauhtinchan, they comprise one of the largest collections of Nahua paintings in this genre that date from the sixteenth century and have a well-established provenance.

3 Constructions of identity can be set into place even if subjects or communities do not remain unified or recognizable as the same entity over time. On the fluidity of identity and the implications of this in colonial contexts, see Homi Bhabha 1986: 5–11.

4 For a more extensive discussion of the *altepetl* as a corporate unit, see James Lockhart 1991: 1–64; 1992: 14–58.

5 Popoloca and Mixtec were also spoken in Cuauhtinchan, but Nahuatl was the predominant language (Gerhard 1972).

6 One other cartographic image which dates from the mid- to late-sixteenth century has been preserved from Cuauhtinchan. Known today as the Mapa de Cuauhtinchan No. 4, this painting exhibits only a few dates and makes no explicit visual references to historical events. Therefore, because it stands outside the cartographic-history genre, the painting has been set aside.

7 For descriptions of the "Mapas de Cuauhtinchan," see John Glass 1964 and 1975; Luis Reyes García 1977; Bente Simmons 1968; and Keiko Yoneda 1981.

8 On pre-Hispanic painting conventions see Elizabeth Boone 1982 and Donald Robertson 1959; for sources see Simmons 1968 and Yoneda 1981.

9 These maps include the *pinturas* of the Relaciones Geográficas and those currently housed in the Tierras section of the Archivo General de la Nación in Mexico City. For discussion of these maps, see Donald Robertson 1975; Serge Gruzinski 1987; Walter Mignolo 1989; Dana Leibsohn in press; and Barbara Mundy 1993. Illustrations of some of these maps appear in volumes 2, 3, 4, and 5 of the *Catálogo de Ilustraciones* (1979), and in the *Relaciones Geográficas* volumes edited by René Acuña (1984).

10 Throughout the colonial period (and into the present), cartographic histories gained legitimacy as "authentic" records of the past in a number of ways. In nearly every instance, the document derives its "authenticity" from the social and historical contexts in which it circulates, as well as from the images it displays, its painting style, and the narrative it cues.

11 This is also marked by the date 13 Reed and signs for the length of Acamapichtli's reign (Dibble 1951: 73).

12 The ambiguity between time and space may even be accentuated by the use of footprints, which can refer to genealogical ties as well as to travel (Dibble 1951; Smith 1973).

13 In Cuauhtinchan the primary subdivisions were known as teccalli; there apparently were seven in number and, like the calpolli described earlier, each had its own leaders, territories and history. Calpolli also existed in Cuauhtinchan, but these groups seem to have figured less prominently. See Reyes García (1977) and Lockhart (1992: 24, 98).

14 This is Yoneda's translation of the term given in the Historia (1990). The expression may refer to a kind of maguey plant, in which case the translation could be "Centipede-Maguey Hill." Kirchhoff, Odena, and Reyes cite another sixteenth-century document that gives the name as Tepematlazolco rather than Petlazolmetepec (1976: 193 n. 3).

15 The word *tzouac* may be translated more specifically as a type of maguey plant (Galarza and Yoneda 1979: 56), and *xilotl* refers to tender ears of green maize (Karttunen 1983: 325). It remains unclear whether *Tzouac* and *Xilotepec* should be translated as two distinct locatives. Because they appear together in text and image, the translation here (rough as it may be) has tried to give the sense of this pairing.

16 There is also evidence for this from written texts. One Nahuatl document from Cuauhtinchan, the Manuscript of 1553, explicitly links a subgroup of the *altepetl* with Tzouac Xilotepec (for a transcription of this document, see Reyes García 1988: 87). This suggests that, in the sixteenth century, certain places were in fact associated with particular lineages and/or ethnic groups. Moreover, in his ethnographic work on contemporary Nahua communities, Alan Sandstrom describes complex and multifaceted practices for naming places within towns and local regions. He has found that patterns of naming betray internally focused, local

orientations; furthermore, official "imposed" names do not necessarily occult other appellations (1991: 106–107).

17 Whether these events "really happened" is not at issue here. They constitute part of the indigenous past because they were deemed worthy of record and, hence, of memory.

18 See Hayden White (1981: 1–24) for a cogent discussion of morality and historical narrative; on the partisan nature of indigenous histories, see Lockhart (1992: 376–392).

19 For insight into this process in Cuauhtinchan, see the Manuscript of 1546–1547, which records a land suit between Cuauhtinchan and Tepeaca, and the Manuscript of 1553, which concerns inter-*altepetl* conflicts (Reyes García 1988: 11–79, 80–104).

20 Located near the center of the Puebla-Tlaxcala region, Cholula was renowned as a religious center and giant market site in pre-Hispanic times (Carrasco 1982: 133). This seat of sacred power was also thought to be the home of Quetzalcoatl. According to the Historia, the town was ruled by Toltecs—people associated with high cultural achievement, religious sanctity, and great wisdom (Kirchhoff, Odena, and Reyes 1976; Carrasco 1982).

21 Mapa 1, which presents a more explicitly factional perspective, is the only exception in this regard. Because this cartographic history focuses on Tollan Calmecauacan rather than Cuauhtinchan (as "Home of the Eagle"), Teuhctlecozauhqui, the founder of "Home of the Eagle," is not present. See Reyes García 1977: 13–14.

22 See Reyes García 1977: 47–51 for a discussion of this arrangement and its implications.

References

Bhabha, Homi. 1986. Interrogating Identity. In *The Real Me: Post Modernism and the Question of Identity,* ed. Homi Bhabha, 5–11. London: Institute of Contemporary Arts.

Boone, Elizabeth Hill. 1982. Towards a More Precise Definition of the Aztec Painting Style. In *Pre-Columbian Art History: Selected Readings,* ed. A. Cordy-Collins, 153–168. Palo Alto: Peek Publications.

———. 1991. Migration Histories as Ritual Performance. In *To Change Place: Aztec Ceremonial Landscapes,* ed. D. Carrasco, 121–151. Boulder: University of Colorado Press.

———. In press. Manuscript Painting in Service of Imperial Ideology. In *Aztec Imperial Strategies,* ed. F. Berdan et al. Washington, D.C.: Dumbarton Oaks.

Brumfiel, Elizabeth. 1989. Factional Competition in Complex Society. In *Domination and Resistance,* ed. D. Miller, et al., 127–139. London: Unwin Hyman.

Bryson, Norman, and Mieke Bal. 1991. Semiotics and Art History. *Art Bulletin* 73, no. 2: 174–208.

Carrasco, D. 1982. *Quetzalcoatl and the Irony of Empire.* Chicago: University of Chicago.

Catálogo de Ilustraciones. 1979. Mexico City: Archivo General de la Nación.

Certeau, Michel de. 1984. *The Practice of Everyday Life.* Berkeley: University of California Press.

———. 1988. *The Writing of History.* New York: Columbia University Press.

Dibble, Charles, ed. 1951. *Códice Xolotl.* Mexico: UNAM.

Eagleton, Terry. 1991. *Ideology: An Introduction.* London: Verso Press.

Galarza, Joaquin, and Keiko Yoneda. 1979. *Mapa de Cuauhtinchan No. 3.* Mexico City: Archivo General de la Nación.

Gerhard, Peter. 1972. *A Guide to the Historical Geography of New Spain.* Cambridge: Cambridge University Press.

Gibson, Charles. 1964. *The Aztecs Under Spanish Rule.* Stanford: Stanford University Press.

Glass, John. 1964. *Catálogo de la Coleccion de Códices.* Mexico City: INAH.

———. 1975. Survey of Native Middle American Pictorial Manuscripts. In vol. 14 of *Handbook of Middle American Indians,* ed. H. Cline, 3–80. Austin: University of Texas.

Gruzinski, Serge. 1987. Colonial Maps in Sixteenth-Century Mexico. *RES* 13: 46–61.

———. 1988. *La Colonisation de l'Imaginaire: Sociétés indigènes et occidentalisation dans le Mexique espagnol XVI–XVII siècles.* Paris: Editions Gallimard.

Harley, J. Brian. 1988. Silences and Secrecy: The Hidden Agenda of Cartography in Early Modern Europe. *Imago Mundi* 40: 57–60.

Harrison, Bernard. 1982. Description and Identification. *Mind* 91: 321–338.

Historia Tolteca-Chichimeca. See Kirchhoff, Paul, et al.

Karttunen, Frances. 1983. *An Analytical Dictionary of Nahuatl.* Austin: University of Texas Press.

Kirchhoff, Paul, Lena Odena Güemes, Luis Reyes García. 1976. *Historia Tolteca-Chichimeca.* Mexico: CISINAH, INAH-SEP.

Kristeva, Julia. 1978. Place Names. *October* 6: 94–111.

Leibsohn, Dana. In press. Colony and Cartography: Shifting Signs on Indigenous Maps in New Spain. In *Cultural Migrations: Reframing the Renaissance*, ed. Claire Farago. Niwot: University Press of Colorado.

Lockhart, James. 1991. *Nahuas and Spaniards: Postconquest Central Mexican History and Philology.* Stanford: Stanford University Press.

———. 1992. *The Nahuas After the Conquest: A Social and Cultural History of the Indians of Central Mexico, Sixteenth through Eighteenth Centuries.* Stanford: Stanford University Press.

Mignolo, Walter. 1989. Colonial Situations, Geographical Discourses and Territorial Representations: Toward a Diatopical Understanding of Colonial Semiosis. *Dispositio* 14, nos. 36–38: 93–140.

Miller, Arthur. 1991. Transformations of Time and Space: Oaxaca, Mexico, circa 1500–1700. In *Images of Memory: On Remembering and Representation,* ed. S. Küchler and W. Melion, 141–175. Washington: Smithsonian Institution Press.

Mundy, Barbara. 1993. *The Maps of the Relaciones Geográficas 1579–1584: Native Mapping in the Conquered Land.* Ph.D. Diss., Yale University.

Nicholson, Henry B. 1971. Prehispanic Central Mexican Historiography. In *Investigaciones contemporáneas sobre historia de Mexico, memorias de la tercer reunión de historiadores mexicanos y norteamericanos,* 38–81. Mexico City and Austin: UNAM, El Colegio de México, and University of Texas.

Noonan, Harold. 1989. *Personal Identity.* London: Routledge.

Rappaport, Joanne. 1988. History and Everyday Life in the Columbian Andes. *Man,* n.s. 23: 718–739.

———. 1990. *The Politics of Memory: Native Historical Interpretation in the Colombian Andes.* Cambridge: Cambridge University Press.

Reyes García, Luis. 1977. *Cuauhtinchan del siglo XII al XVI: Formación y desarrollo histórico de un señorio prehispánico.* Wiesbaden: Franz Steiner Verlag.

———. 1988 [1978]. *Documentos sobre tierras y señoríos de Cuauhtinchan.* Mexico City: Fondo de Cultura Económica.

Robertson, Donald. 1959. *Mexican Manuscript Painting of the Early Colonial Period.* New Haven: Yale University Press.

———. 1975. The Pinturas (Maps) of the Relaciones Geográficas. In vol. 12 of *Handbook of Middle American Indians,* ed. H. Cline, 243–278. Austin: University of Texas.

Sandstrom, Alan. 1991. *Corn is Our Blood: Culture and Ethnic Identity in a Contemporary Aztec Indian Village.* Norman: University of Oklahoma Press.

Simmons, Bente Bittman. 1968. *Los mapas de Cuauhtinchan y la Historia Tolteca-Chichimeca.* Mexico: INAH.

Smith, Mary Elizabeth. 1973. *Picture Writing from Ancient Southern Mexico.* Norman: University of Oklahoma Press.

White, Hayden. 1981. The Value of Narrativity in the Representation of Reality. In *On Narrative,* ed. W.J.T. Mitchell, 1–24. Chicago: University of Chicago Press.

Yoneda, Keiko. 1981. *Los mapas de Cuauhtinchan y la historia cartográfica prehispánica.* Mexico: AGN.

———. 1990. *Migraciones y Conquistas: Descifre Global del Mapa de Cuauhtinchan No. 3.* Thesis, Universidad Iberoamerica, Mexico City.

Tom Cummins

Representation in the Sixteenth Century and the Colonial Image of the Inca

It is difficult to gauge the impact of native systems of representation on Latin American colonial culture. It is equally difficult to gauge what real impact the European system of representation had on native cultures. Instead, we are told quite simply that one of the immediate results of the Spanish conquest was the destruction of the Inca and Aztec artistic systems,[1] and that these native systems had almost no effect on European art in the colonies.[2] But were the differences of what the Spaniards saw in Mexico and Peru of no account for what came afterward because the Hegelian "spirit of Western culture" was so overwhelming? Was the Spanish imposition of a common body of architecture and imagery so complete and unmediated that Mexican and Peruvian concepts of representation did not, in some fashion, enter into the colonial staging of those places?

To ask such questions does not mean to look for some pre-Hispanic stylistic traits that lingered in the Spanish colonial works produced by native artists or to explain pre-Hispanic iconographic features that were smuggled into the compositions and edifices of colonial art.[3] Rather, I will argue that if Peruvian and Mexican concepts of representation did, in some sustained way, fashion colonial representation, they can be recognized first in those rare instances in which the foreign cultures so recently conquered were presented visually in a forum that was European but that was based on images produced in the New World. Such presentations permit us to articulate unaccountable differences and thus allow for a discussion of what those differences mean in terms of the construction of native colonial imagery in Peru.

One forum in which Mexicans and Andeans were presented together to a European audience is in the engravings made for Antonio de Herrera y Tordesillas's *Historia general,* a four-volume work published in Madrid between 1601 and 1615 (Figures 1 and 2).[4] Of concern are two title pages, one for the "Descripción de las Indias Occidentales" and the second for the "Decada Quinta." The engravings precede Herrera's compilation of the histories of Mexico and Peru. The sources for both prints come from colonial images, two from Mexico and one from Peru, and the kinds of colonial sources chosen for the two engravings frame the fundamental differences, in the sixteenth-century Spanish reception and uses of the native two-dimensional arts, between Mexico and Peru. These differences are important because they mark the independent course that each colony took for the next three hundred years in terms of the colonial use of native imagery and language. That is, how are we to explain why in Mexico there are any number of colonial legal documents written in native languages and illustrated with native colonial imagery

Figure 1. Title page for the Descripción de las Indias Occidentales in the *Historia* (Herrera 1601–1615).

Figure 2. Title page for the Decada Quinta in the *Historia* (Herrera 1601–1615).

derived from pre-Hispanic sources, whereas in Peru there are very few legal documents written in Quechua, the language of the Inca,[5] and there is only one extant document composed and profusely illustrated by a native Andean?[6]

The answer, in part, lies in the sixteenth century, when Spaniards first encountered the two dominant cultures of the New World, the Aztec and the Inca, and in the different reactions of the Spaniards to the physical manifestations of the conceptual forms of native knowledge, the artistic systems of each culture. It is here that Peruvian and Mexican concepts of representation entered into the fashioning of colonial representation, but in very different ways. The difference rests in the fact that for the Andeans to be presented visually to a European audience, the Andean system of representation was the subject of a greater form of transformation than what occurred in Mexico. This is because, whereas both the arts of Mexico and Peru were deemed by the Spaniards to represent demons and idolatry, the Peruvian system of representation could not even be used to depict that idolatry to interested Europeans, because Andean art did not correspond in any sense to European notions of representation.[7]

The historical differences in the conquest and early settlement of the two areas accounts partially for the contrast, and certainly the fact that Mexicans had a form of illustrated manuscript is a crucial factor. Yet, clearly, to depict Peru for Europeans meant eschewing forms and representational concepts employed by the Peruvians themselves, and when pictorial images of Peru were desired, European modes of representation, based on mimesis, were employed.

With this introduction we can turn to the two engravings found in Herrera (Figures 1 and 2). Both title pages display the same system of organization, and of interest are the side panels of each. In the title page for the "Descripción de las Indias Occidentales," each side panel contains four separate illustrations representing Mexican gods or festivals. A single source was used for the top three vignettes: the *Libro de Figuras* (ca. 1529–1553), the earliest copy of a manuscript produced between 1528 and 1533 for a mendicant friar, who commissioned a native artist to paint preconquest-style images of deities, calendars, and customs.[8] The manuscript is divided into two discrete parts: text and image. The text written by the friar on the verso precedes the related image and offers a description of the iconographic details and the Nahuatl terms. In Herrera's frontispiece the discrete pages of textual and visual information are collapsed; so, for example, the kneeling figure in the upper left vignette is identified simply as "el dios de los finados."

Nonetheless, Herrera's image of the Aztec goddess Cihuacoatl reproduces the kind of imagery encountered by the Spaniards when they first entered Mexico. Native imagery, mediated through its compilation in a book by a friar, is employed as a source for Herrera's title page because it is accepted as capable of representing knowledge about Mexicans to Europeans. The image is pictorial, confirming visually what is claimed in the text. That is, the Spaniards were able to accept, as it is presented here, that the relation between the Nahuatl words for a deity and its attributes, either in oral Aztec or written Spanish form, and the Aztec deity image to which the Nahuatl words referred was similar to their own forms of text and illustration.[9]

This is not only true for images of deities, but for historical characters as well. Thus, the lower left-hand image is taken from another colonial source using a pre-Hispanic pictorial style. Here a figure is seated in profile with a number of symbols surrounding him. The symbols are pictographs and name glyphs which identify the figure as Acamapichtli, the first Aztec king, and the four towns he conquered. Herrera's image is based on the compression of Aztec pictorial elements used in colonial manuscripts such as the Codex Mendoza, perhaps commissioned in the 1530s by the first Viceroy of New Spain, Don Antonio de Mendoza, to record Aztec history and tribute.[10] What is important here is that an Aztec image is employed to represent a pre-Hispanic historical character and his deeds. The gloss above Herrera's figure, "Acamapichtli primero rey de Mexico," is all that is needed to establish the identity of what is represented.

If we turn to the second engraving, there are ten bust portraits in circular frames which compose the side panels (Figure 2). The figures are presented in a variety of poses, and, like the image of Acamapichtli, these are historical portraits representing the thirteen Inca kings, beginning with the dynastic founder, Manco Capac, in the top central rondel and proceeding clockwise around the frame, ending with Huascar, the last legitimate Inca king according to certain Inca factions. Each of the kings is identified by name, and each is shown wearing some form of the Inca imperial crown, the *mascaipacha,* a red woven tassel worn at the forehead. Other features, such as the shields, are more or less faithful to items worn or carried by Inca monarchs. Yet for all the iconographic correctness of these images, they are not taken from Andean representations of Inca kings, but from European-style colonial paintings depicting what Inca kings should look like. That is, Herrera took for his source a colonial painting produced in Peru but intended for a European audience. There was no Peruvian Codex Mendoza from which to derive Inca portraits even though the first Viceroy in Peru was the very same person who, as Viceroy of Mexico, commissioned several pictorial manuscripts, including possibly the Codex Mendoza.[11]

Herrera's probable source was a painting commissioned by the descendants of Inca kings, who intended to have the painting entered into court as evidence to establish their hereditary rights as recognized by Spanish law. The painting, now lost, was seen by Garcilaso de la Vega el Inca in Spain in 1603, and he describes it as being about four and one-half feet high with the portraits of the Inca kings painted from the waist up.[12] This painting, like a series of portraits sent to Philip II by the Peruvian Viceroy Francisco de Toledo in 1570, was painted by native artists. But, unlike the native artists employed in Mexico, they did not use autochthonous forms of representation.[13] Rather they used European models. And it was this colonial source, a Western mimetic kind of image produced in Peru and shipped back to Spain as a representation of the kings of Peru, that was chosen to illustrate Herrera's title page. Thus, two different types of sources are employed by Herrera: a native-style source for the Mexican images, and a European-style source for the Peruvian images.

The difference between the kinds of sources employed for Herrera's two title pages is not just a matter of chance. There was opportunity for employing Andean imagery. As early as 1553, a royal cedula sent to Peru requested that "whatever painting, tablets, or other means that there was at that time" be gathered in order to discover and record Andean history.[14] Later chroniclers, such as Sarmiento de Gamboa and Cristóbal de Molina, write that they had seen Andean paintings on wooden boards that recorded Inca history.[15] None of these authors describes what they looked like; rather they mention the information contained in the images. That is, their texts translate the content of these Andean paintings into a narrative form rather than describe the form of the images themselves.

As both the textual accounts and Herrera's title page demonstrate, Peruvian representation does not seem to have been used to represent itself or things Andean for a Spanish audience, but needed to be translated into European modes. The question is what was being translated? What made Peruvian art so different from what the Spaniards found in Mexico?

We can begin to address this issue by paying attention to the few Spaniards who were familiar with both Mexico and Peru and who described some of the differences they perceived. Agustín de Zárate, who was in Peru less than thirteen years after the Spanish arrival, notes: "que en el Peru no ay letras que conseruar la memoria de los hechos pasados ni aún en las pinturas que sirven en lugar de libros en la Nueva España, sino unas ciertas cuerdas de diversos colores añundadas."[16] The same sentiment is voiced by Cabello de Valboa, who writes that the natives of Mexico used "pinturas y dibujos" in which were "figuras" that represented the histories that the Mexicans wished to remember. He then goes on to write that "nuestros Peruleros antiguos" began using knots tied in strings of various colors, and there were experts who used these knots and colors to know and remember Inca accounts and deeds just as Spanish *escribanos* (scribes) record ours.[17] Cabello de Valboa and Zárate are describing the Andean *quipu,* a mnemonic device of knots and strings used to remember various categories of Andean knowledge, and both authors classify them along with Aztec pictorial manuscripts (Figure 3a and b). Spanish chroniclers and legal authorities acknowledged the accuracy of this Inca mode of recording information,[18] but unlike the Mexican figural images, the *quipu* as a form of representation never entered directly into the record.

Strings, knots, hundreds of meaningful colors, tactile sensitivity, non-

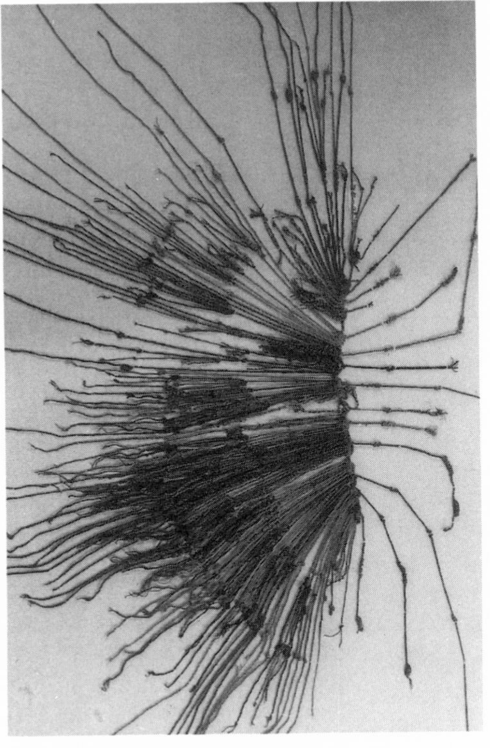

a

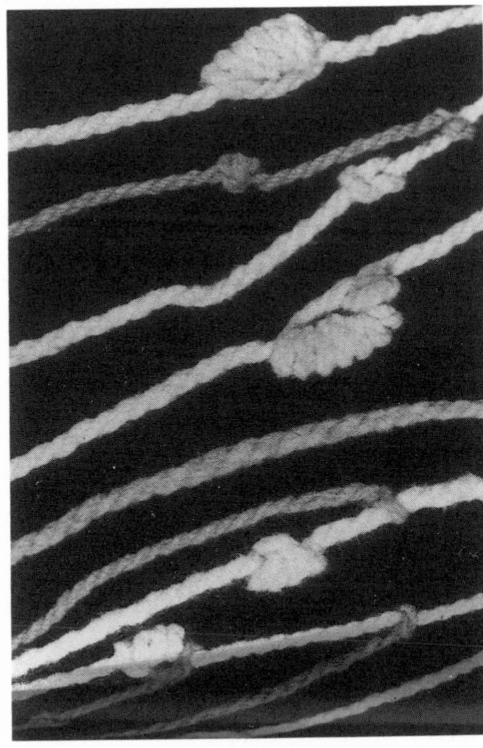

b

Figure 3. An Inca *"quipu,"* (a) and details of the knots (b). *Circa* 1500. Amano Museum, Lima.

linear recording with no surface, these are the essential elements for the composition and use of a *quipu* as a device for memory.[19] They are hardly something that one might expect to draw European Renaissance attention. However, the devices of artificial memory were extremely important to the Spaniards in the sixteenth century, especially in the New World.[20] For example, the most extensive discussion of *ars memorativa* by a Spanish-speaking author is in the six chapters dedicated to this topic in the *Rhetorica Christiana,* published in 1579 in Italy and written in Latin by Diego Valadés, a Mexican mestizo of the Franciscan order.[21] In fact, Valadés makes reference to the *quipu* as part of his evidence that Indians possessed the arts of artificial memory, but without acknowledging that it is an Inca device.[22]

The mention of colored strings is made only in passing, however, and as an example of a lesser form of native abilities, and attention is given instead to the images used by the Mexicans, the community with which Valadés was familiar. Moreover, the Mexican images conform, more or less, in form and use to those employed in the system of *ars memorativa* of classical rhetoric as mentioned by Cicero, in *De Oratore,* and fully explained in the anonymous *Rhetorica ad Herennium.* These and Quintilian are the classical authors to whom Valadés ultimately refers, and in their writings the system of artificial memory, one of the five parts of *Rhetorica,* is based upon two crucial elements, *loci* and *imagines.* The first step in the system is to imprint in the mind a series of places or *loci.* The best structure of such places is architecture. Then one is to go around the building placing in it different things, *imagines,* for example an anchor, a crown, or a sword. Each one of these things relates to a point that one wishes to remember, and as one begins a discourse one goes around the building mentally, seeing the *imagines* that have been ordered in a proscribed sequence and place.[23] This system described by Valadés was to be employed by his fellow priests to aid in teaching doctrine in the New World. What is clear is that memory as part of learning in a European sense is conditioned by mimetic images in terms of both *loci* and *imagines,* and this is what could be read into the Mexican pictorial manuscripts. The same could not be inscribed into the *quipu,* and thus, although the *quipu* is acknowledged as a device of artificial memory, it is not similar.

The incommensurability between the form of the *quipu* and European forms of memory meant that the *quipu* was not immediately the object of early campaigns of destruction as were the "books" of Mexico that were burned by Bishops Juan de Zumárraga and Diego de Landa. It is only after the threat posed by the Taqui Onkoy movement in the 1560s and the subsequent concern with Andean memory as addressed in the Third Lima Church Council (1582) that the *quipu* came under the destructive power of Spanish surveillance.[24] Aztec and Maya screenfolds, however, immediately approximated European books because they were laid out on paper or parchment and their pictorial contents were arranged in a sequential display. The fact that the Mexicans had forms similar to the book could only be explained by seeing them as products of the devil, and therefore they had to be destroyed, whereas *quipus* were not associated with the devil and thus escaped the iconoclasm of early Spanish extirpation campaigns. Yet, in the period of that destruction, copies of Mexican images were made in order to record and understand what was being destroyed or assimilated. Appropriation included retooling the *tlacuilos,* the Mexican scribes, who were placed under the direction of the missions and taught to produce new books and images for the colonial system.[25] In Peru on the other hand, *quipucamayocs,* those who made and read *quipus,* were called to present their evidence orally in law

Figure 4. Contador Maior: Tezorero Tavantin Suio Qvipoc Curaca Condos Chava. In Guaman Poma, *Nueva Corónica i Buen Gobierno,* folio 360 (362). *Circa* 1613.

Figure 5. Quiuta Calle. In *Nueva Corónica i Buen Gobierno,* folio 202. *Circa* 1613.

suits or other situations, but there is no indication that *quipucamayocs* were retrained so as to work with European forms, as Mexican *tlacuilos* had been.

Quipus had no resonance with European forms, and while they were not categorized as creations of the devil, neither could they be adapted to simulate anything directly in the Spanish colonial system. Thus, the *quipu* was transcribed into a European form simply as an illustration or as a written text. In fact, there are only eight colonial depictions of a *quipu,* seven of which are in Guaman Poma's *Nueva Corónica i Buen Gobierno.*[26]

In Guaman Poma's drawings the *quipu* is displayed by a man in order to signify his office as a *quipucamayoc* (the accountant who reads the *quipu*) (Figure 4). Guaman Poma never attempts a depiction of the *quipu* as a sign capable of signifying its content. In fact, the *quipu* is so enigmatic as a pictorial sign capable of revealing what it is that the first time the *quipu* appears in Guaman Poma's drawings it is identified by a placard displaying the Spanish word *carta* (Figure 5). The word on the placard is turned toward the viewer and held in the same hand as the *quipu. Carta* refers both to the *quipu* itself and the fact that the youth carrying the *quipu* is serving as a messenger.

What is extraordinary about this image is that most of Guaman Poma's 397 drawings depict individuals holding objects, many of which are Andean items such as *keros, chuspas,* and *chakitacllas.* These are the Quechua words for these objects, but neither these terms nor their Spanish equivalents are necessary to the identification of the objects by a

European viewer. It is clear by their familiar forms that they are a cup, a bag, and a footplow, and are thus left unglossed. The *quipu* reveals nothing about its identity by its pictorial form, so this becomes the only image by which the object is glossed, by a kind of meta-image.[27]

These images of the *quipu* and *quipucamayoc* are to be contrasted with Guaman Poma's image of the native scribe who replaces the *quipucamayoc* in the colonial period (Figure 6). Here, instead of displaying the objects of his craft in an iconic fashion, the scribe is shown engaged in the act of writing, with a legible, partially written text on the page before him. The scribe's pen is joined to the last letter so that he is literally in the act of communicating.[28]

Figure 6. Escrivano de Cabildo Nombrado de su Majestad. In Guaman Poma, *Nueva Corónica i Buen Gobierno,* folio 814. *Circa* 1613.

The *quipu* also communicated through the *quipucamayoc,* but in an oral form, and the information which it represented could be extensive, as revealed in the *Relación de la Descendencia, Gobierno y Conquista de Los Incas,* a text derived from the 1542 testimony of several *quipucamayocs,* the experts referred to by Valboa.[29] The historical information they provided was, however, translated and organized according to Spanish notions of a written narrative structure. The Andean form and organization of knowledge was thus translated into a European form. Moreover, one finds very few Quechua terms entering into the text because there are no illustrations to which there could be a visual correspondence to explain them. The element of the *quipu* to which the Quechua text agreed would have been as unintelligible to a European as the Quechua words themselves, because their relationship was not based on text/illustration—so that neither could be used to explain the other to a European. Information for a European audience therefore needed only to be given in Spanish because the two Andean forms from which this information was gathered both needed to be interpreted.[30]

Quipus are not a distinct element of Andean representation but are a part of the Andean development of weaving technology as a primary medium of expression. And although Europeans understood the value of textiles as a commodity form, they found it difficult to recognize that the structure of the textile, as in the case of a *quipu,* was as significant as the design on the surface. There is, however, at least one attempt by a Spaniard to find an equivalence rather than an illustration, although still within European forms, for the nonpictorial structure of the signification of Andean textiles, and it demonstrates how problematic cross-cultural equivalences could be. The example occurs on the last page of the Loyola Manuscript version of Murúa's *Historia del Pirú* (Figure 7). Murúa abandons on this page the European-style illustrations used throughout this and the other versions of his work.[31] Instead he presents a transcription of the structure of the weave of a *chumbi,* a belt, and the Quechua prayers that may be related to it, perhaps in the way that the *quipu*'s structure and color are related to the data it represents. Murúa first introduces the weaving pattern by indicating the importance of the object, writing: "Memoria de un famoso chumbi de lujo o cumbi que solian traer las coyas en las grandes fiestas que llamaban çara, lleba ciento y cuatro y cuatro hilos [*sic*] duplicados. Los ocho son los extremos, cuatro en un lado y cuatro en otro."

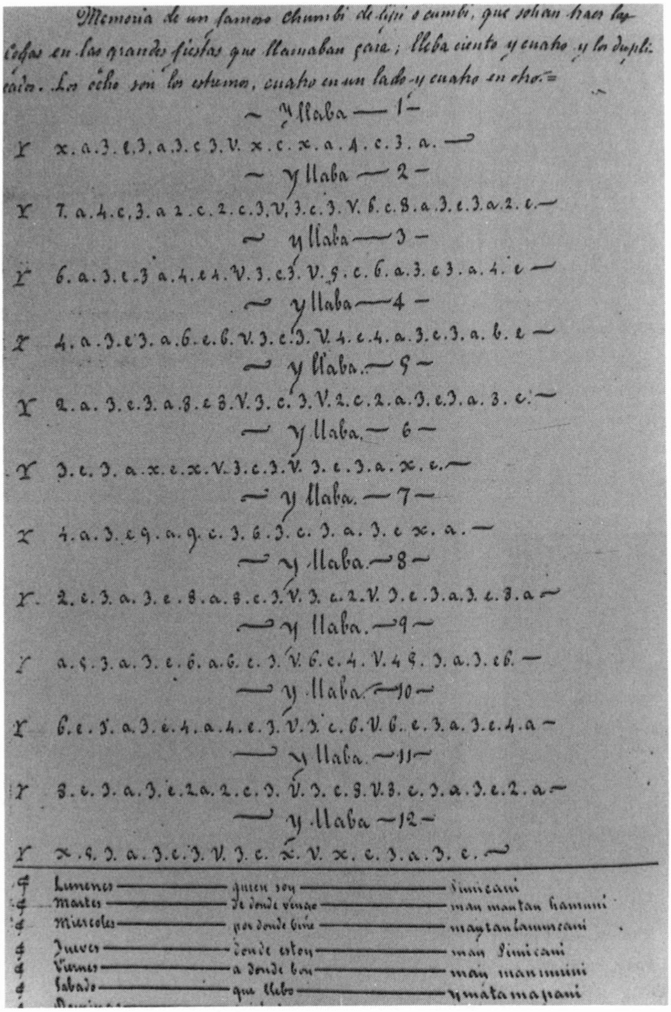

Figure 7. Last page of Martín de Murúa's *Historia General del Perú. Circa* 1590. Loyola, Spain: Archives of the Jesuits.

The textual introduction is followed by a draft of the *chumbi* weave created by a coded pattern of symbols. Below this is a linguistic pattern arranged in three vertical columns. The first column is a list of the seven days of the Western week written in Spanish. The second column is a Spanish translation of the Quechua text, which appears in the third column. How the prayers, the pattern in which they are arranged, and the weaving pattern are connected, if at all, is unclear, and it may be that an explanation was on a now lost folio. But it is significant that this is the only example in which both a Quechua text and an Andean image are decoded by a sixteenth-century Spaniard on the same page, and the arrangement and relationship of meaning is completely obscure.[32]

Murúa's page makes it clear why only the data from a *quipu* would be of any real importance to a European audience. That is, the form of evidence, the *quipu* itself, which signified through its structure as a textile, never entered directly into the Spanish account as did native forms of signification in sixteenth-century Mexico, where both native languages and pictorial forms continued to enter into official records throughout the colonial period.

Quipus were not the only way of recording information among the Inca. As mentioned there were paintings, but as I shall show, these were equally abstract, dependent upon form and color as signifying agents. Again it is important to heed the comparisons between Mexico and Peru made by sixteenth-century Spaniards. Acosta writes that Andeans made up for their lack of writing in part by "pinturas," paintings, like those of the Mexicans; however, the Peruvian paintings were by comparison very crude and rough, and in the main they used *quipus.* Acosta draws a parallel between both Mexican and Peruvian paintings and between Peruvian paintings and the *quipu.*[33] He does not, unfortunately, go on to discuss what he means by his qualitative judgment on the crude or rough nature of the Peruvian paintings. However, his pejorative assessment can be understood, if we attend to Acosta's implied relationship between these paintings and the *quipus.* What will become clear is that the images he mentions are not necessarily inferior in artistic quality; rather Andean painted images did not correspond to his received ideas of how such an image should look. In other words, the images that Acosta was describing were as abstract and intractable, as a direct source of Andean information, as the *quipus.*

The equally abstract nature of Andean paintings and *quipus* is revealed by the 1582 testimony of the mestizo Bartolomé de Porras and two unidentified native Peruvians. Responding in Cuzco to a questionnaire sent by the Viceroy Martín Enríquez, the three witnesses declared that the

Inca had a court of law formed by judges who "knew and applied the law which they understood by means of signs they had in their *quipus* which are knots of different colors and by other signs which they had on some wooden tablets painted in different colors."[34] It is clear from this testimony that Inca paintings existed, as mentioned by other chroniclers discussed above, but it is equally clear that the paintings were not images that reproduced forms corresponding to the known world; they were not mimetic. They were abstractions based on color and formal arrangement, like the *quipus,* and they revealed their content through the interpretation of informed individuals.

What constituted the difference between Mexican pictorial images and the images that appeared on the boards is revealed first by an entry in the Quechua/Spanish dictionary of 1586. The Quechua word *tocapu* is translated as a form that was woven in textiles or painted on wooden boards like those just mentioned.[35] There are no surviving Inca boards with *tocapu,* but there are a number of textiles that give a very good idea of what these forms are. *Tocapu* are abstract geometric forms composed within square or rectangular borders. Each *tocapu* is a discrete unit which, on textiles, can be placed either in a linear pattern across the waist or in a grid pattern covering the entire surface (Figure 8).

These abstract designs probably demarcated ethnic, political, and religious status when woven into textiles and worn for ceremonial occasions.[36] However, it is apparent that *tocapu* were painted onto wooden boards like the ones used by the Inca judges, or they were used to record Inca history, as suggested by Sarmiento and Molina, or these images could communicate other forms of information. The only equivalence that any Spaniard offers for the form of a *tocapu* comes again from Martín de Murúa, who, as already indicated, seems to have understood the degree to which Andean representation stood outside European norms. To explain *tocapu* to his Spanish readers, he appeals to their familiarity with a more approximate "other" to offer an analogy: the most recently expelled Moors. Writing about the designs of Inca textiles he states: "esculpin en ellos marabillosas labores de tocapu que ellos dizen que significa dibersidad de labores con mil matices de subtil manera, al modo de los almaisares Moriscos. . . ."[37]

Murúa's comparison does not reveal much about the *tocapu* except that its abstraction can only be assimilated by its equation with another, more familiar "other." But unlike the Andeans, the Moors had writing as well as pictorial representation outside of Islamic prohibitions, so that the comparison ends here. Moreover, Murúa's reference is not descriptive. It does not reveal what these Andean forms would have looked like

Figure 8. Tunic with *tocapu* design covering entire front and back. *Circa* 1500. Dumbarton Oaks, Washington, D.C.

if they had been presented as an image of Andeans to a European audience instead of the familiar European conventions, such as the portrait forms used by Herrera.

One of the very few Andeans who availed himself of the European form of writing gives us the answer to this hypothetical question and reveals how strained and awkward the use of such imagery would be. This is Juan de Santa Cruz Pachacuti Yamqui's drawing of the three caves of Inca origin at Pacaritambo from which emerged the Inca dynastic founder Manco Capac (Figure 9). Pachacuti produced his work in the southern highlands in 1613, and it is the only manuscript that employs an unmediated form of Andean imagery as a source for a manuscript illustration.[38]

The drawing is abstract in form and metaphoric in meaning. The principal cave, Tambotoco, is in the center of the composition. It is represented by a geometric design of three concentric rectangles, in the center of which is an off-axis rectangle that contains a fifth rectangle that parallels the outer three. The two other caves are placed below and to either side of Tambotoco and they are also represented by concentric rectangles, differentiated by the spacing of the lines. The left one represents Marastoco and the right one represents Sutitoco.

These right and left images represent not only caves but also Manco Capac's paternal and maternal great aunts and uncles. Manco's parents, Apotambo and Pacchamamchi, are placed to either side of the central image and are depicted as trees with their roots revealed. Pachacuti Yamqui notes that one tree is gold and the other is silver. If we are to believe Juan de Betanzos, one of the earliest and more reliable chroniclers, the Inca did place a gold and silver tree on either of the caves at Pacaritambo, so it might be suggested that Pachacuti's drawing is a landscape based upon observation, that is, a mimetic representation.[39] But aside from the recognizable form of the trees, the understanding of the image is derived not from mimicry but from the formal organization of the discrete elements. The organization is strictly based on a two-dimensional design. Each shape is stabilized in the space of the page through its relationship to the others. The pattern of the design is what gives the image the coherency of a composition. Thus the absence of a ground, necessary in European landscapes, is disregarded here. We can see this simply by comparing Pachacuti's image of Tambotoco with that of Guaman Poma, where all the European compositional techniques are brought into play so as to suggest place, space, time, and event (Figure 10). Order in Guaman Poma's drawing is used to create a pictorial narrative of ritual in which the representation of the caves specifies the action.

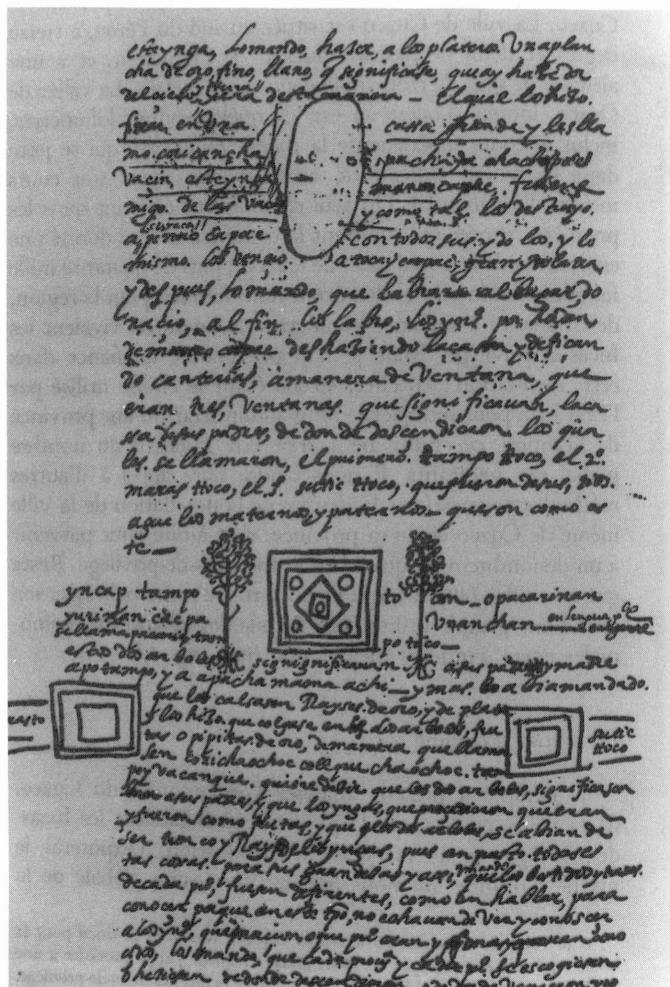

Figure 9. Caves of Pacaritambo. In Joan de Santa Cruz Pachacuti Yamqui Salcamaygua, *Relación de antigüedades del Pirú. Circa* 1613.

Pachacuti's use of non-Western conventions to create the image, on the other hand, indicates part of the overall Andean concept of representation, which is based on geometric abstraction. When a recognizable form is introduced, the image is intended for the viewer to think less about the object in nature that the form imitates and more about the metaphoric associations that the image has within Andean culture, in relation both to the overall composition and to the type of object on which the image is placed. Here, it is clear that Pachacuti's use of trees to de-

Figure 10. De Los Idolos Ingas/ Inti, Vana, Cauri, Tanbo Toco/ Uana Cauri/tanbo Toco/Pacari Tanbo/en el Cuzco. In Guaman Poma, *Nueva Corónica i Buen Gobierno,* folio 264 (266). *Circa* 1613.

pict Manco's progenitors is metaphoric and depends upon the meaning of the Quechua word *mallki,* which means both a plant with its roots and the body of a venerated ancestor.[40] The abstract images of the cave are *tocapu* and are similar to those found on Inca textiles and the incised designs on *keros* (wooden drinking vessels). They denote in Pachacuti's drawing both geographic place and paternal and maternal descent.

Each of these "pictorial" elements is, however, only a symbol of general concepts, so that the composition does not signify by itself. It is dependent upon informed interpretation. In pre-Hispanic Peru this would have been provided by those whom Sarmiento de Gamboa called "learned men."[41] In this case, however, the image appears within a Western written format, which means that, like the text, the images are potentially independent of an oral interpreter. This concept of the Western use of imagery in relation to printed text was clearly understood by Guaman Poma. His drawings are separated from and precede the text to which they are related, sometimes in a contradictory fashion.[42] Here, however, the immediate and inexorable relation between Andean symbolic image and oral interpretation is nonetheless demonstrated by Pachacuti's rendering of words and image as a single compositional unit. That is, Pachacuti does not explain the image in the main body of his text nor does the image appear on a separate page as an illustration. Rather, he physically interrupts his written narrative by placing the image between two paragraphs, with the identifying words and explanatory texts next to the images. Written words are not a gloss as they are in Mexican manuscripts. They are conceptually an equal part of the signifying unity, and it is as if Pachacuti were orally relating this history and had brought out the image as a mnemonic aid.

If one looks at this Andean representation of the progenitors of the Inca dynastic founder Manco Capac and then at the image of Manco Capac as presented to a European audience in Herrera's title page (Figure 2), we can see the kind of transformation in the representation of things Andean that took place in Peru during the sixteenth and early seventeenth centuries. Herrera's frontispiece represents the official sphere of colonial culture; the world in which Spaniards, mestizos, and the most acculturated natives operated. It in no way conforms with the indigenous Peruvian artistic system, as represented by Pachacuti's drawing, which worked in concert with Andean oral forms. Rather the engraving and its source conform to an artistic system that is founded on illustration, and it is this system that was assimilated by acculturated Andean artists. Thus we find portraits and paintings like Herrera's frontispiece, in which Andean cultural objects such as headdresses, textiles, and even *tocapu* designs are part of an iconographic ensemble that denotes Andeanness in the same way that a halo denotes sacredness in colonial Christian paintings. Andean items of symbolic importance become illustrations of things Andean rather than direct conveyances of knowledge within an Andean system of reference. That is, both Andean objects and images such as *tocapu* lost their primary Andean signifying function and became iconographic elements within a European system of symbolic representation. Andean representation could not be reduced to an equivalence in the same manner that it could be in New Spain.

The kinds of paintings just described are a form of acculturation that is to be expected in imagery created for the colonial elite, and it occurred in both Mexico and Peru. Paintings were produced according to European standards, and native artists, representing Andeans or Mexicans who were almost always aristocrats, learned to control these conventions. But the difference is that whereas in New Spain both native languages and forms of representation did find a place in official, legal, Viceroyal culture,[43] they did not in Peru. And what can be argued is that in Peru native forms of representation were sustained only at a different level. But at the same time, the intransigence of the Europeans, which bordered on complete denial, toward Andean representation meant that Andean representation, where it did occur, did not go unaffected. Just as native Mexican imagery ultimately was transformed within the official documents of maps and genealogies, there was a shift in imagery on traditional Peruvian objects that persisted throughout the colonial period—*keros* (Figure 11) and textiles (Figure 12)—and this shift represented not only a change in the form of Andean expression but also a subtle shift in the symbolic content of the objects themselves.

Keros (ritual drinking vessels) and textiles were extremely important symbolic objects among all Andean people, and most especially among the Inca. And whereas they are described by Spaniards as unrelated items of Inca production, *keros* and textiles were conceptually regarded by the Inca as objects to be given together as a single gift. This Inca custom is confirmed by Inca and non-Inca sources throughout the empire. The point is that textiles and *keros,* at one level of Andean understanding, were regarded as a set of symbolic objects each referring to the other and together expressing the significance of the Inca gift. Of course, each object had a symbolic function according to its utilitarian function: *keros,* for example, were used in Andean rituals as drinking vessels in such a way as to express a number of social and political concepts. But what needs to be stressed here is how these two types of objects, *keros* and textiles, could be used together to recall, through their symbolic relationship to each other, notions of Inca historical deeds. At this level, *keros* and textiles served the same mnemonic function as described for Pachacuti's drawing. By first describing this pre-Hispanic symbolic relationship we can then see how the imagery painted on colonial *keros* represents a shift away from the Andean system of representation to a more Europeanized system.

Figure 11. Inca *kero. Circa* 1500. Museum für Völkerkunde, Berlin, VA 10456.

Figure 12. Inca military tunic (*Uncu*). *Circa* 1500. Munich. Staatliches Museum für Völkerkunde.

Keros and textiles were offered as gifts on a number of occasions, but the occasion described in the greatest variety of written sources is the presentation of these items to the leaders of local areas once they had accepted Inca rule. At the same time, a similar set of gifts was presented to the captains from the allied nations who aided in the conquest.[44] Both gifts represented a symbolic gesture of alliance according to Andean forms of reciprocity.[45] However, the significance of the gifts continued after their initial presentation, so that when they were later brought out for ritual display they conjured up the deeds that had originally prompted the gifts. This process is described in Cristóbal de Albornoz's treatise on the extirpation of idolatry, written shortly before 1580.[46] He cautions fellow priests to be on guard against dances in which certain *keros* and textiles are used because the natives worship these objects, as they remind them of past military feats. Albornoz describes the *keros* as being decorated with figures and the textiles as having a chess-board design. The chess-board design refers to the Inca military tunic, as described by many chroniclers (Figure 12). The description of *kero* figures is vague, but there are *keros* that have designs that also implied conquest and military feats (Figure 11).

What is significant is that these objects were brought out together in later ceremonies and that their physical presence and their designs were capable of suggesting a specific type of Inca "historical" event. However, the *keros* and textiles, in relation to their decorative designs, could only convey the type of event in general so that, like the abstract designs used by Pachacuti to represent the place of Inca dynastic origins, the specific content, in this case specific Inca triumphs, was conveyed by the songs and dances that were performed at the time of their appearance. The association between the *keros* and the textiles as elements of a single gift offered by the Inca to commemorate certain events means that the objects acted together as mnemonic forms and that their designs recalled types of events.

In the context described above, *keros* and textiles formed a single signifying unit and the information they conveyed united the past with the present as an undifferentiated part of time. The forms, designs, and physicality of *keros* and textiles therefore had a quasi-linguistic function because their presence made them eyewitnesses to an ancient event and perhaps permitted the accompanying texts to be sung in the eyewitness tense rather than the Quechua reportive verb form "*sqa,*" which is used for any real or supposed action that has occurred in the past in which the speaker has not had direct participation.[47] The objects were things in and of themselves that served as unmediated connections between the past and the present. Albornoz's text is, however, significant beyond the ethnographic information it provides because its purpose was to guide other Spanish priests in destroying not only the objects but the contexts in which they signified. The intent of Spanish acculturation was to rupture the nexus between the objects, their designs, and the cultural arena in which they operated. The signifying unity in Andean art between context, object, and design was, by the late sixteenth century, under siege through the process of acculturation.

To resist this erosion in the seventeenth and eighteenth centuries meant that native artists manufacturing traditional textiles and *keros* could not rely solely on the expressive context as outlined above. Instead, as this context became more obscured as a result of European intervention, the associations and conceptual categories through which these traditional objects signified now had to be made more explicit. They had to be represented.

We can see this first in the pictorializing of the symbolic relationship between *keros* and textiles. Much of the ritual context of Inca presentation that united these objects was absent, so that the bond between them needed to be visualized. Thus, the abstract *tocapu* designs used for one of the objects, textiles (Figure 13), now were placed on the other, *keros* (Figure 14). Moreover, the placement of the textile design on the *kero* corresponded to the location of the same motif on the textile; that is, at the waist. In this sense the design on the *kero,* while still *tocapu,* does not have the same function as in a pre-Hispanic context. It is not abstract mnemonic imagery meant to be used with oral literature; rather it is iconographic imagery meant by its mimetic representation to reproduce the same design on textiles in order to call attention to the *kero*'s traditional symbolic relation to textiles.[48] In pre-Hispanic times this kind of visual reference was unnecessary and *kero* and textile designs are rarely alike. Thus there is no linguistic evidence of this kind of *kero* design in sixteenth-century sources. It is only in seventeenth-century dictionaries that terms for this kind of *kero* decoration appear. The names for these painted *keros, chumpi kero* in Quechua and *huaskaja kero* in Aymara, are newly coined terms, and they express the visual relation between *keros* and textiles needed in order to retain their traditional associations. *Chumpi* and *huakasaja* are textile terms originally referring to either the woven design or the sash designs that appeared on textiles but which now are applied to *kero* designs.[49] Thus, although operating for a different audience, the abstract *tocapu* designs become iconographic elements like those features found in Herrera's portraits because they are used to illustrate things Andean rather than directly to convey Andean concepts within a traditional artistic system.[50]

Figure 13. Inca textile with *chumpi* band. Private collection.

If we look at the scenes in the upper register of the *kero,* we can see an even more emphatic declaration of these traditional associations (Figure 14). Here the European representational system is fully employed, with figures arranged in narrative compositions depicting rituals in which *keros* and textiles were used together. All the contextual elements of the pre-Hispanic signifying system—textiles, *keros,* and rituals—are now illustrated. They are composed of iconographic elements that represent the Andean symbolic system rather than being signifiers within such a system, as described for Pachacuti's drawing and Inca traditional textiles and *keros.*

The *kero* itself has been transfigured from being a discrete Andean symbolic object operating within a purely Andean context to being an object that bears the representation of its meaning. The *kero* can no longer directly conjure up the Andean sense of "historical" remembrance, because that remembrance was not now directly part of present experience. Inca, or, better said, pre-Hispanic, past was a memory medi-

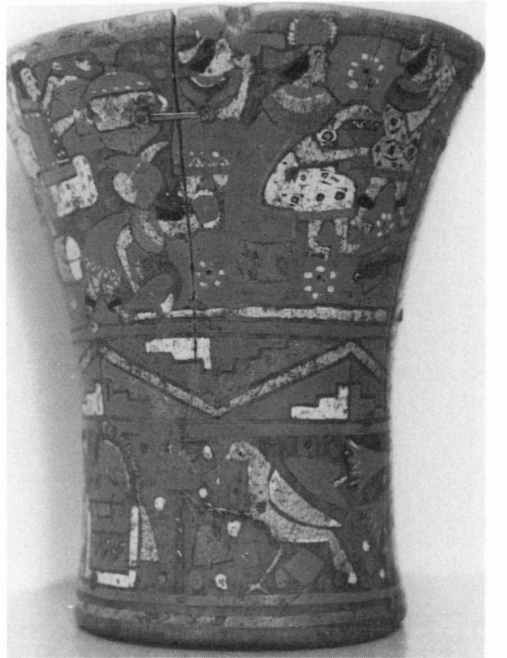

a

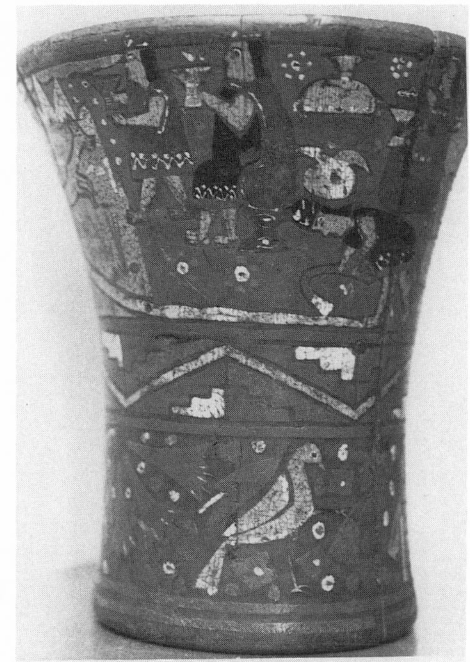

b

c

Figure 14. **(a, b) Photographs of a *kero;* (c) line drawing of the upper register of a *kero. Circa* 1700. Museum für Völkeskunde, Berlin, 63959 (a, b), and Musea de Arqueología, Cuzco (c).**

ated by the experience of conquest and colonial cultural repression. The past was no longer real in the sense that traditions were uninterrupted; rather the past was an ideal, something to go back to in order to escape the present. *Keros* and textiles therefore refer to that imagined past in their imagery.

But the imagery itself signifies the impossibility of such a return because the signifying system is European. It is narrative and the narrative frame of reference is allegory, a category of meaning nonexistent in pre-Hispanic art. That is, these scenes, in which only archaic, pre-Hispanic figures operate, are a response to the sense of estrangement from tradition. They at once acknowledge the remoteness of the past and a desire to redeem it for the present. As allegory, the pictorial scenes are one text through which another can be read.[51] In this case, in the Andean case, the text is messianic. It is the return of the Inca and the restitution of native autonomy, a desire to which the scene shown here ultimately refers in the form of the colonial myth *Incari,* a myth that is still held in the areas around Cuzco and which posits the return of the Inca.[52] Thus the past that is signified through a European system, the artistic form of acculturation, conveys an entirely different sense of the past; the past now is painted as a form of resistance to the present.

Finally, if we return to Herrera's two engravings I think we can see what the differences between the kinds of sources chosen for them meant in terms of colonial art in Peru and Mexico. Almost from the beginning in Mexico there was a much greater form of synchronization between Native and European art. This meant, among other things, that certain Native pictorial forms such as maps and genealogies entered into official colonial culture. This did not happen in Peru. There the artistic system was so vastly different that there was an almost complete loss of Andean forms in official colonial culture. This meant that Andeans were required to adopt European means of representation, almost right from the beginning, to portray themselves to a European audience as indicated by Herrera's engraving. This irreconcilable difference meant that in the late seventeenth and eighteenth centuries, when the pre-Hispanic past became of interest in both New Spain and Peru in the quest for identity, Mexican creoles could turn to the real thing.[53]

But in Peru the terms were different. In fact, the constructed image of the sixteenth century became what was believed to be the authentic image; that is, the engraving for the "Decada Quinta" became the real thing when a 1726 reprint became the source for a series of eighteenth-century Peruvian oil portraits of the Inca kings. But even as Andeans came to represent themselves or see themselves represented in an alien form, they were able to reinterpret this European system by applying it to traditional objects, most especially in the eighteenth century, and thereby to create an alternative to the official art of colonial Peru.

Notes

1 See, for example, George Kubler's often cited essay (1964).

2 Donald Robertson 1976.

3 See, for example, Stephen Greenblatt 1991: 150–151.

4 Herrera's *Historia general de los hechos* is not just one of the many chronicles describing the conquest of the Americas. Antonio de Herrera y Tordesillas was named Major Chronicler of the Indies of the Royal and Supreme Council of the Indies in 1596 and Chronicler of Castile in 1598, and his *Historia general de los hechos* was published in Madrid by the Emprenta Real. Although he never traveled to the Americas, he had access, as the official chronicler, to the vast documentation that had been accumulated by royal officials. His work is the first systematic history of the conquest and settlement of America by Spain up to 1554 (Manuel Ballesteros Gaibrios 1973).

5 Texts written in Quechua are extremely few, and almost all surviving sixteenth and seventeenth-century examples are either grammars, dictionaries, Catholic religious texts, or isolated Inca prayers incorporated into chronicles written in Spanish; see P. Rivet and G de Créqui-Monfort 1951. There are only two known fragments of notarial records written in Quechua, which are cited by Bruce Mannheim (1991:143–144). He suggests that the lack of notarial records in Quechua in comparison to the long of run of Nahuatl records in Mexico is possibly due to the strict enforcement by Viceroy Toledo of a (1576) royal decree forbidding mestizos from occupying the office of notary. Aside from the fact that many laws enforced or promulgated by Toledo were to no lasting effect and that the law refers to mestizos and not natives, even if this law were enforced throughout the colonial period, this does not explain the extreme paucity of other forms of autochthonous Quechua writings and images of any kind including, most especially, maps. Moreover in the only known representation of a native Peruvian scribe, he is shown writing in Spanish, not Quechua; see Guaman Poma de Ayala 1980: folio 814 (828) (Figure 6).

6 There are at least 418 examples of colonial Mexican illustrated manuscripts or documents; see John B. Glass 1975. Not only were there many more illustrated manuscripts and legal documents produced in Mexico, but many of them were produced to be used in Nueva España, while the two illustrated manuscripts from Peru, the Andean Guaman Poma de Ayala's *Nueva Corónica i buen Gobierno* and the Spaniard Martín de Murúa's *Historia General de Peru,* these were produced for European consumption and were sent to Spain.

7 The "encounter" between Europe and the New World is too often seen as a single event in which the only variable is the European. Thus, the "encounter"

with Mexico is often taken as an inclusive paradigm through which the conquest of America can be measured. For example, in T. Todorov's extremely influential study, Mexico and the Aztec come to stand for all the Americas and its collective defeats because Todorov (1982: 121) suggests that it is the difference between the technologies of symbolism—writing versus orality, ritual versus improvised action—which led to the defeat of the Aztec and, by extension, the Inca and all others. Essentially, the possession of a superior representational technology, the ability to write and, by extension, the Renaissance perspective, enabled the Europeans accurately to describe for themselves the "other" in order to improvise their actions in a war of complete assimilation. The difference between the colonial representations of the Aztec and the Inca is as much about the inflexibility of European Renaissance discourse(s), as provided through its various modes of representation, as it is about the differences between these two cultures. In short, Todorov could not have written his book as he has if he had taken Peru, or for that matter the Maya, as his paradigm.

8 E. Boone 1983: 3–6, 45–53.

9 The great attention that sixteenth-century Spaniards paid to Aztec culture and iconographic conventions has had a profound affect on Aztec studies in particular and on Mesoamerican studies in general in the twentieth century. Aside from iconographic studies of specific monuments, especially in the Maya and Aztec fields, an increasing number of Mesoamerican studies have centered on the relation of text and image using colonial texts, newly deciphered hieroglyphs, and pictorial images; see for example, Janet Berlo 1983.

10 H. B. Nicholson 1992: 1–11.

11 Certainly it would have been difficult for Antonio de Mendoza to accomplish in Peru what he had done in New Spain. He was old (seventy) and infirm when he arrived in Peru, which was then embroiled in internal strife, and he died within two years of his arrival. Nonetheless, it is significant that no succeeding viceroy of Peru, including Mendoza's nephew, who had arrived in the first viceroy's retinue from New Spain, had a pictorial manuscript produced as had been done in New Spain. Rather, the first official Inca history, as generated through the viceregal structure of power, based directly on native sources, is Juan de Betanzos's written narrative *Suma y narración de los Incas,* which was produced for the viceroy Hurtado de Mendoza in 1551.

12 Garcilaso de la Vega 1960; see also Enrique Marco Dorta 1975: 67–78.

13 At the same time that the artistic image of the Inca was being constructed according to European conventions, Inca imperial mythology was also being reconfigured in colonial historical accounts according to European standards. Both changes were engendered by the political and cultural policies of Viceroy Toledo in the 1570s, and the first set of Inca portraits were made to accompany Toledo's commissioned history of the Inca. The reconfigured Inca mythohistory and the constructed Inca portraits were used to further both acculturated indigenous and

Spanish colonial agendas; for the "rewriting" of Inca mythohistory see Gary Urton 1990.

14 "Y demas de la información que hubiéredes de los testigos haries traer ante vosotros cualesquier pinturas ó tablas ó otra cuenta que haya de aquel tiempo por do se pueda averiguar lo que está dicho" (Fernando de Santillán 1950 [1563]: 38).

15 Sarmiento de Gamboa 1988 (1572): 49. Molina's exact phrase "la vida de cada uno de los yngas y de las tierras que conquistó pintado por sus figuras en unas tablas y orígen que tuvieron" implies that figures were used; however, he gives no indication of their form (Cristóbal de Molina 1916 [1573]: 4).

16 Agustín de Zárate 1555: 10.

17 Miguel Cabello de Valboa 1951 (1586): 239.

18 For the accuracy of the information presented by a *quipu* within a colonial context, see John Murra 1975a: 243–254.

19 The best description of the *quipu*'s functional and aesthetic attributes is found in M. Ascher and R. Ascher 1981; see also L. Locke 1923.

20 See René Taylor 1987: 45–76.

21 Ibid., 47.

22 "Sic nostri (licet alioqui crassi et inculti videantur) veluti polygraphia quadam utentes variis modis arcana sua absque literis, sed signis et figuris mandabant. Succedebant interdum in locum eiusmodi characterum, fila, diversis coloribus pro qualitate nuncii ipsius tincta" (Valadés 1579: 94). Valadés had no personal experience in Peru and had never seen a *quipu;* however, he was familiar with writings and images referring to Peru, such as G. Benzoni's *La Historia del Nuevo Mundo* (1565).

23 René Taylor 1987: 48–52.

24 "Y porque en lugar de libros los indios han usado y usan unos como registros hechos de diferentes hilos que ellos llaman quipos, y con estos conservan la memoria de su antigua supersitción y ritos y ceremonias y costumbres perversas, procuren con dilegencia los obispos que todos los memoriales o quipos que sirven para su superstición se les quiten totalmente a los indios" (*Tercer Concilio* [1584] 1982: 103). As Pierre Duviols (1977: 305) notes, *quipus* up until this point were used in learning catechism and prayers, and as objects they occupied an ambiguous place between licit and illicit things. This ambiguity continued well past the decree of the Third Lima Council. For example, there is evidence of the occasional destruction of *quipus* as recorded by Diego d'Avalos in 1602 (cited in Locke 1923: 105), who mentions the burning of a *quipu* in Jauja that recorded all that had happened in the valley since the arrival of the Spaniards in anticipation of the account that would have to be rendered to the Inca upon his return. But this account stands out by its singularity, and *quipus* continued to be used for confessional practices into the seventeenth century, as evidenced by Bocanegra's remarks on why they should not be allowed.

25 The use of native Mexican artists to produce colonial images is discussed in J. Peterson 1988: 273–294. Valadés has two different prints in which these new images are used for native instruction (1579: 211 and 207 [*sic*]).

26 The eighth is in Murúa 1613: folio 51v.

27 By meta-image is meant the fact that the reference of the placard and the word "carta" are internal and refer to what the image is supposed to convey. Moreover, the placard does not carry a text but a nomitive word referring to what the placard is, which in turn refers to the *quipu* and the young man's actions. Guaman Poma does not resort to using European objects to explain Andean objects in any other of his drawings about Andean society before the conquest. Moreover, in images about colonial writing he does not need internal references to explain what it is. If text appears, it is not a reference to the act in general but is specific to what the actor is actually writing. For example, in the drawing of a native colonial scribe seated at a table, he is depicted in the act of writing a will with the first part written out and legible up to the point that the viewer intrudes upon the act (Guaman Poma de Ayala 1981: folio 814 [828] see also R. Adorno 1981: 56–60, 64–65).

28 This is a remarkable image in that the line of the written word is continuous and becomes the outline of the pictorial image, so that the two acts in which Guaman Poma as an author and an illustrator is himself engaged are unified. In a sense, this is a reflective image about the ambiguity that Guaman Poma holds for the distinction between writing and drawing (Tom Cummins 1992: 46–60).

29 Cristóbal Vaca de Castro 1974 (1542–1544).

30 The most extensive explanation of how the *quipu* was manipulated to record historical events is not provided until the mid-seventeenth century by Antonio de la Calancha (1974–1981: 206–209).

31 According to Guaman Poma, Murúa knew about Andean textiles intimately. Although he does not present the acquisition of this knowledge as anything more than part of Murúa's maltreatment of Andeans, he writes: "Este dicho Morúa fue comendador del pueblo de Yanaca de la prouincia de los Aymarays el qual destruyyó grandemente, a los yndios con el mal y daño y trauajos ajuntar los solteras, hilar texer y hazer cunbi y ausca . . ." (Folio 684 [662]). The drawing preceding this text shows Murúa standing behind an old man and making him weave.

32 The intent of Murúa's attempt is inexplicable, at least to modern scholars, both historians and weavers. The editor of the published version added in a footnote to the page: "Estos dos fragmentos terminan el libro de Murúa, como pegadizos. Declaro que no enténderlos" (Martín de Murúa 1946 [1611]: 431). Sophie Desrosiers (1986: 219–241) simply dismisses the third part of the page with Quechua and Spanish texts because it "does not make any mention of textiles."

33 José de Acosta 1940 (1590): 102.

34 "No podían arbitrar, sino en cuanto a juzgar, juzgaban por las leyes que ellos tenían, las cuales entendían por unas señales que tenían en quipos que son nudos de diferentes colores, y por otras señales que tenían en una tabla de diferentes colores por donde entendían la pena que cada delincuente tenía" (Bartolomé de Porras 1904 [1582]: 197).

35 "Tocapu—labrar en lo que se borsla o texe o en vasos, tablas, etc." (Anonymous 1951 [1586]: 84).

36 For a discussion of some *tocapu* motifs, see R. Tom Zuidema 1991: 151–202.

37 Murúa 1613: Folio 205. Murúa's mention of the *"almaizares"* is not the first occasion that this object was used to categorize difference as it was observed by Europeans. Columbus, on his third voyage, wrote of the natives of Trinidad that "they had their heads wrapped in scarves of cotton, worked elaborately and in colors which I believe were *"almaizares"* (cited in Greenblatt [1991: 86]).

38 Joan de Santa Cruz Pachacuti Yamqui 1950 (1613): 207–281. The survival of this manuscript along with the only Andean mythology written in Quechua reveal how rare these colonial forms of Andean expression are. They both were collected and kept with the papers of Francisco de Avila, a perhaps mestizo Jesuit, who was an active member in the campaign of extirpation in the early seventeenth century. Both manuscripts are bound together in Seville with other manuscripts collected by Avila to aid him in his investigations. Without the material collected by Avila and the manuscript of Guaman Poma, twentieth-century knowledge about early colonial native expression in Peru would be considerably different. Mexican scholarship is not so dependent on serendipity.

39 Juan de Betanzos 1987 (1551): 288. The relative reliability of Betanzos is based on his knowledge of Quechua and his marriage into one of the ruling families of the Inca only a decade after the conquest.

40 Jeanette Sherbondy 1986; Regina Harrison 1989: 65.

41 Sarmiento (1988: 49) says that the Inca, Pachacuti, "constituyo doctores que supiesen entenderlas y declararlas."

42 Rolena Adorno 1986: 84.

43 See, for example, James Lockhart 1991.

44 For example, Fernando de Santillán 1950: 49.

45 John Murra 1975b: 145–70.

46 Cristóbal de Albornoz 1967: 22.

47 This verb form is used in Spanish by native writers like Pachacuti Yamqui (1950), and one can see how the form changes when he uses images. He translates this voice as "dicen que," followed by the past tense in his telling of historical deeds. When, however, his text begins to wrap around the image of the caves, he becomes absolutely assertive and changes to the present tense as the images are introduced. Thus Pachacuti writes "eran tres ventanas [cuevas] que significauan

la cassa de sus (Manco Capac) padres, de donde descendieron los quales se llamaron, el primero Tampottoco; el segundo Marasttoco; el tercero Suticttoco, que fueron de sus tios, aguelos maternos y paternos, que *son* como este" (my italics). At this point the text breaks off and the drawing begins.

48 There is at least one colonial textile in which the process is reversed and the abstract *tocapu* band at the waist is replaced by a pair of repeated figures of an Andean male and female, with the female offering a pair of *keros* to the male.

49 Diego González de Holquín 1952 (1608): 304; Ludovico Bertonio 1879 (1612): 290; see also John Rowe 1961: 317–341.

50 There is an odd corollary to the transposition of the *chumpi* band from the textile to the *kero,* in that it is a *chumpi* design that is drafted on the last page of Murúa's Loyola Ms. discussed earlier (Figure 7).

51 Craig Owens 1980.

52 Tom Cummins n.d.

53 The collections of Carlos de Sigüenza y Góngora in the seventeenth century and Lorenzo Boturini Benaduci in the eighteenth century are the most prominent examples of early colonial Mexican manuscripts gathered by *criollos.*

References

Acosta, José de. 1940 (1590). *Historia natural y moral de los Indias.* México.

Adorno, Rolena. 1981. "On Pictorial Language and the Typology of Culture in a New World Chronicle." *Semiotica* 36, nos. 1–2: 51–106.

Adorno, Rolena. 1986. *Guaman Poma Writing as Resistance in Colonial Peru.* Austin: University of Texas Press.

Albornoz, Cristóbal de. 1967 (c. 1580). Instrucción para descubrir todas las huacas del Pirú y sus camayos y haciendas. *Journal de la Société des Américanistes* (Paris) 56: 17–39.

Anonymous. 1951 (1586). *Vocabulario y phrasis en la lengua General de los indios del Perú llamada Quichua, y en la lengua española.* Ed. Antonio Ricardo. Lima.

Ascher, Marcia, and R. Ascher. 1991. *Code of the Quipu.* Ann Arbor: University of Michigan Press.

Ballesteros Gaibrios, Manuel. 1973. Antonio de Herrera, 1549–1625. In *Handbook of Middle American Indians,* ed. H. Cline, 13: 241–255. Austin: University of Texas Press.

Benzoni, Girolamo. 1565. *La Historia del Nuevo Mundo.* Venice.

Bertonio, Ludovico. 1879 (1612). *Vocabulario de la Lengua aymara.* Leipzig.

Betanzos, Juan de. 1987 (1551). *Suma y Narración de los Incas.* Madrid.

Boone, Elizabeth. 1983. *The Codex Magliabechiano and the Lost Prototype of the Magliabechiano Group.* Los Angeles: University of California Press.

Cabello de Valboa, Miguel. 1951 (1586). *Miscelánia Antártica.* Lima.

Calancha, Antonio de la. 1974–1981 (1638). *Crónica Moralizada del Orden de San Augustín en el Perú.* Lima.

Cummins, Tom. 1988. Abstraction to Narration: Kero Imagery of Peru and the Colonial Alteration of Native Identity. Unpublished Ph.D. diss., UCLA.

———. 1992. The Uncomfortable Image: Words and Drawings in Guaman Poma's *Nueva Corónica i buen Gobierno.* In *Guaman Poma de Ayala: The Colonial Art of an Andean Author.* New York: Americas Society.

Desrosiers, Sophie. 1986. An Interpretation of Technical Weaving Data Found in an Early 17th Century Chronicle. In *The Junius B. Bird Conference on Andean Textiles,* ed. Ann Pollard Rowe. Washington, D.C.

Duviols, Pierre. 1977 (1971). *La Destrucción de las Religiones Andinas.* Trans. A. Maruenda. Mexico D.F.: Universidad Nacional Autónoma de México.

Garcilaso de la Vega. 1960 (1609). *Comentarios Reales,* vols. 134–135. Madrid: Biblioteca de Autores Españoles.

Glass, John. 1975. A Survey of Native Middle American Pictorial Manuscripts. In vol. 14 of *Handbook of Middle American Indians,* ed. Robert Wauchope, 3–80. Austin: University of Texas Press.

González de Holquín, Diego. 1952 (1608). *Vocabulario de la Lengua general de Todo Perú llamada Qquichua o del Inca.* Lima: Imprenta Santa Maria.

Greenblatt, Stephen. 1991. *Marvelous Possessions: The Wonder of the New World.* Chicago: University of Chicago Press.

Guaman Poma de Ayala, Felipe. 1981 (c. 1615). *El primer nueva corónica i buen gobierno.* Ed. John Murra and Rolena Adorno. Mexico: Siglo XXI.

Harrison, Regina. 1989. *Signs, Songs and Memory in the Andes.* Austin: University of Texas Press.

Herrera y Tordesillas, Antonio de. 1601–1615. *Historia general de los hechos de los castellanos en las islas y Tierra Firme del Mar Océano.* Madrid: Imprenta Real.

Kubler, George. 1964. On the Colonial Extinction of the Motifs of Pre-Columbian Art. In *Essays in Pre-Columbian Art and Archaeology,* ed. S. Lothrop et al., 14–34. Cambridge: Harvard University Press.

Locke, L. Leland. 1923. *The Ancient Quipu.* New York: The American Museum of Natural History.

Lockhart, James. 1991. *Nahuas and Spaniards, Post Conquest Central Mexican History and Philology.* Stanford: Stanford University Press.

Mannheim, Bruce. 1991. *The Language of the Inka since the European Invasion.* Austin: University of Texas Press.

Marco Dorta, Enrique. 1975. Las Pinturas que envio y trajo a España don Francisco de Toledo. *Historia y Cultura* 9.

Molina, Cristóbal de. 1916 (c. 1575). *Relación de los fabulas y ritos de los Incas.* Colección de Libros y Documentos Referentes a la Historia a la Historia del Perú, 1st ser. 1.

Murra, John. 1975a. Las etno-categorías de un khipu estatal. In *Formaciones económicas y políticas del mundo andino.* Lima: IEP.

———. 1975b. La Función de Tejido en varios contextos sociales y políticos. In *Formaciones económicas y políticas del mundo andino.* Lima: IEP.

Murúa, Martín de. 1613. *Historia General del Perú.* J. Paul Getty Museum, MS. Ludwig XIII 16.

———. 1946 (c. 1590). *Historia de orígen y genealogía de los Reyes Incas del Perú.* Ed. Consantino Bayle. Madrid.

Nicholson, Henry. 1992. "The History of the *Codex Mendoza.*" In *The Codex Mendoza,* ed. F. Berdan and P. Anawalt; 1: 1–13. Berkeley: University of California Press.

Owens, Craig. 1980. The Allegorical Impulse: Toward a Theory of Postmodernism. *October* 12: 67–86; 9: 59–80.

Peterson, Jeanette. 1988. The *Florentine Codex* Imagery and the Colonial Tlacuilo. In *The Work of Bernardino de Sahagún,* ed. Jorge Klor de Alva, H. B. Nicholson and E. Quiñones Keber. Austin: University of Texas Press.

Porras, Bernarbé. 1904. Testimony of Bartolomé de Porras, 1582. In *La Imprenta en Lima,* ed. J. Toribio Medina, vol. 1. Santiago de Chile.

Rivet, Paul, and G. de Créqui-Monfort. 1951. *Bibliographie des langues aymará et kicua,* vol. 1. Vol. 51 of *Travaux et Mémoires de L'Institut D'Ethnologie.* Paris.

Robertson, Donald. 1976. Mexican Indian Art and the Atlantic Filter: Sixteenth to Eighteenth Centuries. In *First Images of America,* ed. F. Chiappelli, 1: 483–494. Los Angeles: University of California Press.

Rowe, John. 1961. The Chronology of Inca Wooden Cups. In *Essays in Pre-Columbian Art and Archaeology,* ed. S. Lothrop et al., 317–341. Cambridge: Harvard University Press.

Santa Cruz Pachacuti Yamqui Salcamaygua, Joan de. 1950 (1613). Relación de antigüedades deste reyno del Pirú. In *Tres Relaciones de Antigüedades Peruanas,* ed. M. Jimenez de la Espada. Asunción del Paraguay.

Santillán, Fernando de. 1950 (c. 1563). Relacion del Orígen, Descendencia, Política y Gobierno de los Incas. In *Tres Relaciones de Antigüedades Peruanas,* ed. M. Jimenez de la Espada. Asunción del Paraguay.

Sarmiento de Gamboa. 1988 (1572). *Historia de los Incas.* Buenos Aires.

Sherbondy, Jeanette. 1986. *Mallki: Ancestors y Cultivo de árboles en los Andes.* Documento de Trabajo No. 5 Proyecto FAO-Holanda. Lima.

Taylor, René. 1987. El Arte de la Memoria en el Nuevo Mundo. In *Iconología y Sociedad Arte Colonial Hispanoamericano.* México: UNAM.

Tercero Concilio Limense 1582–1583. Versión castellana original del los decretos con el sumerario del Segundo Concilio Limense. 1982. Lima: Facultad Pontificia y Civil de Teología de Lima.

Todorov, Tzvetan. 1982. *The Conquest of America: The Question of the Other.* New York: Harper & Row.

Urton, Gary. 1990. *The History of a Myth.* Austin: University of Texas Press.

Valadés, Diego. 1579. *Rhetorica Christiana.* Perugia.

Vaca de Castro, Cristóbal. 1974 (1543). *Relación de la Descendencia, Gobierno, y Conquista de los Incas.* Lima.

Zárate, Agustín de. 1555. *Historia del Descurbrimiento y Conquista del Perú.* Antwerp.

Zuidema, R. Tom. 1991. Guaman Poma and the Art of Empire: Toward an Iconography of Inca Royal Dress. In *Transatlantic Encounters,* ed. K. Andrien and R. Adorno. University of California Press.

Walter D. Mignolo

Signs and Their Transmission: The Question of the Book in the New World

Who Is Naming That Object a Book?

Alejo Venegas was a well-known humanist and man of letters in the Spain of Carlos I. He was the teacher of Cervantes de Salazar, who went to Mexico toward 1550 and became the first professor of rhetoric at the Universidad Real. In 1540, in Toledo, Alexo Venegas published the first part of an ambitious project titled *Primera parte de las diferencias de libros que hay en el universo.* He provided the following definition of the book:

> [A] book is an ark of deposit in which, by means of essential information or things or figures, those things which belong to the information and clarity of understanding (*entendimiento*) are deposited.

Following the rules of logical discourse at the time, Venegas proceeded to analyze each component of the definition. The book is an "ark," he said, because it is derived from the verb "*arredrar*" (to frighten), and, according to Venegas's interpretation, the book frightens ignorance. The book is a "depository" because, in the same way that the ark was invented to contain things, books keep the treasures of knowledge. Furthermore, things are deposited "by means of essential information" because the Divine Book contains the information and knowledge that God has of Himself and through which He knows everything past, present, future, and possible. Because of His divine essence, God produces and engenders the eternal Verb by means of which He creates everything. Venegas's definition also includes "things" because "things" are signs which bring information about something else. Finally, he says "by means of figures" because of the diversity of "written letters." Thus, "figures" basically means "written letters."

After defining the book, Venegas introduced the distinction between the "Archetype Book"[1] and the "Metagraph Book." He called the first "*exemplar*" or "*dechado*" and the second "*trasunto*" or "*traslado.*" The first is the uncreated book read only by the angels; the second is the book read by wordly human beings. The idea of the book as presented by Venegas is that it is an expression of the Divine Word and also the container of All Knowledge. God as the supreme writer has expressed the truth in the Book of Nature and in the Holy Book (Archetype), which has been inscribed in alphabetic characters. The human book (Figure 1) has two functions: to know the creator of the Universe by reading His Book and, at the same time, to censure every human expression in which the Devil manifests itself by dictating the false books.

The idea that the Holy Book was the expression of the Divine Word and the human book a container of knowledge and the inscription of the human voice in alphabetic writing was taken for granted during the sixteenth century and still has validity in communities of believers. In the sixteenth century, what missionaries and men of letters perceived in Amerindian sign carriers was molded by an image of the book to which Venegas's definition largely contributed. One can also surmise that the concrete examples that Venegas, as well as any educated person in sixteenth-century Castile, had in mind were medieval codices and recently printed books (Glennison 1988; Febvre and Martin 1958). This hypothetical person had probably forgotten the story about what a "book" might have been before papyrus was replaced by vellum and the roll by the codex (Kenyon 1932: 86–119; Reynolds and Wilson 1991: 122–163), and perhaps also that writing did not imply the need of a "book" (Figure 2a and b). He might not necessarily have been aware

Figure 1. Writing and an actual sign carrier: a medieval codex. Berlin, Deutsche Staatsbibliothek.

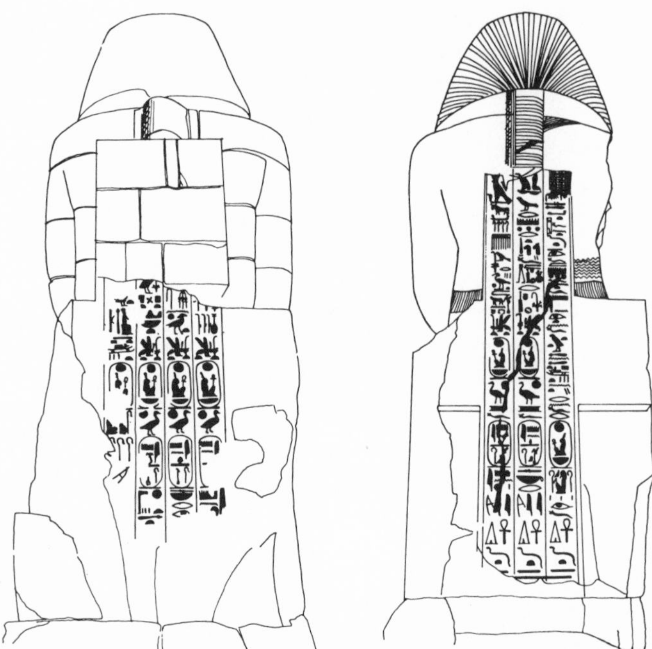

Figure 2a. Writing without books: graphic inscriptions on stone (the Colossus of Memnon; Royal Mortuary Temple of Amenhotep III). Figure 2b. Writing without books: inscription of an ancient Maya battle scene on a polychrome vase (from Michael Coe, *The Maya Scribe and His World*).

that in the transformation and subsequent use of the codex form, Christianity and the reproduction of the Bible played a crucial role (Skeat 1969: 54–79).

Thus, when the missionary, the educated soldier, or the man of letters was exposed to the artifact the Mexicas called *amoxtli* and which the Maya called *vuh,* the Europeans described it as an object folded like an accordion, and it was translated as "book" (Figure 3a and b). In China and Japan, during the fifteenth century, narratives painted on folding screens and hanging scrolls were still very common, and the bound "book" familiar to European men of letters, like Venegas, one among other alternatives.[2] But since the Spanish were not sure what *kind* of "books" the Amerindian "books" were, they feared that the words of the Devil were registered in them, without suspecting that the notion of "book"[3] might have been alien to Amerindians and the very idea of the Devil questionable. The Spanish took action consistent with what they believed a book was and what they perceived Amerindians to have. One reaction was to burn them, perhaps in the calm and secure spirit which characterizes the following description by Friar Diego de Landa, one of the first Franciscans in the Yucatan Peninsula:

> These people used certain characters or letters, with which they wrote in their books about their antiquities and their sciences; with these, and with figures, and certain signs in the figures, they understood their matters, made them known, and taught them. We found a great number of books in these letters, and since they contained nothing but superstitions and falsehoods of the devil we burned them all, which they took most grievously, and which gave them great pain. (Landa, ch. xli)[4]

Misunderstanding was entrenched in the colonization of language. Landa presupposed equal means of communication and social practices in such a way that reading and writing was the same both for the Spanish and the inhabitants of the Yucatan peninsula; he also presupposed the concept of letters among the Maya, which he distinguished from "characters." Finally, because he was accustomed to seeing Medieval illuminated books, he assumed that the Maya *vuh* (translated by the Spanish as "book") were also written and illustrated with pictures.[5] It did not occur to him that such a distinction may not have been relevant to the Mayas. Landa, toward 1566, gave a physical description (instead of a definition) of the Maya "book." It would be worthwhile when reading it to keep in mind Venegas's definition:

> They wrote their books on a long sheet doubled in folds, which was then enclosed between two boards finely ornamented; the writing was on one side and the other according to the folds. *The paper they made from the roots of a tree, and gave it a white finish excellent for writing upon.* Some of the principal lords were learned in these sciences, from interests, and for the greater esteem they enjoyed thereby; *yet, they did not make use of them in public.* (Landa, vii; italics mine)

Landa might not have had any choice but to talk about "their letters" and "their books," rather than think in terms of "our *vuh*" and

Figure 3a. Writing and an actual sign carrier: a Mexica *amoxtli* (*Codice Borbonico,* author's collection).
Figure 3b. Writing and the transformation of *amoxtli* into book: the *Codice Tudela,* a hybrid of pictograms and alphabetic writing, bound in book form (author's collection).

ask what concept or concepts the Maya used for designating the basic units of their writing. Nor did he ask whether the distinction between painting and writing made sense for them and, consequently, what was the purpose of describing "their" books as having pictures illustrating their writing if the Maya did not care to make a distinction between writing and painting. Landa could also have asked whether there was, among the Maya, a distinction between "book" and "paper," since *vuh* seems to refer to the surface on which signs were inscribed and to the object created by written signs on a solid surface made out of tree bark (*vuh*). But there is still more: why did Landa believe that Maya writing was to be understood in terms of books, and why did he not think that they could have had other surfaces on which signs were inscribed and on which they practiced writing?[6] I assume that for Landa, in the latter half of the sixteenth century, writing was naturally conceived in terms of papers and books, and books in terms of the medieval manuscript and the printing press, which were also the examples Venegas might have had in mind some twenty-five years before Landa's report.

In the lake of Mexico, the term regularly employed to refer to the surface on which painted narratives were inscribed was *amoxtli.* Fray Toribio de Benavente (Motolinía), who arrived in Mexico in 1524, reported on the Mexica "books." Contrary to Landa, Motolinía's description oscillates between the material inscriptions and the conceptual "genres" he perceived in Mexica's books. In a letter Motolinía (1903) wrote to Lord Antonio Pimentel, he reported:

> I shall treat of this land of Anáhuac or New Spain . . . according to the ancient books which the natives had or possessed. These books were written in symbols and pictures. This was their way of writing, supplying their lack of an alphabet by the use of symbols. . . . These natives had five books, which, as I said, were written in pictures and symbols. The first book deals with years and calculations of time; the second, with the days and with the feasts which the Indians observed during the year; the third, with dreams, illusions, superstitions and omens in which the Indians believed; the fourth, with baptisms and with names that were bestowed upon children; the fifth, with the rites, ceremonies and omens of the Indians relative to marriage. Only one of all these books, namely the first, can be trusted because it recounts the truth.

The quotation above, taken from Borgia Steck's translation, has left out some important words in the original—namely, Motolinía's statement that only the first book can be trusted *because* the other four were invented by the Devils. It is curious to note that a similar observation was made by Landa, although not in section 7 of his *relación,* from which the previous statements by him were quoted, but from section 41, where he talks again about writing and the books in connection with the Maya concept of time. In this section, he precisely translates Maya glyphs into alphabetic writing and reports:

> The sciences which they taught were the reckoning of the years, months and days, the festivals and ceremonies, the administration of their sacraments, the omens of the days, their methods of divination and prophecies, events, remedies for sicknesses, antiquities, *and the art of reading and writing by their letters and the characters wherewith they wrote, and by pictures that illustrated the writings.* (Landa, vii; italics mine)

Venegas's dual typology, distinguishing between the archetype and the metagraph book, did not take into account a third type which emerged in almost every report about writing and books in the New World: the book of the Devil, which contained not science but superstition, not truth but falsehood. The material differences in writing practices, in the storage and transmission of information, and the construction of knowledge became—in the Spanish conceptualization—a process of analogizing by which the material aspects of reading and writing practices across cultures was erased in the name of God and His fight with the Devil.

The game of the word became, thus, a conceptual game which impinged on understanding across cultures (what is "behind" words such as *amoxtli, vuh,* and book?), on the exercise of power (who is in a position to decide whose knowledge is truth; what container and sign carrier is preferred and should be trusted?), and on the colonization of language. The only kind of artifact that Motolinía trusted he called *xihutonal amatl,* which he translated as "book counting the years." *Amatl* is derived from *amoxtli,* a plant which grew in the lake of Mexico and from whose bark sign carriers were prepared. *Amatlacuilo* was a name for the individual whose social role it was to paint on the *amatl;* this was translated as "scribe." Other expressions related to social roles in writing activities have been derived, such as *uei amatlacuilo,* which Remi Siméon (1963) has translated as "secretary or principal writer"; and also *amoxtlacuilo,* which he has translated as "scribe, author." Simeon's translation of the first as "secretary" and of the second as "author" suggests that *amoxtli* might have referred to "books" and *amatl* to "paper." In any case, not only was the material of the artifact different, but also the conceptualization associated by each culture with the signs (letters or painting), with the sign carrier (*amoxtli* and book), and with social roles (*tlacuilo* and scribe) and activities (writing/reading and looking at/telling a story).

These conceptualizations varied according to the respective traditions, cultural and social uses, and the materiality of reading and writing interactions. The Spanish, however, had the last word and took for granted that their reading and writing habits, their human and divine books, and their ways of organizing and transmitting knowledge were for some reason better and exempt from devilish design. The spread of Western literacy, then, not only took the form of reading and writing; it was also a massive operation in which the materiality as well as the ideology that Amerindians built around their own semiotic interactions began to be combined with or replaced by the materiality and ideology of Western reading and writing cultures.

Writing without Words, without Paper, without Pens

Writing does not necessarily presuppose the book, although during the sixteenth century, under the influence of the celebration of the letter, the meaning was narrowed down almost exclusively to just that. Its image is so strong in cultures of the book[7] that peoples who do not belong to these cultures are not always aware of what a book means. The complicity between writing and the book was such that alternative sign carriers (like newspapers) were not yet available, and the possibility of writing on clay, animal skin, tree bark, and the like was just beyond the cultural horizon of the time. Venegas's definition of the book, very much like the Spanish humanist Elio Antonio de Nebrija's celebration of the letter, erased previous material means of writing or denied coeval ones that were not alphabetically based.

Keeping with examples from the Yucatan peninsula, the large number of Spanish descriptions and reactions to Mayan writing practices make it seem as if Western books and the equivalent of Western paper were the only sign carriers. Less attention was paid to writings carved in stone and painted on pottery, which had very wide use and significant social functions.[8] The reader of these descriptions was invited to conceive of Maya literacy in terms of European literacy and never invited to imagine what Europeans might lack if the point of reference were Maya script and sign carriers (see Houston, this volume).

A few years after Landa wrote his *relación,* another Franciscan, Antonio de Ciudad Real, observed in his report on the life of Fray Alonso Ponce that the Maya should be praised above all other people of New Spain for three things. He was impressed, first, by the characters and figures (he called them *letras*) with which the Maya wrote their narratives and recorded their past (which he called *historia*). Second was their religion with its sacrificial rites devoted to their gods (which he called *idols*). Third was the Maya calendars inscribed on artifacts made of tree bark. He described these artifacts as consisting of very long strips almost a third of a *vara* (thirty-three inches) wide, which were folded "and came to be more or less like a quarto-bound book." He made some observations revealing the spread of Maya literacy. Only the "priests of the idols" (*ah kins*) and every so often a noble person (said Antonio de Ciudad Real [1976]) understood such "figures and letters." After the conquest however, "our friars understood them, knew how to read them, and even wrote them."

The analogy with "a quarto-bound book" is indeed quite revealing. The medieval bound manuscript was basically similar in format to the printed book during the Renaissance (Figure 1). When paper was introduced in Europe toward the end of the thirteenth century, replacing previous sign carriers (such as parchment), it was folded into two or four leaves (in-folio or in-quarto) and then assembled into segments (*fasciculus*) of four to six sheets. Medieval and Renaissance printed books acquired a very distinctive material format in relation to the previous rolls or scrolls. According to standard histories of the book, the first books were in scroll form. The implication is that the original material format (i.e., of the Medieval and Renaissance book) was imperfect when invented and that, in its final form, the book achieved an essential quality that had been *in potentia* since its inception. This evolutionary model of writing and the book was to a great extent an invention of the European Renaissance, and it was precisely the model used by missionaries and men of letters when they described Amerindian writing practices and sign carriers. What is somewhat curious is that if the evolutionary model was used, the analogy was made between the Amerindian *amoxtli* or *vuh* and the "quarto-bound book" instead of the scroll to which new pieces could be added. The famous dictum of Bernal Diaz del Castillo (one of Cortes' soldiers during the conquest of Mexico-Tenochtitlan) that Mexican books were folded like Castilian fabric conveyed the image of the scroll rather than the bound "book."

I would like to elaborate on this point, taking an example from current observations about writing. An evolutionary model seems to prevail according to which "true writing" is alphabetic writing; writing is, in this view, indistinguishable from the "book," which, in turn, is indistinguishable from the material form of the European medieval and Renaissance examples.

Following D. Diringer (1962), three kinds of writing can be visualized: embryonic, non-alphabetic, and alphabetic. He calls the last two "pure" writing. While it is possible, he says, "to count as 'writing' any semiotic mark . . . an individual makes and assigns a meaning to," the antiquity of writing is perhaps comparable to the antiquity of speech. But, he states, a "critical and unique breakthrough into new worlds of knowledge was achieved within human consciousness not when simple semiotic marking was devised but when a coded system of visible marks was invented whereby a writer could determine the exact words that the reader would generate from the text" (1962: 84). Writing thus conceived is restricted to syllabic and alphabetic writing.

If this distinction is valid from the standpoint of the history of writing, ethnography, or paleography, it is not as satisfactory from a semiotic point of view. I am less concerned with the change of *name* than with the change of *level,* which directs us away from the lexicon and expressions of a culture linked with the representation of a particular mode of interaction and toward the lexicon and expressions of the discipline in which a concept is bonded to its theoretical definition. One needs, first, a theoretical definition of graphic signs and of graphic semiotic interactions before moving into a historical classification of different stages in the development of writing. Semiotically, a graphic sign is, then, a mark on a solid surface made for the purpose of establishing a semiotic interaction. Consequently, a human interaction is a semiotic one if there is a community and a body of common knowledge according to which: (a) a person can produce a visible sign with the purpose of conveying a message (to somebody else or oneself); (b) a person perceives the visible sign and interprets it as a sign produced for the purpose of conveying a message; and (c) that person attributes a given meaning to the visible sign. Notice that in this theoretical definition of writing the links between speech and writing are not necessary.

In this sense, writing is a common communicative device in a large number of cultures all over the world, although not every member of a community has access to writing. For its part, the "book" is a concept united with "writing" only in the conceptualization of a culture in which "writing" is understood in the restricted sense defined by Diringer.[9] To avoid the ambiguities caused by the use of concepts which preserve, in a disciplinary context, the same meaning they hold in cultural (nondisciplinary) expressions, a theoretical definition is needed. Before giving a definition of "book," I will first attempt a description. In what follows I rely on D. Diringer's classic study (1982) devoted to the book before printing. My own recognition of his important contribution will not prevent me from challenging some of his basic presuppositions. The most relevant of Diringer's presuppositions for the issues explored in this chapter is his consistency in using the term "book" in the restricted sense furnished by the expression of his own Western and contemporary culture and projecting it into different times and places. Let me illustrate this statement. Diringer writes:

> *Libri Lintei* ("linen books") are mentioned by Livy not as existing in his own time, but as recorded by Licinius Macer . . . who stated that linen "books" were kept in the temple of Juno Moneta. They were not "books" in the modern sense, but simply "very ancient annals and libri magistratum ("books of magistrates").

Despite the caution ("they were not books in the modern sense"), Diringer translates "*libri*" as "books." It is known, as Diringer certainly knows, that *libri lintei* designates ancient chronicles of the Romans which were written on linen and preserved in the Temple of Juno Moneta. But it is not known for sure that they were books, since *libri* may have been used to designate the solid surface on which writing was performed (a possible extension from the original meaning: inner bark of a tree, or just "writing on linen"—and *libri magistratum* could also be translated as "writings of the magistrates").

A second example comes from the idea that *papyrus* was the "main writing material for books" in the Greco-Roman world. Although *papyrus* was indeed the primary writing material, it does not follow that it was "for writing books," but rather just for writing and a multitude of other purposes (e.g., recording data for future use, communicating on a synchronic level, communicating with gods).[10] To be inscribed and transmitted, a graphic sign needs, certainly, a medium. But from this point to the "book" is a long road. Diringer states that the Greek word *biblos* means the "pith of the papyrus stalk"; this gave origin to the word *biblion,* which was the common word for "papyrus scroll" or "papyrus roll," whose plural was *biblia,* "papyrus rolls"; hence *tá biblía,* "the scrolls." In this case, Diringer translates "the scrolls" as the equivalent of "the book."[11] In the Roman lexicon, Diringer relates that the modern word "volume" derives from the Latin *volumen* (a thing rolled up); it is formed from the verb *volvere* (to roll), and is the Latin rendering of the Greek *kylindros* (cylinder). It is in this context that *evolvere, folia volvere* (to unroll) was often used in the sense of "to read" (*folia conjicere*). When, after all this information, Diringer relates that the term *volumen,* like *liber* (to peel, the inner bark of a tree), was in common use for "book," the quotation marks do not solve the problem of the manner in which a community represents its own objects and social interactions. For an educated member of Western culture, the word "book" is associated with a body of knowledge (and representations) far from the meaning of a roll (*volumen*) from the inner bark of a tree (*liber*) or the frame in which a roll was cut (*tómos*), which in all probability were among the meanings associated with these words in the Roman community.

Certainly the entire problem of the book cannot be reduced to the meaning of the words coined to designate the material aspects of writing ("roll," "cut," "unfold," "bark of a tree," etc.), and we cannot view the "book" only as an object (or a class of objects). With the increasing complexity of literacy, the practice of writing on *liber, boc, papyrus,* and *biblos* changed. A change in a given practice and in the object affected by that practice is accompanied, sooner or later, by a change in the conceptualization of the practice and of the object. The meaning of the original words related to the practice of writing and the graphic sign carrier entered a process of transformation. I am mainly interested in two aspects of this transformation: (a) the plural of *biblion—biblia*—came to indicate "Sacred Scriptures" and "The Book" par excellence;[12] (b) from *biblos* (the inner bark of the papyrus) was formed the Greek *bibliothéke* (house of papyrus), which came to mean "wisdom" or "knowledge."[13] In other words, the representation of the semiotic system of interaction achieved by inscribing and transmitting graphic signs on solid surfaces began to change with the increasing complexity of literacy and became strongly associated with religion and knowledge.

This long detour through the house of words leads me to believe that a more accurate translation of *amoxtli* would be *biblos, papyrus, liber,* or *boc,* rather than "book" or "*libro,*" as shown through a closer look at some of the Aztec words related to *amoxtli:*[14]

> *Amoxcluiloa,* whose roots are *amoxtli* and *icuiloa,* "to paint," "to inscribe something";
> *Amoxcalli,* whose roots are *amoxtli* and *calli,* "house," "room";
> *Amoxitoa/amoxpoa,* both of which have as their roots *amoxtli; itoa* means "to say" or "to narrate something by heart"; and *poa* means "to tell," "to summarize a process," "to count."

The translation of *amoxitoa/amoxpoa,* offered by Simeon as "*lire un livre*" (to read a book), is quite misleading if it is understood either in the sense of "to go over a written page with the eyes" or "to pronounce out loud what is written," for the romance words "*lire*" or "*leer*" (to read) come from the Latin *legere* meaning "to collect" (*lectio,* a gathering, a collecting). The sense of "collecting" is absent from the Nahuatl word designating the "same" activity, and the emphasis is on "telling or narrating what has been inscribed or painted on a solid surface made out of *amoxtli.*" The difference is not trivial. It gives us a better understanding of the idea of the sign carriers in societies with alternative literacies.[15]

Now it is possible to attempt a definition of "book" which, contrary to that of "sign," will be culture-specific: (a) a solid surface is a book as an object to the degree to which it is the sign carrier for some kind of graphic semiotic interaction; (b) a book as an object is also a book as a text to the degree to which it belongs to a specific stage in the development of writing ("pure writing," according to Diringer's classification) and the members of a given culture represent the system of graphic semiotic interaction in such a way that it attributes to the sign carrier (the book as an object) high and decisive functions (theological and epistemological) for their own organization.

According to this definition, the book as text implies "pure" writing, although "pure writing" does not necessarily imply the idea of the book. The necessary connections are founded in the presuppositions underlying cultural expression. A rereading of the seminal chapter by Curtius on "The Book as Symbol" (in his *European Literature and the Latin Middle Ages*), will show that he devotes a great deal of time to metaphors about writing; and that he seems to assume that they are plain and simple synonyms of metaphors for the book.

Be that as it may, some example needs to be drawn from Curtius in order to back up our definition of the book as text. In 1948 Curtius called attention to the amount and the significance of the images that different cultures had constructed to represent their ideas about writing and the book. He began his survey with the Greeks, noting that they did not have any "idea of the sacredness of the book, as there is no privileged priestly caste of scribes." What is more, one can even find a disparagement of writing in Plato. There is the familiar last part of Plato's *Phaedrus* in which Socrates attempts to convince Phaedrus that writing is not an aid to memory and learning but, to the contrary, can only "awaken reminiscences" without replacing the true discourse lying in the *psyche* of the wise man, which must be transmitted through oral interactions. It should be emphasized that Socrates is mainly concerned with "writing" in its relationship to knowledge and its transmission, but not with the "book." If one thinks of the rich vocabulary associated with graphic semiotic interactions inherited from the Greeks and also remembers that the idea of the sacred book was alien to them, for they were more concerned with "writing" than with the "book," it should again be concluded that to translate "*biblos*" as "book" implies imposing our meaning of what a book is upon theirs, rather than fully understanding their meaning of "*biblos.*" This observation, amounting to the general problem of "fusion of horizon" or "fusion of cultural expressions," is also valid in the case where *amoxtli* is translated as "book."

Contrary to the corrupted nature of writing in which Plato represented graphic semiotic interactions, nothing is found but the utmost praise (and with God as the archetypal writer) in Christianity. In this form of representation, the tongue becomes synonymous with the hand[16] and the Universe with the Book. While Socrates anchors knowledge in the *psyche* and conveys it through the oral transmission of signs, Christianity secures knowledge in the *Book* and conveys it through the graphic transmission of signs. One could surmise that "the idea of the book" may have entered into the system of representation of graphic semiotic interaction at the point when "writing" gained its autonomy from orality and the "book" replaced the "person" as a receptacle and a source of knowledge. It is quite comprehensible that when the word was detached from its oral source (the body), it became attached to the invisible body and to the silent voice of God, which cannot be heard but can be read in the Holy Book. However, the theological view of writing developed by Christianity and the epistemological view of knowledge provided by Socrates/Plato (where God is not only the archetype of the writer but also the archetype of wisdom) joined forces during the Middle Ages (Le Goff 1957: 90–97; Glennison 1988: 115–163) and continued into the Renaissance. Nature is the book that God wrote, and to know nature is the best way to know God. Curtius quotes a telling passage from Fray Luis de Granada's *Símbolo de la fé,* in which Granada uses the expression "to think philosophically in this great book of earthly creatures" to mean that because God put us in front of the "marvelous book of the entire universe" we must read the creatures as live letters and thus, through them, come to know the excellence of their Creator.

Christianity is not, of course, the only religion having a holy book or scriptures (take, e.g., the Koran, or the Torah). But it shares with these others the disequilibrium of power between the religions that possess the Book and those that do not. What is at stake here is the role played by "the book as a text" during the process of colonization carried on by literate societies. As a matter of fact, the role of the book in our understanding of the colonial period in the New World may not have been entirely exploited. One could, perhaps, profit by taking an example from

J. Goody as an analogy. To practice the Asante religion, observes Goody, you have to be Asante. Due to the lack of a written narrative that traces the border between the internal and the external space, between what is prescribed and permitted and what is proscribed and forbidden, the "idea" attached to the Asante religion varies considerably over time. Religions founded on alphabetic writing and the corresponding idea of the book are, concludes Goody, "generally religions of conversion, not simply religions of birth. You can spread them, like jam. And you can persuade or force people to give up one set of beliefs and practices and take up another set" (Goody 1986: 5). What is important here is not the "content" of the Book but rather the very existence of the object in which a set of regulations and metaphors were inscribed, giving to it the special status of Truth and Wisdom.

It is now easier to understand Motolinía's metaphorical language when he refers to and describes Aztec "books." One can also understand the context of meaning underlying the epistemological metaphors he employs to describe these "books." By talking about "the five books" the Aztecs had, he projects the cognitive component of the idea of the book; by deciding which ones are "true" and which "false," he draws from the theological component of the idea of the Book in which truth finds its warranty. If Motolinía cast the Devil as the author of the false books it was not only because the Devil was guilty of all wrongdoing in this world, but also because he had a thousand faces. In this case, the face he showed was related to the sacralization of the Book in Christianity.

The model of writing and the book imbedded in the European mind during the Renaissance, and generally defined by Venegas, erased many of the possibilities for missionaries and men of letters to inquire into different writing systems and sign carriers rather than simply describe them by analogy with their own model. Because the paradigmatic example of writing was alphabetic and referred to the medieval codice and the Renaissance printed book, the Peruvian *quipu* was virtually eliminated from the perspective one might get concerning the materiality of reading and writing cultures—when reading and writing was mainly conceived in terms of inscribing letters on paper and then composing and printing books. There was certainly more than a reading and writing culture both in Renaissance Europe and in the colonial New World, as we have seen in the first chapter. However, the model provided by the alphabet and the book was a paradigmatic example of the material facets of reading and writing.

The *quipu* certainly did not go unnoticed among those who were in Peru observing Amerindian cultures during the first century of the conquest (see Cummins in this volume). Acosta, in his *Historia natural y moral de las Indias* (1590), devoted several chapters (Book VI) to descriptions of Amerindian writing systems, comparing them with alphabetic as well as Chinese writing. Acosta referred to the *quipu* when he spoke about memory and recordkeeping in Peru. He began his description by noticing the differences between the *quipu* and other writing systems:

> Los indios del Pirú, antes de venir españoles, ningún género de escritura tuvieron, ni por letras ni por caracteres, o cifras o figurillas, como los de la China y los de México; más no por eso conservaron menos la memoria de sus antiguallas, ni tuvieron menos su cuenta para todos los negocios de paz, y guerra y gobierno.
>
> The Indians of Peru, before the Spaniards came, had no sort of writing, not letters nor characters nor ciphers nor figures, like those of China or Mexico; but in spite of this they conserved no less the memory of ancient lore, nor did they have any less account of all their affairs of peace, war and government. (IV: viii)[17]

The *quipu* was considered by Acosta a valid sign for recordkeeping but not equivalent to writing since it did not consist of letters, characters, or figures (see p. 21). Acosta's definition of writing, then, presupposed that a graphic sign (letter, character, or image) inscribed on a solid surface (paper, parchment, or bark of a tree) was needed in order to have writing. A bunch of knotted strings of different colors would not qualify as such for an insightful observer as analytically minded as Acosta. However, when Acosta had to describe what a *quipu* was and how it was used, he could not avoid using the notion of "writing"; even more, he made a perfect analogy between writing with letters and writing with strings, colors, and knots. Acosta defined the *quipu* by saying: "*Son quipos, unos memoriales o registros hechos de ramales, en que diversos ñudos y diversas* [*sic*] *colores, significan diversas cosas*" (*Quipus* are a kind of recordkeeping or registers made out of a set of branches in which a diversity of knots and a diversity of colors mean different things).

What attracted Acosta's attention, however, was not the material appearance of the *quipu,* but what the Inca did with it. Acosta thought that whatever could be done with books in matters of recording the past, of keeping track of the law, of ritual, and of business matters could be also done with the *quipus* ("*los libros pueden decir de historias, y leyes y ceremonias, y cuentas de negocios, todo eso suplen los quipos tan puntualmente, que admira.*") Thus Acosta's hesitation between the fact that *quipus* are *not* considered writing or books and the fact that they perform like writing and books. More striking in this respect is the analogy Acosta established with alphabetic writing:

> Y en cada manojo de éstos, tantos ñudos y ñudicos, y hilillos atados; unos colorados, otros verdes, otros azules, otros blancos, finalmente tantas diferencias que así como nosotros de veinte y cuatro letras guisándolas en diferentes maneras sacamos tantas infinidad de vocablos, así estos de sus ñudos y colores, sacaban innumerables significaciones de cosas.
>
> And in every bundle of these, so many greater and lesser knots, and tied strings; some red, others green, others blue, others white, *in short, as many differences as we have* with our twenty-four letters, arranging them in different ways to draw forth an infinity of words: so did they, with their knots and colors, draw forth innumerable meanings of things. (VI: viii; emphasis mine)[18]

It seems evident, after reading Acosta as well as other writers who described the *quipu,* that not only the material image of a roll or scroll has been forgotten and replaced by the "quarto-bound book," but the meaning of *textum* has also faded out of the vocabulary of the time. *Texo* in Latin meant "to make" and more specifically "to weave." By transference, it was also used in the sense of "join or fit together," to interlace or to intertwine. Hence, *textum* evoked the idea of something woven or made into a web. It was also transferred by the Roman rhetorician to alphabetic, written compositions to denote the texture of a composition ("*dicendi textum tenue*"). What Acosta missed, because he assumed that writing presupposed graphic signs inscribed on flat surfaces, was the tactile aspect of the *quipu.* Modern scholars who have recently studied them in detail have observed that the *quipu* maker produced meaning, recorded memory, and worked with numbers by tracing figures in space. In the process of organizing or weaving strings and colors, and of knotting them, the *quipucamayoc* had to change the direction of the strings and the position of the colors relative to each other. This process, the author observed, was not simply preparatory to the "real stuff" of making a record. It was an integral part of "*quipu* making" or "writing." The materiality of *quipu* making invites interesting comparison with the brush and the stylus, the instruments of Mexica and European writing practices:

> . . . the quipumaker's way of recording—direct construction—required tactile sensitivity to a much greater degree. In fact, the overall aesthetic of the quipu is related to the tactile: the manner of record-

ing and the recording itself are decidedly rhythmic; the first in the activity, the second in the effect. We seldom realize the potential of our sense of touch, and we are usually unaware of its association with rhythm. . . . In fact, tactile sensitivity begins in the rhythmic pulsating environment of the unborn child far in advance of the development of other senses. (Ascher and Ascher 1981: 61–62)

The tactile sensitivity perceived today in the *quipu* maker would have been difficult to perceive by Renaissance men of letters who were thinking in terms of letter writing and books as the paradigmatic model of producing meaning and keeping records. Acosta, as we have seen, certainly did not miss the similarities between *"guisar"* (to organize or weave letters, strings, little stones, or beans) and constructing the *quipu* in order to produce meaning and to keep records. But he failed to see the tactile dimension in *quipu* making.

Quipu making was, then, an important activity in Inca society, important enough to be associated with a social role—that of the *quipu* maker. Guaman Poma de Ayala, in his *Nueva Corónica and Buen Gobierno,* left a few drawings which illustrate what a *quipu* and a *quipucamayoc* looked like (Figure 4). For Acosta to consider the *quipucamayoc* as a social role equivalent to a medieval scribe (Figure 5), a Renaissance secretary, or a man of letters (Figure 6) would perhaps have been beyond his horizons. Or perhaps he was also seeing, from a different perspective, the transformation that Guaman Poma de Ayala saw when he depicted an Inca colonial secretary (Figure 7); this, we can imagine, resulted from the social transformation of the ancient *quipu* maker in colonial society.

Writing and Social Roles

In medieval Europe (as well as in the Islamic world), the practice and conceptualization of writing was closer to physical labor than an intellectual pursuit (see Figure 1). *Dictare* was the verb used to describe the type of activity that one would use today for *writing* and composition. The generation of a text began with a dictation inscribed on a wax tablet by the *scribe;* then, after the corrections were made by the *dictator,* the text was transcribed onto parchment. Writing, then, required not only physical dexterity, but also the knowledge of how to prepare the instruments involved (stylus, feather, ink, parchment, etc.). The transformation by which the roles of dictator and scribe were consolidated in one person began to take place perhaps around the sixteenth century.[19] However, the idea that writing implied a voice might not have vanished as quickly as one might suppose after the transformation of reading brought about by the increase in the production of manuscripts during the early fourteenth century, and the invention of the printing press in the second half of the fifteenth century. Titu Cusi Yupanki reported, in 1570, how people from northern Peru witnessed the arrival of the first Spaniards, and described them as bearded men who talk to themselves looking at pieces of white fabric.

In Mexico, the *tlacuilo* was the social role equivalent to the Peruvian *quipucamayoc,* the medieval scribe, or the Renaissance secretary. He

Figure 4. Writing and social roles: Andean *quipucamayocs* and the administration of the Inca empire (Guaman Poma de Ayala, *Nueva Coronica y Buen Gobierno* toward 1615).

Figure 5. **A Medieval scribe (Dijon, Municipal Library, ms 493, fol. 29).**

Figure 6. Writing and social roles: a Renaissance man of letters (National Gallery of Art, Washington; Rosenwald Collections).

Figure 7. Writing and social roles: a colonial secretary—a possible transformation of a *quipucamayoc* (Guaman Poma de Ayala, *Nueva Coronica y Buen Gobierno,* toward 1615).

did not deserve as much attention from the Spanish writers, however, as those who had the wisdom of the word (*tlamatinime* in Nahuatl; *amauta*[20] in Aymara; *qo ru naoh* in Maya-Cachiquel), translated as "orators" or "philosophers" by Spanish chroniclers. Sahagún ([1578] 1969, book 6), for instance, who did such a thorough job in researching and describing Mexica culture, devoted an entire chapter, out of the twelve in his Florentine Codex (1578), to rhetoric and moral philosophy. The *tlacuilo* was practically hidden in a chapter he devoted to the craftsmen, and disguised under the name of the "oficiales de la pluma" ("feather craftsmen") (Figure 8). The Mendoza Codex, gathered under the mandate of Viceroy Mendoza toward 1550, has the *tlacuilo* and his son in the context of artisans in Mexica society (Figure 9).

Francisco de San Antón Muñón Chimalpaín, born around 1579 in Chalco-Amaquemecan,[21] left several *relaciones,* written in Nahuatl and in Latin script, about the origin, peregrination, and memories of people of his area. In his "Octava Relación" ("Eight Relation"), Chimalpaín described in detail his sources as well as the process of writing about them. In regard to the sources, he specified that the information came from "five parts or books, from ancient painted papers, very old and painted by elder and dear nobles from the towns of Tzacualtitlan Tenanco Chiconcóhuac, who wrote them before I arranged them, and wrote this story" (*De cinco partes o libros, de antiguos papeles pintados muy viejos hechos por los antiguos queridos nobles que fueron de Tzacualtitlan Tenanco Chiconcóhuac, antes que yo los arreglara, fue compuesta esta historia*). The reference to five units or parts (also called *"libros"* by Chimalpaín) reminds us of Motolinía's classification of Aztec "books" or "partes" (pieces). What those pieces might have been can be surmised by what Chimalpaín refers to as five units of painted *amoxtli.* He described, furthermore, where the information comes from:

> Estos viejos relatos fueron hechos durante el tiempo de los señores nuestros padres, nuestros antepasados. Y estas pinturas del pueblo y la historia de los linajes antiguos fueron guardados mientras a Dios plugo darle vida, por Don Diego Hernández Mochintzetzalohuatzin, Príncipe reinante quien se hizo español y murió en Ce-Calli, 1545.
>
> Entonces, el papel pintado y la historia de los linajes antiguos fueron dejados a su querido hijo el señor don Domingo Hernández Ayopochtzin, quien se instruyó en la cuenta de los libros y pintó un libro escribiéndolo con letras, sin añadirle nada, sino como un fiel espejo de las cosas que de allí se trasladó.
>
> These old stories were made during the time of the lords our fathers, our ancestors. And these paintings of the people and the history of the ancient nobility were kept, as long as it pleased God to grant him life, by Don Diego Hernández Mochintzetzalohuatzin, reigning Prince who became a Spaniard and died in Ce-Callí, 1545.
>
> Then, the painted paper and the history of the ancient nobility were left to his beloved son, the esteemed Don Domingo Hernández Ayopochtzin, who instructed himself in the telling of the books and then painted a book, writing it in letters, adding nothing, but rather as a faithful mirror of the things translated from there.[22]

Figure 8. Writing and social roles: a *tlacuilo* with feather artisans (Bernardino de Sahagun, *Florentine Codex,* toward 1578. Biblioteca Medicea Laurenziana).

In the same way that the proper names are already a clear manifestation of colonial semiosis,[23] so are the vocabulary and the cognitive structures of those who lived, thought, and narrated between the world of the painted *amoxtli* and the alphabetic written books. The learning process alluded to by Chimalpaín ("*se instruyó en la cuenta de los libros,*" "instructed himself in the telling of the books") also indicates the superposition of two kinds of schooling: the old, in which part of learning was to look at and to interpret books; and the new, in which Chimalpaín himself was educated and learned to replace the "*pinturas*" by "alphabetic writing," and to approach speech through written prose. The fact that Chimalpaín still maintained in his writing the repetitive structure of the oral is indicative of the fractures of colonial semiosis in the conflict between oral narratives, in which repetition is a part of everyday speech, to an alphabetic, written prose (in both Latin and Spanish) from

Figure 9. Writing and social roles: a *tlacuilo* and his son (*Codex Mendoza,* Bodleian Library, Oxford).

which Chimalpaín learned to write in Nahuatl. By the sixteenth century, this repetition had already clearly established its distinction with versification. Even in modern Spanish translation, the echoes of a rhythmic speech could be heard: "*el papel pintado y la historia de los linajes antiguos*" (the painted paper and the lineage history), "*ahora yo he pintado, he escrito con letras un libro*" (to paint a book, writing it with letters), "*el me lo prestó, el libro de sus antepasados, me lo proporcionó*" (he loaned it to me, the book of his ancestors; he made it available to me) (Chimalpaín [ca. 1600] 1982: 20–21).

If there were at least five "ancient books," as Motolonía and Chimalpaín mentioned, perhaps the *tlacuilo* was not just one single person, generally trained to paint any of them, and perhaps there was a division of labor and a division of training also. Don Fernando de Alva Ixtlilxochitl was a descendant of the same Tezcocan family who hosted Pedro de Gante around 1523. What emerges from the words of Mexican chroniclers such as Chimalpaín and Ixtlilxochitl is what the Spanish chronicals had some difficulty in understanding (or at least in sorting out in a way that would still be satisfactory for today's reader): that both Spanish and Amerindians recorded their past as well as their wisdom in graphic and oral forms; that both equally treasured those records, even if they had different perspectives on the values that should be attributed to the oral and the written; and that the *quipu* in the Andes and the painted signs in Mesoamerica were the equivalent of letters. The Spanish never understood that if the Amerindian lacked letters they (the Spanish) by the same token lacked *quipu* and *amoxtli.* And while the Spanish had men of letters, the Incas had *quipucamayoc* and *amauta,* and the Mexica had *tlacuilo* and *tlamatini.*

Ixtlilxochitl and Chimalpaín left an extensive description of their working method. Ixtlilxochitl's written Spanish was quite impressive, even though he always criticized the Spanish interpretation of Mexican history. As a historian writing in agreement with the conventions of Western historiography and alphabetic writing, he found his source of information in ancient painted *amoxtli* as well as in oral reports and in the memories of the elders (*huehue*). In order to find out the truth about the past of New Spain, Ixtlilxochitl could not trust the contradictory opinions of the various authors (most, if not all, of them Spanish) who wrote its history. He decided to look into the painted records of the Mexicans themselves, as well as at the song they used to register their memories (". . . *y de los cantos con que las observaban, autores muy graves en su modo de ciencia y facultad*"). The authority, according to Ixtlilxochitl, was in the hand of the "most distinguished and wise people" (*gente muy ilustre y entendida*), who looked at the events as carefully and intelligently as "the most serious and trustworthy authors and historians of the world" (*los más graves y fidedignos autores y históricos del mundo*). Ixtlilxochitl backed up his assertion by saying that the distinguished and wise people he trusted and relied upon as the ultimate authority had, for each genre of recordkeeping, their scribes (*escritores, tlacuilo*):

> . . . unos que trataban de los anales poniendo por su orden las cosas que acaecían en cada año, con día, mes y hora. Otros tenían a su cargo las genealogías y descendencias de los reyes y señores y personas de linaje, asentando por cuenta y razón los que nacían y borraban los que morían, con la misma cuenta. Unos tenían cuidado de las pinturas de los términos, límites y mojoneras de las ciudades, provincias, pueblos y lugares, y de las suertes y repartimientos de las tierras, cuyas eran y a quién pertenecían. Otros, de los libros de las leyes, ritos y ceremonias que usaban en su infidelidad; y los sacerdotes, de los t empos, de sus idolatrías y modo de su doctrina idolátrica y de las fiestas de sus falsos dioses y calendarios. *Y finalmente, los filósofos y sabios que tenían entre ellos, estaba a su cargo el pintar todas las ciencias que sabían y alcanzaban, y enseñar de memoria todos los cantos que observaban en sus ciencias e historias; todo lo cual mudó el tiempo con la caída de los reyes y señores,* y [con] los trabajos y persecuciones de sus descendientes y la calamidad de sus súbditos y vasallos. (1975, I: 527)

. . . some dealt with the annals, placing in order the things that had occurred in each year, [recording the] day, month, and hour. Others were in charge of the genealogies and descent of the kings and lords and persons of noble birth, noting faithfully those who were born and erasing those who died, in the same manner. Some took care of painting the limits, boundaries, and borders of the cities, provinces, towns, and villages, and the parceling and distribution of lands: whose they were and to whom they belonged. Others [looked after] the books of laws, rituals, and ceremonies that they practiced in their unbelief, and the priests [recorded] the times of their idolatries and the manner of their idolatrous doctrine, and the feasts of their false gods and calendars. *And finally, the philosophers and wise men among them were entrusted with painting all the knowledge they possessed and had attained, and with teaching from memory all the chants they observed in their histories and lore; all of which time altered with the fall of the kings and lords,* and the labors and persecutions of their descendants and the calamity of their subjects and vassals. (1975, I: 527)[24]

Ixtlilxochitl's distinction, or lack thereof, between the "scribes" (*escritores; tlacuilo*) and "wise men" (*filósofo; sabio; tlamatini*), established in other chronicles an attractive analogy with the situation in the European Middle Ages. It is not obvious that both functions were part of the same social role, since there were distinctly different names for those who had wisdom and those who had skill. It is not surprising, then, that Sahagún placed the *tlacuilo* among the crafstmen, although, according to the sources, there seems to be a closer connection between the *tlacuilo, tlatoani* (one skilled in speaking, but also governor), and *tlamatinime* (having the wisdom of the word) than between the *tlacuilo* and the expert in several crafts. In Ixtlilxochitl, this connection is perhaps due in part to the process of transculturation and the changing patterns (as he himself noticed at the end of the paragraph) which blurred the distinction between *tlatoani* and *tlamatini.* For the Spanish, very much used to the idea that philosophers and wise men were at the same time scribes, the distinctive and complementary functions of the *tlamatini* and the *tlacuilo* went almost unnoticed. The Spanish erased the differences between the two cultures by using their description of themselves as a universal frame for understanding different cultural traditions. Venegas's definition of the book stands as a paradigmatic image of a cultural product which was at once a distinctive material object, written in alphabetic characters by a wise man, that had to be read or explicated by intelligent people. Today, from the perspective opened by Venegas's description, we can understand part of the difficulty the Spanish had in understanding the material aspects of Amerindian reading and writing culture, as well as the action the Spanish took, either in burning the Amerindian "books" or in slowly erasing them by teaching the Amerindian to change the material configuration of reading and writing as well as the format in which signs were inscribed and information graphically recorded and orally disseminated.

Concerning Graphic Signs, Sign Carriers and Persons of Knowledge and Wisdom

By the time the Franciscans arrived in Mexico on their mission to convert the Amerindian to Christianity, a historical dialogue took place between the twelve Franciscans and representatives of the Mexica nobility and men of wisdom. The dialogue was apparently recorded at the time it took place, probably over several weeks in 1524, and the record was found by Sahagún 1565. He rewrote it and put it into the form of a document on Christian Doctrine, with the title of *Coloquios y doctrina christiana con que los doce frailes de San Francisco enbiados por el papa Adriano Sexto y por el Emperador Carlos Quinto convirtieron a los Indios de la Nueva España. En lengua Mexicana y Española.* The manuscript was found in the Vatican's secret archives and was published for the first time in 1924 (Pou y Martí 1924). The fact that it was found in Rome and not in Seville suggests once more that the Christianization and Hispanicization of the Amerindians were two different programs, even during the period in which Carlos I of Castile and Aragon and Carlos V of the Holy Roman Empire combined both programs in one person.

Alphabetic writing allows for the inscription of what is said but not for a description of the scene of speaking. Mexica writing, on the contrary, allowed for the inscription of the scene but not for what was said. Near 1550, in the Colegio Santa Cruz de Tlatelolco, Sahagún found the scattered notes, probably left by one of the twelve Franciscans or by an Amerindian already familiar with alphabetic writing. He put the pieces together and provided a free and somewhat distorted translation of what was said by the Mexica nobles and wise men. Around 1560 it was still possible to believe that conversion was quick and easy and that the Mexican recognition of Christianity was so obvious that there was no room for doubt. But my interest here is to "listen" to the dialogue again, to that particular moment when the question of reading, writing, books, and knowledge came into the discussion. Let us first look at the transcription of the dialogue, which includes the original in Nahuatl and the close Spanish translation provided by León-Portilla, as well as an English translation provided by Kłor de Alva (1980: 52–193; Sahagún 1986). The scene is roughly the following. The twelve Franciscans friars, in a meeting with the nobles and *tlatoani* (governors) explain to them their own mission, and their roles as agents of God and the Emperor (Charles I of Spain and Charles V of the Holy Roman Empire). The *tlatoani* respond to the Franciscans in the terms transcribed below, and ended their speech at the moment in which they decide to consult with the *tlamatinime* (the wise men):

761 Auh inhin, totecujyoane
(Y, he aquí, señores nuestros,)
And these, oh our lords,[25]

ca oncate in oc no techiacana,
(están los que aún son nuestros guías)
indeed, they are there, they still guide us

in techitquj, in techamama
(ellos nos llevan a cuestas, nos gobiernan,)
these who carry us, these who govern us,

yn jpampa in tlaiecultilo
(en relación al servicio)
in relation to these being served

765 ca in toteoua yn jntlacaceuhcava
(de los que son nuestros dioses, de los caules es el merecimiento)
indeed, these who are our gods, these who have their merit

cujtlapillj ahtlapallj
(la cola, el ala [la gente del pueblo]:)
that of the tail, of the wing:

In tlamacazque, in tlenamacaque,
(los sacerdotes ofrendadores, los que ofrendan el fuego,)
the ones who offer things, the ones who offer incense,

auh in quequetzalcoa mjtoa
(y también los que se llaman quequetzalcoa)
and those named the feathered serpents,

in tlatolmatinjme
(Sabios de la palabra,)
These are knowers of the word,

auh in jntequjuh in qujmocujtlauja
(su oficio, con el que se afanan,)
and their charge, with which they trouble themselves,

in ioalli in cemjlhuitl
(durante la noche y el día,)
by night, by day,

in copaltemaliztli
(la ofrenda de copal)
is the act of burning copal,

in tlenamaqujliztlj
(el ofrecimiento del fuego)
the act of offering incense,

in vitztlj, in axcoiatl,
(espinas, ramas de abeto)
thorns, *axcoyatl,*

in neçoliztli.
(la acción de sangrarse)
the act of blood letting.

in qujtta, in qujmocujtlauja
(los que miran, los que se afanan con)
These see, these trouble themselves,

yn johtlatoquiliz ini jnmatacacholizq in jlhuicatl
(el curso y el proceder ordenado del cielo)
with the journey, the orderly course of the heavens,

in iuh iovalli xelivi.
(cómo se divide la noche)
according to how the night is divided.

Auh in quitzticate,
(los que están mirando [leyendo],)
And these continually look at it,

in qujpouhticate,
(los que cuentan [o refieren lo que leen])
these continually relate it,

in qujtlatlazticate in amoxtlj
(los que despliegan [las hojas de] los libros,)
these continually cause the book to cackle,

in tlilli, in tlapalli,
(la tinta negra, la tinta roja,)
the color black, the color

in tlacujlolli quitaqujticate
(los que tienen a su cargo las pinturas.)
is in the painting they continually carry.

Ca iehoantin techitqujticate,
(Ellos nos llevan,)
Indeed, they are the ones who continually carry us,

techiacana, techotlatoltia
(nos guían, nos dicen el camino.)
they guide us, they cause the path to speak to us.

tehoantin qujtecpana
(Los que ordenan)
They are the ones who put it in order,

in iuh vetzi ce xivitl,
(cómo cae el año,)
such as how a year falls,

in iuh otlatoca in tonalpoallj,
(cómo siguen su camino la cuenta de los destinos y los días)
such as how the count of the destinies-feasts follows its path,

auh in cecempoallapoallj
(y cada una de las veintenas,)
and each one of the complete counts.

qujmocujtlauja,
(de esto se ocupan)
They trouble themselves with it,

iehoantin yntenjz, incocol,
(de ellos es el encargo, la encomienda,)
they have their charge, their commission,

y mamal in teutlatollj
(su carga: la palabra divina)
their duty which is the divine word,

Auh in tehoantin
(Y nosotros,)
and we are those

ca ça ye iyo totequjuh
(sólo es nuestro oficio:)
indeed, who but have as our sole task,

795 (in mjtoa) teuatl tlachinollj.
(Lo que se llama el agua divina, el fuego [la guerra])
(what is called) divine water, fire.

auh ça iehoatl ypan titlatoa,
(y también de esto tratamos,)
And only we speak on it,

tictocujtlauja yn jtequjuh
(nos encargamos de los tributos)
we trouble ourselves with the tribute,

yn cujtlapillj, yn atlapallj
(de la cola y el ala [del pueblo])
of the tail, the wing.

. . . .

803 Ma oc tiqujnnechicocan
(Permitidnos que reunamos)
Let us, for now, assemble them,

yn tlamacazque, in quequetzalcoa
(a los sacerdotes, a los quequetzalcoa).
the ones who offer things, the feathered serpents.

ma tiqujmacaca
(Que podamos darles)
Let us give them.

in jhyotzin, yn jtlatoltzin,
(su aliento, su palabra)
His precious breath,[26] His precious word.

The dialogue continues with the meeting between the *tetecuchtin* (in charge of the military apparatus) and the *tlamatinime* (members of the noble class in charge of the religious apparatus), where they discuss the answer they would give to the twelve Franciscans. This scene is followed by another in which the *tlatoani* and the *tlamatinime* return to talk with the Franciscans; this time, the words are in the mouths of the *tlamatinime.* Their answer is a respectful disagreement with the Christian Doctrine presented by the Franciscans. One of the central points is the discourse about the Christian God and the Mexica *in Tloque in Nauaque* (The Owner of Nearby and Together). The *tlamatinime* refer to the Christian God as *in Tloque in Nauaque* and they express their admiration that the Spanish had come "from the clouds, the fog, from the very inside of the immense water" in order to bring "his book, his painting, the celestial word, the divine word" (990—*yn jamux, yn jtlacujlol;* 991—*in ilhuicac tlatolli, in teotlatolli*). After listening to the *tlamatinime,* the twelve Franciscans begin their reply as follows:

1098 ca muchi tamechilhuizque
(Todo os lo diremos)
Indeed, we will tell you everything,

tamechcaquitizque
(os lo haremos escuchar,)
we will cause you to hear it,

1100 intla anquinequ
(y si es que vosotros queréis)
if you desire it.

yoa uel tamchilpachiuitizque
(Y os habremos de tranquilizar)
And we will be able to cause you to have a full heart,

iehica in tehoantin ticpia
(porque nosotros guardamos)
because we guard it,

in teuamuxtli in teutlatolli
(el libro divino, la palabra divina)
the divine book, the divine word,

in oncan neztoc ycuiliouthoc
(en donde se ve, está escrita)
there, where it lies visible, it lies painted

1105 tlatlamantitoc
(está debidamente dispuesta)
it lies arranged,

in ixquich ytlatoltzin
(toda la que es su palabra),
all that is His precious word,

in tloque naoque
(del Dueño del cerca y del junto)
this one the Possessor of the Near, Possessor of the
Surrounding.

Briefly stated, this scene is relevant for an understanding of conflicting religious views that impinged on ideas related to writing, the book, and the social roles associated with reading and writing practices. León-Portilla was inclined to offer alternative readings when he translated the activities performed by *tlatolmatinjme* (those who have the wisdom of the word) (line 769). The translation of line 779 is "those who are looking at," and León-Portilla added "reading." The following line is translated "those who narrate," and the parenthetical portion specifies "those who refer to what they read," which, following the logic introduced in the previous paragraph, could be translated as "those who narrate what they look at," instead of "read." The following could be interpreted without parenthetical clarification as "those who unfold the book," although in this case the parenthetical portion further specifies that it is indeed "the pages of [the book]" which are being unfolded. At this point it is necessary to introduce Sahagún's ([ca. 1565] 1986) own free translation of lines 761 to 803, which he summarized in one paragraph, and more specifically what corresponds, more or less, to lines 761 to 781:

> Demás de esto sabed, Señores nuestros, que tenemos sacerdotes que nos rigen y adiestran en la cultura y servicio de nuestros dioses; ay también otros muchos que tienen civersos nombres, que entienden en el servicio de los templos de noche y de días, que son *sabios y ábiles, ansí cerca de la rebolución y curso de los cielos como cerca de nuestras costumbres antiguas, tiene los libros de nuestra antiguallas en que estudian y ojean de noche y de día.*
>
> And furthermore may you know, good sirs, that we have priests who direct and train us in the culture and service of our gods; there are also many others who have diverse names, who understand the service of the temples by night and by day, who are as *wise and skillful in regard to the revolution and course of the heavens, as they are in regard to our ancient customs; they hold the books of our ancient lore, which they study and look upon, by night and day.*[27]

Sahagún distinguished between understanding the trajectory of the stars and the configuration of the sky from "[to] *ojear* the books day and night." As we shall see, such a distinction is less clearly made in the paleographic edition and in León-Portilla's and Klor de Alva's translations. Since Spanish orthography was not clearly established in the mid-sixteenth century, despite Nebrija's efforts, I was tempted to translate *ojear* (to look at; Spanish definition: *echar los ojos, mirar con atención a determinada parte;* Latin: *oculos conjicere*) as "peruse" (to read through, to read with attention), which would be more akin to *hojear* (going through the pages of a book; Latin: *folia volvere*). This second option would be close to León-Portilla's clarification of his translation in which *"estan mirando"* (they are looking at), replaces the verb *"estan leyendo"* (they are reading). What is also notable in León-Portilla's translation that is absent in Sahagún's version is the verb *"despliegan"* (they unfold), which once again corresponds to Bernal Díaz's description of the Mexica *amoxtli:* "they unfold them like Castilian pieces of fabric." Sahagún could not have been aware, by 1565, of what a Mexica painted artifact was and what differences there were between "reading" in fifteenth- and sixteenth-century Spain and Mexico-Tenochtitlan.

While Sahagún placed the accent on the book, the Nahuatl version (as well as León-Portilla's translation) emphasized the spoken word and their agents, *tlatolmatinime* (those who have the wisdom of the word, *tlatol* + *tlamatinime*). Molina, in the sixteenth century, translated *tlatolli* as "word" while Simeón, toward the end of the nineteenth century, was more generous in his rendering and translated it as "speech, discourse, exhortation, history, story"; and he also rendered the derived expression *tlatollotl* as "history, process, life, biography."[28] More recently, León-Portilla interpreted the same word in the context of the Mexica conception of *toltecayotl,* which would be closer to what, in late fifteenth- and sixteenth-century Europe, was understood as cultural tradition and civility. In this context, *tlatollotl* was a word designating, at the same time, speech or discourse and a discourse in which the memory of past events and deeds was preserved. León-Portilla (1980: 53–71) rendered this second meaning by the expression "discourse-memory" (*palabra-recuerdo*).

The discourse of the "principales" who were in charge of the military apparatus, but who were also skilled in speaking (*tlatoque*),[29] introduced a difference between two social roles—their own and that of the *tlamatinime*—and consequently two concepts of discourse: the first derived from skill in speaking, the second from possession of the wisdom of the word. On top of the Aztec hierarchy, *tlatoani* and *tlamatinime* (which, interestingly enough, is written *tlatolmatinime* in line 769 on the paleographic version) were the social roles in which the power of the spoken word was embodied.

What did it mean "to be in charge" of the paintings, to read the red and black ink? Did it mean to be in charge of interpreting them or of writing them? Was the *tlamatini* also a *tlacuilo?* Apparently not. Those who had the wisdom of the word were those who could "look" at the sky or at the painted books and interpret them, to tell stories based on their discerning of the signs. The oral narrative of the wise men seems to have had a social function as well as a rank superior to the *tlacuilo,* who was placed by Sahagún among those who were skilled craftsmen.

The Spanish understanding of Amerindian writing practices and sign carriers was tinted with an emerging idea of progress, which went hand in hand with the origin of comparative ethnology. The model organized the world and intercultural relations in terms of what Fabian (1983) expressed in the formula "the denial of coevalness." Such a denial comes with particular force and clearness in Juan Bautista Pomar. Pomar was born in the same town as Ixtlichochitl, around 1535. He was well informed about the Amerindian past, well informed about Tezcoco (capital of Acoluhacan and one of the cities of the Triple Alliance, with Mexico-Tenochtitlan and Tlacopan), was literate and probably educated in the schools founded by Gante in the same city a decade before he was born. It was from the perspective of an educated person that he described the education of the nobles in his native town. As was already pointed out, Pomar placed the power of knowledge in letters and in the body, since without letters knowledge is limited. It seems that, disregarding the difference in societies and traditions, that there was a lack of letters was an observation made in different times and different places. Martín de Murúa ([1590] 1986), talking about the Incas, made observations similar to those of Pomar while talking about the Mexica:

> Aunque al Ynga y a sus reinos les faltó el arte tan industriosa de saber leer y escribir, medio tan famoso y conveniente para comunicarse las gentes de unas provincias a otras, y para salir los hombres de las tinieblas de la ignorancia, y alcanzar el título tan deseado de sabios, y trascender y alcanzar los secretos desconocidos, y aun casos sucedidos de tantos millares de años como tenemos, sabemos y gozamos mediante las letras.

> Although the Inca and his kingdoms lacked the most industrious art of knowing how to read and write, a most famous and convenient

> means for people to communicate among different provinces, and for men to sally forth from the shadows of ignorance and reach the most desired title of wise men, and transcend and reach unknown secrets, and even events transpired over many thousands of years, such as we possess, know, and enjoy by means of letters. . . .[30]

Both Pomar and Murúa recognized that Mexica and the Incas had their ways of knowing, although the lack of letters put them in a lower position in relation to the Spanish. Before introducing the letter as a warranty of knowledge, Pomar mentioned that in the education of the nobles there was a particular branch in which "they specialize in the knowledge of the star and the movement of the sky in order to predict the future" (see lines 775–785, above).

The whole range of questions regarding the material aspects of reading and writing cultures seems to be summarized in these two examples. The increasing relevance of alphabetic writing in Western culture contributed to the change in meaning of the Latin verb *legere* (to read). One of its original meanings was "to discern." Its meaning changed when it began to be applied to discerning the letters of the alphabet in a text, thus acquiring the modern sense of reading. One can surmise that *legere,* in the sense of looking at and discerning the meaning of whatever one is looking at, is precisely what is implied in what Pomar reported about the Mexica's "knowledge of the stars and the movement of the sky," and what the *tlatoque* who spoke to the twelve Franciscans had in mind when they referred to those who have "the wisdom of the word" as those who are "looking at," and why León-Portilla was inclined to add "*leyendo*" (reading) next to "they are looking at." In the same way that the *tlamatinime* looked at the sky they also looked at the inscriptions in solid surfaces made out of tree bark, which they unfolded and looked at.[31] Thus, the Spanish and the Mexica had not only different material ways of encoding and transmitting knowledge but also—as is natural—different concepts of the activities of reading and writing. The Mexicas put the accent on the act of observing and telling out loud the stories of what they were looking at (movements of the sky or the black and the red ink). The Spanish stressed reading the word rather than reading the world, and made the letter the anchor of knowledge and understanding. Contemplating and recounting what was on the painting (*amoxtli*) was not enough, from the point of view of the Spanish concept of reading, writing, and the book, to ensure correct and reliable knowledge.

This conflicting view reached its peak in Sahagún's *Coloquios* at the moment when the twelve Franciscans had to explain for the second time

Figure 10. Young Fray Bernardino de Sahagún surrounded by "books" (oil painting by Cecil O'Gorman, private collection).

to the *tlamatinime* ("those who have the wisdom of the word") what they had explained previously to the *tlatoque* ("governor and skillful in speaking").

Sahagún provided his own interpretation of Mexica discourse (see lines 1098–1105, above) and furnished it with the connotations surrounding the Spanish concept of writing and authority (Figure 10):

> . . . todo esto os declararemos muy por extenso si lo queréis oyr y satisfazeros emos en todo, *porque tenemos la sagrada escriptura*

donde se contiene todo lo que os diremos, que son palabras de aquel que da el ser y el vivir en todas las cosas. Esta sagrada escriptura, de que muchas vezes os emos hecho mención, es cosa antiquísima; son palabras muy verdaderas, certíssimas, dignas de todo crédito.

> . . . we shall explain all of this at great length if you wish to hear it and we shall satisfy you with all our explanations, *because we have the sacred scripture wherein are contained all the things we shall tell you, for they are the words of He who gives being and life to all things.* This sacred scripture, of which we have spoken many times, is very ancient, its words are most true, definite, and worthy of belief. (León-Portilla 1986: 90A, italics mine)

It would have been difficult for the *tlamatinime* to understand the connections between human writing and the writing of God, or between the "archetype book" and the "metagraph book," according to Venegas's distinction, which was naturally imbedded in the answer provided by the twelve Franciscans. It would have been equally difficult for them to understand a concept of truth that presupposed both a philosophy of language that prioritized the letter and a religious belief that attributed the final truth to the written version of the spoken words pronounced by God.[32] At the same time, it was just as difficult for the twelve Franciscans to understand that the material aspects of Mexica reading and writing culture drove them to a conceptualization of the word, the painted "books," and the relations of words and signs with the *in Tloque in Nauaque* (the Owner of the Near and the Together), which were not necessarily constructed around alphabetic writing.

God's metaphor of writing, according to which His words are dictated to men, is so well known that we need not press the idea further (Curtius 1973: 301–348). Less familiar to scholars dealing with similar topics are communicative situations across cultures in which agents are, so to speak, on different sides of the letter. The Mexica had a set of concepts to outline their semiotic interactions and their negotiations with the spoken words, written signs, and social roles and functions attached to such activities. They also had an articulation of the social and religious functions of spoken words and written signs which could hardly be translated into Western categories (e.g., philosopher, man of letters, scribe, or poet) without suppressing (and misunderstanding) similar activities in a context in which the conceptualization of semiotic interactions is based on a different material configuration of the reading and writing cultures. On one side of the dialogue, the agents were members of a learned culture in which the ideology of the letter and the book was equated with learning and wisdom.

On the other side, the participants were members of a society in which wisdom and learning were deposited in the body of the elders (*huehue*), were looked at in the sky and in painting, and were transmitted in oral discourse (*tlatolli*; López Austin 1985). The image of the "other" that members of each group constructed changed with the changes in the personal pronoun designating, in the dialogue recorded in Sahagún's *Coloquios,* the speaker and the listener, relating them to the context of a particular reading and writing culture. The mobility of the locus of enunciation was, in this case, loaded with the ideology of the book, and *amoxtli* with the spoken word and the diversity of graphic signs. The "other" depended on and changed with the change of speaker, which, in this case, belonged to two disparate, discursive situations and cultural traditions.

How could the Mexica understand that "the sacred writings" and the "Divine Book" were proof of God's existence and the warranty of Truth when alien to them were not only such a configuration but also the Western notion of truth?[33] Quite simply, the Mexica were unable to understand because, instead of reading the Letter of the Book, they were accustomed to listening to the Sages of the Word as well as to looking, recounting, and displaying the paintings of their *amoxtli.* How could the Spanish understand and accept the position expressed by the "Sage of the Word" if they believed that a lack of alphabetic writing was not only a sign of civil barbarism but also one of religious marginality? How could a group of lettered men whose very social role presupposed the concept of the letter understand the "Sages of the Word," whose very social role presupposed the oral transmission of knowledge?

"To read" meant unmatched activities for the Spanish and for the Mexica, as well as other Amerindian communities. The story of Atahualpa, in the episode of Cajamarca, in which he holds the Bible to his ears expecting to hear the Book talk, is as well known and revealing as the metaphor of the "talking book" in the autobiography of Frederick Douglass.[34] Mexicans described as "contemplating and recounting what is in the picture and on the sky" what the Spanish described as "reading the pages of a book" and, by extension, "reading" the universe as a book written by the hand of God. There is a double interpretation of this analogy. One interpretation would tell us that what Mexica and the Spanish were doing with the artificial signs inscribed on solid surfaces and with the natural signs wandering around the universe was basically the same, since they were looking at and making sense of them.

The second interpretation could be formulated as a question: why did the Spanish, in their accounts, leave the impression that the Mexica were doing well in reading and writing matters, although they were not yet at the level of Spanish intelligence and cultural achievement? Chronicle after chronicle of the first encounters described the material aspects of the reading and writing cultures and showed the difficulties the Spanish had in understanding how the Mexicans could have been satisfied with an oral description of what they saw in the paintings. On the other hand, there are few and scattered pieces of evidence that the Amerindians had difficulty understanding how a book or a page could "talk," and how their "painted signs" (the alphabet) could tell what could have been told by way of speaking. They were both, so to speak, on opposing sides of the letter. The Mexicas were not aware of its existence, while the Spanish were perfectly aware and convinced that the lack of letters placed human communities in the realm of the absences: the illiterates. The Mexicas were aware of the significance of being skilled in the art of speaking and the meaning of having the wisdom of the word.

It was the speech of those who knew how to "look at the stars and the sky" and to "unfold the *pinturas*" that they referred to as the authority, not to writing and the book. On the contrary, the Spanish, if they were aware of the power of the spoken word, also accepted the warranty of the written word and the book. It is to writing and the book that the Franciscans referred in their dialogue with the *tlatoque* and the *tlamatinime,* who underlined spoken discourse. The other experience of Anahuac was that the veracity of one god and the falsity of others could be judged by invoking the graphic inscription of the letter in an object which did not look like their *amoxtli.* How could the *tlamatinime,* routinely contemplating the paintings drawn by the *tlacuilo* and, telling stories, exercising at the same time the power of the spoken word, be reconciled with the idea that the true meaning was contained in the silent Words of the Sacred Book? Conflicting ideas about speech and writing, about the material aspects of reading and writing cultures, is what the process of colonization brought about during the first encounters between Spanish men of letters and Mexicas skilled in painting and speaking. The seed was planted for similar interpretations and behaviors during the colonization by other European nations in the nineteenth and twentieth centuries (Clammer 1976; Mudimbe 1988; Bloch 1989; Calvet 1974; Loufti 1971).

A Book Is Not Necessarily a Book: The Material Aspects of Signs and Their Descriptions.

The Spanish translated as "book" certain kinds of sign carriers. Writing that appeared on stone, for instance, was neither translated as "book" nor seriously considered as a sign carrier. The previous discussion has suggested, I hope, the implications of such a translation, given the fact that the network of meaning that Amerindians associated with the material aspects of their reading and writing cultures was suppressed and supplanted by the network of meaning that Spaniards created around similar kinds of cultural practices. While the translation of *amoxtli* as "book" or *libro* may be correct inasmuch as this rendering offers the best alternative in the English or Spanish lexicon, it is also misleading, since it does not take into account the etymological meaning of these words and the social function related to these translations in the respective languages. As a consequence, the "idea" associated with the object designated by a word is suppressed and replaced by the idea and the body of knowledge associated with that word in the lexicon and the expressions of the culture in which the original is translated. Thus, the translation of *amoxtli* as "book" does not capture the differences in the conceptualization of the activities related to the object (book, *amoxtli*), such as "to write"/"*tlacuiloliztli*" and "to read"/"*amoxitoa.*" A partial description of the knowledge associated with the word "book" and the verbs "to write" and "to read" in fifteenth- and sixteenth-century Spain, and a comparison with their Nahuatl equivalents (*amoxtli, tlacuiloliztli, amoxitoa*) would soon make it evident that the Aztecs could hardly have had books in the same sense that Castilians understood that word. The Aztecs did, nevertheless, have books.[35]

The point I am trying to make here is that while it is possible to generalize by saying that writing (in the sense of scratching on solid surfaces or using any kind of material meant to codify meaning) is an activity common to several cultures (and it is conceivable that every culture with writing systems has expressions to designate these activities), the *conceptualization* (i.e., the "meaning network") associated with the word and with the conceptualization of the activity is *culture specific* (see King, in this volume, for some illustrative examples). The same statement could be made in relation to the material aspects of sign carriers and their conceptualization in different cultures. "Book" is neither the universal name nor the universal concept associated with solid surfaces on which graphic signs are inscribed, preserved, and transmitted. It is only from the point of view of a culture capable of applying its own regional concept to similar practices and objects in other cultures that the clay tablet of the ancient Middle East and the papyrus in Egypt could be seen as forerunners of Western and Christian books.[36]

If the hypothesis that "book" designates the object and implies its representation in a network of semiotic interactions then the question "What is a book?" should be answered in the same way that the question "What is writing?" can be answered: a "book" is not a class of objects whose essential property can be identified, but rather a cultural and regional interpretation of a specific kind of object. Writing, although it refers to an activity rather than to an object, follows the same logic. The Mexica used "red and black ink" to describe an activity similar to what the Spanish referred to as "writing."[37] The development of speech and the extension of hands to scratch solid surfaces (originally "to write" came from the Anglo-Saxon *writan* and meant "to scratch" marks with something sharp; in Icelandic it was *rita,* "to scratch"; in Swedish *rita,* "to draw, to trace"; in Dutch *rijten;* and in German *reissen,* "to tear") have increased the complexity of semiotic behavior among the species *Homo sapiens* and, together with speech, have contributed to the consolidation of features we recognize as "human." Because in the West the concept of writing had been associated with the activities of scratching or the drawing of graphic signs on solid surfaces, Peruvian *quipus* presented a lot of difficulties to be interpreted and accepted also as writing.

If the properties which make an object into a book are neither in the object nor in the class of objects of which the "book" is one element (mainly because there is no such thing as an essential meaning supporting all different ideas of the "book" but, rather, changing conceptions of sign carriers), then we have to seek an answer to the question from among the specific cultural descriptions of similar kinds of objects. The question now becomes "What kind of conception/description does a culture associate with a class of physical objects made of graphic marks on a solid surface or of knotted and colored strings?"—or something equivalent, such as: "For whom is a physical object with a given set of characteristics a 'book'? How much is the idea of the 'book' based on the alphabet and on literacy? What kind of 'books' do we find in societies with nonalphabetic writing systems?"

One possible answer to this set of questions seems obvious: "*amoxtli*" and "*vuh*" were words coined to designate a class of objects within a society with picto/ideographic writing systems, while "book," during the fifteenth century, was a word used to designate a class of objects within a society at a complex stage of alphabetic literacy. This answer, however, does not tell us much about the kind of representation associated, in each culture, with the word in question. To explore this issue, it is necessary to relativize the notion of the "book" that we all bring with us and become observers of our own cultural presuppositions. Let us explore first the question of writing and then the question of the book.

According to current estimates, the biological line of the hominids to which human beings belong is a lineage about fifteen million years old. The human features to which one is accustomed today were consolidated far more recently (about three million years ago). One of the crucial aspects of this consolidation was the emergence of a particular kind of semiotic interaction: speech. All animals can be characterized by their ontogenetic, communicative, and semiotic behaviors. The first behavior accounts for all the actions of the individual; the second, for their tendency to live in "common union" with other individuals of the same species; the third, for their ability to exchange signs. To live in "common union" implies a communicative behavior and, therefore, the transmission and exchange of signs. If speech and writing distinguish the species *Homo sapiens* from other species, reading (from the Anglo-Saxon *raeden,* "to discern") seems to be one aspect of the sphere of semiotic interactions shared by all animal species—although not every animal species uses its hands "to write," all are certainly able "to discern" (e.g., to read) the semiotic behavior of other animals as well as changes in the cycles of nature.

If it is true that with speech a form of semiotic interaction was introduced that had a significant impact on biological configuration (enlargement of brain size) as well as on the organization of communal life (law, family life, planning, etc.),[38] with writing (visible signs) both a restructuring of thought and a reorganization of social life was attained.[39] Writing (in the general sense of the use of hands and the extension of hands through a sharp instrument, brush, pen, fabric, or knotted strings, etc.), together with speech, distinguishes the network of semiotic interactions proper to humans from the more limited ones found in other animal species. Writing, which is of interest here for its ties to the book, seems to have a larger extension than the book. Writing is a practice, the book a regional object resulting from a particular practice and its corresponding conceptualization. The "book" could be conceived as a general object among communities with different writing systems, only if there is agreement to call that a "book" any kind of material or solid surface on which graphic signs are inscribed (i.e., the book as mere object); it is culture-specific if there is agreement that what a culture understands by "book" (e.g., Holy Book) transcends the object and becomes a text: the idea of the object on which graphic signs are inscribed as conceived by the culture producing and using it.

Concluding Remarks

I have attempted to avoid the dangers of placing an all-powerful colonizer in front of a submissive native by taking a mountain detour in which the winding road that I have followed has offered the reader a vast scenic view. You may have perceived, in the distance, that colonial semiosis implies constant interactions, where relations of domination cannot be avoided, adaptation by members of cultures in conflict takes place, and opposition (from "inside") and resistance (from "outside") to the official power structure are enacted in various forms. Speaking, writing, and sign carriers, as well as their conceptualization, constitute one set of relations or network in which colonization took place. Thus, the spread of Western literacy linked to the idea of the book was also linked to the appropriation and defense of cultural territories, of a physical space loaded with meaning. The Western book became a symbol of the letter, in such a way that writing was mainly conceived in terms of the sign carriers: paper and the book, and the practices associated with reading and writing more and more came to be conceived in terms of the sign carrier; reading the word became increasingly detached from "reading the world," as the *tlamatinime* would have preferred to say.

Paradoxically, modern technology has returned us to the "beginnings of the book" (*biblos*) in that microfilms, screens, floppy disks, and tapes have become the new kind of surface on which writing is inscribed. The new forms of storage and retrieval of information are in the process of eliminating our bookish habits. Soon, we will have no need to peruse pages to find the necessary pieces of information. We already have access to alphabetical and thematic menus from which to obtain what we need. The metaphor of the Divine Book could be replaced, then, by the metaphor of the Electronic Book, an international data bank in which all knowledge will be contained. A professor of literature, teaching Borges's "The Library of Babel" will have to explain to his or her students what a "book" and a "library" were.

During the process of colonization, however, the book was conceived by the Spanish as a container in which knowledge from the New World could be deposited, as a carrier by means of which signs could be transmitted to the metropolis, and, finally, as a text in which Truth could be discerned from Falsehood, and the Law imposed over chaos. The book, furthermore, also played a very important role in the reverse process of sign transmission: from the metropolis to the colonial periphery. Printed books facilitated the dissemination and reproduction of knowledge and replaced, in the New World, the practice of the *tlacuilo* and the function of the *amoxtli,* thus contributing to the colonization of languages.

Notes

A first version of this paper was delivered at the conference "The Book in the Americas," organized by Norman Fiering at the John Carter Brown Library (1987). I am indebted to Norman Fiering for his confidence in and support of my preliminary ideas about the "book" across cultures. I am also indebted to Michael Palencia-Roth and Paul F. Gehl for their critical remarks, and to Elizabeth H. Boone for her enthusiastic reactions as well as her helpful comments. This essay is a revised version of chapter 2 of my *The Darker Side of the European Renaissance: Literacy, Territoriality and Colonization* (Ann Arbor: The University of Michigan Press, forthcoming).

1 This idea is far from original in Venegas. It has a long history, related to both Jewish and Arabic holy traditions. Widengren has summarized the trajectory of the idea of the Archetype or Heavenly Book from the Babylonian Tablets of Destiny and Israelitic-Jewish literature to the Koran. He has also traced the trajectory of the manifestation of the Heavenly Book in outward form ("Metagraph book," in Venegas's conception): "There are accordingly two different conceptions of the outward form in which the Heavenly Writing is written: it is *either* written as a sheet, or a scroll, or as a *kitab,* a real book, or even in a way—at least partly—identical with a special Jewish-Christian Book, the single *zabur,* or this Heavenly Scripture is not a book, but tablets, or rather one tablet, *lauh* (Widengren 1968: 215–216).

2 Folding-screen, scroll, and wall-hanging narratives from China and Japan are reproduced and described in the National Gallery's catalogue (Levenson (ed.), 1991: 305–362). But, alas, they are presented as "art" and "painting," not as "books." This image was already in place in fifteenth-century Europe. Roger Bacon observed that "The people in Cathay to the east write with the same instrument with which painters paint, forming in one character groups of letters [*sic!*], each group representing a sentence" (Bacon 1962). In Japan, printed flat surfaces in the form of scrolls were called *kansu,* and *orihon* was used to name folding-screen.

3 Among the many examples available to illustrate this assertion, the best I could find comes from the Canadian-Australian movie *Black Robe,* about the Jesuit mission among the Hurons, around 1630. Black Robe, the French missionary, writes down on a piece of paper a sentence pronounced by an Amerindian and then takes the piece of paper, fifteen feet away from where he wrote it,

and asks another French member of the expedition to read it. He reads it out loud, surprising the Amerindians, who do not understand how the things he said could have been carried that distance and pronounced by someone who did not hear him.

4 See Friar Diego de Landa ([1566], 1978). On Landa's mission see Clendinnen 1987, chapters 7 and 8.

5 The *Thesaurus Verborum* of Maya-Cachickel compiled by Thomas de Soto has an extended vocabulary related to sign carriers that is related to Western "books": *Nima vuh,* large book; *qhuti vuh,* small book; *bixabal vuh,* book of songs; etc. And, it is added: "This name *vuh* is applied to any kind of paper, notebook, breviary, etc." The same dictionary has *Q,ib* as "escritura" and the action of writing *q,ibanic* or *q,ibaxic* (Coto [1647], 1983).

6 Michael D. Coe (1973), provides several examples of different surfaces on which writing was inscribed. It includes also a description of the *Grolier Codex,* one of the four supposedly pre-Columbian codices from the Yucatan peninsula (the other three are the *Dresden, Madrid* and *Paris*); it is a folding screen painted on bark paper coated with stucco (p. 150).

7 See García Pelayo 1965: 45–70; Brandon 1968: 1–20; Widengren 1968: 210–216; Pedersen 1984: 12–20; and Graham 1987: 49–115.

8 Michael Coe has observed: "Maya hieroglyphs are obviously highly pictorial.... Because of these factors, *the Maya calligrapher was basically a painter, and probably both professions were joined in the same man.* This is reminiscent of China, of course. As in China, brush pens of various sizes were used. It is likely that for the relief carving of a text the master calligrapher would first brush on the characters, the rest of the job being finished by the sculptor; in the case of carved pottery, the calligrapher himself may have incised the still-damp clay" (Coe 1973: 8). Keightley (1989: 171–202) has observed that "Literacy in China involved not only a profound knowledge of the written classics but also the ability to wield a brush effectively, either to paint a landscape, usually with a poem inscribed at its side, or to write Chinese characters in their meaning but also their aesthetic vitality and the taste of their composer." If indeed the Maya were fully literate, to be literate in such a society meant something different than being literate in the European Middle Ages. The material aspects of signs, of communicative interactions and the discourse about them, had a different configuration.

9 See also Ong (1982).

10 See Oppenheim (1964: 230ff) and Michalowski (1990: 53–69). A clear presentation of Egyptian writing is in Fischer (1986).

11 A roll was conceptualized in terms of the frame, where either it stopped or was cut, and was called *tómos* (a cutting); hence our idea of "tomes." The Romans translated it as *volumen,* a thing that is rolled or wound up. Since long inscriptions, such as those dealing with the law or theological narratives, needed more than one volume, they were called "voluminous." The Greeks also coined the

word *bibliotheke* to name the place (boxes or rooms) in which *biblos* or *papyrus* rolls were kept. The ancient Mexicans also named the object after the material it was made from, *amoxtli,* and they derived from it the name of the place where it was stored, *amoxpialoya, amotlacentecoyan.* The logic of naming is the same: the name of the object derives from the material of which it is made, plus the name designating a place in which the object is stored.

12 One can surmise, after this collection of words, that there was a moment in the configuration of the system of representation of different cultures in which the name of a tree was used to designate the medium on which graphic signs were inscribed and transmitted. The Spanish *Diccionario de Autoridades,* published in the eighteenth century, describes the "book" as a volume of paper sawed and covered with parchment or something else. It is quite interesting to note that eighteenth-century Spanish has already eliminated the connection with the Latin *liber* (the inner bark of a tree, on which surface the ancients wrote) and has retained only the equivalence between "book" and "work" (*obra*) or "treatise." Here I have in mind the comment made by Diringer after drawing the etymological map of the word "book": "The exact connection, says Diringer, between 'book' and 'beech tree' is not known." The comment draws attention to the semantic and not to the phonetic aspect of the word. I suspect a connection could be suggested by departing from the system of representation associated with the words, instead of taking into account only the change in their meanings.

13 Curtius ([1948], 1973: 306) quotes a Greek epigram, engraved on a stone of a *bibliothéke,* which reads: "Say that this grove is dedicated to us, the Muses, and point to the books (*ta biblios*) over there *by the plane tree-grove.* We guard them here; but let him who truly loves us come to us: We will crown him with ivy" (italics mine).

14 Siméon ([1885] 1963) gives, as the first meaning of *amoxtli, "Plante abondante dans le lac de Mexico"* and, as the second meaning, *"livre, ouvrage."*

15 I cannot resist the temptation to recall that, according to Curtius ([1948] 1973: 313), *exarare* (to plough up) could also mean "to write," which, on the one hand, explains the comparison between "book" and "field" and, on the other, the fact that *legere* is used in noncultivated Latin in the sense of "gathering and collecting."

16 *"Lingua mea calamus scribae velociter scribentis"* (My tongue is the pen of a ready writer) (Curtius [1948], 1973 p. 311).

17 Translated by Maureen Dyokas.

18 Translated by Maureen Dyokas.

19 See Zumthor (1987: 107–154); Schmitt (1990: 239–251); Goldberg (1990).

20 *Amauta,* which Garcilaso de la Vega (*Comentarios reales de los Incas,* bk. 2, chap. 27) translates as "philosopher," is not clear. The word is not registered before Garcilaso. Some Andeanists surmise that it might have been Garcilaso's invention. Either that or, because of the image of the *letrado* (men of letters) in

Spanish society, early missionaries failed to see the similarities between those in the Andes who had the wisdom of the word (which Garcilaso called *amautas*) and those in Castille who possessed the written word. The solution seems to be that *amaota* is an Aymara word, not a Quechua one. See Mignolo (1993).

21 An area located southeast of Mexico-Tenochtitlan, between Mexico and Puebla. In colonial times, Chalco was under the administration of Mexico, both in economic and religious matters.

22 Translated by Maureen Dyokas.

23 I use the expression "colonial semiosis" to indicate precisely the conflictive interactions of alternative literacies in colonial situations.

24 Translated by Maureen Dyokas.

25 In Klor de Alva's translation (Klor de Alva 1980), the first verse quoted here has the number 770 instead of 761.

26 "Breath" designates oral discourse, speech. In the codices it is generally indicated by the depiction of air going out of the mouth.

27 Translated by Maureen Dyokas.

28 See Molina ([1571] 1971) and Siméon ([1885] 1963).

29 There are no unified criteria regarding the name of the person in charge of the military apparatus and the sovereign head of a well-organized religious and military community. Some suggest *tlatoani,* others *tlatoqui* (plural *tlatoque*). What is important, however, is that both are skillful in speaking, and their names have the same root, *tlatoa,* which means "to speak" and also to sing (Siméon, 1963). The relationship between being skillful in speaking and being in a position of power is well known in case studies of the ethnography of speaking.

30 Translated by Maureen Dyokas.

31 It has been observed that in the European Middle Ages "reading" was an activity quite different from what is understood by reading today (Riche 1579; Richaudeau 1969; Zumthor 1987).

32 Although according to the Christian idea the verb does not become the book (as is believed by Jews and Muslims [Pedersen 1984]) but flesh, and it reveals itself in the words and deeds of Christ, the idea of writing and the book is incorporated into Christian ideology with the New Testament (also García Pelayo 1965: 46–49).

33 "Otherness," as well as personal pronouns, is an empty and movable category. It is not just Europe the "self-same" and the rest the "others!" See Mignolo (1988: 28–53) and Krammer (1989: 107–123).

34 See MacCormack (1989). Gates (1989: 131) has perceived a similar phenomenon in nineteenth-century slave narratives and used the metaphor of the "talking book" to describe communicative situations across writing boundaries. Gates's essay indirectly shows that similar episodes related to the interpretation of written signs repeat themselves in colonial situations. The trope of the "talking-

book" is an ur-trope of the Anglo-American tradition which reveals the tensions between the Black vernacular and the literate White text, between the oral and the printed form of literary discourse: "Literacy, the very literacy of the printed book, stood as the ultimate parameter by which to measure the humanities of authors struggling to define the African self in Western letters."

35 This is nothing new. The fact that Aztec books were different from Spanish books is quite obvious. Robertson, for instance, places the word within quotation marks, but then proceeds to compare pre-Columbian painting with the European Renaissance(!). The problem does not lie in the "perception" of the different but in thinking within its framework. Donald Robertson does perceive the difference although his description of the Aztec "books" makes you doubtful (Robertson 1958: 29ff).

36 For a perspective on the practice, transmission, and conceptualization of writing in the Arabic World see the wonderful book by Johannes Pedersen (1984). Pedersen is writing for a Western audience and naturally uses the word "book" in the title. According to the previous discussion, the title should have been *The Arabic Kitab and al-Kitab,* where the emphasis is on human and holy writing rather than on the object (book) resulting from the inscription of graphic signs on solid surfaces.

37 Wood (1985) has transcribed several autobiographical accounts from Kerala, according to which learning the alphabet was coupled with the ritual of having the letters inscribed (physically) on the tongue.

38 See Ecles, 1989: 71–97; and Bickerton, 1990: 164–197. I am following the approach developed by Humberto Maturana and Francisco Varela, (1987) in particular, "Linguistic Domains and Human Consciousness" (pp. 205–239).

39 By "restructuring of thought" I am not referring to the supposed qualitative jump achieved by alphabetic writing. One of the difficulties of this thesis is that the paradigmatic example is always the classical tradition in the West (see for instance, Havelock, 1982: 314–350. I am referring rather to the extension of brain function once the visual means for recording and classifying information began to develop in human cultures. See Claiborne, 1974. And for a more sophisticated approach, although heavily rooted in the ideology of the consequences of (Western) literacy and in Greek "beginnings," see De Kerchove and Lumdsen (eds.), 1988: 235–321.

References

Ascher, Maria and Robert Ascher. 1981. *Code of the Quipu: A Study in Media, Mathematics and Culture* Ann Arbor: The University Press.

Bacon, Roger. 1962. *The Opus Majus of Roger Bacon* R. B. Burke, trans. New York: Russell and Russell.

Bickerton, Derek. 1990. *Language and Species* Chicago: University of Chicago Press.

Black Robe. 1991. 100 min. Distributed by Samuel Goldwyn.

Bloch, M. 1989. "Literacy and Enlightenment," in *Literacy and Society* Karen Schousboe and Mogens Trolle Larsen, eds. Copenhagen: Akademiske Forlag: 15–37.

Brandon, S. G. F. 1968. "The Holy Book, the Holy Tradition and the Holy Ikon," in *Holy Book and Holy Tradition: International Colloquium Held in the Faculty of Theology University of Manchester,* F. F. Bruce and E. G. Rupp, eds. Grand Rapids: William B. Eerdmans Publishing Company: 1–20.

Calvet, Louis-Jean. 1974. *Linguistique et colonialisme. Petit traité de glottophagie* Paris: Payot.

Ciudad Real, Antonio de. 1976. *Relación breve y verdadera de algunas cosas de las muchas que sucedieron al Padre Fray Alonso de Ponce* 1873, Madrid. México: Universidad Nacional Autónoma de México, Instituto de Investigaciones.

Claiborne, Robert. 1974. *The Birth of Writing* New York: Time-Life.

Clammer, J. R. 1976. *Literacy and Social Change: A Case Study of Fiji* Leiden: E. Brill.

Clendinnen, Inga. 1987. *Ambivalent Conquests: Maya and Spaniard in Yucatan,* 1517–1570. N.Y.: Cambridge University Press.

Coe, Michael D. 1973. *The Maya Scribe and His World.* New York: The Grolier Club.

Coto, Thomás de. 1983. *Thesavrvs Verborvm. Vocabulario de la lengua cakchiquel v el Guatemalteca, nueuamente hecho y recopilado, com summo estudio, trauajo y erudición* [ca. 1647]. René de Acuña, ed. México: Universidad Nacional Autónoma de México.

Curtius, E. R. [1948] 1973. *European Literature and the Latin Middle Ages* Princeton: Princeton University Press.

Curtius, Robert. 1953. *European Literature and the Latin Middle Ages* (1948). New York: Pantheon Books.

De Kerchove, D. and Charles J. Lumdsen, eds. 1988. *The Alphabet and the Brain: The Lateralization of Writing* London: Verlag.

Diringer, David. 1962. *Writing* New York: F. A. Praeger.

Diringer, David. 1982. *The Book before Printing* 1953. New York: Dover Publications.

Ecles, John C. 1989. *Evolution of the Brain: Creation of the Self* London: Routlege.

Fabian, Johannes. 1983. *Time and the Other: How Anthropology Makes Its Object* New York: Columbia University Press.

Febvre, Lucien and Henri-Jean Martin. 1958. *L'apparition du livre, 1450–1800.* Paris: Albin Michel.

Fischer, Henry George. 1986. *L'écriture et l'art de l'Egypte ancienne. Quatre Leçons sur la paléographie et l'épigraphie pharaoniques* Paris: Press Universitaires de France.

García Pelayo, Manuel. 1965. "Las culturas del libro." *Revista de Occidente* 24/25: 45–70.

Gates, Henry L. 1989. *The Signifying Monkey* New York: Oxford University Press.

Glennison, Jean, ed. 1988. *Le livre au Moyen Age* Paris: Presses du CNRS.

Goldberg, Jonathan. 1990. *Writing Matters: From the Hands of the English Renaissance* Stanford: Stanford University Press.

Goody, Jack. 1986. *The Logic of Writing and the Organization of Society.* N.Y.: Cambridge University Press.

Graham, William A. 1987. *Oral Aspects of Scripture in the History of Religion* New York: Cambridge University Press.

Havelock, Erick. 1982. "The Aftermath of the Alphabet" in *The Literate Revolution in Greece* Princeton: Princeton University Press.

Keightley, David N. 1989. "The Origins of Writing in China: Scripts and Cultural Contexts," in *The Origins of Writing,* W. Senner, ed. Lincoln: Nebraska University Press: 171–202.

Kenyon, Frederic G. 1932. *Books and Readers in Ancient Greece and Rome* Oxford: Clarendon Press.

Klor de Alvae, Jorge, trans. 1980. "The Aztec-Spanish Dialoques 1524" *Alcheringa, Ethnopoetics* 4/2: 52–193.

Krammer, Fritz. 1989. "The Otherness of Europe" *Culture and History* 16: 107–123.

Landa, Diego de. 1978. *Yucatan before and after the Conquest* William Gates, trans. New York: Dover Publication.

Le Goff, Jacques. 1957. *Les intellectuels au Moyen Age* Paris: Editions du Seuil.

León-Portilla, Miguel. 1980. "El testimonio de la historia prehispánica en náhuatl," in *Toltecayótl: aspectos de la cultura náhuatl* México: Fondo de Cultura Económica.

Levenson, J. A., ed. 1991. *Circa 1492: Art in the Age of Exploration.* Washington and New Haven: National Gallery of Art and Yale University Press.

López Austin, Alfredo. 1905. *La Educación de los Antiquos Nahuas.* México: UNAM. 2 vols.

Loufti, Martine Astier. 1971. *Litterature et colonialisme: L'expansion coloniale vue dans la littérature romanesque francaise, 1871–1914* Paris: Mouton.

MacCormack, Sabine. 1989. "Atahualpa and the Book" *Dispositio,* special issue on *Colonial Discourse,* R. Adorno and W. D. Mignolo, eds. 33–36.

Martin Rubio, María del Cármen, ed. 1988. *Instrucción del Ynga D. Diego de Castro Tito Cussi Yupangui* Madrid: Ediciones Atlas.

Maturana, Humberto and Francisco Varela. 1987. *The Tree of Knowledge: The Biological Roots of Human Understanding* Boston: New Science Library.

Michalowski, Piotr. 1990. "Early Mesopotamian Communicative Systems: Art, Literature, and Writing," in *Investigating Artistic Environments in the Ancient Near East,* Ann C. Gunter, ed. Washington: Smithsonian Institution: 53–69.

Mignolo, Walter D. 1988. "Anáhuac y sus otros: la cuestión de la letra en el Nuevo Mundo" *Revista latinoamericana de crítica literaria* 28: 28–53.

———. 1993. "Sujetos dicentes, roles sociales y formas de inscripcíon." Academic lecture, Berkeley, November 11.

———. Forthcoming. *The Darker Side of the European Renaissance: Literacy, Territoriality and Colonization* Ann Arbor: University of Michigan Press.

Molina, Alonso de. 1971. *Vocabulario en lengua castellana y mexicana y mexicana castellana* (1571) México: Editorial Porrúa.

Motolinia, Toribio de. 1903. *Memoriales.* Manuscrito de la colección del Señor don Joaquín García Icazbalceta. Publicado por primera vez por su hijo Luis García Pimental, Méjico. 1951. *Motolonia's History of the Indians of the Indians of New Spain,* Francis Borgia Steck, trans. Washington: Academy of American Franciscan History.

Mudimbe, V. Y. 1988. *The Invention of Africa: Gnosis, Philosophy and the Order of Knowledge* Bloomington, Indiana University Press.

Muñon Chimalpahin Francisco de San Antón. [ca. 1600] 1982. *Relaciones originales de Chalco Amaquemecan,* paleografiadas y traducidas del Náhuatl con una introducción por Silvia Rendón. México: F.C.E.

Murúa, Martín de. 1986. *Historia general del Perú* (1590) Manuel Ballesteros, ed. Madrid: Historia 16.

Ong, Walter. 1982. *Orality and Literacy* New York: Methuen.

Oppenheim, A. L. 1964. *Ancient Mesopotamia: A Portrait of a Dead Civilization* Chicago: University of Chicago Press.

Pedersen, Johannes. 1984. *The Arabic Book* G. French, trans. Princeton: Princeton University Press.

Pou y Martí, José María. 1924. "El libro perdido de las pláticas o Coloquios de los doce primeros misioneros de México," in *Estratto della Miscellanea Fr. Ehrle III* Roma: Tipografia del Senato, del Dottore G. Bardi.

Real Academica Española. 1964. *Diccionario de Autoridades,* edición facsimilar. Madrid: Editorial Gredos.

Reynolds, L. D. and N. G. Wilson. 1991. *Scribes and Scholars: A Guide to the Transmission of Greek and Latin Literature* Oxford: Clarendon Press.

Richaudeau, Francois. 1969. *La lisibilité* Paris: Denoel.

Riche, Pierre. 1979. *Ecole et enseignement dans le haut Moyen Age* Paris: Denoel.

Robertson, Donald. 1958. *Mexican Manuscript Painting of the Early Colonial Period* New Haven: Yale University Press.

Sahagún, Bernardino de. 1969. *Florentine Codex* (1578) Charles E. Dibble and Arthur J. O. Anderson, ed. and trans. Utah: The School of American Research.

Sahagún, Bernardo de. 1986. *Los diálogos de 1524 según el texto de Fray Bernardino de Sahagún y sus colaboradoes indígenas* (ca. 1565) Edición facsimilar del manuscrito original, paleografía, versión del Náhuatl. Miguel León-Portilla, ed. México: Universidad Nacional Autónoma de México.

Schmitt, Jean-Claude. 1990. *La raison des gestes dans l'Occident médiéval* Paris: Gallimard.

Siméon, Remi. 1963. *Dictionnaire de la langue Náhuatl ou Mexican* (1885) Verlagsanstalt, Austria: Akademische Druck-U.

Skeat, Thomas. 1969. "Early Christian Book Production: Papyr and Manuscripts," in *The Cambridge History of the Bible,* G. N. Lampe, ed. New York: Cambridge University Press.

Tito Cusi Yupangui. Inga D. Diego de Castro [1570] 1988. *Instrucción,* ed. by Marie del Carmen Martin Rubio, prólogo de Francisco Valcárcel. Madrid: Ediciones Atlas.

Widengren, Geo. 1968. "Holy Book and Holy Tradition in Islam," in *Holy Book and Holy Tradition: International Colloquium Held in the Faculty of Theology University of Manchester,* F. F. Bruce and E. G. Rupp, eds. Grand Rapids: William B. Eerdmans Publishing Company: 210–236.

Wood, Ananda. 1985. *Knowledge before Printing and after: The Indian Tradition in Changing Kerala* Bombay: Oxford University Press.

Zumthor, Paul. 1987. *La lettre et la voix. De la "literature" médiévale* Paris: du Seuil.

Joanne Rappaport

Object and Alphabet: Andean Indians and Documents in the Colonial Period

Introduction

As the early seventeenth-century Quechua-speaking author of the Huarochirí manuscript tells us, alphabetic literacy exerted a considerable influence in the reconstruction of a native Andean world view and historical memory under European domination:

> Runa yndio ñiscap machoncuna ñaupa pacha quillcacta yachanman carca chayca hinantin causascancunapas manam canancamapas chincaycuc hinacho canman himanam vira cochappas sinchi cascanpas canancama ricurin hinatacmi canman.

> If the ancestors of the people called Indians had known writing in earlier times, then the lives they lived would not have faded from view until now. As the mighty past of the Spanish Vira Cochas is visible until now, so, too, would theirs be. (Salomon and Urioste 1991 [Anonymous n.d.]: 157)

What the narrator neglects to add is that the written word was also instrumental in erasing the past as indigenous people had remembered it.

This paper will examine the role played by alphabetic literacy in the process of domination of native northern Andean peoples during the colonial period: how the power of European institutions was constituted and maintained through the spread of literacy in indigenous communities from the late sixteenth to early nineteenth centuries. On the one hand, it will investigate the impact of the contents of written documents on indigenous readers. In it, I will suggest the ways in which written documents influenced the definition of new forms of political process within and across aboriginal communities. I will also inquire into the role of literacy in redefining cosmological, ecological, social, and spatial referents as political, through their inclusion in administrative documents. On the other hand, I will also be concerned with documenting the process by which literacy influenced the nature of the historical memory, which had formerly depended upon the interplay of oral narrative and mnemonic device. To this end, I will explore the ways in which memories encoded in objects were translated into written form and the eventual replacement of mnemonics by alphabetic writing.

The backbone of Andean ethnohistorical investigation is traditionally constituted by a corpus of anomalous documents, written in Spanish, Quechua, or some combination of the two, by elite, educated native authors, and directed toward a primarily European audience.[1] On the one hand, these native treatises have been mined as sources of historical evidence for the reconstruction of Incaic social, political, economic, and religious organization (Murra 1980; Zuidema 1990). On the other hand, they have been analyzed as literary texts, as examples of indigenous efforts at communicating native concepts and values using a foreign idiom and medium (Adorno 1982, 1986; González Echevarría 1990).

In this paper I will take a different approach, concentrating on legal documents—land-titles, wills, royal decrees, dispute records—as opposed to narrative histories, such as the *relación*. It is more properly within the legal document, accessible to native authorities and carefully guarded for posterity by them, that the impact of literacy among Andean native peoples is most clearly evident, for it is with this type of writing that aboriginal communities came most frequently into contact. In other words, from the colonial period to the present, the legal document has constituted the major genre of written expression and of communication across the two cultures and of codification and transmission across time of indigenous oral and spatial memory (Rappaport 1990; Rivera 1986). The particular characteristics of this administrative genre are fundamental to an understanding of the impact of official documents upon indigenous people, for in records of lawsuits, notarial entries, and land titles, the power of history is codified according to Spanish linguistic and legal criteria. When historical evidence is read through them, it is filtered through the institution of private property, Spanish notions of heredity, and colonial definitions of the nature of the process of transmission of lands, movable wealth, political rule, and prestige.

Although I perceive literacy as playing a central role in the transformation of native Andean thought and organization, I do not consider it as a neutral technology that molds thought in predictable ways, as do the more evolutionary theorists (Goody 1977; Ong 1982). In contrast, I look for explanation within the social and political matrix in which specific literacies are employed to comprehend the impact that the written word had on native Andean peoples (Street 1984). It is not so much literacy itself, but the legal idiom in which the contents of documents are cast and thereby legitimized, and the administrative structure through which they are operationalized, that has determined the transformation of Andean society through the domination of the written word. Steve Stern (1982) has asserted that by operating within Spanish legal conventions, even if to secure protection against exploitation, colonial native authorities relinquished control over their own structures of authority and were forced not only to continue to play by European rules, but to defend them against challenges to European authority. Similarly, growing native participation in the literate conventions of the Spanish legal world, characterized by the exclusivity of its language and the individualization of legal claims, undermined other modes of expression and of communication, fostering the restructuring and repositioning of formerly oral, pictorial, or ritual genres (Gruzinski 1988). Thus, in keeping with Stern, it is not so much the technology of writing as the impact of its operationalization within a specific colonial context that will be central to my analysis.

The focus of this investigation will be the Pasto and, to a lesser degree, the Páez. Both are ethnic groups located beyond the borders of the Inca empire of Tawantinsuyu. The Pasto—today known only by their community names—inhabited the territory that comprises the southern portion of the modern Colombian department of Nariño and Carchi province of northern Ecuador; the Inca presence among the Pasto lasted only a decade or so, and was confined to the three southern chiefdoms (*cacicazgos*) of Tuza, Huaca, and Tulcán (Landázuri 1990). The Páez live on the slopes of the Central Cordillera of Colombia in the northeast corner of the department of Cauca. These northern Andean ethnic groups were characterized by a decentralized political structure and the absence of a state level of sociopolitical integration (Rappaport 1988b, 1990; Salomon 1986). Consequently, official state histories such as are documented for the Inca were absent in this area. Indigenous narrative histories, such as those of Guaman Poma or Pachacuti Yamqui, which build upon the official Inca version of the past, are likewise unknown for the region. Legal documents constituted the only channel of written expression available to these northerners.

Colonial Literacy

It would be a mistake to assume that the scribes of the Spanish colonial administration perceived literacy in the same functional way as we do today. Until the end of the sixteenth century language was an "absolutely certain and transparent sign for things, because, it resembled them" (Foucault 1970: 35). Writing was, in other words, an image of the truth lodged in things (Ibid.: 36–41). As a consequence, the relationship between orality, literacy, and object was different from what we perceive today. Colonial-era Spanish writing was fundamentally oral in nature, replicating in space the temporal dimension of oral communication through a refusal to appropriate the economy of expression that characterizes written communication. In other words, colonial literacy can be understood as oral communication set down in writing or as ritual acts described in detail, over and over again.[2]

The clearest examples of the orality of colonial Spanish writing are the numerous documents (ANE/Q 1685, 1693) that record the process by which aboriginal communities were divested of their lands. These documents are especially ubiquitous for the towns around the administrative center of Pasto, where the native Quillacinga population fell precipitously during the first half-century of conquest (Padilla et al. 1977: 40–41), leaving the Spanish with an opening for usurping what they saw as underutilized lands. In order that such lands be freed for public auction, public announcement by a town crier was necessary. Frequently, the town crier was obliged to repeat his message some thirty times; his words—or a translation into Spanish of them—are reproduced, verbatim, as thirty identical sentences in the documentary record.

Just as orality is reproduced in writing in colonial Latin American documents, ritual practice is relived through its inclusion in the legal record. Once again, Spanish scribes neglected the economy of expression that writing could afford: instead of briefly mentioning that certain rituals took place at designated sites with designated participants, they are described in painstaking detail, over and over again. For example, in the numerous records of disputes over cacicazgos, we are given repeated descriptions of the ceremony whereby political authority was bestowed upon a hereditary chief (*cacique*) through the ceremonial offering of woven mantles by neighboring caciques and the carrying of the new office-holder in procession around the plaza (ANE/Q 1694, 1735a).[3]

The replication of selected acts and statements repeatedly in the documentary record would ultimately dictate the memory of future generations. The impact of conventions of documentary writing upon native thought in the colonial period are convincingly recounted by Gruzinski (1988), who details the contents of eighteenth-century community titles fabricated by Mexican Nahuas, who had used Spanish documents as a model (see also Lockhart 1982, 1985). To jump ahead a few centuries, in my own experience in Panán, Colombia, those who asked me to read their eighteenth-century land title listened most carefully to the text of the possession ceremony. In nearby Cumbal, the text of the ceremony, which is still practiced today, is a central part of oral historians' description of the creation of their reservation (Rappaport 1988a). Memory is condensed into those oral and ritual acts that have been set in writing.

It is not as easy to gauge the extent to which the writing down of oral narrative and of ritual practice left its mark on the indigenous oral memory in the colonial period. The Spanish legal system required that written evidence be submitted to substantiate native claims; this could be either written versions of oral testimony or archival documents, both of which were used by colonial Indians in their lawsuits. Clearly, once memory was inscribed on paper and no longer lived in ceremony, bodily movement, and social relations (Connerton 1989), it became univocal; its meaning was transformed.[4] But the documentary record provides us with no clues to the nature of the lively oral tradition that certainly coexisted with the written word; my only entry into the oral domain is the ritual object that, as I will demonstrate later, was inserted into the written record.

Transformations in memory originating in the written channel can almost certainly be ascribed in part to the fact that most of these documents were written in Spanish, not in the various aboriginal languages used in the area.[5] In fact, unlike in Central Mexico, where a lively scribal tradition recorded thousands of documents in a variety of aboriginal tongues (Lockhart 1982, 1985), the number of legal documents in Andean languages can be counted on the fingers of one hand; Mannheim (1991: 143–44) surmises that their preparation was restricted by colonial decree. Guaman Poma's illustration of an indigenous scribe at work (Guaman Poma 1980: f. 814) portrays a man drawing up a will in Spanish. Legal documents from the Pasto Province are all in Spanish and, with only the exception of the wills (for example, ABC/I 1642), produced by non-Indian scribes. Thus, when eighteenth-century Pasto readers consulted sixteenth- or seventeenth-century wills, their understanding of these documents was mediated by the translations to which they had been subjected.

The Andean voice is thus severely limited in the colonial legal record. Less constrained were the authors of Mexican documents, who wrote in Nahuatl and illustrated their briefs with modified pictorial imagery (Gruzinski 1988). Here, the native voice enters not only into the language of the document, but into its very structure. In the Viceroyalty of Peru and of New Granada, in contrast, both Spanish and native legal documents such as land titles, wills, and suits are univocal, all written in Spanish. Only toponyms and proper names of important Andean items are recorded in an aboriginal language. More importantly, native documents are not amplified or presented through any form of a native representational system, although such a system existed, based primarily on color and abstract geometric design, as Cummins (this volume) so clearly explains.

Literacy and Power

Our first task is to understand why legal documents should be so key to the development of indigenous literacy in the colonial period. Because legal papers were drafted by individuals active in community activities and retained and read by them and by their heirs, they exerted such a great influence on the community. An examination of the social matrix in which such documents were written, used, and transmitted illustrates, moreover, why legal writing was so influential in transforming native categories of thought and of social organization.

Legal documents conferred privileges upon those who enjoyed access to them. In colonial-era Pasto Province this meant the caciques, who served as intermediaries between the community and the colonial administration, and who controlled the means of preparing such papers. In the first instance, caciques were enfranchised through their monopoly of the technology of writing. In a day and age in which political power was exercised to a great extent through writing, only those who knew how to write, or who were able to communicate with scribes, either in Spanish or through an interpreter, could lay any claim to the reins of power (Phelan 1967). Pasto caciques, like their Incaic counterparts to the south, were educated in special schools, where they learned to read, to write, and to speak Spanish. Such was the case with sixteenth-century caciques Don Andrés Guachag y Mendoza of Huaca and Don García Tulcanaza of Tulcán, both of whom were also active in the European conquest of the Pacific lowlands (Hartmann and Oberem 1981; Moreno 1986); their military experience won them the support of the Spanish and the allegiance of conquered lowlanders, while their command of the written word would maintain their ascendancy after the war was over.

But it was not only the literate cacique who was enfranchised by the legal document. Similarly empowered were those with access to the legal arena through the services of scribes. In some cases, we do not know whether certain caciques were literate or not, but we do know that they were able to cement political claims through recourse to writing. Especially interesting evidence in this respect are chiefly wills, which list those objects which their authors perceived as important signs of status during their lives and which, by hereditary transmission, could possibly affect the status of their heirs. Good examples are the testaments of two early caciques of Tuza, in what is today Carchi Province, Ecuador. Both Don Cristóbal Cuatin and Doña Catalina Tuza, living at the turn of the seventeenth century, encoded in their wills a series of power-objects of Incaic origin, including laquered wooden drinking-vessels called *keros* (*limbiquiros* in the testaments), silver keros called *aquillas,* and various types of finely woven cloth called *qompi,* that made it clear to the colonial administration and to their heirs that they had been recognized as authorities by the Incas (ABC/I 1592: f. 1v; 1606: f. 2v).[6] Note the central role played by these Incaic symbols of authority in the process by which the *Spanish* recognized the *colonial* authority of Pasto chiefs, achieved not simply through the possession of such objects, but even more so through their inclusion in a written document. A good indicator of this is the presence in a 1624 will from Túquerres (ANE/Q 1735b: f. 88r) of another pair of *keros,* objects not present in earlier such documents from north of the Inca frontier (such as, for example, a 1589 will from Guachucal, ANE/Q 1695: ff. 48r–49v). It was under European authority that certain Incaic symbols were revalidated and recontextualized in the colonial political arena, operationalized in part through writing. This is why Incaic symbols of recognition of political authority begin to crop up far to the north of Tawantinsuyu almost a century after the Spanish invasion.

Similarly, legal writing revalidated in a new political context certain northern Andean signs of political authority. Thus for example, Don Cristóbal Cuatin's 1592 will lists *caracoles,* or snail shells, among the objects he valued (ABC/I 1592: f. 1v). Even more intriguing is Cuatin's mention of two *mates,* or gourds—similar in function to *keros* or *aquillas*—sold him by Juan Quaya, principal of Tuza (Ibid.: f. 2r). Quaya is undoubtedly the same *mindalá* or status-trader, cited by Grijalva (1937: 81–84) as having used his special access to trade goods as leverage for usurping political control from a cacique (see also Salomon 1986: 208–210).

Just as Gruzinski (1988) discovered in his analysis of Central Mexican community titles authored by Nahuas, the northern Andean documentary record contains intriguing references to native-authored documents that bestowed legitimacy upon their owners by virtue of their written character, even if the documents were not recognized as legitimate by the Spanish administration. One example will suffice. Antonio Tandazo Montoya y Minchala, a native of Loja in what is today southern Ecuador, established his legitimacy over the early nineteenth-century Pasto by displaying royal decrees:

> Repreguntado, como dise que todo lo que se le pregunta es falzo, quando resulta de la misma sumaria decia publicamente a los yndios ser casique de muchos pueblos y que traia siete cedulas reales para poder radicarse donde le pareciese y que tambien traia breves pontificios. . . . Dixo: Que es cierto traia consigo siete reales cedulas y que profirio tambien ser casique de muchos pueblos y podia vivir donde mejor le acomodase. . . .

Asked again how he could say that all asked of him is false, when

> the written record states that he publicly told the Indians that he was the cacique of many towns, and that he carried seven royal decrees [*cedulas reales*] so that he could establish himself where he desired, and that he also carried papal briefs. . . . He responded: That it is true he carried seven royal decrees on him and that he also claimed to be cacique of many towns and could live where he was most comfortable. . . . (ANE/Q 1803: f. 7v; Moreno 1976; Oviedo 1987)

Later in the record, we learn that some of these documents were concocted by Tandazo himself:

> Preguntado si eran suyas las bulas viejas que se le han manifestado y tambien el papel que empiesa la Asia dibidido y concluye Pasto y doze de mil ochocientos tres, finalizando con la firma que dice Antonio Montoya y Minchala con su rubrica. . . . Dixo: Que es cierto que las bulas y pedasos son suyas, y lo mismo el papel referido y que no lo ha escrito por si sino que se formó de su orden por un cavallero a quien no lo conose ni sabe su nombre, porque era pasajero, de quien dice ser la firma y rubrica, y que el fin fue de poblar el citio de Mataconchoy.

> Asked if the old bulls [*bulas*] which were shown to him were his, and also the paper that begins with divided Asia and ends with Pasto 12 of 1803, ending with a signature that says Antonio Montoya y Minchala with its rubric. . . . He responded: That it is true that the Bulls and pieces [of paper] are his, as well as the referred paper, and that he did not write it himself, but that a man he does not know, nor does he know his name, formed it under his supervision, because he was a passenger, and the signature and rubric are his, and that he did it in order to found a town in the place called Mataconchoy. (Ibid.: ff. 9v–10r)

Despite the fabricated nature of the documentation, the Spanish administration was deeply concerned about the use of the written word to cement native authority, because they themselves recognized the tremendous force of authority that the written word wielded within their own system. And the indigenous actors who responded to these written symbols of political control had, like the caciques who included material symbols of chiefly authority in their wills, capitulated to a new system of legal legitimization of authority, which, from their perspective as the underdog, crystallized most perfectly in the symbol of the written word.

Finally, and in a similar vein, officially recognized written documents bolstered chiefly authority by affording caciques the possibility of registering their control over posts of authority and over community lands in their wills. In other words, not only the form, but the contents, of writing legitimized chiefly status. A number of caciques named their political heirs in their wills. Don Feliz Quastuza, cacique of Huaca, writing in 1711, stated the following:

> Yten declaro que el casicasgo le toca a mi hermano Don Julian de la Bastida o a alguno de sus hijos y hasta en tanto que parescan estos que mi hijo Don Bartholome Quastuza lo mantenga como io lo e tenido.
>
> Yten declaro que para el descargo de mi consiensia que este casicasgo no le toca a mi sobrino Don Gabriel de la Bastida hijo de Doña Maria Bastida mi hermana porque su padre fue Don Joseph Changona Garsia del pueblo de Pimanpiro y asi no le toca el casicasgo declaro para que conste como tambien lo sauen todos los principales del pueblo de Guaca.
>
> I also declare that the cacicazgo passes to my brother Don Julian de la Bastida or to one of his sons and until one of them appears, my son, Don Bartholome Quastuza, should maintain it as I have.
>
> I also declare, to ease my conscience, that this cacicazgo does not pertain to my nephew, don Gabriel de la Bastida, son of Doña Maria Bastida my sister, because his father was Don Joseph Changona Garsia from the town of Pimanpiro and for this reason the cacicazgo does not belong to him. I so declare so that it is on record and so that all of the authorities [*principales*] of the town of Guaca are aware of it. (ANE/Q 1734: f. 6v)[7]

Others, such as Doña Gregoria Chimachanag of Jongovito and Mocondino, near Pasto, sought out witnesses to prove that at one time there had existed legal papers documenting her inheritance of the cacicazgo (ANE/Q 1765). Don Ambrocio Fernández Táques declared in his 1713 will that he was cacique of Taques " . . . *por testamentos de mis antepasados*" (ABC/I 1787: f. 29r)—by testament of his ancestors. And most telling is the will of Doña Micaila Puenambas, cacica of Guachucal in 1691, who not only refers to legal documents to ensure that her nephew, Don Juan Bautista Ypialpud, would inherit the cacicazgo, but wills him the legal patent of nobility and the royal provision that she had inherited from her father (ANE/Q 1695: f. 38r).

Indigenous Authors and the Technology of Writing

The increasing centrality of writing in caciques' lives can be traced in Pasto wills from 1592 to 1759. In the late seventeenth century, *escritorios* or portable desks begin to appear in testaments.[8] In at least one of these cases, we even learn what was kept in them, as is outlined in Don Sebastián Yaputa's 1681 testament, in which the cacique's son is left a locked box:

> . . . para que guarde las memorias de las cobransas de los rreal tributos. . . .
>
> so that he keeps [in it] the records of collection of royal tribute. . . . (ANE/Q 1736: f. 9r)

Such documents are repeatedly cited in the wills as evidence of ownership of land; the use of documents to prove land ownership appears to have depended upon the physical presence of the written word in the hands of the witness, since possession of title meant possession of the object.[9] A good example of this is the 1711 will of Don Feliz Quastuza, of Huaca, who was forced by necessity to deposit title to his lands with a Spaniard in Otavalo, in exchange for a debt, and in another instance was robbed of his titles and, consequently, of his lands:

> Yten declaro que tengo otras mas tierras en este Mumiar y asimesmo en el pueblo de Guaca y como los papeles me los tiene usurpados Don Gabriel de la Bastida me e quedado yndefenso mando a mi hijo Don Bartholo si en algun tiempo paresieren con los mesmos demande y quite las tierras que en ellos mensionare.
>
> I also declare that I have other, further lands in Mumiar and also in the town of Guaca, and as Don Gabriel de la Bastida has usurped the papers, I am without defenses [and] I order my son, Don Bartholo, that if they should ever appear, he should sue them and take from them the lands mentioned in [the papers]. (ANE/Q 1736: f. 9r)

These were expensive papers to prepare: in the early eighteenth century, Don Mathias Quatimpas of Tuza paid out four mares in exchange for the cost of preparing an inventory of possessions, a good example of the fact that access to the written word was confined to the privileged few (ANE/Q 1746: 9r).

Before considering the transformations wrought by the written word, let us turn briefly to how these documents were read by native people. For the most part, they were probably only consulted by a few caciques and by their legal representatives. This is certain in a number of instances in which the originals have been retained by the community, but are barely legible:

> . . . Con la solemnidad nesesaria [Don Simon Mainbas, cacique de Tuza y Puntal] manifiesta vnos ynstrumentos antiquados pertenecientes a vnas tierras que posee para que de ellas se cirba Vuestra Merced de mandar que el presente escribano le de vn tanto de todo lo que se hallare legible porque con las hinjurias del tiempo se ban consumiendo por lo que se nesesita su refacsion. . . .
>
> With the necessary solemnities [Don Simon Mainbas, cacique of Tuza and Puntal] submits some ancient instruments belonging to some lands that he owns, so that Your Honor will order that the present scribe copy over what he finds legible, because with the ravages of time they are being consumed and are in need of repair. (ANE/Q 1757: f. 3r)[10]

In other instances, they were read in rituals (ANE/Q 1747: f. 11v). And in others, we know that they were owned by caciques, as is evident from the legend of a bound volume of documents held by the caciques of Tuza, Puntal, and El Angel:

> Contiene este quaderno los ynstrumentos antiquisimos desde el año de quinientos ochenta y seiscientos veinte y nueve, con vna real provision y otros mandamientos de amparo y possecion de las tierras de Mumial en fabor de Don Diego y Don Francisco Paspueles casiques principales de todos tres pueblos de Tusa, Puntal y el Angel: esta en posesion Don Agustin, Don Manuel Tussa: onse fojas.
>
> This notebook contains the very ancient instruments [dating] since the year fifteen eighty and sixteen twenty-nine, with a Royal Provision and other writs of protection and possession for the lands of Mumial, in favor of Don Diego and Don Francisco Paspueles, principal caciques of all three towns of Tusa, Puntal, and El Angel: it is owned by Don Agustin, Don Manuel Tussa: eleven pages. (ANE/Q 1792: cuaderno 1)

Legal papers retained by caciques were, clearly, read only in certain legal contexts. And then, their contents were examined for specific reasons, such as to ascertain boundaries or to prove that the cacicazgo was inherited properly. As I will illustrate below, the ways in which these documents were employed and the form in which they were cast forced their owners to shift their own vision of space and of time, so that it corresponded more closely to Spanish legal dictates, which emphasized boundaries over toponymic essence and chronology over nonlinear notions of temporal process.

Legal Documents and Social Transformation

Colonial-era legal documents codify in the political arena ritual acts that themselves encode political, social, and religious referents through the use of geographic and temporal space, experienced through bodily movement (Connerton 1989). That is, documents reduce multivocal practices to univocal texts by confining them to the domain of social administration.

A good example of this is the enumeration of boundary markers in the mid-eighteenth-century title to the Pasto community of Cumbal (NP/I 1758). Cumbal's boundaries, as described in the title, include a number of named boundary markers, as well as natural features of supernatural importance, such as rivers and lakes. The colonial cacicazgo of Cumbal, like its twentieth-century counterpart, was organized into a hierarchy of sections, arrayed from north to south in parallel bands of territory. Participation in colonial, nineteenth-century, and contemporary political organizations has always been structured according to the territorial hierarchy, with authorities from different sections assuming key administrative positions in a fixed rotational order that corresponds to the path of the sun between the summer and winter solstices, and which has also determined participation in festival sponsorship (Rappaport 1988a, 1988b). Interestingly, the enumeration of Cumbal's boundaries in its title follows precisely the hierarchical order that structures ritual and political life in the community. Nevertheless, in the title, the symbolism of the section hierarchy is condensed into the political domain, and this is how the boundaries have been read by later generations of Indians, who seek ritual referents in other sections of the title—in particular, in descriptions of the possession ceremony whereby land title was granted to the community—and not in the list of boundary markers (ibid.).

References to specific forms of historical interpretation and of ethnic identification become decontextualized political material in legal papers. Succeeding generations with access to documents, deprived of the sociocultural context of these referents, can reconstitute them in novel ways. Such is the case of the title to the community of Vitoncó, Tierradentro, prepared by the eighteenth-century cacique, Don Juan Tama de la Estrella, who legitimized his rule over the community by associating himself in the title with heavenly bodies and with streams, both of supernatural importance in the Pre-Columbian period. He also identified himself in this document with conquest-era military leaders, probably themselves participants in shamanic activity (ACC/P 1883 [1708]). The title to Vitoncó, nevertheless, simply states that Don Juan Tama was the "son of the Star of the Tama Stream" and that he acquired his political authority by triumphing over the neighboring cacique Calambás, taking his head. In an uninformed reading of the title, such information appears extraneous to the central point of the document: the Spanish administration's legitimization of Don Juan Tama's political authority and of Vitoncó's boundaries. The written word has, thus, politicized formerly multivocal symbols. Nevertheless, these seemingly odd facts probably served as points of legitimacy for Tama in the eyes of his own people. As late nineteenth and early twentieth-century Páez reread Tama's title, they recontextualized these demythified and politicized symbols within the framework of post-Independence civil wars, adding to them a mythic flavor that does not correspond to their significance at the time of the writing of the title (Rappaport 1990).

Not only was cosmological reality subsumed under the administrative rubric of the legal document, but the multivocality of place names and the very meaning of space were transformed as they were committed to paper. A chronological comparison of indigenous wills demonstrates that along with the particular brand of legal writing used by Andean peoples and their Spanish overlords came a shift in the ways in which land ownership was described. In early testaments, for example, plots were identified by toponyms, sometimes by the names of the owners of adjacent parcels, but never by a detailed enumeration of boundaries (ABC/I 1592, 1787). By the end of the seventeenth century, though, listings of boundary markers begin to appear in the documents.[11] This transformation is equally true in notarial records pertaining to European holdings; both indigenous and Spanish documents are altered in response to increasing pressure on land (Jeanette Sherbondy, personal communication).

The passage from identification by toponym to circumscription by boundary marker was a significant one for native people. Toponyms are considerably less complex in documents produced by Spaniards than they are in the notarial records of indigenous lands. For the most part, the differences lie in the use of an array of suffixes by Pasto landholders. As we know almost nothing about the lexicon and grammar of Pasto, it is virtually impossible to appreciate the layers of meaning concealed in these toponyms. Given the symbolic importance throughout the Andes of the organization of topographic space and the use of geographical markers to encode historical knowledge, however, it is certain that the abandonment of toponymic references to landholdings resulted in the further circumscription of the native voice in the written channel. Significantly, this also reverberated in the impoverishment of the historical memory since the rich texture of toponyms would be lost to future indigenous readers, who, even as early as the turn of the eighteenth century, were becoming monolingual Spanish speakers in ever-increasing numbers.[12]

Object and Alphabet

As Cummins demonstrates in his paper in this volume, Andean mnemonics and the European representation of discourse through alphabetic writing are very different processes (see also Cummins 1988). Mnemonic devices such as the *quipu,* an article composed of colored and knotted strings used in Andean cultures to recall various categories of information (Ascher and Ascher 1981), do not abstractly communicate knowledge in the same way that writing does. Rather, the knots of the *quipu* stand for categories of knowledge that are specified by an interpreter, who has memorized the data that they represent. This intimacy between object and person is equally true of other Incaic modes of representation, such as the checkered patterns of textiles and the geometric designs called *tocapu* on Pre-Columbian *keros.* These abstract design elements were used by the Inca to conjure up specific historical associations, such as memories of military conquest, when displayed in tandem on specific occasions, accompanied by oral interpretations of their import (Albornoz 1976: 23). They were not, however, narrative devices that brought to mind specific events; instead, these designs represented generic classes of incidents whose specificity had to be supplied by the interpreter.

Early in the colonial period, Andean people confused mnemonic device and alphabetic writing, as Bird (1943) discovered in a sixteenth-century burial of a southern Peruvian indigenous authority. Along with Andean objects of symbolic importance, a printed papal bull dated 1578 was neatly folded and carefully placed on the cacique's chest. We will never know whether the deceased could read the document, or whether, like *quipus* found in burials (Menzel 1976: 230), its contents had been interpreted to the chief by an intermediary. But a much later example from the Páez area demonstrates that written documents were perceived as ordered lines of abstract shapes whose meaning had to be interpreted by specialists. Undachi, the leader of an early eighteenth-century messianic movement, asserted his leadership by virtue of letters he received from God, but he could not read them:

Estando en la dicha prision el dicho indio dixo sin ser preguntado ablando con este declarante y los demas que auian ydo con Su Merced que si no querian creer que dios le auia ablado le mostraria vna carta que Dios le auia dejado escrita y que le soltasen, la yria a traer y que de lo qual dio noticia a Su Merced dicho señor Gobernador quien mandó lo sacasen de la dicha pricion y que yendo con Su Merced entregase la dicha carta y que pasando con el dicho yndio a otra casa mandó le bajasen vna mochilita pequeña que estaba colgada a la serca de la casa y que abierta la dicha mochila allaron en ella vnos pliegos de papel blanco y que tomando el dicho yndio vno de los pliegos en la mano dixo ser aquel la carta que Dios le auia dejado escrita sobre el altar de la capilla y que asi viesen lo que decia dicha carta porque el no la entendia y que siendo reconosida por Su Merced alla era solo vno de los pliegos de papel blanco y que hauienle dicho [que] no auia en el dicho pliego ninguna cosa escrita lo pidio y estandolo reconociendo dixo en su lengua señalando la marca de la imprenta: que aquello era lo que auia quedado escrito. . . .

While in said prison, said Indian stated in an unsolicited declaration while talking with this witness and the rest of those who had accompanied Your Honor, that if they did not want to believe that God had spoken to him, he would show them a letter that God had written and left for him and if they would free him, he would bring it. The Governor informed Your Honor, who sent for him to be taken from prison and, accompanying Your Honor, to deliver the aforementioned letter. Going with said Indian to the other building he ordered that they take down a small woven bag which was hanging on the wall. When the aforementioned bag was opened, in it they found some sheets of white paper. When said Indian took hold of one of the sheets he said that this was the letter that God had left him on the altar in the chapel, and that they should look at what was written in the letter, because he could not understand it. Once inspected by Your Honor, it was seen to be simply one of the several sheets of white paper. When he was told that there was nothing written on said sheet, he asked for it and examined it and spoke in his own language, pointing to the water-mark: that that was what had been written. . . . (AHT/B 1727: ff. 160r-v)

This role of writing as object did not remain static in the colonial world; the power and meaning inherent in the function of documents, as well as in Andean articles of symbolic importance such as *keros,* textiles, and their designs, were not constant. Colonial *keros,* unlike their Pre-Columbian predecessors, were not decorated with abstract motifs, but were pictorial and narrative in character; designs from a number of media, including textiles, were condensed on their surfaces (Cummins 1988). Clearly, the same processes were occurring in the visual and the alphabetic channels. Multivocal referents, hailing from a broad range of sources, were compressed onto univocal surfaces: the transposition of designs onto *keros* is reminiscent of the abandonment of cosmological, historical, and social referents in favor of the political and administrative realm in legal discourse.

As literacy increasingly became a reality among high-ranking caciques, the concept of the possession of a document moved from the ritual sphere it occupied, in the two examples I have given, to the political and social spheres, in which objects of Andean importance—both land and symbolic paraphernalia—were legally constituted by their appearance in documents, as we have already seen in indigenous wills. But the inclusion of these objects in testaments also transformed alphabetic writing into a mnemonic device. Catalina Tuza (AHT/B 1606: f. 4r), for example, specifically identified a piece of cloth she owned as *tucllapacha* (probably *ticllapacha*), a type of weaving bearing checkered patterns (see González Holguín 1989: 341), which represented a particular class of historical events associated with warfare. Similarly, paintings and statues representing religious themes began to be used to jog the historical memory, and were included as property in native wills (ABC/I 1592). But as literacy dug deep roots into the social fabric of Andean society, historically charged objects dropped out of the written record, replaced, by the seventeenth century, by references to written forms of historical evidence, such as wills, royal decrees, and other documents. Mnemonics gave way to alphabetic literacy, not because the latter was superior, but because its inception in America was accompanied by the spread of a legal ideology, born of colonial domination and carried by the written word.

Notes

The research upon which this paper is based was conducted with support (1) in 1978–1980 from the Fundación de Investigaciones Arqueológicas Nacionales, Banco de la República (Bogotá), (2) in 1990 from the University of Maryland, Baltimore County, Designated Research Initiative Fund, and (3) in 1989 from the Wenner-Gren Foundation for Anthropological Research. This is a revised version of "Literacy and Power in Colonial Latin America," written in collaboration with Thomas Cummins, and presented at the World Archaeological Congress II (Barquisimeto, Venezuela, 1990). I am thankful to Tom for his insights into the parallels between the written word and the pictorial image in the Andes, and hope that I have adequately summarized his ideas. I am also grateful to a number of people for their stimulating commentary on the paper, including Catherine Allen, Elizabeth Boone, Anita Cook, Jean-Paul Dumont, David Gow, Andrés Guerrero, Kirsten Hastrup, Sven Erik Isacsson, Dana Leibsohn, and Jeanette Sherbondy.

1 For examples of such writings, see Guaman Poma de Ayala (1980 [1615]); Pachacuti Yamqui (1967 [1613]); and Salomon and Urioste (1991 [Anonymous n.d.]).

2 Clanchy (1979) describes a similar state of affairs in medieval England, where objects and rituals were never wholly supplanted by the written word, but, instead, bestowed legitimacy upon written documents.

3 Spanish holders of *encomiendas* received these tribute grants in similar ceremonies (ANE/Q 1727a).

4 The dependence upon written documentation for historical evidence was particularly dangerous when fabricated texts were inserted into the legal record by the Spanish, as Isacsson (1987) documents for the Chocó.

5 In addition to Pasto—or the "mother tongue," as it is called in the documents—many witnesses from southern villages testified in Quechua—the "general language of the Inca." Although the Incas controlled the chiefdoms of Tuza, Huaca, and Tulcán for a decade or so, it was most probably under Spanish control that Quechua was introduced into the area.

6 The role of gifts, especially cloth, in the expansion of Tawantinsuyu is discussed by Murra (1975: 145–170). The use of *aquillas* as ceremonial vessels is explained by Grijalva (1923), and their presence in sixteenth-century Otavaleño chiefly wills is mentioned by Caillavet (1982).

7 See also the 1681 will of Don Sebastian Yaputa in ANE/Q (1736: f. 7r).

8 For example, the 1681 will of Don Marcos Taques of Tulcán (ANE/Q, 1727b); the late-seventeenth century will of Don Sebastian Calisto of Carlosama (ANE/Q 1747); and the 1709 testament of Don Mathias Quatimpas, principal of Tuza (ANE/Q 1746).

9 As early as 1606, Doña Catalina Tuza distributed land to her subjects through the use of documents (ABC/I 1606: f. 1v). See also the 1689 testament of Don Francisco Paspuel Guachan de Mendoza, cacique principal of Guaca, in ANE/Q 1757: f. 12r; the 1713 will of Don Ambrocio Fernandez Taques, in ABC/I 1787: ff. 29r–v; and the early eighteenth-century will of Jacoba Heznam, a commoner from Tuza, in ANE/Q 1792.

10 See also the testament of Andrés Yazam (ANE/Q 1772: f. 3r).

11 For the late seventeenth-century: "Testamento de Don Sebastian Calisto . . ." (ANE/Q 1747); "Testamento de Don Francisco Paspuel Guachan de Mendoza . . ."

(ANE/Q 1757). For the eighteenth century: "Testamento de Don Feliz Quastuza . . ." (ANE/Q 1734); "Testamento de Don Mathias Quatimpas . . ." (ANE/Q 1746).

12 This shift also brought material transformations to the lives of Indians, as outsiders took advantage of the simplification of toponyms to grab lands from communities (Jeanette Sherbondy, personal communication).

References

(a) Archives

ABC/I (Archivo del Banco Central, Ibarra). 1592. Testamento de Don Christobal Cuatin, principal del pueblo de Tuza. 1339/244/1/M.

ABC/I. 1606. Testamento de Doña Catalina Tuza, principal del pueblo de Tuza. 1335/295/1/M.

ABC/I. 1642. Protocolos y testamentos a cargo de Juan Francisco Guapastal, escribano nombrado de Tulcan. 1140/39/6/M.

ABC/I. 1787. Demanda que hace Pedro Ramon de Rueda . . . en nombre de Bernardo Garcia Tulcanaza y otros, a Francisco Perez, quien se ha introducido en las tierras que estan a beneficio del comun de los indios. 979/232/3/J.

ACC/P (Archivo Central del Cauca, Popayán). 1883 [1708]. Titulo del resguardo de Vitoncó. *Fondo Notarial*, Partida 757.

AHT/B (Archivo Histórico de Tierradentro, Belalcázar). 1727. Tierras de los ocho pueblos . . .

ANE/Q (Archivo Nacional del Ecuador, Quito). 1685. Materia seguida por Lucas Falconi, cacique de Botana, sobre licencia de venta de tierras. *Fondo Popayán,* caja 8.

ANE/Q. 1693. Autos del Alferes Real Nicholas Gregorio Zambrano sobre el remate de un pedaso de tierra del pueblo de Quina, jurisdiccion de Pasto. *Fondo Popayán,* caja 12.

ANE/Q. 1694. Materia seguida por don Ambrosio de Prado y Sayalpud, sobre el cacicazgo de Cumbal. *Fondo Popayán,* caja 13.

ANE/Q. 1695. Don Juan Ipialpud contra Rafael Assa, sobre el cacicazgo de Guachocal. *Fondo Popayán,* caja 13.

ANE/Q. 1727a. Doña Juana de Basuri y Sanbursi, sobre que se le entregue la encomienda de Buesaquillo en Pasto. *Fondo Popayán,* caja 45.

ANE/Q, 1727b. Patricio Cisneros contra Maria Taques Garcia Tulcanasa, cacica principal de Tulcan, por las tierras de Carampuer. *Fondo Indígenas,* caja 46.

ANE/Q. 1734. Autos de Domingo Yaputa, Francisco Paspuel Tuza y demas caciques de Guaca, sobre las tierras nombradas San Bartolome. *Fondo Indígenas,* caja 53.

ANE/Q. 1735a. Autos de don Reymundo Guaycal sobre el casicasgo de Cumbal. *Fondo Popayán,* caja 55.

ANE/Q. 1735b. Testamento de Doña Luisa Actasen, viuda de Pedro Queasa, principal del ayllu de Chaytan, en Túquerres. *Fondo Popayán,* caja 55.

ANE/Q. 1736. Don Domingo Garcia Yaputa, Gobernador del pueblo de Carlosama, sobre el cacicazgo de Carlosama. *Fondo Popayán,* caja 58.

ANE/Q. 1746. Autos en favor de Miguel Garcia Paspuel Tuza por tierras que heredó de su abuela. *Fondo Indígenas,* caja 63.

ANE/Q. 1747. Autos de Don Visente Garcia Yaputa, gobernador, y el comun de yndios del pueblo de Carlosama, con Don Mariano Pareces, sobre las tierras nombradas Yapudquer y San Sevastian, en los Pastos. *Fondo Popayán,* caja 75.

ANE/Q. 1757. Cuaderno de los instrumentos de la escritura de venta, otorgada por Don Pedro Guatinango a Don Andres Gualsago y testamento de Don Francisco Paspuel Guachan en la causa que siguen Don Hernando de Cuatinpas y Don Pedro Garcia, principales del pueblo de Tusa, con Don Antonio Luna, sobre tierras. *Fondo Indígenas,* caja 77.

ANE/Q. 1765. Autos de Don Manuel Pirtajoa y Chimachanag sobre el cacicasgo de Jongobito y Mocondino en Pasto. *Fondo Popayán,* caja 114.

ANE/Q. 1772. Autos de Don Juan Rosero, vecino de la Provincia de los Pastos, con los indios de Tulcan, sobre unas tierras. *Fondo Indígenas,* caja 97.

ANE/Q. 1792. Titulos y ynstrumentos de los yndios y casiques del pueblo de Tusa sobre la propiedad de vnas tierras. *Fondo Cacicazgos,* caja 3 (Carchi), cuaderno 14.

ANE/Q. 1803. Expedientes relativos a los autos criminales contra Antonio Tandazo. *Fondo Rebeliones,* caja 6.

NP/I (Notaría Primera de Ipiales). 1906 [1758]. Expediente sobre los linderos del Resguardo del Gran Cumbal. Escritura 997.

(b) Published Sources

Adorno, Rolena, ed. 1982. *From Oral to Written Expression: Native Andean Chronicles of the Early Colonial Period.* Foreign and Comparative Studies, Latin American Series, no. 4. Syracuse.

Adorno, Rolena. 1986. *Guaman Poma: Writing and Resistance in Colonial Peru.* Austin: University of Texas Press.

Albornoz, Cristóbal de. 1967 [1582]. Instrucción para descubrir todas las guacas del Pirú y sus camayos y haciendas. Ed. Pierre Duviols. *Journal de la Societe des Americanistes* 56, no. 1: 17–39.

Ascher, Marcia, and Rober Ascher. 1981. *Code of the Quipu: A Study in Media, Mathematics, and Culture.* Ann Arbor: University of Michigan Press.

Bird, Junius. 1943. Excavations in Northern Chile. *Anthropological Papers of the American Museum of Natural History* 38, no. 4: 171–319.

Caillavet, Chantal. 1982. Caciques de Otavalo en el siglo XVI: Don Alonso Maldonado y su esposa. *Miscelánea Antropológica Ecuatoriana* (Quito) 2: 38–55.

Clanchy, M. T. 1979. *From Memory to Written Record: England, 1066–1307.* Cambridge: Harvard University Press.

Collier, G. A., R. I. Rosaldo, and J. D. Wirth, eds. 1982. *The Inca and Aztec States, 1400–1800: Anthropology and History.* New York: Academic Press.

Connerton, Paul. 1989. *How Societies Remember.* Cambridge: Cambridge University Press.

Cummins, Thomas B. F. 1988. *Abstraction to Narration: Kero Imagery of Peru and the Colonial Alteration of Native Identity.* Ph.D. diss., UCLA.

Foucault, Michel. 1970. *The Order of Things: An Archaeology of the Human Sciences.* New York: Vintage.

González Echevarría, Roberto. 1990. *Myth and Archive: A Theory of Latin American Narrative.* Cambridge: Cambridge University Press.

González Holguín, Diego. 1989 [1608]. *Vocabvlario de la lengva general de todo el Perv llamada lengua qquichua o del Inca.* Lima: Universidad Nacional Mayor de San Marcos.

Goody, Jack. 1977. *The Domestication of the Savage Mind.* Cambridge: Cambridge University Press.

Grijalva, Carlos E. 1923. *Cuestiones previas al estudio filológico-etnográfico.* Quito.

Grijalva, Carlos E. 1937. *La expedición de Max Uhle a Cuasmal, o sea, la protohistoria de Imbabura y Carchi.* Quito: Ed Chimborazo.

Gruzinski, Serge. 1988. *La colonisation de l'imaginaire: sociétés indigènes et occidentalisation dans le Mexique espagnol, XVIe-XVIIIe siécle.* Paris: Gallimard.

Guaman Poma de Ayala, Felipe. 1980 [1615]. *El primer nueva corónica y buen gobierno.* Critical edition by John V. Murra and Rolena Adorno. Mexico: Siglo XXI.

Hartmann, Roswith, and Udo Oberem. 1981. Quito: un centro de educación de indígenas en el siglo XVI. *Contribuçoes à antropologia em homenagem ao Profesor Egon Schaden.* Sao Paulo: Coleçao Museo Paulista, serie ensaios 4.

Isacsson, Sven Erik. 1987. The Egalitarian Society in Colonial Retrospect: Embera Leadership and Conflict Management under the Spanish, 1660–1810. In Skar and Salomon 1987: 97–129.

Landázuri, Cristóbal. 1990. Territorios y pueblos: la sociedad Pasto en los siglos XVI y XVII. *Memoria* (Quito) 1, no. 1: 57–108.

Lockhart, James. 1982. Views of Corporate Self and History in some Valley of Mexico Towns, Late Seventeenth and Eighteenth Centuries. In Collier, Rosaldo, and Wirth 1982: 367–393.

Lockhart, James. 1985. Some Nahua Concepts in Postconquest Guise. *History of European Ideas* 6, no. 4: 465–482.

Mannheim, Bruce. 1991. *The Language of the Inka since the European Invasion.* Austin: University of Texas Press.

Menzel, Dorothy. 1976. *Pottery, Style and Society in Ancient Peru.* Berkeley: University of California Press.

Moreno Yánez, Segundo E. 1976. *Sublevaciones indígenas en la Audencia de Quito.* Estudios Americanistas de Bonn, 5. Bonn.

Moreno Yánez, Segundo E. 1986. De las formas tribales al señorío étnico: Don García Tulcanaza y la inserción de una jefatura en la formación socio-económica colonial. *Miscelánea Antropológica Ecuatoriana* (Quito) 6: 253–263.

Murra, John V. 1975. *Formaciones económicas y políticas del mundo andino.* Lima: Instituto de Estudios Peruanos.

Murra, John V. 1980. Waman Puma, etnógrafo del mundo andino. In Guaman Poma de Ayala 1980: xiii–xix.

Ong, Walter J., S.J. 1982. *Orality and Literacy: The Technologizing of the Word.* London and New York: Methuen.

Oviedo, Ricardo. 1987. Antonio Tandazo. *Revista Obando* (Ipiales) 3: 47–50.

Pachacuti Yamqui Salcamaygua, Joan de Santacruz. 1967 [1613]. Relación de antigüedades deste Reyno del Pirú. *Crónicas peruanas de interés indígena,* 281–319. Biblioteca de Autores Españoles, vol. 209. Madrid.

Padilla, Silvia, María L. López, and Adolfo L. González. 1977. *La encomienda en Popayán (tres estudios).* Escuela de Estudios Hispano-Americanos de Sevilla. Sevilla.

Phelan, John L. 1967. *The Kingdom of Quito in the Seventeenth Century.* Madison: University of Wisconsin Press.

Rappaport, Joanne. 1988a. History and Everyday Life in the Colombian Andes. *Man,* n.s. 23: 718–739.

Rappaport, Joanne. 1988b. La organización socio-territorial de los pastos: una hipótesis de trabajo. *Revista de Antropología* (Bogotá) 4, no. 2: 71–103.

Rappaport, Joanne. 1990. *The Politics of Memory: Native Historical Interpretation in the Colombian Andes.* Cambridge: Cambridge University Press.

Rivera C., Silvia. 1986. *"Oprimidos pero no vencidos": luchas del campesinado aymara y qhechwa, 1900–1980.* La Paz: HISBOL.

Salomon, Frank L. 1986. *Native Lords of Quito in the Age of the Incas.* Cambridge: Cambridge University Press.

Salomon, Frank, and George L. Urioste, trans. 1991 [Anonymous n.d.]. *The Huarochirí Manuscript: A Testament of Ancient and Colonial Andean Religion.* Austin: University of Texas Press.

Skar, Harald O., and Frank Salomon, eds. 1987. *Natives and Neighbors in South America: Anthropological Essays.* Göteborg: Göteborgs Etnografiska Museum.

Stern, Steve. 1982. *Peru's Indian Peoples and the Challenge of Spanish Conquest.* Madison: University of Wisconsin Press.

Street, Brian V. 1984. *Literacy in Theory and Practice.* Cambridge: Cambridge University Press.

Zuidema, R. Tom. 1990. *Inca Civilization in Cuzco.* Austin: University of Texas Press.

Walter D. Mignolo

Afterword: Writing and Recorded Knowledge in Colonial and Postcolonial Situations

At the time of the writing of this afterword, four books dealing directly or indirectly with the question of writing in Mesoamerica and the Andes have been published,[1] and a manuscript dealing with similar topics is in press.[2] All of these, in one way or another, cast doubt on current conceptions of writing and bring new light to the understanding of the kinds of writing systems that were not considered to have played a very important role, from a Western perspective, in the histories of writing. They all contribute, directly or indirectly, to the understanding of alternatives as well as conflicting literacies during the colonial period.

In her introduction to this volume, Boone addressed the issue of evolutionary models, which cast the history of writing as an ascending and triumphant move toward the invention of the letter and its conceptualization as the representation of speech. Pre-Columbian writing systems in the New World have more often than not been left out of the picture, though they have sometimes been used, locally, as a prehistory to the introduction of the Latin alphabet. In what follows, I would like to address the coexistence and interactions, during the colonial period, of alternative and conflictive literacies in Mesoamerica and the Andes, seeing them as a consequence of the Occidentalization of the globe and as a challenge to canonical histories of writing based on evolutionary models and monotopical hermeneutics. The coexistence of conflictive literacies brings about the need, first, to theorize coevolutionary histories of writing and, second, to move toward a pluritopical interpretation of the history of writing in colonial situations when alphabetic literacy coalesced with non-Western writing systems.

One of the consequences of alphabetic writing in the history of the West was its close association with speech and the increasing distinction between writing and drawing. While, in medieval illuminated books, connections were made between the forms of letters and the expressions of the human body and manual labor, the printing press detached the hand from drawing and writing and contributed to the subordination of drawings and illustrations to alphabetic writing and to the conception of alphabetic writing as an inscription of speech. Writing and painting became, in the European Renaissance, more autonomous than ever before.

Reents-Budet (1994) has observed, in the introduction to *Painting the Maya Universe,* that

> The origin in painting of Maya pictorial pottery, and of much of Maya art, is underscored by the fact that in all Mayan languages

> there is no linguistic or semantic differentiation among the words for painting, drawing and writing; all are referred to by the verb stem *ts'ib.* The distinction among painting and drawing is an occidental feature probably stemming from the two primary kinds of implements, the *stylus* and the *brush,* with which those of us from the Western tradition make marks on paper, and from a conceptual distinction between inking characters which represent language versus brushing on pigment to create an image. . . . For the Classic Maya, then, the making of images was born from the brush, be it writing, drawing or painting. Technically and conceptually, all were the same creative activity.

A similar point about the materiality of reading and writing cultures in China has been advanced by Michael Sullivan:

> From the merchant who hoists up his newly written shop-sign with ceremony and incense to the poet whose soul takes flight in the brilliant sword-dance of the brush, calligraphy is revered above all other arts. Not only is a man's writing a clue to his temperament, his moral worth and his learning, but the uniquely ideographic nature of the Chinese script has charged each individual character with a richness of content and association the full range of which even the most scholarly can scarcely fathom. (Sullivan 1973: 183)

To this David Keightley has added that "A man absorbed with writing was absorbed not just with words but with symbols and through the art of writing with the brush, with a form of painting and thus with the world itself." (Keightley 1989: 171)

Contrary to Mesoamerican and Chinese traditions, the European Renaissance witnessed the emergence of a theory of writing grounded on the examples of the invention of the letter and of alphabetic writing, such as the one introduced by the Spanish humanist, Antonio de Nebrija. Letters were, according to Nebrija, one of the greatest inventions of humankind, and an indication of their greatness was the possibility that alphabetic writing could tame the voice. If one can argue that taming the voice was implicit in the very invention of the alphabet, it was during the European Renaissance, at the fringes of Occidentalization and colonial expansion, that writing was first theorized and conceptualized as an instrument for taming (not representing) the voice and language, conceived in connection with territorial control. Nebrija's Castilian grammar became a cornerstone for the politics of language, implemented by the Crown for the purpose of expanding the Castilian empire in what was called the (West) Indies (Heath 1972; Mignolo 1992). Nebrija's Latin grammar was widely used in the Spanish colonies (the New World as well as the Philippines [Rafael 1992]) to write grammars of Amerindian languages and, directly or indirectly, to replace the Amerindian writing systems with European ones.

But, of course, the march of alphabetic writing over Amerindian writing systems was not without conflicts and tensions. To understand the conflict of consciousness which may have arisen, it should be remembered—first—that in Mesoamerica the writing systems in place did not distinguish writing from painting, as they did not consider writing a surrogate or a tool for controlling the voice, even if in Maya writing phonetic instructions were part of their logograms. Second, the Andean *quipu* challenged a concept of writing that, in the European Renaissance, was being established on the experience of the alphabet. Finally, Amerindian writing systems also challenged the Christian distinction between the Holy and the secular book. The missionaries believed that Amerindians did not have a language sufficient to explain the mysteries of the Holy Catholic Faith, but the missionaries did not consider the possibility that their own language was equally insufficient to account for Amerindian matters, among them the Amerindian uses and conceptualization of painting, carving, and weaving (e.g., writing) and the role that these played in society.

Although the understanding of Amerindian writing systems has expanded significantly over the years (Marcus 1992), the conflicts between Mesoamerican, Andean, and European literacies have yet to be explored. Two remarkable contributions in this direction, however, are Serge Gruzinski's *La colonization de l'imaginarie* (1988), a book in which the author explores some of the aspects of the conflict of literacies, from the valley of Mexico to the valley of Oaxaca, and from the beginning of the sixteenth to the middle of the seventeenth centuries, and James Lockhart's *The Nahuas after the Conquest* (1992), a book which examines the interactions and transformation of Nahuatl culture under Spanish rule.

Gruzinski emphasizes the period of persecution, which extended from approximately 1525 to 1540. This was also the period when alphabetic literacy was introduced and strategies of adaptation and resistance were developed by the Mexican intelligentsia in order to save their written records and to negotiate the conflict of literacies with the newcomers. For it was not only in oral form that information was given to or hidden from the Spanish. Most of the Mesoamerican codices known to us today were painted after the conquest, at the request of Spanish administrators.

The *Codex Borbonicus* (Mexico), the *Tonalamatl Aubin* (Tlaxcala), and the *Codex Selden* (the Mixtec region in Oaxaca) are all examples of the survival of ancient writing systems during the colonial period (Nowotny and Durand-Forest 1974; Aguilera 1981).

Lockhart has placed more emphasis, instead, on the overwhelming evidence of the extant documents showing that Amerindians were quick to adopt alphabetic writing and used it, during the sixteenth century, to register oral speech as well as oral narratives complementing the picto-logographic codices. He has also looked in greater detail at the transformation of the Latin alphabet that was used as the script of the Nahuatl language. Lockhart remarked that the notion of "word" was alien (at least during the sixteenth century) to the Nahuatl population that was using alphabetic writing, as they transcribed sound, syllables, and sentences but not words. From this example one can surmise that even when the adoption of alphabetic writing was quick and became widespread among the Aztecs, it cannot be inferred that the Western *philosophy* of writing was adopted and that writing was also conceived of as the representation of speech. The fact that *icuiloa,* which could be translated as "writing" or "painting" (for its literal meaning is "spreading colors on solid surfaces"), continued to be used to refer to Western "writing" indicates that although the practice of alphabetic writing was adopted, its conceptualization in the Western tradition was not. Nahuatl people had to negotiate, during the sixteenth century, not only the association between speech and alphabetic writing but also the relationship between writing and their own traditional writing practices.[3]

A parenthesis on weaving and plowing is necessary here. Tedlock (1985) translated the opening line of the *Popol Vuh* as: "This is the beginning of the Ancient Word, here in this place called Quiche. Here we shall *inscribe,* we shall *implant* the Ancient Word."

And Tedlock and Tedlock (1985) suggested that *inscribe* and *implant* could be replaced by *design* and *brocade,* so that the last line will read: "Here we shall design, we shall brocade the Ancient Word."

The analogies between writing and weaving in the Maya traditions have also been perceived in the Latin Middle Ages (see Mignolo, this volume). But of further interest are the connections between writing, weaving, agriculture, and distribution of labor according to gender. In the Latin Middle Ages (again see Mignolo, this volume) writing was analogized with *plowing* and the analogy was twofold. On one hand, because of the need of carving implied in the act of writing in certain solid surfaces as well as in the act of plowing. On the other hand, the analogy reflected the back-and-forth movement implied in plowing a field. *Boustrophedon,* a way of reading and writing common in Mesoamerica (See Boone, Pohl, van der Loo and Mignolo, this volume), is a word of Greek origin whose meaning is related to the act of turning like the oxen in the act of plowing, in the sense of moving horizontally in one direction and then reversing the direction in the next line like an ox plowing a field.

Thus the links between weaving, agriculture, and writing overcame the colonization shock and remained until nowadays (in Mesoamerica, Morris 1991, Berlo 1991; in the Andes, Seibold 1992; Cummins, this volume) as alternative literacies. Berlo (1991: 446) has underlined, based on Franquemont and Franquemont (1987: 70), that among the Quechuas of Chinchero, Peru, textile and agriculture maintain their traditional complicity. The word "pampa" in that community refers to both "the agricultural plain and to the large single color sections of hand woven textiles." Furthermore, *Khata* means "a furrowed field ready for planting as well as the textile warp configuration ready for pattern formation." The links between "pampa-*khata*" is that of "a broad plain broken by fields and ready to plant or to the broad plain-colored expanse of the textile broken by the design sections in their raw form (Franquemont and Franquemont 1987: 70)."[4]

There are several reasons why Amerindians would maintain, even after the conquests, their own oral traditions and writing systems. The first is so obvious that it is always forgotten: discoveries and conquests are not the only necessary conditions for an automatic replacement of the conquered way of life by the conquerors. It is also a generational issue. Those who were adults at the time of the conquest would have had more difficulties in changing their habits than would their children, who were born under new social conditions and were formally educated in the manners of the new rulers, living their everyday lives in a new society, whether at its center (where Spanish institutions were first established) or at its periphery (where Spanish institutions arrived late or not at all). One can argue that the new situation was not radically different, for communities living under Inca or Aztec rule, from the previous one. The social transformation, particularly in Mesoamerica and the Andes, from a world order rooted in a cosmology totally alien to the new and unfamiliar Christian cosmology impinged on the transformations of the writing systems, which ended up fading away after two or three generations, approximately one century after the conquest.

The suppression of Amerindian writing systems during the colonial period involved a process of adaptation and transformation during which the scribes had to adapt to a new social situation while at the same time learning a new writing system. The adaptation and transformation had an effect on both writing as such and on the reasons and motives that Amerindian scribes had had to weave *quipu,* to paint codices, or to carve stones for public places and institutional buildings. Let us address first the transformation of the writing system as such, which is a good example of the coexistence of both alternative and conflictive literacies.

Speech and writing, in Amerindian societies, were not related and were not conceived in the same way that they were in Greece and in the construction of the Western tradition, as critically analyzed by Derrida in his seminal work (Derrida 1967). The coexistence of alphabetic writing, the politics of languages introduced by the missionaries on the one hand and the Crown on the other, and the official philosophy of writing advanced by Nebrija in the preface to his Castilian grammar further complicated matters. As a result, a new dimension appeared when traditional writing systems among Amerindians began to merge with alphabetic writing. This encounter brought to the foreground the increasing distinction, in the European tradition, between writing and drawing and caused the Amerindians to change their practices of painting, carving, and weaving, as well as their conceptualization of writing practices. Antón de Muñon Chimalpain offers a good example of this merging in Mexico, toward the beginning of the seventeenth century. In writing a report on the deeds and memories of his people, addressed to the Spanish institution in Mexico City, he had to "read" ancient painted codices and to "translate" them into alphabetic writing. This is the way Chimalpain described this transaction:

> These old stories were made during the time of the lords our fathers, our ancestors. And these paintings of the people and the history of the ancient nobility were kept, as long as it pleased God to grant him life, by don Diego Hernández Mochintzetzalohuatzin, reigning Prince who became a Spaniard and died in Ce-Calli, 1545.
>
> Then, the painted paper and the history of the ancient nobility were left to his beloved son, the esteemed Don Domingo Hernández Ayopochtzin, who instructed himself in the telling of the books and then painted a book, writing it in letters, adding nothing, but rather as a faithful mirror of the things translated from there. (Rendón 1965)

The "red ink, the black ink" is one well-known Nahuatl expression in which writing and drawing were conceptualized as one and the same.

Finally, as far as there was coexistence and merging of different writing systems, there was also the conflict between the social roles of performing, in each society, the activities related to drawing and writing matters.

If these are some of the issues related to the adaptation and transformation of writing or, better, to the materiality of reading and writing cultures, there are also questions concerning the motives inviting or forcing Amerindian intellectuals to resort to their writing systems in a colonial situation, in which the alphabetic system was the one employed by the colonial administration in all of its transactions. Gruzinski explored the increasing control over the Amerindian population as one reason for the significant amount of codices painted by Amerindian *tlacuiloque* in Mexico-Tenochtitlan, in the nearby city of Texcoco and in the important Amerindian intellectual center of the Mixtec region, in Southern Mexico. It may sound like a contradiction to say that the Spanish persecution of Mexican society, which resulted in the destruction of ancient codices by the Inquisition (in order to eliminate the physical traces of their cultures) as well as by Amerindians themselves (in order to hide from the colonizers the physical traces of their cultural memory), would generate contemporary documentation equivalent to what was being eliminated.

But perhaps there is no contradiction—just a different set of circumstances and social situations in which what was destroyed in one place, for a given set of contradictory reasons, emerged as a new form of cultural production in a different social setting under a new set of circumstances. For instance, new codices were painted for a variety of reasons: as new reconstructions of Amerindian cultural memory requested by members of Spanish institutions, in response to the Amerindians' need to negotiate economic and legal matters with Spanish institutions in the colonies or to negotiate their own cultural identity under new social circumstances (see Leibsohn, this volume). Although there was a significant number of legal transactions and claims written by Amerindians in their own languages, using alphabetic writing (Lockhart 1992), the legacy of the ancient system was still in force—in Central Mexico and the Valley of Oaxaca—at least until the seventeenth century.

The preservation of preconquest forms of writing as well as their sign carriers (*amoxtli, book, quipu*) began to show the symptoms of its transformations with the intensity of colonization. Such transformations have already been significantly studied, and the mixture of European signs with the legacy of Amerindian traditions has been detailed and enumerated (Robertson 1958; Glass 1975; Glass and Robertson 1975: 81–252). Pioneering works on ancient Mexican writing systems, such as the one by Robertson (1958), insisted on the coexistence, on the same surface (writing or painting), of Amerindian and Spanish signs. The question, however, is not so much that Amerindian and Spanish writing systems coexisted on the same surface but, rather, what the meaning and implications of such a coexistence were in relation to the needs and social situations in which such paintings or writings were produced. This conflict of consciousness can be traced from one generation to the next, and it resulted in the almost total extinction of ancient writing systems by the late sixteenth and early seventeenth centuries. One of the most interesting implications is that in such "paintings" we find not just "information" (intentionally or unintentionally transmitted from the "native informants" to the Spanish administrators or missionaries), but mainly the ways in which Amerindians "wrote" their past as well as current events in Mexico and Spain, as they saw them impinge on their own social situation. If ancient codices are important documents to understand both the preconquest systems of writing and culture and situations and events during the colonial period, they are also truly alternative and conflictive acts of enunciation in colonial situations.

II

While most of the essays in this volume concentrate on Pre-Columbian legacies regarding writing, recordkeeping, and conceptualizing territories, they cannot avoid dealing in one way or another with the colonial period and the confrontations between people with different writing systems and, consequently, with different conceptualizations of speech and writing. As I have already mentioned, Nebrija's belief in the power of the letter to tame the voice and the Greek legacy of the power of the letter to represent speech have had serious consequences in the ways missionaries perceived Amerindian writing systems. Torquemada (1977), for instance, bitterly complained about the limitations of Aztec pictographic over alphabetic writing:

> One of the things which causes the most confusion in a republic and which greatly perplexes those who wish to discuss its causes, is the lack of precision with which they consider their history; for if history is an account of events which are true and actually happened and those who witnessed them and learned about them neglected to preserve the memory of them, it will require an effort to write them down after they happened, and he who wishes to do so will grope in the dark when he tries, for he may spend his life collating the version which he is told only to find that at the end of it he still has not unravelled the truth. This (or something like this) is what happens in this history of New Spain, for just as the ancient inhabitants did not have letters, or were even familiar with them, so they neither left records of their history. (I: xi)

The supposed disadvantage of pictographic over alphabetic writing began to fade away in more recent studies of Aztec writing systems. Hanns J. Prem (1992), for instance, suggested that

> Pictographic should not be considered a defective method, since it has undeniable advantages, the most important of which is that pictographic recording is not confined to a particular language but resembles in many respects a language of its own. Every story rendered in narrative pictography can be retold verbally in virtually any spoken language—certainly quite a useful feature in multilingual ancient Mexico. Even a modern reader can at least vaguely trace the complex scenes of unknown rituals, such as those depicted in the Codex Borgia, even though the language of its painter remains unknown. The second advantage has been less noted until now: narrative pictography allows readers to vary the length of their verbal renditions. This stands in contrast to textual writing, where the reading of a coherent story can be modified neither in wording nor in completeness.

For better or worse, the conflict of writing during the colonial period witnessed the victory of the alphabet and, with it, the overwhelming quantity of printed pages in Castilian over the relatively few written documents in Amerindian languages (Lockhart 1992). One of the consequences of alphabetic literacy was the change taking place in the semiotic configuration of speech and writing in Amerindian cultures. Certain uses of the writing systems practiced in Mesoamerica and the Andes needed an oral narrative to be interpreted (for instance, those referred to by Torquemada). Consequently, they allowed for linguistic diversity around the same system of writing. Eventually, alphabetic writing, in complicity with the language of the state and the printing press, overpowered linguistic diversity and established a linguistic hierarchy largely supported by the power of national languages and their inscription in alphabetic scripts. When Amerindian languages began to be written in alphabetic characters, they were used in legal transactions between Amerindians and Spanish or among the Amerindians themselves, and then remained in the archives without transcending their context of use. This represents an overwhelming consequence of the theory according to which the function of alphabetic writing was to tame the voice, and also provides a clear example of the connections between national languages, alphabetic scripts, and territorial construction. Thus, the conflict of literacies in the colonial period went hand in hand with a redistribution of forces according to which European languages became the language of the empire, and Amerindian languages survived in oral form, in marginal adaptations of alphabetic script, and in the decreasing influence (and eventual disappearance) of Amerindian writing systems.

During the Essex conference on Europe and its others, organized by Frances Baker et al. in 1987, Gordon Brotherston addressed the question of writing in the New World in the context of the discussion opened by Claude Lévi-Strauss's well-known "Leçon d'écriture" (1958) and Jacques Derrida's thesis developed in *De la grammatologie* (1967). Brotherston boldly stated that "no literary approach to the texts of the New World can avoid the problem of 'grammatology' raised by Derrida in his book of that title." The essays in this collection extensively and provocatively dealt with the "texts" of the New World without explicit references, comments, or discussions of the thesis advanced by Derrida's book. Brotherston argued in favor of a conciliation of the two positions by accepting, on the one hand, a "grammatology" in the terms formulated by Derrida and by including, on the other hand, Lévi-Strauss's contributions: there was a need to look into non-Western semiotic practices in the Americas.[5] This is, of course, Brotherston's own contribution, as a British scholar, to a debate between two French intellectuals about the question of writing and civilization in a non-European context.

The essays collected in our volume have a different pedigree, although most of the questions they address could be related to the European debate between Lévi-Strauss and Derrida taken up by Brotherston. But I would argue, consequently and contrary to Brotherston's earlier suggestion, that Derrida should be circumvented in dealing with questions of writing and cultures in the New World for at least three reasons. First, ancient Mesoamerican writing systems are totally alien to the idea of writing as representation of speech that Derrida traced back to ancient Greece. Second, the idea of writing in colonial situations is totally alien to the grammatological program founded in the regional history of Western philosophy of writing. And third, the foundation of national languages during the European Renaissance conceived writing as having control of the voice and the construction of territoriality rather than as the representation of speech. I am not saying that Derrida should be ignored and that a "new" way of looking at the history of writing be proposed. I am just suggesting an "alternative" way of looking at writing which circumvents the perennial Western foundation located in Greece and the perennial Western trajectory traced from Greece to Italy (during the Renaissance) to France (during the Enlightenment). Instead of taking Derrida's grammatology as a model, I would like to explore the possibility of rereading Derrida's grammatology *from* the experience of the Americas.

While the debate framed by Brotherston remains within a European politics of intellectual inquiry, what I am suggesting is the possibility of imagining not only *alternative literacies* but also *alternative politics of intellectual inquiry* and *alternative loci of enunciation.* I am assuming that research agendas are anchored in local debates and that, as a consequence, Derrida's motivations to address the question of writing in the intellectual debate of the sixties, as well as his political intervention in France, cannot be projected toward the question of writing in the preconquest and colonial Americas without risking an academic colonialism which uses a new laboratory to discuss old problems. Colonization of language is simply not a relevant issue in Derrida's influential grammatological reflections.

His entire argument in *De la grammatologie* rested on the assumption that, in the West, speech has been conceptualized as more fundamental than writing, which was understood as a mere surrogate or representation of speech. His paradigmatic examples go from Plato to Rousseau and from them to Saussure and Lévi-Strauss. In this scheme, the European Renaissance's contribution to the debate in the context of colonial expansion is glossed over, since Derrida's agenda was to debunk the pervasive idea that writing *is* representation of speech. Although the European Renaissance is not central to Derrida's argument, it is unavoidable when the issue at stake is the expansion of the West and the conflict of literacies in colonial situations.[6] Thus, the initial question is no longer a grammatology of the Americas, but alternative literacies in non-Western societies and the conflict of literacies in colonial situations. In other words, while Derrida has articulated a devastating critique of the Western philosophical tradition that privileged speech over writing, the essays in this volume indirectly suggest that his thesis—although relevant in the process of alphabetization—is not automatically relevant to account for Mesoamerican and Andean writing practices before the conquest and the coexistence and transformation of them during the colonial period.

III

Let us explore this issue further. There are indeed two related contexts in which reflections on writing traditions of the Americas and their transformations after the conquest and colonization could be framed. Both could be related to Lévi-Strauss's influential "Leçon d'écriture." One is, of course, Derrida's dismantling of Lévi-Strauss in his *De la grammatologie* (part 1, chapter 1), and the second is Jack Goody and Ian Watt's influential article on "The Consequences of Literacy," originally published in 1963. M. Bloch has convincingly shown the connections between Goody and Watt's concept of literacy and the colonialist ideology of the eighteenth-century French "philosophes."[7] Certainly the network could be extended back toward the European Renaissance, when a powerful ideology of alphabetic writing began to be articulated as a justification of colonial expansion.

The basic critique that Derrida addressed to Lévi-Strauss, because of his conflation of a notion of writing in a narrow sense with a notion of writing in a larger sense (or archi-writing), is a useful starting point because it is a critique valid, mutatis mutandis, for Goody and Watt as well as for sixteenth-century missionaries and men of letters trying to make sense of Mesoamerican and Andean writing systems. Let us pause for a moment to look at some of the basic concepts advanced by Derrida in his critique of the Western conceptualization of writing.

Derrida (1974) offers one of his many versions of his own concept of writing in his comment on one of the passages in which Lévi-Strauss deals with the effects that alphabetic literacy produces in a Nambikwara:

> A native—said Lévi-Strauss—, still in the period of the stone age, had realized that even if he could not himself understand the great instrument of understanding he could at least make it serve other ends.

Derrida's comments underline that Lévi-Strauss calls "writing" what indeed is writing in a narrower sense, for writing in a larger sense also covers the field of unwritten speech. "Writing in the narrow sense," which is one of the cornerstones of Derridian criticism, is more clearly articulated in the pages he devotes to the notion of "supplement" in Rousseau and Rousseau's definition of "writing in the narrow sense":

> Languages are made to be spoken, writing serves only as a supplement to speech. . . . Speech represents thought by conventional signs, and writing represents the same with regard to speech. Thus the art of writing is nothing but a mediated representation of thought. (1974: 144)

Since Derrida takes his paradigmatic example from a philosophy of writing so pervasive in the Western tradition, he has to invent the notion of "difference" or "archi-writing" in order to escape the notion of "writing in the narrow sense," conceptualized as a supplement to or representation of speech. If, instead of theorizing writing based on the Western tradition, one takes Mesoamerican and Andean examples as starting points, one comes up with a different notion of writing that allows for a rethinking of the relationship between speech and writing which does not make the second subservient to the first. And if one takes the spread of Western literacy, and not Greece, as a starting point, one will come up with a different agenda. For example, one can start with the principle of minimal rationality which will place ancient Greece, ancient Mesoamerica, and the Andes at the same level in regard to the uses of the mouth to produce and the ears to receive sounds that the brain will organize according to cognitive competence and social needs. Similar statements could be made with regard to the use of the hands to produce and the eyes to look at visible signs. The principle of minimal rationality (Taylor 1985) not only allows for the execution of the practice, but also for its conceptualization: why one kind of practice or one kind of conceptualization should be given a privileged status is a question that goes beyond the principle of minimal rationality and enters the realm of power and domination. Thus, by rethinking the question of writing from the Mesoamerican and Andean legacies, as well as from colonial situations (rather than from the Greek legacy as interpreted by Renaissance Humanists and Enlightenment "philosophers"), new articulations of the complicities between speech and writing are possible. Furthermore, the picture may be subsequently changed if we take into account and rehearse the discussion in Lévi-Strauss's "Leçon d'écriture" from the point of view of *alternative* literacies in preconquest Mesoamerica and the Andes and *conflictive* literacies during the colonial period.

Let us return to the principle of minimal rationality. In the 1940s, von Uexküll (1982) suggested a very attractive theory of meaning which went unnoticed in the humanities and the social sciences. Meaning, according to von Uexküll, was not a question of "words" or even man-made signs, but a question of a living organism creating its environment by sorting out the good and the bad and insuring survival as well as figuring out how to expand its philogenetic and ontogenetic domain of interactions. From brainless to brainful living organism, meaning as a set of processes and a question of life and death seems to be a common feature.

Von Uexküll's notion of "meaning" is perhaps not too far removed from Derrida's notion of "archi-writing." The differences could be accounted for in the examples—and the enemies—that this Austrian biologist of the forties and the French philosophies of the sixties were working against. Von Uexküll was dealing with a positivistic and physicalist notion of "living" grounded in biological rather than humanistic theories. Derrida was dealing with a narrow description (in time and space as well as in conceptual scope) of writing. Von Uexküll is relevant to the humanist and social scientist interested not only in transcending Western metaphysics by redefining writing, but also in transcending Derrida and moving beyond the speech-writing dichotomy as well as the trajectory of the letter from the southeast to the northwest Mediterranean—in other words, to move beyond Occidentalism as it manifests itself in the ideology of language subservient to colonial expansion (Mignolo 1991: 357–392).

In order to overcome both the dichotomy between speech and writing and the surrogate roles given to writing over speech in the European classical tradition, Derrida introduced the notion of "archi-writing" and made a significant move to anchor his argument in the human process of signification, rather than in the distinction between speech and writing. While this move opened up a panoramic vista, Derrida's argument—however—remained very much within the narrow European classical tradition, from the invention of the alphabet to contemporary linguistics and anthropology. That is to say, it remained within the fabrication of the European self-belief in the superiority of speech over writing and a conception of a civilizing process in which writing played a crucial role within a wide range of social activities.

I would like to maintain the distinction which Derrida attempted to blur. The distinction is relevant because it allows us to understand that the characterization of humanness based on speech has a different articulation from the characterization of humanness based on writing. Humans share, with other animals, the possibility of coordinating interactions by the production of sounds. Humans distinguished themselves from other animals in the animal kingdom with the use of the hand to "manu-facture" a wide range of tools and instruments for the organization of communal life and for the interaction with and creation of a satisfactory environment (Leroi-Gourhan 1964: 261–300; Marshack 1971: 118–130). Among the many "manu-factures" one can describe across cultures and times, there is a wide range of activities involving scratching signs on solid surfaces or knotting strings and using colors to coordinate (human) behavior, either by keeping a record of past events, transmitting knowledge, or providing instructions for a course of action. The interrelations of visible signs with sounds to coordinate behavior is certainly diverse. How it happened, then, that in the history of humanity a set of visible signs closely connected with sounds has been achieved, and why it became so pervasive in a region of the globe north of the

Mediterranean Sea which extended itself over the Atlantic, is a story that has not yet been told in any detail. Derrida's spectacular deconstruction of a short period of time (from the fifth century B.C. to the twentieth century A.D.), and of a narrow spatial domain (from the eastern to the north-central Mediterranean) is no doubt a significant contribution to dismantling an ideology of writing working in complicity with imperial expansion and with postcolonial nation-building.

Basically, the connivance between alphabetic writing and the major languages of the colonial powers (Spanish, Portuguese, English, and French) extended itself beyond the colonial period and remains pervasive in postcolonial nation states, from the earliest examples in Latin America (at the beginning of the nineteenth century) to more recent cases in the Caribbean, as well as in Africa and Asia. Thus, it is not so much the metaphysics of the presence criticized by Derrida that I am trying to underline in this afterword as it is the colonial and postcolonial politics of writing in colonial empires and postcolonial states. But, of course, the quick move from meaning and signification among living systems to postcolonial nation-states that I have made in this paragraph needs some clarification, even if this is not an essay in itself but a set of concluding remarks.

Beyond the conflated example of the Nambikwara in French philosophical discussions of the sixties, there is also the hidden splendor of Andean and Mesoamerican writing systems, whose fairly recent "discovery" in literary scholarship,[8] opened up the possibility of rethinking the canonical histories of writing in which the Andes and Mesoamerica were left off the map (see Boone's introduction), as well as Derrida's dismantling, in the European tradition, of a regional ideology prioritizing speech over writing and presupposing, by the same token, that writing must be "visible speech." The history of Mesoamerican and Andean writing systems has at least two parts. Part of the history occurs before 1524 in Central Mexico, before 1532 in the Yucatan Peninsula, and before 1533 in the Andes. Even if this dating is still schematic it is at least more generous than the flat "Pre-Columbian times" homogeneously but misleadingly dated to 1492.

Between 1492 and 1524 no radical changes took place in any of the three main centers of Spanish colonization. The same could be said for the Yucatan Peninsula and the Andes, between 1492–1532 and 1492–1533, respectively. A systematic campaign to teach alphabetic reading and writing did not begin in Mexico-Tenochtitlan until the arrival of the Franciscans and the transplantation of the Spanish school system, which began to replace the Mexican *calmemac.* Although Amerindian social roles did not vanish immediately after the conquest, as schooling continued among Amerindians under different circumstances, they were placed in a subaltern position. Despite the fact that Amerindian scribes and Andean *quipucamayoc* played an important role in maintaining their communal identity and social organization during (approximately) the first century after the conquests (see, for instance, Leibsohn and Cummins in this volume), they also became crucial pieces of the imperial intellectual machinery gathering information from Amerindian cultures. In the first case, they began to be marginalized and, in the second, they began to occupy a subaltern position in the new world order.

The spread of Western literacy in the colonies had different goals, and the consequences were not always consistent with those goals. While Franciscan missionaries were (mainly) interested in teaching reading and writing in order to make good Christians, the Crown was interested in teaching reading and writing Castilian in order to make good vassals. However, when Amerindians learned how to read and write, they chose to write in their own languages, either to negotiate with colonial authorities or to conduct their own business. A minority of the Amerindian population began to use alphabetic writing in order to preserve their own traditions. Because of such transformations in the practices of writing, we have today examples such as the *Popol Vuh* (Tedlock 1985) and the *Chilam Balam,* (Edmonson 1986) which, together with the painted codices of the knotted *quipu,* bear witness to the complexity of writing in colonial situations. Traditional narratives preserved in the memory of living persons and inscribed in stone, deerskin, or tree bark, or in knotted and colored strings, began to be fixed on paper with alphabetic writing.

Thus, this particular moment in the history of writing not only shows signs of coevolution of different writing systems (Maya, Mexica, Inca, Spanish) but also a conflict of consciousness within the Amerindian population and a form of domination among the Spanish administrators. Writing and recorded knowledge in colonial America, at least in areas with strong written traditions, became a battlefield, a complex system of interactions and transformations both of writing systems and of sign carriers (see Mignolo's chapter in this volume). The complexities of the history of writing in the colonial period impinged not only on the writing systems themselves, but on the materiality of reading and writing cultures as well. The discontinuity of both the European classical tradition and the Amerindians' own legacies in colonial situations is, at the same time, a discontinuity of the logocentric ideology built around the idea that writing is a surrogate of speech (which Derrida dismantled in his grammatological project) and of the evolutionary model assuming that there is an ascending line moving naturally from the oral to the written tradition.

IV

While writing in colonial situations staged a conflict of literacies, writing in neocolonial situations became the decisive victory of Western literacy and of the languages of the colonizers as the languages of the new and emergent nation-building processes. The Crown's colonial project to teach Castilian in order to make good vassals was transformed into a national project of teaching Castilian in order to make good citizens. The Amerindian nobility, decimated over the years, left the image of their glorious past in opposition to a marginalized Amerindian population, which became the burden of the present for nineteenth-century nation builders. The nineteenth century was also the period in which new colonial expansions, enacted by the British and French empires, allowed travelers and businessmen to collect the traces of ancient civilization and begin to transform the conflict of literacies during the colonial period into dead and decontextualized pieces for the museum or the archives.

Thus, while writing in postcolonial situations went together with the consolidation of ancillary national languages (Spanish in Latin America and the Caribbean; English in North America and the Caribbean; Portuguese in Latin America; and French in North America and the Caribbean), ancient writing systems became the treasure trove of and a commodity for travelers and businessmen for whom the economic expansion of their countries allowed a transformation of cultural legacies into exotic commodities. As a consequence, writing in colonial and postcolonial situations requires, more than a grammatology, theories of the materiality of reading and writing cultures and their relevance to understanding colonial expansions and ideologies of domination. At the close of the twentieth century, when colonial empires are almost a chapter of the past in the history of humankind, academic colonialism is still alive and well. The legacy of the European Renaissance, its celebration of knowledge attached to alphabetic literacy, is the legacy enacted in the major centers of research and learning in Europe and the United States and, in a more conflictive manner, in postcolonial states which, after the Second World War, became the "third world." Whether rethinking alternative and conflictive literacies would point toward alternative and conflictive ways of knowing it is perhaps both overly ambitious and premature. However, it is sufficient to realize that the recognition of alternative literacies is not only an interesting subject matter but an important indication of alternative ways of knowing which may impinge on our current conceptions of knowledge, understanding, and the politics of intellectual inquiry.

Notes

1 The four books are: Coe 1992, particularly ch. 1; Lockhart 1992, particularly chs. 7, 8, and 9; Marcus 1992 and Brotherston 1992.

2 Reents-Budet 1994. This volume argues a similar issue in relation to the Eurocentric conceptualization of Art. One of the basic points made in the Introduction to the book is related to the criteria constructed upon the materiality of painting practices to define what is and what is not Art. For instance, according to the Western tradition, great paintings are created in oils and tempera, ruling out the possibility that great Art can be actualized using slip-based paints on low-fired pottery. Similar arguments have been advanced in our volume regarding the concepts of writing, books, and maps. (I am grateful to Reents-Budet for letting me read the manuscript.)

3 Enrique Florescano has also observed that the introduction of alphabetic literacy among the Nahuatl-speaking population opened a new dimension in their own recording of the Past. As Amerindian intellectuals interpreted the painted codices in alphabetic writing, they replaced—in certain contexts—the variety of oral interpretations with a written one—this, of course, from the European perspective (e.g., one of such "certain contexts") (Florescano 1992).

4 For the relationships between weaving as writing and cultural identity, capitalist economy and tourism in a (post) colonial situation, see Morris 1991.

5 An expanded and revised version of this essay was reprinted as chapter 2 of his recent *Book of the Fourth World: Reading the Native Americas through Their Literature* (New York: Cambridge University Press, 1992), pp. 40–81. Brotherson dropped his claim for a "grammatology" of the Americas and replaced it, instead, with a long discussion on the social role of the Mesoamerican scribes and the sign carriers (*amoxtli, quipu,* etc.).

6 It is certainly possible to interpret Renaissance writing manuals within the grammatological project, as Goldberg did. But, once again, such reading remains within the history of the West and neither impinges on non-Western writing cultures nor on the question of writing in colonial situations, which is my concern here. See Jonathan Goldberg (1990).

7 Bloch 1989: 15–37. See also Stephen Houston's contribution in this volume.

8 See Gordon Brotherston, *The Book of the Fourth World,* for a general overview of writing, mapping, and recordkeeping in Mesoamerica and the Andes.

References

Aguilera, Carmen, ed. 1981. *Tonalamatl Aubin.* Tlaxcala: ITC.

Berlo, Janet Catherine. 1991. Beyond Bricolage: Women and Aesthetic Strategies in Latin American Textiles. In *Textile Traditions of Mesoamerica and the Andes: An Anthology,* Margo Blum Schevill, et al., eds., 437–482. New York: Garland Publishing.

Bloch, Maurice. 1989. Literacy and Enlightenment. In *Literacy and Society* Karen Schousboe and Mogens Trolle Larsen, eds., 15–37. Copenhagen: Akademiske Forlag.

Brotherston, Gordon. 1992. *The Book of the Fourth World: Reading the Native Americas through Their Literature.* New York: Cambridge University Press.

Codice Selden. 1964. México: Sociedad Mexicana de Antropologiá.

Coe, Michael. 1992. *Breaking the Maya Code.* New York: Thames and Hudson.

Derrida, Jacques. 1967. *De la grammatologie.* Paris: Minuit.

Derrida, Jacques. 1974. *Of Grammatology,* Gayatre Chakravorty Spivak, trans. Baltimore: Johns Hopkins University Press.

Edmonson, Munro, ed. and trans. 1986. *Heaven Born Merida and Its Destiny: The Book of Chilam Balam of Chumayel.* Austin: University of Texas Press.

Florescano, Enrique. 1992. La conquista y la transformación de la memoria indígena. In *Los conquistados: 1492 y la población indígena de las Américas,* Heraclio Bonilla, comp. Ecuador: FLACSO.

Franquemont, Christine and Edward Franquemont. 1987. Learning to Weave in Chinchero. *The Textile Museum Journal* 26: 55–78.

Glass, John B. 1975. A Survey of Native Middle American Pictorial Manuscript. In *Handbook of Middle American Indians,* Vol. 14, H. Cline, ed., 3–80. Austin: University of Texas Press.

Glass, John B. and Donald Robertson. 1975. A Census of Native Middle American Pictorial Manuscripts. In *Handbook of Middle American Indians,* Vol. 14, H. Cline, ed., 81–252. Austin: University of Texas Press.

Goldberg, Jonathan. 1990. *Writing Matters: From the Hands of the English Renaissance.* Stanford: Stanford University Press.

Goody, Jack and Ian Watt. 1963. The Consequences of Literacy. *Comparative Studies in Society and History* 5: 304–345.

Gruzinski, Serge. 1988. *La colonization de l'imaginaire.* Paris: Gallimard.

Heath, Shirley Brice. 1972. *La política del lenguaje en México: de la colonia a la nación.* México: Secretaría de Educación.

Keightly, David. 1989. The Origins of Writing in China: Scripts and Cultural Contexts. In *The Origins of Writing,* Wayne Senner, ed. Lincoln: Nebraska University Press.

Leroi-Gourhan, André. 1964. *Le Geste et la Parole.* Paris: Albin Michel.

Lévi-Strauss, Claude. 1958. *Tristes Tropiques.* Paris: Gallimard.

Lockhart, James. 1992. *The Nahuas after the Conquest.* Stanford: Stanford University Press.

———. 1991. *Nahuas and Spaniards: Postconquest Central Mexican History and Philosophy.* Stanford: Stanford University Press.

Marcus, Joyce. 1992. *Mesoamerican Writing Systems: Propaganda, Myth and History in Four Ancient Civilizations.* Princeton: Princeton University Press.

Marshack, A. 1971. *The Root of Civilization: The Cognitive Beginning of Man's First Art, Symbol and Notation.* New York: McGraw-Hill Book Co.

Mignolo, Walter D. 1992. Nebrija in the New World. *L'Homme: Revue Francaise d'Anthropologie* 122–124: 187–209.

———. 1991. (Re)modeling the Letter: Literacy and Literature at the Intersection of Semiotics and Literary Studies. In *On Semiotic Modeling,* M. Anderson and I. Merrell eds., 357–392. Berlin: Mouton de Gruyter.

Morris, Walter F., Jr. 1991. The Marketing of Maya Textiles in Highland Chiapas, Mexico. In *Textile Traditions of Mesoamerica and the Andes: An Anthology.* Margot Blum Schevill et al., eds., 403–436. New York: Garland Publishing.

Nowotny, Karl A. and Jacqueline Durand-Forest, eds. 1974. *Codex Borbonicus.* Graz: Akademische Druck.

Prem, Hanns J. 1992. Aztec Writing. In *Epigraphy: Supplement to the Handbook of American Indians,* Victoria R. Bricker, ed., 53–69. Austin: University of Texas Press.

Rafael, Vicente. 1992. *Contracting Colonialism.* Durham: Duke University Press.

Reents-Budet, Dorie. 1994. *Painting the Maya Universe: Royal Ceramics of the Classic Period.* Contributions by Joseph W. Ball, Ronald L. Bishop, Virginia M. Fields and Barbara McLeod. Durham: Duke University Press.

Rendón, Silvia, trans. 1965. *Relaciones originales de Chalco-Amaquemecan* (toward 1610). México: Fondo de Cultura Económica.

Robertson, Donald. 1958. *Mexican Manuscript Painting of the Early Colonial Period.* New Haven: Yale University Press.

Seibold, Katharine E. 1992. Textiles and Cosmology in Choquecanche, Cuzco, Peru. In *Andean Cosmologies Through Time: Persistence and Emergence,* Robert V. H. Dover et al., eds., 166–201. Bloomington: Indiana University Press.

Sullivan, Michael. 1973. *The Art of China.* Berkeley: University of California Press.

Taylor, Charles. 1985. *Philosophical Papers.* New York: Cambridge.

Tedlock, Barbara and Dennis Tedlock. 1985. Text and Textile: Language and Technology in the Arts of the Quiche Maya. *Journal of Anthropological Research* 41 (2): 121–146.

Tedlock, Dennis, trans. 1985. *Popol Vul: The Mayan Book of the Dawn of Life and the Glories of Gods and Kings.* New York: Simon and Schuster.

Torquemada, Juan de. 1977. *Monarquía Indiana,* 1615, Miguel León-Portilla, ed. México: Universidad Nacional Autónoma de México.

Uexküll, J. von. 1982. The Theory of Meaning. *Semiotica* 42/1: 25–82.

Index

Contributors

Elizabeth Hill Boone has been working with Aztec manuscripts since her graduate work at the University of Texas at Austin, where she received a Ph.D. degree in art history. Since 1980 she has been at Dumbarton Oaks in Washington, D.C. where she is Director of Pre-Columbian Studies. She is the author of *The Codex Magliabechiano and the Lost Prototype of the Magliabechiano Group* and *Incarnations of the Aztec Supernatural: The Image of Huitzilopochtli in Mexico and Europe.*

Walter D. Mignolo received a Ph.D. from the Ecole des Hautes Etudes in Paris. Currently he is Professor of Romance Studies and in the Graduate Program in Literature at Duke University. He has been working on literary theory, the European colonization of the New World, and rethinking the idea of (Latin) America. *Elementos para una teoria del texto literario* (1978) and *Teoria del texto e interpretacion de textos* (1986) speak to the first concern; *The Darker Side of the European Renaissance: Literacy, Territoriality and Colonization* (1994) and the edited volume *The Americas: Loci of Enunciation and Imaginary Constructions* (1994) speak to the second.

Tom Cummins is Assistant Professor in the Department of Art at The University of Chicago. He is the author of "The Madonna and the Horse: Alternative Readings of Colonial Images," "Tradition in Ecuadorian Pre-Hispanic Art: The Ceramics of Chorrera and Jama-Coaque," "The Uncomfortable Image: Pictures and Words in the *Nueva Corónica i Buen Gobierno*" and "We are the Other: Peruvian Portraits of Colonial Kurakakuna."

Stephen D. Houston is Assistant Professor in the Department of Anthropology at Vanderbilt University. He is the author of *Hieroglyphs and History at Dos Pilas* and *Maya Glyphs,* and co-editor of the journal of *Ancient Mesoamerica.*

Mark B. King is Assistant Professor in the Department of Anthropology at Georgia State University. He has been working with Mixtec symbolism and writing for eighteen years.

Dana Leibsohn is Assistant Professor of Art History at Ithaca College. In the 1992–93 academic year she received an Ittleson Fellowship from the Center for Advanced Study in the Visual Arts at the National Gallery of Art.

John Monaghan is Assistant Professor in the Department of Anthropology at Vanderbilt University. He is the author of *Sacapulas: Continuities in Highland Maya Social Organization* (with Robert Hill) and *The Covenant with Earth and Rain: Exchange, Sacrifice and Revelation in Mixtec Society.*

John M. D. Pohl is a documentary film writer-producer and a research associate with the Fowler Museum of Cultural History at the University of California at Los Angeles. He is investigating ancient Mexican kingship, government, and religion in relation to how political ideology is symbolized in pictographic and hieroglyphic writing systems. He is the author of *The Politics of Symbolism in the Mixtec Codices* (1993).

Joanne Rappaport teaches anthropology at the University of Maryland, Baltimore County. She is the author of *Cumbe Reborn: An Andean Ethnography of History* and *The Politics of Memory: Native Historical Interpretation in the Colombian Andes.*

Peter L. van der Loo is Assistant Professor in the Department of Humanities and Religious Studies at Northern Arizona University. He is the author of *Codices Costumbres Continuidad, Un Estudio de la Religion Mesoamericana* and an editor of *Continuity and Identity in Native America.*